IMPROVING HEALTH CARE SAFETY AND QUALITY

Law, Ethics and Governance Series

Series Editor: Charles Sampford, Director, Key Centre for Ethics, Law, Justice and Governance, Griffith University, Australia

Recent history has emphasised the potentially devastating effects of governance failures in governments, government agencies, corporations and the institutions of civil society. 'Good governance' is seen as necessary, if not crucial, for economic success and human development. Although the disciplines of law, ethics, politics, economics and management theory can provide insights into the governance of organisations, governance issues can only be dealt with by interdisciplinary studies, combining several (and sometimes all) of those disciplines. This series aims to provide such interdisciplinary studies for students, researchers and relevant practitioners.

Recent titles in the series

Idealism and the Abuse of Power
Lessons from China's Cultural Revolution
Zhuang Hui-yun
ISBN 978-0-7546-7208-1

Integrity Systems for Occupations
Andrew Alexandra and Seumas Miller
ISBN 978-0-7546-7749-9

Promoting Integrity
Evaluating and Improving Public Institutions
Edited by Brian W. Head, A.J. Brown and Carmel Connors
ISBN 978-0-7546-4986-1

Protracted Displacement in Asia
No Place to Call Home
Edited by Howard Adelman
ISBN 978-0-7546-7238-8

Governing the Heroin Trade
From Treaties to Treatment
Melissa Bull
ISBN 978-0-7546-7121-3

Improving Health Care Safety and Quality

Reluctant Regulators

JUDITH HEALY
The Australian National University, Australia

ASHGATE

Published by
Ashgate Publishing Limited
Wey Court East
Union Road
Farnham
Surrey, GU9 7PT
England

Ashgate Publishing Company
Suite 420
101 Cherry Street
Burlington
VT 05401-4405
USA

www.ashgate.com

British Library Cataloguing in Publication Data
Improving health care safety and quality : reluctant regulators. – (Federalism studies)
1. Health services administration—Europe. 2. Health services administration—North America. 3. Health services administration—Australia. 4. Health facilities—Risk management—Europe. 5. Health facilities—Risk management—Australia. 6. Health facilities—Risk management—North America.
I. Series II. Healy, Judith.
362.1'068-dc22

Library of Congress Cataloging-in-Publication Data
Healy, Judith.
Improving health care safety and quality : reluctant regulators / by Judith Healy.
p. cm. — (Series law, ethics and governance)
Includes bibliographical references and index.
ISBN 978-0-7546-7644-7 (hardback : alk. paper) — ISBN 978-0-7546-7645-4 (ebook : alk. paper) 1. Medical care—Law and legislation. 2. Medical care—Evaluation. 3. Medical care—Safety measures. 4. Health facilities—Safety measures. I. Title.
K3601.H43 2010
363.15'56—dc22

2010035140

ISBN 9780754676447 (hbk)
ISBN 9780754676454 (ebk)

MIX
Paper from responsible sources
FSC www.fsc.org FSC® C018575

Printed and bound in Great Britain by the MPG Books Group, UK

Contents

Tables

Figures

Boxes

Preface: Why This Book?

Trends in Health System Governance

Health care systems around the world are undergoing cycles of governance reform that show no signs of abating. Health care systems usually are in transition from one mode of governance to another: the *Health Systems in Transition* series published by the European Observatory on Health Systems and Policies has proved remarkably prescient. For example, the devolutionary trend of the last decade is being reversed in a presidential direction in terms of central control over policy and top-down structural change and surveillance. Such oversight is controversial when applied to clinical performance since the state traditionally does not watch encounters between doctors and patients. But 'trust me, I'm a doctor' is no longer a persuasive mantra. Complacent assumptions that health care is a low-risk activity are being shed, as is the view that scrutiny is best left to doctors. Medical scandals have shaken public confidence that health care providers can be trusted to put the interests of patients first.

'Trust me, I'm a politician', however, is even less persuasive. Can a presidential style of regulator in the national office of a prime minister or a president or office of a state premier understand the realities of working in a hospital emergency department? Typically what happens in a top-down approach is that a regulator targets some politically salient and measurable performance indicator, such as emergency department waiting times, and punishes a hospital financially if it does not meet the target. Health professionals are clever people, however, and good at 'gaming the numbers', as a legion of stories attest. Further, does the measurable drive out the important? Consequences flow from changing one element when every part of a health care system connects to another. Will the result of a top-down edict be to pull health professionals away from other important tasks and will that produce better outcomes overall for patients?

Good Governance Builds on Cultural and System Strengths

The first principle of good governance is that it should build on a foundation of strengths not weaknesses. Pick the strengths and expand on them. The strengths of a health system lie essentially in its people. Health care depends upon highly trained professionals – a distinctive characteristic of the health sector compared to other sectors of the economy. The implications for regulation are that, first, health professionals generally have internalized a strong ethical code and aim to provide a social service. Second, the health professions are built on a learning culture and good professionals continue to learn and to reflect upon their practice over their working life (and continuing professional development often is a pre-requisite for maintaining registration). Third, the medical profession values its clinical leaders so that health reforms must engage champions for change as a key strategy. The Darzi health system reforms for the British NHS and the new hospital network boards in Australia now promise to engage clinicians more in hospital governance.

One problem with a reliance on top-down regulation is that it risks killing off cultural strengths within health care systems by squashing local innovation and individual commitment. Health professionals are experts in the arcane workings of health services and when encouraged are quite capable of finding solutions to pressing problems. There are also are many weaknesses in health care systems. For example, the medical culture needs to face up to the magnitude of medical error, consider collective good practice solutions, and redesign service delivery as patient-centred (not professional-centred) care.

key argument

The conclusion from my peroration so far is that improving health care involves multiple regulators and multiple strategies; in other words, networked governance. One single and central regulatory actor cannot expect to have all the knowledge, to have command over all actions, and still less have the necessary cunning to implement change in a complex system. Making health care better and safer involves everyone: politicians, administrators, doctors, nurses, allied health professionals and support staff, as well as patients and families.

Why Should We Regulate for Safety and Quality?

The problem is that an alarming number of things go wrong in health care – and often patients are not told about them or euphemistic mention is made of 'complications'. Patient safety increasingly is recognized as a big issue and a body of knowledge is accumulating on how to fix or at least lessen the problem, the regulatory aim being to reduce the risk that patients will be inadvertently harmed by health care itself. The public expects a high standard from health care but confidence has been shaken by revelations of unsafe practice, dawning realization that health care can be risky, and accumulating evidence that quality varies enormously. The Hippocratic Oath injunction to doctors, 'first, do no harm', remains as relevant to modern medicine as to ancient Greece. That errors occur is not surprising. An acute care hospital, for example, is a complex organization where a patient's treatment involves many technical procedures carried out by many staff working in a high-pressure environment. A regulatory revolution is underway in the twenty-first century as governments around the world strengthen the regulation of professionals and organizations in order to ensure better and safer health care for patients. England's Chief Health Officer has pointed out that this is overdue as the health care industry, compared with other high-risk industries, has been slow to inculcate a safety culture and to install safety procedures.

Efforts to ensure patient safety have been prompted by a series of medical scandals, by studies from the mid 1990s onwards which reported that between 4 and 12 per cent of patients experience an adverse event in hospital, and by influential reports from the United States and in the United Kingdom that galvanized politicians into action. The magnitude of adverse events in health care came as a big surprise to many. Consider that this could be you – a one in ten chance of medical error in your next hospital admission, and a one in four risk of error over the next year or so related to your GP consultations, medication or diagnostic tests. Patient safety has emerged as the focus of international efforts within the broader push to improve health care quality – unnecessary deaths among patients are much more compelling argument for regulatory reform than less than optimal treatment.

The central purpose of regulation, according to Malcolm Sparrow, is the abatement or control of risks to society while the essence of the regulatory craft is to 'pick important problems and fix them' (Sparrow 2000). What gives the state, or other bodies, the right to regulate others? The scope and scale of risks to patients indicate that regulatory intervention is normatively justifiable. The World Health Organization argues, for example, that the state has a duty of 'stewardship' in ensuring that its population has access to good quality health care.

Mapping Regulatory Actors and Strategies

This book is timely, given the dramatic expansion in the twenty-first century in regulatory actors and regulatory strategies and the myriad safety and quality activities that are underway. There is much to be optimistic about and many lessons to learn – although we have no good measures on whether this ferment of activity has made health care safer and whether the number of adverse events has been reduced. Who are the regulatory actors, what patterns of regulatory activities are underway, what have been the implementation experiences, and what is known about the outcomes of efforts to install systems and change behaviour?

This book takes a new approach to mapping what is happening in health care systems internationally and in Australia. We cannot effectively govern a health care system without some meaningful picture of how the parts connect, what needs to be fixed, and how one might go about fixing things. People working in a health system know their own bit of it but usually have only a hazy idea about the other parts. It reminds me of the story of the three blind men and the elephant: one grasped an ear and said the elephant looks like a fan, the second grasped a leg and said it is like a tree trunk, while the third grasped the trunk and said that an elephant is like a snake. In planning a strategy, a map of the contours of the land is essential in order to look for promising paths. A scoping study is a necessary first step, as the terrain of health sector regulation is expanding very rapidly and new regulatory features are in the process of emerging. We need to identify the regulatory bodies, the regulatory principles that are espoused, and the implementation strategies they adopt. Before identifying promising regulatory paths it is necessary to survey the regulatory terrain:

> That is, one must identify the range of instruments and actors available for recruitment to the regulatory cause; the policy levers which government can pull to activate their engagement; the underlying properties of instruments and parties which determine complementary regulatory combinations; and the means of avoiding dysfunctional combinations. (Gunningham and Grabosky 1998: 20)

This work is informed by my colleagues in the Regulatory Institutions Network (RegNet) at the Australian National University, whose theory-building draws on interdisciplinary and intersectoral research using principles of induction and integration. The principle of induction prompts the gathering of quantitative and qualitative data, using a variety of methods, including mapping, which ground the process of theory-building. The principle of integration looks to combine insights from different disciplines and from studies in different sectors of the economy to achieve greater explanatory power. RegNet applies regulatory knowledge from several disciplinary perspectives (economics, criminology, law, sociology) and from several fields (business and finance, criminal justice, the environment, occupational health and safety, taxation, and health and welfare systems). I also draw on my experience in analysing the health care systems of over a dozen countries for the European Observatory on Health Systems and Policies and currently for the Asia-Pacific Observatory on Health Systems and Policies.

This book reviews experiences in regulating the safety and quality of patient care mainly in Antipodean, European and North American countries. Health policy makers in a globalized world are interested in the experiences of others. While international datasets are desirable and are the basis of much comparative analysis, contextual analysis also is needed in order to understand the story behind the statistics. As well as searching for common principles and investigating the possibilities and pitfalls of different strategies, a comparative analysis can consider whether strategies applied in one area might be applicable in another. Context is crucial in considering regulatory actors and strategies since regulation is a socially constructed task: 'how regulators approach their role and function appears to be highly culturally dependent, and similar regulatory problems result in quite different regulatory solutions'(Walshe 2003: 35). The regulatory literature does not lend itself to a rulebook or 'how to' guidebook, therefore, but indicates regulatory patterns and a way to order strategies for contextual consideration: while evidence is accumulating on the success of different strategies, regulation like policy analysis also is an art and a craft (Wildavsky 1979).

This book explores what is known about the impact of regulation upon the quality and especially safety of patient health care. The problem has been well described and the research emphasis now is upon identifying the solutions. But while evidence is accumulating on clinical practices that make patient care better and safer, there is very little evidence so far on what regulatory strategies and mechanisms ensure that these practices are put in place and are working well. This is the domain of regulatory research. This knowledge currently has to be pieced together from various sources, including case studies and from exponents of the regulatory craft, given the paucity of the sort of studies that lend themselves to systematic reviews. Leape and Berwick thus bemoan the lack of evidence on progress despite a ferment of activity:

> The diversity and level of engagement in improving safety in health care is impressive. Ten years ago, no one was talking about patient safety … Now, the majority of health care institutions are involved to some extent and public awareness has soared. A growing patient safety movement is afoot. But if so much activity is going on, why isn't health care demonstrably and measurably safer? (Leape and Berwick 2005: 2387)

Framework for this Book: Responsive Regulation

There is a better way to regulate than opting for polar opposites such as calling in the central bureaucrats or leaving it to the doctors. Effective regulation should combine the strengths and offset the weaknesses of different regulatory approaches – since each has it advantages and disadvantages. I acknowledge that regulation is a problematic word that is unpopular among health professionals, and so I use it interchangeably with governance as a softer word. Many regulators seek to avoid enforcement connotations by referring only to quality improvement. I cannot avoid the R word, however, as my argument is that regulation covers persuasion as well as coercion, while there is a large and scholarly research literature on regulation and governance – and a journal of that name.

Regulation has many meanings but is used here in its broad sense, meaning much the same as governance conceived in its most general sense: both meaning steering the flow of events (Ayres and Braithwaite 1992). How can a health care system best be steered? Again, the elephant metaphor is helpful since a health system can be conceived of as an intelligent animal with a mind of its own and quite capable of charging off and doing considerable damage. Steering an elephant calls for rewards with punishment as a last resort. Regulatory strategies that seek to influence behaviour use both incentives and disincentives. Mapping a potentially large array of rewards and sanctions requires a framing theory. It should not be a dogmatic theory that asserts a health system is best steered by one type of strategy – whether the law, economic incentives, top-down leadership, clinical governance, or patient-led. Rather a regulator should learn from the responses of those being regulated and be flexible enough to try a different approach if the first does not work. Regulators also need some guidance on what to try first and what should be a last resort. A regulatory theory also needs to make sense from the perspective of multiple actors involved in a health care system (politicians, managers, clinicians, patients) and the multiple strategies already underway (legal instruments, financial incentives, information strategies, persuasion).

The theory that informs the contours of this health system map is the responsive regulation model as it gives a conceptual framework for mapping the multiple regulatory actors and the multiple regulatory strategies, for explaining and predicting behaviour, and for indicating when to persuade and when to punish. The large base of the regulatory pyramid suggests that most regulatory activity takes place voluntarily in response to persuasion (see Figure 0.1). The model argues that regulators should respond to the behaviour of those being regulated by choosing from a range of supports and sanctions, but in the first instance, they should begin with dialogue and persuasion, before ascending to enforcement-type sanctions such as criminal or civil penalties and licence suspension or revocation. Responsive regulation is an appropriate framework for the health sector given the absence of a single and central regulator, a proliferation of regulatory actors and activities, a tradition of personal and professional voluntarism, strong ethical norms, and a learning model commitment to knowledge and reflective practice (Healy and Braithwaite 2006).

This book maps the many regulatory actors and examines the many regulatory strategies they use ranging from persuasion to coercion. The problem of patient safety has focused the minds of regulators from government actors on down to clinical leaders. While initially reluctant regulators, government actors now are adopting strategies from all parts of a regulatory pyramid. Health care managers

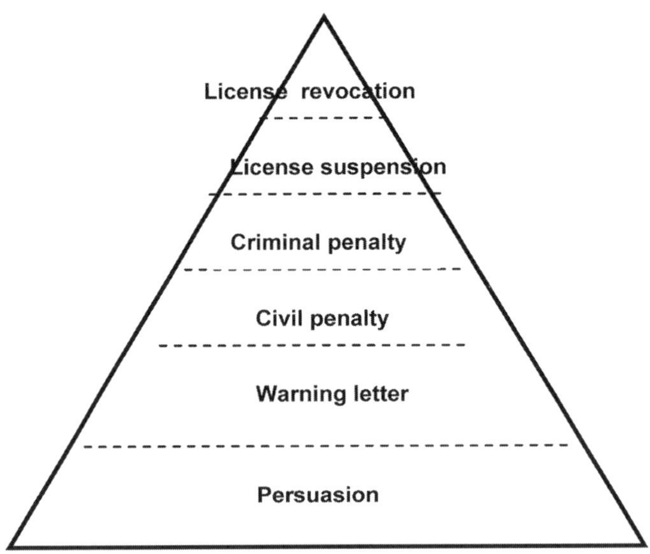

Figure 0.1 Example of a regulatory pyramid

Source: Ayres & Braithwaite 1992: 35

are increasing regulatory pressure but also seek to draw upon the cultural strengths and creativity of health professionals. As the following quote drawn from my interviews for this study indicates, managers, such as hospital clinical leaders, are learning how to bring about change:

> We have learned a lot on how to go about putting a procedure in place in the hospital. First, you need clinical leaders. For example, if it mainly involves the surgeons you need the strategy to be surgeon-led, or if it is about the operating theatre then you need the whole theatre group. Second, we need to be clear on the level of authority. Is it a mandatory directive or a clinical alert? Third, the procedure needs to be well-designed in its forms and processes. You need pictures of activities and a well-designed suite of tools, such as forms and checklists. Fourth, the education strategy needs to be multi-tiered, including posters, other kinds of information, case studies, personal experiences and training sessions. Fifth, the rationale has to be based on better patient care rather than just saying 'thou shalt do this'. Finally, you need to decide on what is to be audited and to develop a good audit tool. These are the things we will definitely do better next time. (Hospital clinical governance director)

References

Ayres & Braithwaite 1992 [see p.18, line 32]
Healy J & Braithwaite J (2006) 'Can better governance produce better health care?' Medical Journal of Australia (Supplement); 184(10): S56–S59.
Gunningham & Grabosky 1998 [see p.19, line 16
Leape & Berwick 2005 [see p.19, line 27]
Sparrow M 2000 [see p. 20, line 36]
Walshe 2003 [see p.21, line 7]
Wildavsky A (1979) Speaking Truth to Power: The Art and Craft of Policy Analysis. Chicago: Little, Brown.

Acknowledgements

This book represents part of an Australian Research Council (ARC) Linkages Project (LP0455448), funded by the ARC, and by three research partners: the Australian National University (ANU), the Australian Commission for Safety and Quality in Health Care, and ACT Health (the Australian Capital Territory Health Department). My work has been greatly enriched by my colleagues at the Regulatory Institutions Network at the Australian National University. My biggest debt is to John Braithwaite for his wise and kind support, for his astoundingly broad scholarship and intellectual insights, and for his strategic comments on this manuscript. This book is framed in large part by his work on responsive regulation. I am also very grateful for the helpful comments on the manuscript made by Christopher Baggoley and by Kathleen Ryan: their extensive experience saved me from drawing several unwarranted conclusions. I am also grateful to Paul Dugdale, my co-researcher and co-author on other work, for his comments on this book, and to Brian Johnston for his comments on Chapter 7. Thanks also to Valerie Braithwaite and Kyla Tienhaara for discussions on trust and transparency. Finally, I want to acknowledge my husband and best friend, Tony McMichael. While I have been thinking about the safety of patients he has been thinking about the safety of the world's population.

Chapter 1
Introduction: Why Regulate?

A Patient Safety Regulatory Revolution

Most people enjoy good quality care but an alarming and preventable number of adverse events occur that are caused by health care itself, even when care is provided by the best of professionals and in the best of hospitals. Policy makers in the early twenty-first century have been galvanized into regulatory action by deaths from medical error, rising numbers of adverse event reports, and by influential patient safety overviews including from the United States (Institute of Medicine 2000) and the United Kingdom (Donaldson 2000). Revelations on the scope and scale of patient safety problems have alarmed the public and have prompted governments to set up new regulatory bodies (McLoughlin et al. 2001), while new international initiatives, such as the WHO World Alliance for Patient Safety, also have added campaign momentum.

Studies from the mid 1990s onwards had reported that between 4 and 12 per cent of patients experience an adverse event in hospital (Thomas et al. 2000; Wilson and Van Der Weyden 2005). Mistakes are common also in other health services; for example, over one-quarter of patients in six high-income countries report experiencing medical, medication or laboratory errors (Schoen et al. 2005). Patient safety advocates point out that more people die in health care accidents than in road accidents. Extrapolating preventable deaths from adverse events among Australian hospital patients (Runciman et al. 2000) shows the hospital toll of 4,500 deaths was higher than the road toll of 1,630 deaths (Australian Transport Safety Bureau 2003). But much less attention has been paid to the hospital toll than the road toll.

Medical alerts illustrate the potential risk to patients of some procedures. Alerts are issued by health authorities to warn about serious known hazards in relation to some medications and procedures. The hazards associated with ampoules of concentrated potassium chloride indicate the types of mistakes that can occur in a busy hospital. An alert issued in several countries was prompted by international reports of fatalities. For example, a woman had a cannula site in her arm flushed with what was thought to be saline from the ward medication cupboard but was instead concentrated potassium chloride – the patient stopped breathing within minutes and died. An alert identified the following three types of error, which illustrates the point that an adverse event often results from an unfortunate combination of system failure and people failure, especially when packaging and procedures are not designed to mitigate the risk of mistakes by busy people (Australian Council for Safety and Quality in Health Care 2003):

- wrong ampoule: potassium chloride ampoules are mistaken for ampoules of a similar appearance such as normal saline;
- cognitive mix-up: a potassium chloride ampoule is selected instead of frusemide (a diuretic) since patients often take both drugs thus conditioning staff to the familiar pairing;
- preparation error: an intravenous infusion is prepared incorrectly (for example, confusion between millimoles and grams).

The restoration of public trust is cited by governments around the world as a key rationale for strengthening the regulation of health care. Patients want to feel confident that they can trust doctors and nurses and want to be assured that any problems that might occur will be fixed. But a series of medical scandals have cast doubt on the willingness of professionals to regulate their own performance. In the United Kingdom, for example, several public inquiries into medical scandals led the editor of the *British Medical Journal* to declare that the era of medical self-regulation was over: 'all changed, changed utterly' (Smith 1998). The governance of the medical profession in the United Kingdom subsequently has been transformed under the banner of ensuring patient safety and restoring public trust (Secretary of State for Health 2007). This is a major regulatory shift and similar shifts are underway in other countries. The safety and quality of professional performance previously had not been regulated as strongly as other areas of the health sector, such as pharmaceuticals and funding (Brennan 1998).

What is Regulation?

Regulation is often narrowly understood as meaning the enforcement of administrative rules. The *Oxford English Dictionary*, for example, defines regulation as: 'A rule prescribed for the management of some matter, or for the regulating of conduct; a governing precept or direction; a standing rule'. In this narrow view, regulation means the promulgation of laws or rules accompanied by mechanisms for monitoring and enforcing compliance. But a regulatory rulebook would not work in the health care sector, arguably unlike some other industries, since health professionals must often make rapid and complex clinical decisions in individual patient cases. Health professionals, and particularly doctors, also tend to see regulation in its most narrow and negative sense as 'red tape' imposed by managers that constrains them in their work while the accompanying paperwork reduces the time available for patients.

A second view sees regulation as the prerogative of the state (meaning government and its agents) and refers to any form of direct intervention by the state, often through a public agency third party, in steering the economy or society. This view implies a 'command and control' type of definition: 'Regulation is sustained and focused control exercised by a public agency over activities which are valued by a community' (Selznick 1985: 363).

The third and broadest view, the view taken in this book, sees regulation as a function of governance that might be performed by state or non-state actors, who use a variety of approaches ranging from persuasion to coercion, in order to steer the flow of events (Ayres and Braithwaite 1992). Regulatory theorists generally take a broad behavioural view. For example, another definition of regulation is 'formal and informal norms and expectations that social actors generate about how to act in particular social contexts (Morgan and Engwall 1999: 3). Regulation is essentially an attempt 'to alter the behaviour of others according to defined standards or purposes' (Black 2002: 96).

An analysis of health care regulation requires a broad view of regulation and an appreciation of the potential range of policy instruments. The first reason for a broad view of regulation is the absence in most health sectors of a sole external public agency regulator with powers of enforcement. Second, health sector regulation is carried out, not only by external public agencies, but also by a variety of other regulatory actors, such as professional associations. Third, health systems depend heavily on health professionals who exert considerable formal and informal power and apply mostly soft regulatory strategies. Finally, conventional regulatory mechanisms do not necessarily work in health care organizations since these are fundamentally different from other types of organizations in terms of their highly professional staff and the complex nature of their work.

Responsive Regulation

John Braithwaite and others proposed 'responsive regulation' as a new paradigm to transcend the regulation-deregulation dichotomy and to achieve 'win-win' and just solutions through innovations in regulatory design (Ayres and Braithwaite 1992; Braithwaite 2002). The responsive regulation model argues that regulators are more likely to succeed when they respond to the context, conduct, and culture of those being regulated. Responsive regulation is an appropriate model for the health care sector given its many regulatory actors, tradition of self-regulation, and strong ethical norms among health professionals. Regulators should begin with soft and collaborative mechanisms, rather than opting immediately for hard enforcement, in order to give more respectful (and cheaper) options a chance to work first, since for most of us, a tap on the shoulder is enough to remind us to mend our ways (Braithwaite 2002). The evidence is that most people and most organizations respond well to a respectful and supportive approach. Punitive mechanisms are reserved for the minority of cases where persuasion fails. Responsive regulators use several mechanisms since one is seldom sufficient, and since each has its strengths and weaknesses, the weakness of one mechanism should be complemented by the strengths of another.

These concepts are depicted in a responsive regulation pyramid that encompasses voluntarism at its softer base and 'command and control' at the apex, while the pyramidal design indicates that most regulatory activities should and do occur lower down the pyramid (Figure 1.1). Regulatory actors and options can be categorized according to types of instruments (Gunningham and Grabosky 1998: 424–6) in ascending order of intervention (from soft to harder regulation), with the addition below of meta-regulation and co-regulation as increasingly used strategies in the health sector:

- *Voluntarism* is based on an individual or an organization undertaking to do the right thing without any coercion.
- *Self-regulation* is where an organized group (such as a profession or industry association) regulates the behaviour of its members (for example, by agreeing on an industry-level code of practice).
- *Economic instruments* involve supply-side funding sanctions or incentives for providers, and also demand-side measures that give more power to consumers.
- *Meta-regulation* involves an external regulatory body regulating the self-regulators to ensure they comply with standards.
- *Co-regulation* involves a partnership between external and internal regulators.
- *Command and control* involves enforcement by government or its agents (for example, ensuring compliance with licensing rules).

The pyramid shown here gives examples of mechanisms against broad strategies that aim to improve patient safety. A voluntarist strategy at the base may include information mechanisms; a market strategy may include incentive payments; peer review is a self-regulatory strategy; a co-regulation strategy may include agreement between several parties on a code of standards; while a government using a meta-regulation strategy may require hospitals to publicly report all adverse events. Failure to remedy problems despite formal requests to do so may provoke enforcement from a regulator as a last resort, for example, removing a licence or closing a facility.

An essential element of responsive regulation is that a regulator must have the capacity to escalate upwards if necessary from soft words to hard deeds. Those being regulated must believe in the inexorable nature of sanctions, as polite requests followed by threats only work when everyone knows that sanctions will follow non-compliance. Responsive regulation argues that stern sanctions must loom as a threat in order to ensure that people comply with softer and more conciliatory approaches:

> the greater the heights of tough enforcement to which the agency can escalate (at the apex of the enforcement pyramid), the more effective the agency will be at securing compliance and the less likely that it will have to resort to tough enforcement. Regulatory agencies will be able to speak more softly when they are perceived as carrying big sticks. (Ayres and Braithwaite 1992: 6)

Responsive regulation also encompasses the concept of networked governance where in the context of diffused power any one regulator must mobilize other actors in order to get things done, such as the professional colleges in the case of patient safety. It also encompasses the idea of networked escalation where a regulator enrols increasing numbers of more potent partners in order to increase pressure on those being regulated (Braithwaite 2008: chapter 4). John Braithwaite developed this idea in the hypothetical tale of Nurse Response who progressively enrols more powerful allies throughout the hospital in order to achieve safer patient care (Braithwaite 2009).

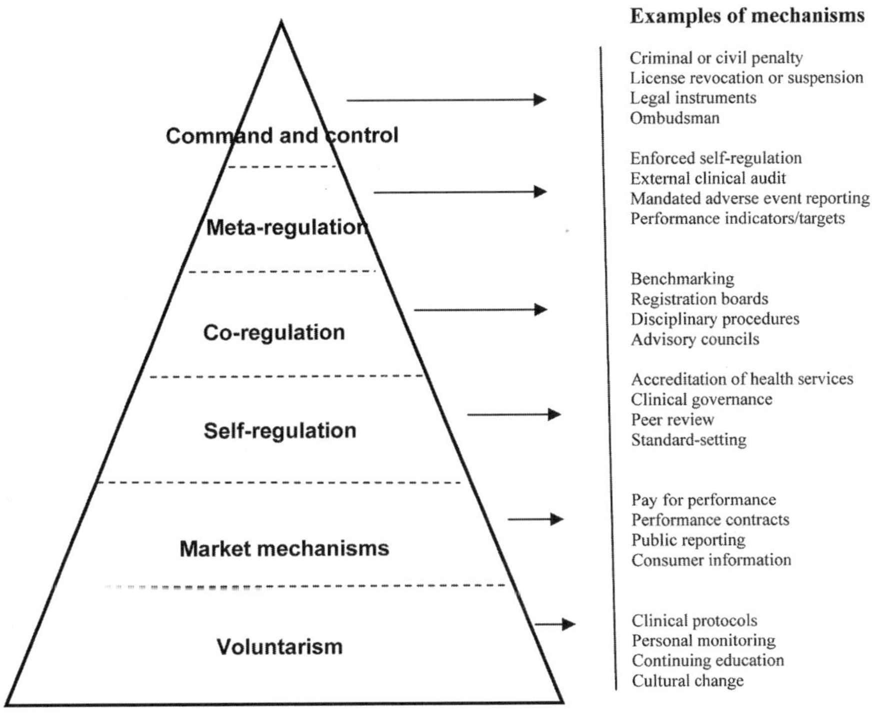

Figure 1.1 Regulatory pyramid of health sector strategies and mechanisms
Source: Adapted from Braithwaite et al 2005: 15

Governance in the Information Age

While the health sector escaped much external regulation until the beginning of the twenty-first century, regulatory agencies were established in other sectors of the economy in the late twentieth century by the 'new regulatory state', a term coined to describe the era when states chose to 'steer rather than row' their developed economies (Osborne and Gaebler 1992). The state set up new authorities to regulate newly privatized activities, particularly when consequences not in the public interest as opposed to shareholder interests became clearer. Recent eras in state governance begin with the 'nightwatchman state' of classical liberal theory from the nineteenth century until the end of the 1930s depression when most steering and rowing was done by civil society; the welfare state from 1945 through the 1970s when the state did much of both steering and rowing; while in the new regulatory state from the 1980s onwards the state steers and civil society does most of the rowing (Jordana and Levi-Faur 2004: 11). The 'nightwatchman state' lives on in the health sectors of many countries, however, in the trust that the state places in doctors, overlaid by welfare state publicly-funded health care, and more recent ventures into regulatory capitalism through market mechanisms and consumer power.

As the history of environmental regulation shows (Gunningham and Grabosky 1998: 5), a command and control approach can provoke opposition from those being regulated. This is important to note in relation to the health sector, since the health industry has a history of organizing very effectively to protect its own interests. Governments in most developed economies in the early 1970s responded to public environmental concern by passing laws to prohibit or restrict environmentally harmful activities. In response to vociferous criticisms, especially in the United States, that regulatory authorities were too bureaucratic, inflexible, adversarial and inefficient, the 1980s saw substantial deregulation. Neo-liberal opponents of the regulatory state mounted a general critique of regulation by the state, calling instead for a market-based and property-rights approach. Gunningham and Grabosky argue that the consequent swing went too far from hard to soft regulation and from state to market-based strategies. Their view is that the regulatory debate should transcend this ideological divide to overcome the inefficiencies of command and control regulation on the one hand, and the pitfalls of deregulation on the other. A smart regulator enlists actors outside the public sector and uses a complementary combination of policy instruments rather than relying on single regulators and single instruments.

Many states from the 1980s introduced market model forms of governance into public sector management, dubbed 'the new public management' in Britain and 'reinventing government' in the United States (Osborne and Gaebler 1992). Malcolm Sparrow maintains that regulatory authorities adopted these ideas too uncritically (Sparrow 2000). He argues that regulators were side-tracked by management fads that peddled customer service concepts, swung too far from enforcement towards voluntary compliance, and failed to take account of the distinctive nature of regulatory obligations. From a health sector perspective, this analysis suggests that the state should take more seriously its regulatory obligation to ensure patient safety.

Regulatory theorists argue that the nature of the contemporary state has changed in fundamental ways in the information age with new networks of institutions emerging that call for different kinds of regulatory strategies. Manuel Castells has re-theorized the relationships between state and society in network terms and argues that: 'Networks constitute the new social morphology of our societies … the power of flows takes precedence over the flows of power' (Castells 1996: 500). The way to govern others is to harness the right networks to a task since a state regulator cannot rely on command and control as in earlier eras.

Regulators in the information age look to more participatory and devolved forms of regulation, especially in complex and highly professionalized industries. One single and central regulator cannot expect to fully understand the nature of an issue, or to have command over all the actions require to implement change via a multitude of state and non-state actors. Traditional agencies, such as government departments, must invest in collaborative partnerships with civil society. This suggests a *co-regulation* strategy (as shown in Figure 1.1), that is, a partnership between multiple external and internal actors. Co-regulation implies a networked governance arrangement between state and non-state regulatory actors. In the health care sector, the language of partnership is far more acceptable to the health professions than the language of enforcement.

Meta-regulation also offers a more acceptable way to regulate in health care sector since it builds upon and strengthens self-regulation by the professions and industry. Meta-regulation allows both the problem-solving creativity of self-regulation and the assurance that a minimum standard of performance is being met.

Why Regulate?

Three arguments essentially are proposed for regulating the health sector. The views of different stakeholders and their different regulatory emphases are reflected in these three normative frameworks: protection of the public, performance improvement, and greater accountability. First, the protection of the public has emerged over the last decade as the main regulatory rationale and this book is based on this rationale. Health care can cure but it also involves significant risks as patients can be inadvertently harmed or killed. The state, therefore, has a responsibility to ensure the reduction of risks to patients, many of whom are already vulnerable through sickness and/or old age. Protecting the public was the state rationale in the nineteenth century for giving statutory powers to medical boards to license and to discipline doctors (Porter 1997). Health care governance essentially was left to the medical profession over the next century, but a regulatory revolution is underway in the twenty-first century. The protection rationale requires, at a minimum, the regulation of basic standards of performance by health care providers and at best the promotion of optimal standards of performance.

Second, pressures to improve performance have gained momentum with accumulating evidence of considerable variation in the quality of care received by patients. For example, a survey of US adult patients found that only about half had received the treatment recommended in clinical protocols (McGlynn et al. 2003). The quality assurance movement gathered momentum in the 1990s with the aim of continually improving the management of patient care (Brook et al. 2000). Patient management based on best practice standards has been strengthened considerably with the rise of evidence-based medicine. The quality movement also promotes the concept of 'patient-centred care' meaning that health care should be designed around the interests of patients not just the interests of providers (Picker Institute Europe 2007). Notably, much of the quality and safety thrust in European Union countries is framed as a 'quality' issue, the aim being to improve clinical performance (Legido-Quigley et al. 2008). European interventions tend to avoid mention of 'regulation' in favour of 'quality improvement' – a term far more acceptable to the health professions.

Performance comparisons within and between countries have become more important in a globalizing world. Globalization is changing the nature of regulation around the world (Braithwaite and Drahos 2000). In the health care sector, people, capital and goods increasingly flow across national boundaries. The global markets of trans-national pharmaceutical corporations continue to expand (Lee 2003), patients seek treatment in other countries ('medical tourism'), while many health systems depend heavily upon doctors and nurses trained in other countries. The dramatic globalization of information has produced convergence in patient safety policies around the world (World Health Organization 2008), and across regions, such as the European Union (Legido-Quigley, McKee et al. 2008). Countries seek to learn lessons from each other about successes and failures in improving the safety and quality of patient care.

Third, there are increasing pressures for greater accountability to the state, to payers and to patients in order to produce high quality clinical performance. Privatization prompted more regulation in the economies of industrialized countries in order to protect the public against the consequences of market failure (Saltman et al. 2002). Although market reform was touted as a way of improving health care quality, there is no consensus on whether quality was affected for better or worse (Harrison 2004). While medical care in many countries has long been delivered by public and private doctors and hospitals, the practice of medicine has become more commercialized, which increases the temptation for doctors to put economic self-interest ahead of the interests of their patients (Walton 1998). Pharmaceutical companies also exert considerable influence upon the prescribing behaviour of doctors (Studdert et al. 2004; Moynihan and Cassels 2005).

Cost containment efforts have driven much health sector regulation in order to strengthen accountability to payers, as rising health expenditures in many countries have prompted cost-effectiveness efforts to constrain costs and to get better value for money. Among European Union countries (the 15 members prior to May 2004) total health expenditure as a percentage of gross domestic product (GDP) rose from 8.6 per cent in 2000 to 9.6 per cent in 2006 (World Health Organization Europe 2009a). Health expenditure will continue to rise with rising treatment expectations by the public, the expansion of technology and the growth of ageing populations (National Research Council 2001). Budget pressures also mean that more attention is being paid to reducing adverse events given their considerable associated costs. For example, preventable adverse events are estimated to cost 2 per cent of total health expenditure in the United States (Institute of Medicine 2000), while an Australian study of adverse events in hospitals estimated the cost at over 18 per cent of inpatient budgets (Ehsani et al. 2006).

The consumer movement wants health care providers to be more accountable to the public and to patients. The patient safety movement initially was slow to pay attention to the point of view of patients (Vincent and Coulter 2002), but patients now are recognized as regulatory actors capable of monitoring their own health care. The WHO World Alliance for Patient Safety has formed an alliance with health consumer groups to help drive the patient safety movement forward (World Health Organization 2009a).

The Regulatory Field

What is the Problem being Regulated?

A very large and diverse number of health sector activities can potentially be regulated. On the supply side, treatment opportunities are expanding dramatically with new technology and advances in medical knowledge and skills. On the demand side, public expectations of health care are rising and the ageing populations will need more health care in future. More diagnostic and treatment procedures, and greater consumption of drugs, especially for older and sicker people, mean there are more opportunities for things to go wrong. People in high income countries increasingly use a variety of health care goods and services. In Australia, for example, men on average consult a doctor 10 times per year and women over 14 times, over one-third of the population are admitted to hospital each year, and medicine prescriptions have grown 3 per cent annually since 1994 (Australian Institute of Health and Welfare 2008).

The regulation of health care broadly covers four spheres of regulatory activity: money (paying health care providers), technology (drugs and devices), health care organizations and services, and people (the health care workforce). While money and technology are strongly regulated and much discussed, this book focuses on professionals and organizations, and specifically on the regulation of clinical performance to improve the care of patients.

Patient safety problems can be classified in several ways; for example, in terms of the type of patient adverse outcome, type of incident, type of procedure, adverse event risk points, and causation factors. While people often think of medical errors in dramatic terms, such as surgery on the wrong patient, many more 'mundane' problems occur although they are eminently preventable. For example, pressure ulcers are preventable and mostly affect people who are bed-ridden with estimates of prevalence ranging from 10 per cent to nearly 15 per cent among hospital patients in high-income countries (World Health Organization 2008: 7), while health care associated infections occur in up to 10 per cent of patients in modern hospitals (Taylor et al. 2001; Spelman 2002). But while there is good evidence on how to prevent or greatly reduce many of these problems, many countries do not require their hospitals to take mandatory action.

Who and What is Regulated?

The health care sector in most countries is a mixed public and private economy. The number and diversity of individuals and organizations presents different challenges to regulation in fields with smaller numbers of large companies, such as the mining industry or the pharmaceutical industry. The public sector in high-income countries generally includes most acute care hospitals, day hospitals and health clinics, population health services (for example, breast cancer screening), and insurance schemes. The private sector includes many or most doctors, some hospitals, a large diagnostic services industry, community-based pharmacies, and private insurance funds. The diverse and highly specialized health workforce generally comprises about 7 per cent of the total workforce of high-income countries (Dubois et al. 2006). Australia, for example, has over 1,290 hospitals, around 6,000 private general practice clinics, and 3,000 residential aged care homes (Australian Institute of Health and Welfare 2008).

Who regulates?

Who should be responsible for regulating the safety and quality of health care? Should the state leave it to the health professions, devolve governance to other sectors, set up co-regulation arrangements, or regulate directly? Pluralist health sectors contain a multitude of potential regulatory actors that can be classified according to their location in four quadrants of society: government, the professions, the market, and civil society. Figure 1.2 depicts regulatory actors located in concentric spheres of regulation in Australia's federal system of government, radiating out from employers, states, national-level, inter-governmental level, and the supranational. This large array indicates the many different regulatory actors that are involved in different aspects of health care governance and also indicates that big health care issues can involve a whole-of-society approach.

The regulatory style adopted by a country depends upon its history, culture, legal and governmental systems, so that government is the dominant regulatory actor in some countries but in others is one of several actors. The main approach to regulation in the health care sector traditionally has been self-regulation by the professions and this remains the preferred approach by the medical profession but not by the community. The market plays an important regulatory role in some countries through third-party purchasers, consumers, and industry groups such as private hospital associations. The community sector includes non-government organizations (NGOs) that exert some influence but individuals still have little influence over health care quality.

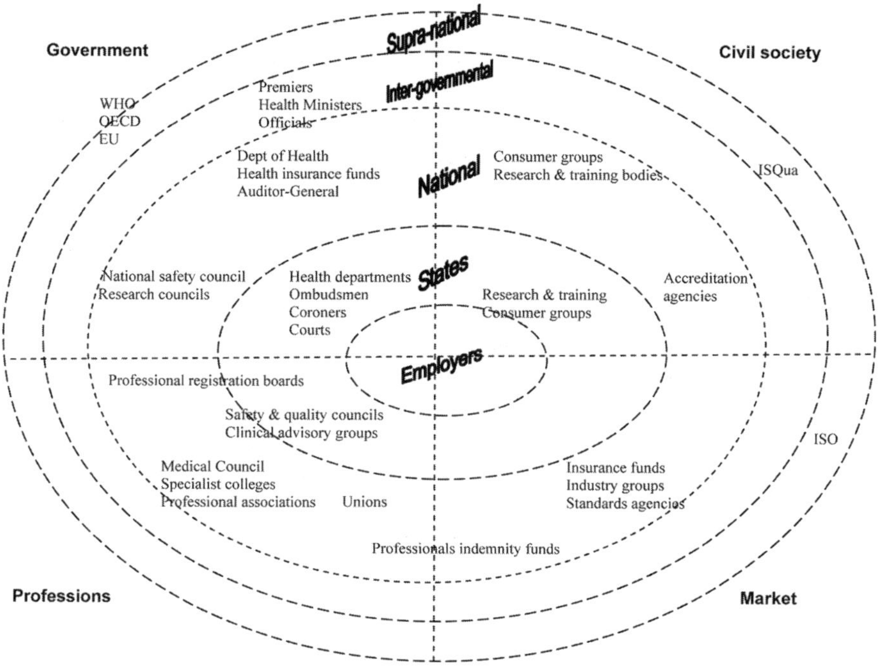

Figure 1.2 Regulatory agencies in the Australian health sector constellation

How regulate?

Regulatory strategies, mechanisms and interventions involve a hierarchy of actions. The *Oxford English Dictionary* defines a strategy (inter alia) as: 'planning of movements' meaning a large-scale plan of manoeuvres rather than a specific action. A mechanism is defined as a 'mode of operation of a process'. An intervention attempts to 'modify the course or result of events'. The commonly used term 'patient safety practice' refers to both mechanisms and interventions. A patient safety practice has been defined as 'a type of process or structure whose application reduces the probability of adverse events resulting from exposure to the health care system across a range of conditions or procedures' (Shojania et al. 2001: 29). A patient safety practice may include computerized prescribing (a mechanism), and the administration of anti-clotting drugs (a clinical intervention).

This book concentrates upon upstream regulatory strategies and mechanisms, rather than downstream and proximate clinical interventions with specific patients. For example, there is good evidence that better hand hygiene by staff (an intervention) is effective in reducing hospital-associated infections among patients, but the regulatory question is what mechanisms would best improve the frequency of hand-washing? Do health professionals improve their hand hygiene because behavioural change is achieved through information, such as posters above handbasins, or through coercion, such as inspections by supervisors, or through system change, such as more bottles of alcohol rub? Or more probably, are all three actions necessary to produce better hand hygiene? Should most regulation in the health sector invoke strategies around the base and middle of a regulatory pyramid or should we be quicker to escalate to the enforcement apex?

Does Regulation Work?

Policy makers want to see evidence that regulation has a positive impact. The proliferation of regulatory innovations suggests the Maoist aphorism: 'Let a hundred flowers bloom, let a hundred schools of thought contend'. But while regulatory actors have scattered many seeds they have had little time so far to walk over the terrain to check which plants have grown, flourished and borne fruit. While evidence on the impact of patient safety regulatory interventions is growing, it is still patchy. These are early days for measuring impacts and health systems research with its real-world complexities is messier to undertake than clinical and laboratory research.

Evidence-based medicine has become a mantra but its evidentiary principle sets the bar high for health systems research and in any case is not always appropriate. First, research on health systems is less developed than clinical research partly because it is difficult to undertake studies across whole organizations, let alone across whole health systems (World Health Organization 2004). Studies on regulatory interventions mostly concern clinical interventions rather than more upstream regulatory interventions, and so fewer studies are available on which to base structured and systematic reviews. There is less research on adverse event reporting systems, therefore, than on proximate patient safety practices, such as administering antibiotics prior to surgery. This patchy evidence does not mean that regulation does not work, but rather that there are few evaluations of strategies and mechanisms.

Second, medicine expects conventional scientific methods and a rigorous standard of evidence but research on health systems uses a wide range of methods. A hierarchy of study designs ranks levels of evidence as follows: systematic review of multiple randomized control trials (RCTs); a large and properly designed RCT; non-randomized control trials; observational studies with controls; before and after case studies; comparative case studies; and expert opinion (National Health and Medical Research Council 2000; Coulter and Ellis 2006). But while a systematic review of RCTs is regarded by many as the gold standard of evidence-based medicine, not all health issues are susceptible to an RCT design (Rychetnik and Frommer 2002; Lin and Gibson 2003).

Hospitals in the real world can seldom be randomly assigned in control trials holding all other factors constant in order to test the impact of a regulatory mechanism, and as not all variables can be identified let alone controlled there may be many possible reasons for successes and failures. Further, health providers usually are subject to multiple interventions so that it is difficult to isolate and evaluate single interventions in a complex field, still less to evaluate a whole package of interventions. The most valuable regulatory interventions are multi-dimensional and multi-organizational and there usually are not numerous enough to assign to randomized studies. Further, knowledge derived from one area of regulation can inform and should be tested in other areas. For example, although the proposition remains to be tested that responsive regulation will work in a complex organization such as a hospital, there is a body of evidence that responsive regulation works in settings such as mines and nursing homes, and in more complex domains, such as finance, oil production and the nuclear industry (Braithwaite 2002: 17–71).

Findings in one context cannot necessarily be generalized with confidence to other contexts, however, and context is crucial in considering regulatory responses. Most studies are undertaken in the United States and northern Europe so that researchers and policy makers must consider whether these findings are applicable elsewhere and in other types of health systems. Finally, as a Hosptital CEO said to me clinicians often demand a more rigorous standard of evidence for a procedural change than they apply to their own clinical practice:

> If I ever try to tackle clinicians on anything they always ask, ‘Where is your evidence?’ I’m increasingly asking ‘Where is yours?’ That stops them in their tracks. It makes them think about why they keep doing things in a certain way. Often there actually is no evidence for what they are doing. (Hospital CEO)

Structured or systematic reviews increasingly are being undertaken on studies of clinical interventions. The US Agency on Healthcare Research and Quality led the way with an influential structured review of 79 patient safety practices, concluding that 11 were based on strong evidence of a positive impact on patient safety. These can be grouped as procedural changes (for example, ask patients to restate what they were told in informed consent), redesign of a device or technical procedure (for example, prevention of ventilator-associated pneumonia), and clinical protocols for specific interventions (for example, ultrasound guidance in central line insertion) (Shojania, Duncan et al. 2001). Another study identified 12 evidence-based practices that can be grouped in three areas: procedural changes (for example, standardizing medication practices), redesign of a device or technical procedure (for example, physician computer order entry), and clinical protocols for specific interventions (for example, perioperative antibiotics) (Leape and Berwick 2005). The World Health Organization now promotes nine ‘patient safety solutions’ based on research and expert consensus: eliminating look-alike, sound-alike medication names; patient identification; communication during patient handover; performance of correct procedure at correct body site; control of concentrated electrolyte solutions; assuring medication accuracy at transitions in care; avoiding catheter and tubing misconnections; single use of injection devices;

and improved hand hygiene to prevent health care-associated infections (World Health Organization 2007).

Moving upstream from proximal patient safety interventions to broader regulatory mechanisms, Table 1.1 sets out an overview of the main patient safety regulatory mechanisms underway around the world and summarizes the extent of their implementation and evidence on their impact. For example, is the structural strategy of standardized procedures being implemented and what is the evidence that this works? From the base of a regulatory pyramid, the list begins with voluntarism as a soft strategy and then actions can move through progressively stronger strategies to enforcement. Systematic reviews have begun to evaluate evidence on the impact of some mechanisms that have proven to be effective in improving patient safety, while many others appear promising although evidence of their efficacy is not yet compelling or has not yet been gathered. For example, positive evidence has emerged from redesigns of physical environments and procedures (systems change), but the evidence on methods for changing the behaviour of individuals (cultural change) is more equivocal. These strategies and mechanisms are discussed in subsequent chapters.

Some Conclusions on Evidence of Impact

The first message from the research for policy makers is that while basing strategies on evidence of regulatory impact is an important principle, these are early days for patient safety research. Many promising mechanisms have yet to be implemented and evaluated. The patchy evidence base means that the design of a regulatory framework often must look to general principles and systems knowledge to guide action. Given the bounded state of knowledge so far on the impact of regulatory mechanisms, policy makers in the short term are forced to opt for adequate not necessarily optimal solutions; that is, rather than optimize they must 'satisfice' (a term coined by Herbert Simon as an amalgam of 'satisfy' and 'suffice'). Policy makers must plot a path across a health system regulatory terrain despite patchy information on implementation let alone impact. The second message is that evidence-based mantras can be an excuse for not thinking and for not applying systemic wisdom. The third message is that given the urgency of the patient safety problem, health policy makers must adopt the precautionary principle and take risk management action when interventions seem promising rather than necessarily proven – they cannot afford to wait for the results of double-blind randomized control trials. The fourth message is that the public will take electoral action if medical scandals continue as health ministers and health department managers are acutely aware.

Table 1.1 Regulatory mechanisms and evidence of impact

Strategy	Mechanism	Implementation	Evidence of positive safety and quality impact
Voluntary strategy	Information to professionals	widespread	some – but low and slow take-up
	Research collaborations	widespread	some – initial success
Market/ consumer strategy	Informed consent	widespread	some – anecdotal
	Consumer participation	widespread	some
	Performance public reports	widespread	some – reputational impact
	Consumer litigation	widespread	some – but may inhibit quality improvement
	Whistle-blowing	variable	strong – trigger to public inquiries
Management strategy	Safety culture	widespread	strong – observational studies
	Clinical governance	widespread	unknown
	Performance contracts	widespread	unknown
	Credentialing	widespread	some – anecdotal
	Qualified privilege	widespread	some – facilitates quality improvement
	Adverse event reports	widespread	some – prompts medical alerts, quality improvement
	Root cause analysis	widespread	some – quality improvement
	Open disclosure	variable	some – patient satisfaction, reduced litigation

Structural strategy	Safe physical design	variable	strong
	Standard procedures	variable	strong
	Technology	widespread	strong
	Safe staffing	variable	some
	Patient management team work	widespread	strong – better staff morale, better patient care
Regulation by professions and industry	Registration of professionals	widespread	strong – normative
	Professional development	widespread	strong
	Disciplinary procedures	widespread	unknown
	Accreditation of health services	widespread	strong – improved processes, outcomes unclear
	Clinical guidelines	widespread	strong
Meta-regulation	Coronial inquiries	widespread	some – case studies
	Health complaints commissioners	widespread	some – case studies
	Performance indicators	widespread	strong
	Adverse event reports	widespread	strong – systemic changes, improved performance
	Mortality registers	widespread	strong – e.g. improved surgical mortality
Command and control	Legislation	widespread	unknown
	Public inquiries	variable	strong – result in major changes
	Prosecution of professionals	rare	unknown –deters fraud and malpractice?

Study Methods in This Book

Regulation is a contested and interdisciplinary research domain since the perspective depends in large part upon who is studying the topic, including economists, lawyers, sociologists and political scientists, each of whom bring their own preconceptions and interests to bear on the task (Walshe 2003: 21). The methods used in this study (while not a linear sequence) involved refining the conceptual framework of responsive regulation, undertaking extensive literature reviews, mapping regulatory actors and activities, interviewing hundreds of health professionals as well as practitioners of the regulatory craft (and illustrative quotes from these interviews are used in this book), collecting micro-studies of quality improvement, and documenting regulatory successes and failures. Since the terminology in the patient safety field can be confusing, this study draws on a WHO glossary of concepts (World Health Organization 2009b).

The breadth of the field required drawing a boundary around the regulatory area of study to concentrate on patient safety as the core issue within the larger quality agenda. This study concentrates upon patient safety issues in high-income countries since most research derives from these countries and since common issues have been identified. Several types of health services were excluded as involving particular expertise and their own forms of regulation: mental health, drug and alcohol services, disability services, complementary and alternative medicine, and population health services. Related fields of health also were excluded, including pharmaceuticals, health technology and therapeutic goods, and laboratory standards.

de-limiting field

Guide to This Book

Chapter 1 has introduced the theories and concepts used in this book and lays out its aims and scope.

Chapter 2 argues that patient safety is an important problem that warrants a regulatory response. It explains the many things that can go wrong in health care, reviews the lessons learned from many public inquiries into medical scandals, and summarizes studies undertaken in several countries on the magnitude of adverse events.

Chapter 3 discusses the complex and distinctive nature of health systems with their multiple regulatory actors, the several sources of regulatory authority, analyses why the tricky nature of health systems governance is characterized by decentred regulation and calls for networked governance.

Chapter 4 argues that the era of sole reliance on the medical profession to regulate health care is now over, and reviews international trends in stronger health profession regulation with greater accountability to the state and to the public.

Chapter 5 argues that the culture of the health sector has distinctive strengths that should be built, that safe design in health care is overdue, and that cultural and systemic change should run in parallel.

Chapter 6 looks at the challenging nature of hospital management – the pessimistic view being that hospitals are ungovernable and riddled by endemic conflicts between different groups. The optimistic view is that managers and clinical leaders are crucial internal regulators in promoting a patient-centred culture and innovative quality and safety solutions.

Chapter 7 examines the growth of external review schemes in regulating health care organizations that increasingly combine the approaches of minimum standards with quality improvement strategies.

Chapter 8 examines the trend towards meta-regulation by external authorities who have the capacity to apply enforcement strategies through laws, monitoring and money.

Chapter 9 points out that the patient has been the missing person in health sector regulatory debates but that patients can play important roles as regulatory actors: informed patients, selective consumers, vocal complainants, entitled citizens and active partners.

Chapter 10 discusses trust and transparency as key and complementary principles in regulatory design.

References

Australian Council for Safety and Quality in Health Care (2003), Medication Alert 1: Intravenous Potassium Chloride can be fatal if given inappropriately. (Canberra: Australian Council for Safety and Quality in Health Care).

Australian Institute of Health and Welfare (2008), *Australia's Health 2008*. (Canberra: AIHW).

Australian Transport Safety Bureau (2003), Road Fatalities, Australia: Monthly Bulletin. (Canberra: Australian Transport Safety Bureau).

Ayres I and Braithwaite J (1992), *Responsive Regulation: Transcending the Regulation Debate*. (New York. Oxford: Oxford University Press).

Black J (2002), 'Critical reflections on regulation.' *Australian Journal of Legal Philosophy* 27: 1–35.

Braithwaite J (2002), *Restorative Justice and Responsive Regulation*. (Oxford. New York: Oxford University Press).

Braithwaite J (2008), *Regulatory Capitalism: How It works, Ideas for Making It Work Better*. (Cheltenham, UK; Northampton, MA, USA: Edward Elgar).

Braithwaite J (2009), 'Leading from behind with plural regulation'. In Healy J and Dugdale P. *Patient Safety First: Strategies for Regulating Health Care*. (Crows Nest NSW: Allen and Unwin): 24–43.

Braithwaite J and Drahos P (2000), *Global Business Regulation*. (Cambridge: Cambridge University Press).

Braithwaite J, et al. (2005) see p. 91 lines 38–9.
Brennan T (1998), 'The role of regulation in quality improvement.' *Milbank Quarterly* 76: 709–731.
Brook R, et al. (2000), 'Defining and measuring quality of care: a perspective from US researchers.' *International Journal for Quality in Health Care* 12(4): 281–295.
Castells M (1996), The Information Age: Economy, Society and Culture. (Oxford: Blackwell).
Coulter A and Ellis J (2006), *Patient-Focused Interventions: A Review of the Evidence*. (London: The Health Foundation).
Dubois C-A, et al. (2006), 'Reshaping the regulation of the workforce in European health care systems'. In Dubois C-A, McKee M and Nolte E. *Human Resources for Health in Europe*. (Maidenhead, Berkshire: Open University Press): 173–192.
Ehsani J, et al. (2006), 'The incidence and cost of adverse events in Victorian hospitals 2003–04.' *Medical Journal of Australia* 184(11): 551–555.
Gunningham N and Grabosky P (1998), *Smart Regulation: Designing Environmental Policy*. (Oxford: Clarendon Press).
Harrison MI (2004), *Implementing Change in Health Systems: Market Reforms in the United Kingdom, Sweden and The Netherlands*. (London. Thousand Oaks. New Delhi: Sage Publications).
Institute of Medicine (2000), *To Err is Human: Building a Safer Health System*. (Washington, DC: Institute of Medicine, National Academy Press).
Jordana J and Levi-Faur D (2004), 'The politics of regulation in the age of governance'. In Jordana J and Levi-Faur D. *The Politics of Regulation: Institutions and Regulatory Reforms for the Age of Governance*. (Cheltenham. Northampton: Edward Elgar).
Leape L and Berwick D (2005), 'Five years after *To Err is Human*: what have we learned.' *Journal of the American Medical Association* 293(19). 2384–2390.
Lee K (2003), *Globalization and Health: An Introduction*. (New York: Palgrave Macmillan).
Legido-Quigley H, et al. (2008), *Assuring the Quality of Health Care in the European Union: A Case for Action*. (Brussels: World Health Organization and European Observatory on Health Systems and Policies).
Lin V and Gibson B (2003), *Evidence-based Health Policy: Problems and Possibilities*. (South Melbourne: Oxford University Press).
McGlynn E, et al. (2003), 'The quality of health care delivered to adults in the United States.' *New England Journal of Medicine* 348(26): 2635–2645.
McLoughlin V, et al. (2001), 'Improving performance using indicators: recent experience in the United States, the United Kingdom, and Australia.' *International Journal for Quality in Health Care* 13(6): 455–462.
Morgan G and Engwall L (1999), 'Regulation, risk and organizations: an introduction'. In Morgan G and Engwall L. *Regulation and Organizations: International Perspectives*. (London: Routledge): 1–14.

Moynihan R and Cassels A (2005), *Selling Sickness: How Drug Companies Are Turning Us All Into Patients*. (St Leonards NSW: Allen and Unwin).

National Health and Medical Research Council (2000), *How To Use the Evidence: Assessment and Application of Scientific Evidence*. (Canberra: Commonwealth of Australia).

National Research Council (2001), *Preparing for an Ageing World: The Case for Cross-National Research.* (Washington DC: National Academy Press).

Osborne D and Gaebler T (1992), *Reinventing Government: How the Entrepreneurial Spirit is Transforming the Public Sector*. (Boston: Addison-Wesley).

Picker Institute Europe, Patient Centred Professionalism, (10 January 2007) http://www.pickereurope.org/page.php?id=9

Porter R (1997), The Greatest Benefit to Mankind: A Medical History of Humanity from Antiquity to the Present. (London: HarperCollins).

Runciman W, et al. (2000), 'A comparison of iatrogenic injury studies in Australia and the USA. II: reviewer behaviour and quality of care.' *International Journal of Quality in Health Care* 12(5): 379–388.

Rychetnik L and Frommer M (2002), *A Scheme for Evaluating Evidence on Public Health Interventions, Version 4*. (Melbourne: National Public Health Partnership).

Saltman R, et al. (2002), *Regulating Entrepreneurial Behaviour in European Health Care Systems*. (Buckingham. Philadelphia: Open University Press).

Schoen C, et al. (2005), 'Taking the pulse of health care systems: experiences of patients with health problems in six countries.' *Health Affairs* Web exclusive 3 November 2005: W5 509–525.

Secretary of State for Health (2007), Trust, Assurance and Safety - The Regulation of Health Professionals in the 21st century. (London: The Stationery Office).

Selznick P (1985), 'Focusing organizational research on regulation'. In Noll R. *Regulatory Policy and the Social Sciences*. (Berkeley, CA: University of California Press).

Shojania K, et al. (2001), *Making Health Care Safer: A Critical Analysis of Patient Safety Practices*. (Rockville MD: Agency for Healthcare Research and Quality).

Smith R (1998), 'All changed, changed utterly.' *British Medical Journal* 316: 1917–1918.

Sparrow M (2000), The Regulatory Craft: Controlling Risks, Solving Problems and Managing Compliance. (Washington DC: The Brookings Institution).

Spelman D (2002), 'Hospital-acquired infections.' *Medical Journal of Australia* 176: 286–291.

Studdert D, et al. (2004), 'Financial conflicts of interest in physicians' relationships with the pharmaceutical industry - self-regulation in the shadow of federal prosecution.' *New England Journal of Medicine* 351(18): 1891–1900.

Taylor K, et al. (2001), *The Challenge of Hospital-Acquired Infection*. (London: Stationery Office).

Thomas EJ, et al. (2000), 'A comparison of iatrogenic injury studies in Australia and the USA: context, methods, casemix, population, patient and hospital characteristics.' *International Journal for Quality in Health Care* 12(5): 371–378.

Vincent CA and Coulter A (2002), 'Patient safety: what about the patient?' *Quality and Safety in Health Care* 11: 76–80.

Walshe K (2003), *Regulating Healthcare: A Prescription For Improvement?* (Maidenhead. Philadelphia: Open University Press).

Walton M (1998), 'Competition policy and the regulation of the medical profession.' *Australian Health Consumer* 1: 10–13.

Wilson RM and Van Der Weyden M (2005), 'The safety of Australian healthcare: 10 years after QAHCS.' *Medical Journal of Australia* 182(6): 260–261.

World Health Organization (2004), World Report on Knowledge for Better Health: Strengthening Health Systems. (Geneva: World Health Organization).

World Health Organization, World Alliance for Patient Safety: Patient Safety Solutions, (2 May 2008 2 May 2008) http://www.who.int/patientsafety/solutions/en/

World Health Organization (2008), *Summary of the Evidence on Patient Safety: Implications for Research.* (Geneva: World Health Organization).

World Health Organization, Patients for Patient Safety, (2 April 2009 2 April 2009) http://www.who.int/patientsafety/patients_for_patient/en/

World Health Organization (2009b), World Alliance for Patient Safety: The Conceptual Framework for the International Classification for Patient Safety: Final Technical Report: Technical Annex 2: Glossary of Patient Safety Concepts and References. (Geneva: World Health Organization).

World Health Organization Europe, Health For All Database, (2 April 2009 2 April 2009) http://data.euro.who.int/hfadb

Chapter 2
How Safe Is Health Care?

Patient Safety: Things that go Wrong in Health Care

Medical errors have always occurred, and cannot be totally eliminated, but realization of the magnitude of adverse events in modern medicine has alarmed policy makers and the public. This chapter maps what is known about the scope and scale of adverse events. Several terms are used to describe the things that go wrong in health care. Medical language uses arcane and euphemistic terms for medical error, such as iatrogenic (healthcare-caused) injury, and nosocomial (hospital-acquired) infections. Most attention so far has concentrated upon hospitals as better data are available and the consequences of error tend to be greater. An *adverse event* is defined as 'an event that results in unintended harm to the patient by an act of commission or omission rather than by the underlying disease or condition' (World Health Organization 2009b). Caused by health care itself, serious cases can result in prolonged hospital stays and even death. There are also a large but unknown number of 'near misses' that do not result in harm to patients but may in future if the causes are not remedied. A *near miss* is defined as 'an event or situation that could have resulted in an adverse event but did not, either by chance or through timely intervention' (World Health Organization 2009b: 28). Up to half of adverse events (although this proportion is disputed) are said to be *preventable*, defined as an 'adverse event that would not have occurred if the patient had received ordinary standards of care appropriate for the time' (World Health Organization 2009b: 32). An adverse event may result from omission, such as omitting to administer antibiotics, or commission, such as administering the wrong dose. A subset of preventable events may involve *negligence*: 'Failure to exercise the skill, care, and learning expected of a reasonably prudent health care provider (World Health Organization 2009b: 28).

Runciman and colleagues discuss the forms of error that underlie the many things that go wrong in the delivery of health care (Runciman et al. 2007: chapter 5). An adverse event may be an unintentional accident, that is, a slip or mistake, which does not involve moral culpability, or more unusually it may be a deliberate violation. A *violation* is 'a deliberate deviation from an operating procedure, standard or rules' (World Health Organization 2009b: 45). 'Cutting corners' is not usually interpreted by staff as a violation since minor violations are common in all workplaces, including hospitals, and usually are not dangerous. *Malpractice* is defined as: 'A failure of care or skill by a professional that causes loss or injury and results in legal liability' (World Health Organization 2009b: 24). From a medico-legal perspective, the law looks for someone to blame in cases of alleged malpractice. Definitions of malpractice and its associated legal liability vary somewhat in different jurisdictions and most cases are pursued under civil rather than criminal law. When evaluating adverse events for the purpose of attributing blame, the law inquires into the actions and thoughts of the practitioner as well as the results (Merry and McCall Smith 2001: 32). An adverse event can be classified in several ways in terms of personal culpability: an accident (unintended, not foreseeable, not preventable); an error (not deliberate); a mistake (a flaw in the plan or procedure); or a violation (a deliberate deviation and hence avoidable).

Adverse events also are classified in terms of the extent of harm or potential harm, such as a serious event that results in permanent disability or death. A subcategory of adverse event is classified as a *sentinel event* that 'signals the need for immediate investigation and response' (World Health Organization 2009b: 40). The term was popularized by the US Joint Commission that requested its accredited hospitals to report such incidents from 1996 onwards to the Commission's reporting system (Joint Commission 2005), and some countries (including Australia) now require their public hospitals to report all sentinel events.

The relationships between near misses and the various types of adverse events can be depicted in a Venn diagram (see Figure 2.1). Gray points out that many errors during episodes of patient care do not result in harm to patients, that not all adverse events arise from errors, that all preventable adverse events involve error, and that all negligent adverse events are preventable (Gray 2003). In addition, there are a very large but unknown number of near misses that do not result in errors or in an adverse outcome for the patient.

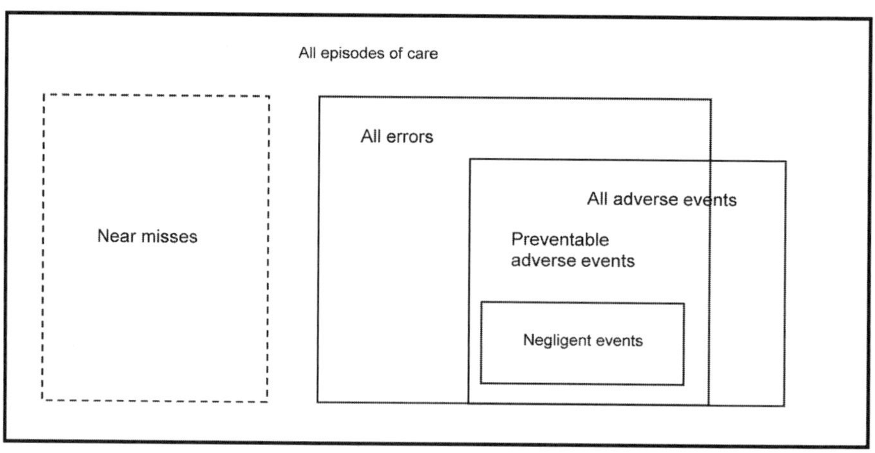

Figure 2.1 Venn diagram representing near misses and adverse events

Source: Derived from Gray 2003: 2

Two influential reports published in 2000, which gathered together the scattered evidence on the extent of patient safety problems, galvanized international action. The US report, *To Err is Human* (Institute of Medicine 2000), extrapolated numbers to estimate that 44,000–98,000 US hospital patients die each year as a result of medical error and more than 1 million are injured. The report pointed out that errors in health care were the eighth most common cause of death, killing more people than motor vehicle accidents, breast cancer or AIDS. The report attracted intense media publicity that led to congressional hearings and prompted the establishment of new safety and quality bodies.

In the UK, the Chief Medical Officer, Sir Liam Donaldson, led the push to improve patient safety and his report, *An Organization with a Memory*, argued that the National Health Service (NHS) should learn from adverse events in order to prevent future occurrences (Donaldson Report 2000). The report scoured information sources to estimate that 4 to 10 per cent of NHS hospital admissions in England involved adverse events that resulted in harm to patients, and that about half of these events were preventable. The main messages of the report were, first, when things go wrong the roots of the failure usually can be traced to systems rather than people, and second, in order to learn from these incidents the NHS should promote a 'safety culture', not a 'blame culture'.

People Failure or System Failure?

The two perspectives on causation, people failure and system failure, are encapsulated in the titles of these reports: *To Err Is Human* (Institute of Medicine 2000), and *An Organization with a Memory* (Donaldson Report 2000). Both reports argued that adverse events mostly are unintentional and that improvements in patient safety are more likely to come from treating adverse events as system failures rather than people failures.

The discussion of adverse event causation previously was mostly couched in terms of individual failure: the legal perspective that someone is to blame. The work of James Reason has been enormously influential in focusing the causation paradigm on systems as well as people (Reason 1995). His argument is that improvements in safety design must take into account both human factors and system/engineering factors, since imperfect decision-making is inherent in complex health care, and human error often is a consequence of system failures. A systems view of causation calls for prevention strategies, such as systems redesign, in parallel with changing the behaviour of organizations and individuals in order to produce a safety culture. Even a well-designed system can fail in a complex hospital environment if several unexpected events coincide; conversely, even the most skilled and knowledgeable person can make mistakes, so that a fail-safe system is required to prevent such mistakes or else to ensure that the consequences of such a mistake are not serious. Health care in hospitals, moreover, is delivered by teams of people so that multiple causes of error may involve several people not just one individual.

Patient safety advocates urge the health sector to reject a blame culture and to adopt a safety culture (Pizzi et al. 2001). From a responsive regulation perspective, the philosophy is to encourage learning from errors and to shift from passive responsibility that holds someone accountable for the past, to active responsibility that encourages a person to take action to make things right for the future (Braithwaite. A safety culture involves both systems and people: 2002):

> In my experience, failures have nothing to do with personality but rather big things going on that directly impact on performance. It is an insult and disrespectful to the surgeons or other people involved to say it is a personality issue. It's not about that. It's about human factors and about working in high-pressure, often stressful situations, and getting a safe outcome for the patient. (Hospital clinical governance director)

Adopting a systems view of causation, however, can gloss over the issue of accountability. While professionals may attribute an adverse event to system failure, the public may want to attribute it to human failure. Malpractice litigation under civil law and public inquiries into medical scandals are both played out in an adversarial atmosphere, and generally look for someone rather than something to blame.

Has Health Care Become Riskier?

Since there are no valid and reliable statistical time series on the extent of adverse events, we cannot be sure whether more, or fewer, things are going wrong in modern hospitals. Charles Vincent and colleagues point out that we do not know whether efforts since the 1990s have produced safer patient care overall, as surgical mortality has improved (in England and Scotland) but reports of health care acquired infections, drug errors and adverse events have increased (perhaps due to better reporting) in countries where such incidents are measured (Vincent et al. 2008).

Medical error is not a new phenomenon, and while there is no reason to believe that contemporary health professionals make more mistakes, there are more opportunities for things to go wrong. In other words, healthcare has become riskier. There are more interventions for each patient, these interventions are more invasive (such as surgery or cocktails of drugs), hospitals are increasingly busy places with rapid patient throughput, and a proliferating number of professionals interact with patients. Treatment opportunities have expanded dramatically so that more people, including the very old and the very sick, who previously would have been cared for but not treated, now receive invasive and technologically advanced medical and surgical interventions (McKee and Healy 2002). All of these factors increase the risk of hospital procedures for patients. One surgeon commented that fewer identity checks are done on people embarking on surgery than those boarding a plane. 'Everything has sped up and that is why we need better checks'; 'Some surgeons don't understand the number of risk points leading up to the person being rolled onto the operating table … That timeout check is the last line of defence against mistakes being made'.

The writings of Roy Porter put contemporary accounts of medical errors into historical perspective. Medical knowledge was rudimentary in seventeenth and eighteenth century England and doctors often were regarded as incompetents who harmed their unfortunate patients, while 'best practice' of the time, such as blood-letting and purging, did more harm than good (Porter 2001). Dramatic advances in medical knowledge and technology came mainly in the twentieth century, accompanied by the rapid rise of medical specialization (Porter 1997). From the 1970s onwards, whole new areas of surgery became common accompanied by a massive expansion of pharmaceuticals and by advances in diagnostic and treatment technologies. From a regulatory perspective, the question is how should the increased risk of adverse events be managed? A first step, therefore, is to examine the extent of the risk.

There are few precise figures on the extent to which patients are harmed by adverse advents in health care. That the risk is significant, however, is estimated in the following sections from several sources: public inquiries into 'medical scandals', retrospective reviews of patient medical records, health system data collections, surveys of patients, and data collections on health care performance.

Public Inquiries

Public inquiries are reviewed first because they have prompted regulatory reforms in many countries, and while inquiries do not necessarily indicate the extent of patient safety failures, they reveal the sort of things that go wrong in health care, and cast light on governance failures that need to be addressed. When things go wrong (or at least when the public finds out), an inquiry is set up, ranging in scope from an internal investigation to a parliamentary inquiry. Public inquiries into 'medical scandals' trigger major regulatory reforms partly because governments then have public backing to insist on more accountability from health care providers. These inquiries usually begin by looking for culprits but end with recommendations for systemic reforms and have all identified similar failings: a secretive medical culture; deficient quality monitoring; lack of accountability since many people knew there were serious problems but did nothing; and a dysfunctional organization whose failures usually were longstanding (Walshe and Shortell 2004; Hindle et al. 2006; Masso and Eagar 2009).

Public inquiries are a major regulatory strategy in the Westminster government systems of the United Kingdom and Australia. By contrast, in the United States, pressure for regulatory action has come from newspaper exposés of medical scandals and from media reporting of litigation on patient deaths, including the Libby Zion case in a New York hospital, the Betsy Lehman case at Boston's Dana-Farber Cancer Institute, and lawsuits at a Philadelphia hospital (Millenson 2002). The following sections review widely-reported public inquiries over the last two decades in the United Kingdom and Australia. The questions are first, whether common internal regulatory failures were identified, and second, whether inquiry findings resulted in effective regulatory reforms.

United Kingdom

Public inquiries have had a major impact upon health sector regulation. The Chief Medical Officer has reviewed a spate of inquiries into 'medical scandals' that revealed inadequate responses by health authorities and medical regulatory bodies to professional malpractice and/or incompetence, and he went on to propose a series of reforms to the governance of the medical profession (Chief Medical Officer 2006: chapter 3). The Bristol inquiry on excess deaths among children (see below), in particular, had a profound impact upon professional and hospital governance (Smith 1998). The regulatory landscape subsequently has been transformed with the establishment of new regulatory bodies and accountability frameworks (Walshe 2003). One of these bodies, the Healthcare Commission (later the Care Quality Commission), has issued several very critical public reports on NHS hospitals. While systematic reviews of hospitals may lessen regulatory recourse to a public inquiry, public outrage means that politicians still respond by setting up an inquiry. For example, an investigation on two hospitals run by the Mid Staffordshire NHS Foundation Trust (Care Quality Commission 2009) was followed by a public review.

Bristol Royal Infirmary

The poor performance of the paediatric heart surgery unit in Bristol went undetected for a decade, until an anaesthetist, Stephen Bolsin, went public. From 1991 to 1995 an excess of 30–35 children under one year of age died after open-heart surgery at Bristol, that is, more than expected compared to other paediatric cardiac surgery units in England (The Bristol Royal Infirmary Inquiry 2001). The General Medical Council found three doctors guilty of professional misconduct and a subsequent public inquiry criticized all the parties: the hospital, doctors, the General Medical Council, and the Department of Health. Among the many failures, the report drew attention to a 'club culture' of doctors closing ranks, and a failure to monitor clinical performance even though 'Bristol was awash with data'.

Ledward and others

Widely-reported inquiries into professional misconduct by several doctors also bolstered calls to reform medical governance (Chief Medical Officer 2006: chapter 3). Rodney Ledward, a gynaecologist and hospital consultant, was struck off the medical register by the General Medical Council in 1998 for bungling the operations of 13 women over 16 years. The subsequent Ritchie Inquiry found serious failings in Ledward's surgical skills, inappropriate delegation to junior staff, poor pre- and post-operative care and judgement, and a culture of silence among the medical profession. In another high-profile case, Dr Clifford Ayling, a general practitioner, in 2000 was convicted of 12 counts of indecent assault relating to 10 female patients, after complaints were made to the police after inaction by health authorities. Other cases included two psychiatrists, Kerr and Haslam, who had long histories of poor performance without any regulatory action being taken.

Harold Shipman

The extraordinary case of Harold Shipman, a general practitioner, also focused attention on medical regulation. Shipman was convicted of murdering 15 patients, a public inquiry, *Death Disguised*, thought he had murdered 215 patients (171 women, 44 men) between 1972 and 1998, while a Department of Health report identified at least 236 suspicious deaths (Dyer 2002). These patients mostly died from overdoses of narcotic drugs. The repercussions of the Shipman case continued with a series of inquiries by Dame Janet Smith, who scathingly criticized medical regulatory bodies, such as the General Medical Council (Shipman Inquiry 2004). Debate followed these cases over whether statistical monitoring could pick up a bad performer (like Shipman) or a poor performer (like Ledward). Could 'a Shipman' be detected by measuring an excess of observed over expected deaths among listed patients in a general practice? No, according to one study (Frankel et al. 2000), but others suggested monitoring the time and place of death (it is unusual for patients to die in a doctor's clinic), and stricter control of death certificates (rather than signed only by the attending doctor). While it is not sensible to design a whole monitoring system to pick up extraordinary situations, an analysis of consultant outcomes using hospital episode statistics (comparing Ledward to 143 other gynaecology consultants), showed that it is possible to pick up statistical outliers, but that the reasons, whether poor performance or difficult cases, then need to be investigated. The researchers argued that statistical monitoring for outlier results is underused in the health sector (Harley et al. 2005).

New Zealand

A public inquiry in 1988, the Cartwright Inquiry into cervical cancer treatment for women at the National Women's Hospital in Auckland, riveted public attention on medical ethics and patient safety (Paul 2000). The Inquiry found that Dr Herbert Green had withheld conventional treatment from patients with a cervical pre-cancerous condition in order to study the natural course of the disease, and that of the 160 women inadequately treated, about 40 eventually developed invasive cancer (Cartwright 1988). The Inquiry found that the hospital had approved the research in 1966 despite the prevailing medical view that a pre-cancerous condition warranted treatment; that the hospital reviewed the trial in 1975 after concerns were raised by two doctors but did not shut down the study; and that women were unaware they were part of a trial.

In another medical scandal, medical error was found to be widespread in the form of misdiagnosis in the national cervical screening programme, as revealed by the Gisborne Cervical Screening Inquiry in 2001. The problem became public when 'Patient A' sued the pathologist and the Crown after discovering that four earlier cervical smears had been reported as normal when in fact they showed evidence of cancer. She said she would not have pursued the matter had she received an apology and an assurance that similar mistakes were not occurring with other women (Lamb 2004).

Public Inquiries into Australian Hospitals

Australia has had a spate of public inquiries into hospital 'medical scandals' over the last two decades (see Table 2.1). (Medical scandals involving individual doctors are discussed in Chapter 4). The regulatory response has been a move to stronger external regulation: the establishment of external regulatory bodies, co-regulation arrangements between the state and other health sector bodies, an increase in legislation, and more monitoring of performance indicators. Public inquiries repeatedly identify the same causal themes when things go wrong which suggests that solving patient safety problems is not easy. There are three views on the outcomes of public inquiries. The 'some improvement' view is that limited reforms to systems do follow but there appears to be little change to clinical practice (Masso and Eagar 2009). The 'no change' view is that public inquiries produce no lasting improvement as the hospital system lacks the capacity to meet rising community expectations (Van Der Weyden 2004; Van Der Weyden 2009). The 'unfair to doctors' view is that public inquiries make doctors the scapegoats for system failures and inadequate funding (Dunbar et al. 2007).

Table 2.1 Public inquiries into poor practice in Australian hospitals

Year	State	Hospital	Public Inquiry	Regulatory outcome
1988–1990	NSW	Chelmsford Private Hospital	Royal Commission into Deep Sleep Therapy	Law strengthened; Health Complaints Commission established
1991	Qld	Ward B, Townsville General Hospital	Royal Commission of Inquiry (Carter Report)	Health department restructured
2000	Vic	Royal Melbourne Hospital	Health Services Commissioner	Hospital improved procedures
2001	WA	King Edward Memorial Hospital	Ministerial Inquiry (Douglas Report)	Hospital improved procedures
2003	ACT	Canberra Hospital	Health Complaints Commissioner	Surgeon's registration revoked
2003–2004	NSW	Campden and Campbelltown hospitals	Health Care Complaints Commissioner; Commission of Inquiry (Walker Report)	Health board dissolved; Health Complaints Commissioner dismissed; Laws strengthened
2005	Qld	Bundaberg Hospital	Commission of Inquiry (Morris) terminated	Public demand for reform
2005	Qld	Bundaberg, Hervey Bay, Townsville, Charters Towers, Rockhampton, Prince Charles	Commission of Inquiry (Davies)	Health department restructured; Health Care Complaints Commissioner powers strengthened
2008	NSW	Acute care hospitals NSW	Garling Commission	139 recommendations – outcomes as yet unclear

Chelmsford Hospital, Sydney, New South Wales

The Chelmsford Private Hospital in Sydney was the scene of a widely-reported medical scandal of the 1980s. Run by Dr Harry Bailey, a well-known psychiatrist, it specialized in deep-sleep therapy, regarded as an innovative but unevaluated technique. Between 1963 and 1979, hundreds of patients suffering depression were put into drug-induced sleep, sometimes for up to three weeks, and often given electric shock therapy while unconscious. One patient, Barry Hart, who was admitted in 1972, received deep-sleep therapy plus electric shock therapy, although he had refused to sign a consent form for the latter, and woke after two weeks with double pneumonia, deep vein thrombosis, a pulmonary embolism, and anoxic brain damage. He sued Dr John Herron and Chelmsford Hospital in 1980 and was awarded damages of A$60,000 for false imprisonment and assault and battery. Reporters from the TV programme, *60 Minutes*, talked to relatives of Chelmsford patients and to staff, uncovering 'a horrifying pattern of people being admitted to Chelmsford with nothing physically wrong and simply dying' (Little 1994). The *Sydney Morning Herald* mounted a campaign that prompted the Royal Commission into Deep Sleep Therapy that ran from 1988 to 1990.

The inquiry found that 24 patients had died as a direct consequence of undergoing 'deep sleep' and that false death certificates had been written. The Royal College of Psychiatrists and the NSW Department of Health had done nothing about earlier complaints. Some 152 patients after many years were awarded payouts totalling A$5.5 million by the NSW Victims Compensation Tribunal. The Royal Commission (which cost some A$15 million) recommended that charges be laid against three doctors (Dr Bailey by then had committed suicide), but all three doctors obtained a High Court ruling granting a permanent stay of disciplinary proceedings, and the Director of Public Prosecutions dropped the charges. The NSW Medical Board took no disciplinary action on the grounds that its legislation covered 'infamous conduct', not poor performance (Thomas 2006). The Chelmsford affair led to new legislation, the *Medical Practice Act 1992* (NSW), that extensively defined the meaning of unsatisfactory professional conduct, and an external regulatory authority, the NSW Health Care Complaints Commission, was established (Thomas 2002). A doctor, who had 'blown the whistle' on the Chelmsford deaths, noted that both the UK Bristol case and Chelmsford involved 'powerful medical men who were beyond reproach and prominent in the medical world' (Boettcher 1998).

Ward B, Townsville General Hospital, Queensland

Complaints had been received over several years about Ward B, the psychiatric unit of the Townsville Hospital, concerning patient abuse and rough handling, and poor medication practices. Nothing was done, even after the local Labor member raised concerns in Parliament, until the media picked up the story in early 1988. The furore contributed to the sacking of the Minister for Health, the establishment of a Health Complaints Unit, an internal inquiry, and an investigation by the Queensland Medical Board that concluded there was insufficient evidence to lay charges against two doctors on grounds of professional misconduct. These actions failed to satisfy the public. A Royal Commission of Inquiry was set up and the resulting report by Mr Justice Carter in 1991 recommended changes to mental health legislation and criminal law, and the Queensland Health Rights Commission was established in 1992. These events contributed to a 1991 reorganization of the Queensland Department of Health with health services regionalized and hospital boards abolished, and promises of better peer review procedures (Hovenga 2002).

Royal Melbourne Hospital, Victoria
The Victorian Minister for Health commissioned an inquiry in 2000 by the Health Services Commissioner into management and performance matters at the Royal Melbourne Hospital, following newspaper allegations of nurses taking drugs and boasting of killing patients. The Commissioner reported in three months at a cost of A$55,000, noting that this was an extremely cost-effective approach compared to other public inquiries (Wilson 2004a). The Commissioner found major problems with the medication management system, inadequate reporting of adverse events, poor documentation, and lack of support and supervision for staff (Health Services Commissioner Victoria 2002).

King Edward Memorial Hospital, Western Australia
With a history of staff concerns unsuccessfully raised with the previous management, the new hospital CEO called for a review of obstetrics and gynaecology services, which was conducted by the metropolitan health authority, followed by a public ministerial inquiry that cost A$7 million and ran for 18 months (Douglas et al. 2001). The Inquiry listed a litany of management deficiencies with the state's maternity services, including substandard patient care, inadequate monitoring of clinical performance, shortages of qualified clinical specialists, inadequate supervision of junior staff, and unclear staff responsibilities and accountability. The report called for stronger leadership, clinical governance, comparisons of performance across hospitals, more rigorous hospital accreditation, open disclosure of adverse incidents, adverse events reporting, and systems for mortality reporting and investigation (McLean and Walsh 2003; Faunce and Bolsin 2004).

Canberra Hospital, Australian Capital Territory
After allegations from a hospital specialist that the Canberra Hospital had not acted on patient safety concerns in its neurological services, and in particular on complaints about the head of neurosurgery, the ACT Minister for Health asked the Health Complaints Commissioner to conduct an inquiry. The inquiry took two years, hampered by clinicians' reluctance to give evidence, and initially was not made public (Faunce and Bolsin 2004). In early 2003, the Commissioner summarized the main findings in his annual report and in December 2003 tabled the full report in the Legislative Assembly. This prompted an external review of all cases over six months managed by the neurosurgeon. During 2009 the ACT Civil and Administrative Tribunal heard an application by the ACT Medical

Board to permanently revoke Raymond Newcombe's registration (by then retired) to practise in the ACT, hearing evidence on patient cases including removal of healthy brain tissue instead of a tumour, spinal fusion to the wrong discs, and a surgical rod left inside a patient.

Campden and Campbelltown Hospitals, New South Wales

The NSW Minister for Health in 2003 ordered investigations into allegations by nurses of management failures to respond to adverse events and to misconduct by surgeons at two hospitals, Campden and Campbelltown, in outer south-western Sydney. The NSW Department of Health sent in a clinical review team that examined the hospitals and made reform recommendations. In response to the Health Care Complaints Commissioner's report, the Minister referred 11 doctors to the NSW Medical Board (and suspended two), commenced disciplinary proceedings against 4 administrators, referred 19 patient deaths to the State Coroner, and dissolved the Macarthur area health board.

The Minister also dismissed the Health Care Complaints Commissioner on the grounds that she should have investigated complaints against individual doctors, and that the report did not go far enough in finding anyone accountable for the hospital failures (Van Der Weyden 2004). The Commissioner had applied a 'no blame' philosophy that held that adverse events are due to faulty systems not faulty people. This proved to be politically perilous since it meant that responsibility for health system failures lay with the NSW Health Minister (Thomas 2006). A Special Commission of Inquiry reported in July 2004, dismissing 91 of the 128 allegations, and referring the remaining 37 cases for investigation (Eagar 2004). The NSW Medical Registration Board cleared four of the 11 doctors of malpractice. Following the inquiry, amendments were made to legislation on patient complaints mechanisms and on the registration of health professionals.

Commentators on the saga proposed different solutions: better protection for whistle-blowers (Faunce and Bolsin 2004), quality managers in every hospital (Wilson 2004b), and peer review of adverse events (Masso 2004). Many hospital staff feared that a culture of blame had ousted a short-lived culture of safety (Frankum et al. 2004). Their view was that quality was compromised by poorly resourced hospitals and over-burdened staff, not because staff were negligent. Eagar, an experienced health services manager, claimed that patient care in the two area hospitals was probably no worse than in similar poorly resourced hospitals elsewhere:

> Macarthur is, on all the evidence I have seen over more than a decade, no different to numerous hospitals we can identify in almost every jurisdiction. These hospitals are typically, but not always, on the urban fringe or in a rural region, without their fair share of senior clinicians and without adequate diagnostic and clinical infrastructure. They simply do not have the resources to provide services at a level commensurate with community political and media expectations. (Eagar 2004: 12).

Queensland public hospitals
The Bundaberg Hospital scandal began with an incompetent surgeon, Dr Jayant Patel, dubbed 'Dr Death' in extensive newspaper coverage (Nason and Fraser 2005), but subsequent public inquiries also found failures on the part of hospital and health department managers, and the Medical Board of Queensland. The situation was brought to light by a whistle-blower, Toni Hoffman, a nurse at the Bundaberg Hospital, who, after her repeated complaints were ignored by hospital managers, went to a Queensland politician who tabled her formal letter of complaint in Parliament in March 2005. A journalist then 'googled' Dr Patel's professional background in the United States, finding his practice had been restricted in Oregon, and also in New York state for 'gross negligence' where he was later required to surrender his licence.

Dr Patel had been located through a private recruiting firm and appointed as staff surgical officer, after the Queensland Medical Board approved his registration, and was quickly promoted to Director of Surgery despite his lack of specialist surgical qualifications. He operated on about 1,000 patients over two years of whom 88 died and many suffered serious complications (Van Der Weyden 2005). A clinical review concluded that Dr Patel contributed to the deaths of 13 patients, may have contributed to the deaths of another four, and contributed to adverse outcomes for 31 surviving patients. A Commission of Inquiry (at a cost of A$5.6 million) run by Anthony Morris QC was terminated in September 2005 on grounds of perceived bias, given the Commissioner's vigorous questioning of hospital and health department managers (Hart and Parnell 2005). The ex-Commissioner then used parliamentary privilege to deliver a damning report on Queensland's health sector (Parnell 2005). The parallel Forster review, set up by the Queensland government into the administration of Queensland Health, produced a report in late 2005 calling for major administrative reforms. A retired appeals court judge was appointed to head a new inquiry with its scope broadened beyond Bundaberg to cover Hervey Bay Hospital, Townsville Hospital, Charters Towers Hospital, Rockhampton Hospital and Prince Charles Hospital. The Davies Inquiry found that in Dr Patel's two years at the Bundaberg Hospital, staff or patients made over 20 complaints about him, which mostly were ignored by the Director of Medical Services and the Queensland Health district manager. The Queensland Medical Board, which had fast-tracked Dr Patel's registration, was found to be negligent (especially since a journalist's Google check had exposed his US malpractice history). The final report referred Dr Patel to the Queensland police for investigation under the Criminal Code in relation to fraud, assault, assault occasioning bodily harm, grievous bodily harm, negligent acts causing harm, and manslaughter (Davies Report 2005).

The Commissioner identified common problems across the Queensland public hospital system: defectively administered and inadequate hospital budgets, negligent administration of registration of doctors by the Queensland Medical Board, an absence of credentialing and privileging by hospital employers (i.e. assessing the credentials and competence of doctors for specific tasks), failure to monitor the performance of doctors, failure to record or to investigate complaints, and the suppression by administrators of complaints. The Commission criticized the Health Minister, hospital managers and health administrators.

These events led to the resignation of the Minister of Health and the Director-General of the health department. The Dr Patel case attracted considerable media interest with the events documented in a book by the investigative journalist, *Sick to Death* (Thomas 2007). The Queensland Medical Board subsequently charged Dr Patel with unsatisfactory professional conduct, he was deregistered by a medical tribunal, Queensland began extradition proceedings with the United States, and Dr Patel returned to Australia in March 2009 to face a committal hearing on manslaughter charges.

Acute care hospitals in New South Wales

A Special Commission during 2008 into acute care services in NSW public hospitals made 139 reform recommendations in a three-volume report (Garling Report 2009). The concerns that led to the inquiry were a parliamentary inquiry into allegations of poor care for several patients at the Royal North Shore hospital, as well as a 2008 coronial report that found that the death of Vanessa Anderson, aged 16 years, at the prestigious Royal North Shore Hospital in November 2005 was preventable and due to systematic errors in her care. (The coroner had found that Vanessa Anderson, who had been hit on the head by a golf ball, died from respiratory arrest in hospital due to the depressant effects of opiate medication after a doctor misread her chart). The Commissioner reported that the state's public hospital system was 'on the brink' of crisis, there was a 'breakdown in good working relations between clinicians and management', and that work practices needed to be streamlined and brought into the twenty-first century. He stated that 'the safety of patients and the quality of their care is paramount' and called for 'new models of care' and for new regulatory agencies to collect information, train staff and monitor performance.

Retrospective Reviews of Patient Medical Records

While public inquiries cast a harsh light on systemic patient safety problems, estimating the scope and scale of adverse events requires different methods. A systematic review of studies of patient medical records concluded that adverse events during a hospital admission affect nearly one in ten patients. The review identified eight studies (from 257 articles) that met criteria for comparable definitions and methodologies on adverse events affecting hospital inpatients (de Vries et al. 2008). Table 2.2 summarizes the eight studies that retrospectively examined samples of medical records of hospital patients using a similar methodology. The advantages of comparing research from several studies and from several countries are, first, similar findings demonstrate that the methodology is robust, and second, similar results show that patient safety is a universal problem for modern hospitals.

Table 2.2 Studies of adverse events from retrospective hospital records reviews

Country	Study	Sample size	Adverse event rate
USA	Harvard Study (Brennan et al. 1991)	30,121 cases in 51 NY State acute hospitals 1984	3.8% of patients with at least one adverse event 58% adverse events preventable 13.6% adverse events led to death (0.28% admissions) 27.6% adverse events negligent (1.0% admissions)
USA	Brigham and Women's Hospital (O'Neill 1993)	3,136 admissions Nov 1990–March 1991	7.5% of patients with at least one adverse event
USA	Utah-Colorado Study (Thomas et al. 2000a)	15,000 acute hospital discharges	3.2% of patients with at least one adverse event 53% adverse events preventable 6.6% adverse events led to death (0.3% of admissions) 0.9% admissions negligent adverse event
Australia	Quality in Australian Health Care Study (Wilson et al. 1995)	14,655 admissions in 28 acute hospitals in NSW and SA	16.6% of patients with at least one adverse event 51% adverse events preventable 2% admissions led to death
Australia	Revised QAHCS estimates (Runciman et al. 2000; Thomas et al. 2000b)		10.6% of patients with at least one adverse event 51% adverse events preventable 0.3% admissions led to death
England	(Vincent et al. 2001)	1,014 admissions in 2 London hospitals	10.8% of patients with at least one adverse event 48% adverse events preventable 8% adverse events contributed to death
England	(Sari et al. 2007)	1,006 admissions one NHS hospital	7.5% of patients with at least one adverse event 44% adverse events preventable
New Zealand	(Davis et al. 2002)	6,579 discharges from 13 general public hospitals in 1988	11.2% of patients with at least one adverse event (12.9% of admissions) 37% adverse events preventable 15% adverse events led to permanent disability or death
Canada	(Baker et al. 2004)	Random sample 37,45 l records 20 hospitals in 5 Canadian provinces in 2000	6.8% of patients with at least one adverse event 36.9% adverse events preventable 20.8% events contributed to death (1.6% admissions)

Note: Selected studies since 1990 with sample size >1,000 cases

A Harvard team study published in 1991 retrospectively examined medical records from 51 New York State acute care hospitals (and developed the methodology used in other studies). They reported that 3.8 per cent of patients incurred harm from at least one adverse event, 58 per cent of errors were preventable, and 13.6 per cent of adverse events (0.28 per cent of admissions) led to death (Brennan et al. 1991; Leape 1994). A study at the Brigham and Women's Hospital reported that 7.5 per cent of patients incurred at least one adverse event (O'Neill et al. 1993). A study of patients discharged from acute care general hospitals in Utah and Colorado found that 3.2 per cent of patients incurred an adverse event, 53 per cent were preventable, 6.6 per cent of adverse events led to death (0.3 per cent of admissions), and 24.7 per cent of adverse events (0.9 per cent of admissions) were due to negligence (Thomas et al. 2000a; Thomas et al. 2000b).

The 1995 Quality in Australian Health Care Study (QAHCS) (using the Harvard methodology) randomly selected hospital medical records in 28 acute hospitals in two Australian states. An adverse event was defined as 'an unintended injury or complication which results in disability, death or prolonged hospital stay and is caused by health care management'. The study estimated that 16.6 per cent of admissions were associated with an adverse event, 51 per cent of events were considered preventable, and 2 per cent of hospital admissions died from an adverse event (Wilson et al. 1995). These findings provoked a furore. The researchers argued that Australian hospitals were not more dangerous than US hospitals but the findings were higher because more minor adverse events had been counted. After a re-analysis adjusting the methodology to better fit the US studies, the estimate was that 10.6 per cent of patients experience an adverse advent in hospital, 51 per cent of these events were considered preventable, 1.7 per cent of admissions experience serious disability, and that 0.3 per cent of patients die from an adverse event (Runciman et al. 2000).

A retrospective review of 1,014 records in two London acute hospitals found that 10.8 per cent of patients experienced an adverse event, 48 per cent of adverse events were judged to be preventable, 25 per cent of adverse events led to moderate or permanent disability, and 8 per cent of adverse events contributed to death (Vincent et al. 2001). Another study of admissions in one NHS hospital found that 7.5 per cent of patients experienced an adverse event (Sari et al. 2007).

In New Zealand, a retrospective review of patient records was carried out in 1998 in 13 acute care hospitals. An adverse event was associated with 11.2 per cent of patients (12.9 per cent of hospital admissions) of which nearly 20 per cent of adverse events had occurred in a health care setting outside the hospital; of all adverse events, 37 per cent were judged to be preventable, and nearly 15 per cent were associated with permanent disability or death (Davis et al. 2002; Davis et al. 2003a; Davis et al. 2003b).

A Canadian study in 20 hospitals across five provinces using the Harvard protocol found adverse events in 6.8 per cent of patient cases, 36.9 per cent of adverse events were judged preventable, with death occurring in 20.8 per cent of adverse events (Baker et al. 2004).

In addition to these eight studies, other countries also have undertaken their own reviews mostly using the Harvard methodology. For example, a study in Danish hospitals found an incidence of adverse events similar to other countries: adverse events occurred in 9 per cent of hospital admissions with permanent harm of death in 0.4 per cent of admissions (Schioler et al. 2001).

Other Data Collections

Other data collections, such as adverse event reporting systems, mortality registers and administrative data sets, examine safety and quality issues from different vantage points. Adverse event reporting has been adopted internationally as a major strategy for addressing patient safety (see Chapter 8). Many countries have established reporting systems, either national systems as in England and Denmark, or regional (state-based) systems as in the United States and Australia. Reporting systems also have been established for particular types of adverse events, for example, hospital associated infections such as methicillin-resistant *Staphlococcus aureus* (MRSA). The early expectation that adverse event reporting is a mechanism to measure and track patient safety has not proved realistic. First, conclusions cannot be drawn on scope, scale and trends since reports mostly are voluntary on the part of staff, and there is considerable under-reporting despite efforts to replace a blame culture with a learning culture. Second, questionnaire-type incident reports may be insufficient for identifying causes and proposing solutions. Clinicians need to undertake in-depth investigations into the events surrounding an incident in order to craft prevention strategies. The consensus, therefore, is that adverse events present a learning opportunity, a 'window onto the system', through which to look for weaknesses in order to prevent future problems (Vincent 2004).

Mortality and morbidity registers with associated audits of clinical practice have been established in many countries mainly by professional associations and are credited with producing significant improvements (see Chapter 8). These methods of self-regulation by the profession are generally well-accepted by doctors. Registers are used more as quality improvement than quality measurement tools, however, since reporting mostly is voluntary.

Administrative datasets also offer a mechanism for regulating safety and quality (see Chapter 8). Hospitals generally have extensive datasets and such routine datasets could be used to monitor safety and quality. For example, in Australia, an analysis of Victorian administrative datasets used for calculating hospital casemix payments found that nearly 7 per cent of patients across 45 public hospitals were coded as experiencing at least one adverse event (Ehsani et al. 2006). Since this result is close to the around 10 per cent of cases identified in retrospective reviews of patient medical records, the argument is that improving routinely collected hospital data offers a cost-effective way to track trends in patient safety.

Surveys of patients offer a new source of information that demonstrates that safety problems are common in community-based health services as well as hospitals. The Commonwealth Fund used a telephone survey to ask people who reported poor health (that is, regular health care users) from six countries (Australia, Canada, Germany, New Zealand, United Kingdom, United States) about their health care experiences. Between 22 and 34 per cent of patients across the six countries said they had experienced a medical mistake, medication error, or laboratory test error in the previous two years (Schoen et al. 2005). Another Commonwealth Fund survey of a representative sample of adults in seven countries (with the addition of the Netherlands) reported that 12–20 per cent had experienced a medical mistake, medication error, or laboratory test error in the past two years (Schoen et al. 2007). In Australia, a telephone survey of a random sample of 1500 adults across five states found that 7.5 per cent reported experiencing an adverse event during a hospital admission and 9.7 per cent during a clinic visit to a doctor (Clark 2004).

General practitioners are not very forthcoming so far on adverse events in their practices. Australian general practitioners are regularly surveyed in the Bettering the Evaluation and Care of Health (BEACH) study, which surveys a random sample of 1,000 general practitioners from a national database who record data from 100 consecutive patient consultations, a total of about 100,000 consultations annually (Britt et al. 2008). These surveys report adverse events in 0.9 per cent of GP encounters with patients (Britt et al. 2003), and that 10.4 per cent of their patients had experienced an adverse drug event in the previous six months (Miller et al. 2006). It seems likely that 1 in 100 general practice patients experiencing an adverse event (compared to 1 in 10 hospital patients) is an under-estimate, especially given the high rate of medication-related problems.

Quality of Health Care Measurements

Quality is a broad term that refers to all the attributes of good health care, one definition being: 'The extent to which health services for individuals and populations increase the likelihood of desired health outcomes and are consistent with current professional knowledge' (World Health Organization 2009b: 33). The US Institute of Medicine proposed that a high quality health care system should aspire to be safe, effective, patient-centred, timely, efficient, and equitable (Institute of Medicine 2001). Patient safety is a key attribute of the broader domain of quality care. Poor quality care does not necessarily mean unsafe care in the sense that it results in an adverse event.

Quality of care is attracting regulatory attention for three reasons. First, only about half of patients overall (in the United States but probably also in other countries) receive treatment in accordance with evidence-based guidelines. Second, there are large variations in the quality of care received by patients with inequities most apparent in rural areas, among the poor and among ethnic minority groups (Healy and McKee 2004). Third, health systems around the world are desperate to make cost-effectiveness savings and to reduce the haemorrhage of funds upon unsafe and poor quality care.

Quality is notoriously difficult to define and measure. A report by the London-based King's Fund concluded, however, that quality measurement despite its many pitfalls has real potential for improving health care (Raleigh and Foot 2010). In monitoring quality, the research thrust is to identify an activity that is easy to measure and track, or if this is not possible, then a proxy measure is sought. The choice of indicators often is pragmatic depending on what data can be gathered conveniently, are least ambiguous (the death of a patient being the least equivocal), and less amenable to being fudged. Measures of quality at the national or health system level, however, may need to be adapted at the local or condition-specific level. For example, while mortality as an indicator of patient outcome is relevant for high-risk procedures, such as heart surgery, it is not relevant for low-risk procedures, such as cataract surgery.

In terms of clinical performance, evidence of sub-optimal or poor quality care can be classified broadly in terms of three measures: overuse, underuse, and misuse of treatments (Institute of Medicine 2000). Examples of the *overuse* of treatments include tonsillectomy, appendectomy, Caesarean births, prostate cancer surgery, episiotomy, screening for prostate cancer, back surgery, and blood transfusions. The argument is that there is 'too much medicine' since many conditions are over-medicalized and over-medicated, especially given the undue influence by the pharmaceutical industry upon doctors' prescribing behaviour (Moynihan 1998; Moynihan and Cassels 2005).

The medical literature also reveals considerable *underuse* associated with the slow take-up of evidence-based medicine. For example, systematic reviews have documented the underuse of beta-blockers to reduce the risk of post-surgical heart attacks (Auerbach 2001). Risk factors that are under-treated include hypertension and high blood cholesterol that predispose to stroke and heart attacks, and there are significant regional variations within countries in treatment and survival rates for ischaemic heart disease (Care Quality Commission 2010), and for cancer (Yu et al. 2004). The underuse of health care is more likely among socio-economically disadvantaged populations, including ethnic minority groups (Whitehead and Hanratty 2004). The goal is to close the gap between evidence and practice by persuading doctors to follow 'best practice' clinical guidelines (Grol and Jeremy 2003). Clinical protocols on many conditions set out recommendations on the treatment that should be provided to patients, so that the proportion of patients who receive the recommended treatment offers a measure of quality care. The Commonwealth Fund has conducted several salutary studies on the gap between good practice and actual practice. A telephone survey of a US patient sample (13,275 across 12 metropolitan areas) found that only 54.9 per cent had received the recommended care, which varied across 30 conditions ranging from 78.7 per cent down to 10.5 per cent of patients (McGlynn et al. 2003). An examination of paediatric outpatient medical records of a sample of US children (1,536 across 12 metropolitan areas) found that only 46.5 per cent received the recommended care, varying across clinical conditions from 92 per cent down to 34.5 per cent (Mangione-Smith et al. 2007).

Examples of the *misuse* of treatment include prescribing an incorrect drug and selecting less effective prostheses. Misuse often involves unsafe practice, such as adverse drug reactions, incorrect blood transfusions and wrong patient surgery. The later section on classification examines definitions and measures of adverse events many of which are misuse of treatment.

Empirical Studies on the Costs of Adverse Events

While there is a clear humanitarian rationale for improving unsafe and poor quality care, there is also a compelling economic rationale. In relation to patient safety, retrospective studies of patient medical records found that adverse events account for a sizeable share of hospital budgets, partly because they increase the length of patient stays in hospital. The Institute of Medicine report estimated that medical errors cost the American health system between US$37.6 and US$50 billion annually, with preventable events equivalent to at least 2 per cent of national health expenditure (Institute of Medicine 2000). In New Zealand, adverse events were estimated to add on average over nine days to a hospital stay and therefore greatly increase hospital costs (Davis et al. 2002). A study of medical records in 13 NZ public hospitals in 1998 estimated that 30 per cent of hospital expenditure went on treating the consequences of adverse events (Brown et al. 2002). In England, adverse events each year were estimated to cost NHS hospitals over £2 billion (Donaldson Report 2000).

The Quality in Australian Health Care Study (QAHCS) concluded that adverse events accounted for 8 per cent of all hospital bed days in 1992, of which over half were potentially preventable. Based on a 1992 cost of A$510 per bed day, adverse events cost the hospital system A$1.68 billion, and preventable adverse events cost A$867 million. The medical costs of potentially preventable iatrogenic injury exceeded A$2 billion annually after adding the costs of treatment outside hospital (Runciman and Moller 2001: 22–25). A study of Victorian public hospitals found that adverse events in 2003–04 added A$6,826 to the cost of an admission and overall cost 18.6 per cent of the total inpatient hospital budget (Ehsani et al. 2006). The study estimated that adverse events cost Victorian hospitals about A$511.5 million a year and cost all Australian hospitals about A$2 billion a year.

Hospital-acquired infections have received particular attention. Patients who acquire infections in UK hospitals spend over twice as long in hospital (Plowman et al. 1999; National Audit Office 2000), and an Australian study estimated that bloodstream infections cost A$686 million (Nimmo and Looke 2001).

The research clearly shows that unsafe care is costly as is poor quality care. The question is do interventions to improve safety and quality save money, in other words, do the savings outweigh the cost? An extensive review of the literature has concluded that there is clear evidence that some interventions are cost-effective, such as prophylaxis before surgery and computer physician entry, but there is less evidence for cost savings on some other effective interventions:

> Does improving quality save money? Sometime, but sometimes not, and mostly we do not know because the research is limited. There is great potential for savings, but it depends what we mean by quality improvement, who makes the savings and when. (Ovretveit 2009: ix)

Whether savings can be made depends in part on the degree of effectiveness of the solution, but also upon whether the solution can be implemented locally at low cost. Simple solutions usually are less costly and easier to implement, while major changes that promise major benefits usually are more difficult and more costly, so that service providers should consider not only the costs and benefits of an intervention outcome but also the ease and cost of its implementation. They should also remember that efficiency is not the only goal:

> Saving money is not a strong motivator for clinical personnel and it is not the only reason to improve quality. There are ethical moral and professional reasons too, but these alone have not proved sufficient. (Ovretveit 2009: xv)

Classifications of Adverse Events

Adverse events can be classified in different ways and so reflect different perspectives on types of errors and their causes. Devising meaningful classifications is a complex undertaking given the enormous number and variety of things that can go wrong in health care. For example, the Quality in Australian Health Care Study (QAHCS) identified 518 principal categories of error involving hospital patients of which the top ten accounted for only 25 per cent of all adverse events (Runciman and Moller 2001: 18). While attention rightly is directed to adverse events that seriously injure or kill patients, regulators should not neglect more numerous and mundane adverse events, because these occur more frequently and are cumulatively costly, accounting for 60 per cent of hospital costs associated with adverse events (Runciman et al. 2002). Their frequency also indicates that the health care system needs to be seriously improved. Adverse event reporting systems generally classify incidents in terms of what, where, when and who, as well as how and why (World Health Organization 2009a). One issue is that some misadventures that befall patients, such as misdiagnosis, are not interpreted by clinicians as error but rather as 'a complication' as Atul Gawande points out in his book *Complications: A Surgeon's Notes on an Imperfect Science* (Gawande 2002).

Classifying Causes of Adverse Events

Crafting the solution to a problem depends upon understanding the cause of a problem and there are still large knowledge gaps in understanding the scope and scale of adverse events let alone the causes. An analysis of causation involves several issues: technical, ideological, and classificatory. The *technical* issue is that incident reports and patient records seldom provide sufficient information to study causation, there is considerable under-reporting, while root cause analyses in individual cases are too expensive to undertake on a scale large enough to detect patterns of causation. The *theory* issue is that classifying 'causes' depends upon the explanatory framework adopted, such as human error versus system error. These two frameworks emerge from different value systems and lead to different regulatory responses, such as investing in staff training versus information technology. The *classificatory* issue is the huge range of types of error and the different causative explanations. Adverse events usually have a multi-cause explanation since modern hospital care involves teams of people and complex procedures. An adverse event analysis also must decide a time frame for the trail of causation and whether attributable to proximate or distal factors. For example, interviews with surgeons at three Massachusetts teaching hospitals found that explanations for surgical error went beyond immediate cognitive causes in citing inexperience or lack of competence (53 per cent of incidents) and fatigue or excessive workload (33 per cent) (Gawande et al. 2003).

Other Categories

Types of errors: Accident researchers study the human dimension of error, and in particular, the types of cognitive processes that lead to error. Research on human error, that is, why people make mistakes, suggests various classificatory frameworks for studying causation; for example, insufficient knowledge, lack of skills, failure in performance, failure to follow rules and protocols, and violations (Reason 1990). Runciman and colleagues discuss 10 types of cognitive errors that expand on the usual typology of errors as knowledge-based, rules-based, skills-based, and technical (Runciman et al. 2007: chapter 4) Understanding the cognitive dimensions of error is crucial in reducing the potential for human failure and understanding the human and system intersections.

Types of patients: Older patients are at higher risk of adverse events than younger patients. First, older people are much more likely than younger people to be hospital patients. For example, in Australia in 2004–05 there were 340 discharges per 1,000 persons for the total population compared to 926 for persons aged 65 years and over (Australian Institute of Health and Welfare 2007). Second, a US study showed that older patients were twice as likely as younger patients to experience an adverse event (Thomas et al. 2000a). The Quality in Australian Health Care Study (QAHCS) showed that patients aged over 65 years old accounted for 40 per cent of all adverse events, with the probability of an adverse event resulting in death being ten-fold higher than for patients aged under 45 years (Wilson et al. 1995). The characteristics of older patients themselves, such as poor balance and deafness, may be contributing factors in adverse events, as well as factors in the hospital environment. In other words, frail and elderly people are high-risk hospital patients. Since populations in OECD countries are ageing, hospitals should improve their risk management for older patients.

Types of hospital units and staff: What areas of the hospital involve the most risk of adverse events for patients? For example, surgery is a major focus (see later) since around half of adverse advents involve surgical patients (Thomas et al. 2000a) and major complications occur in 3–17 per cent of surgical cases (Haynes et al. 2009). Are some types of staff more likely to be involved in adverse events? This is difficult to answer for several reasons: adverse event reports seldom identify individuals as the philosophy is to avoid blame; an adverse event often involves several people; and nurses mostly undertake the reporting task. Sub-optimal care occurs more commonly at both ends of the professional age range. Young and inexperienced doctors learn by practising on patients ('see one, do one, teach one') and their initial training often involves botched procedures – according to anecdotal accounts (Gawande 2002). At the other end of the experience continuum, there is evidence that older doctors provide lesser quality of care than younger doctors (Choudhry et al. 2005).

Types of devices and procedures: Medical treatment involves the use of a huge array of devices and equipment and faulty design or misuse present constant risks especially at the interface between equipment and user. The Global Harmonization Taskforce on medical devices classifies errors as manufacturer-related error, use or design error, and user error (World Health Organization 2007: 16). Equipment may be substandard (for example, poorly designed equipment), may be confusing for users (for example, lack of standardized devices), the user may lack technical competence (for example, faulty insertion of drips, cannulas and catheters), or a hospital may fail to take action to prevent failures or to respond when thing go wrong (for example, lack of staff training, lack of safety procedures, absence of performance monitoring). About 2 per cent of adverse events identified in the Quality in Australian Health Care Study involved a problem with a device (Runciman et al. 2002). In Australia, the Therapeutic Goods Administration runs a Medical Device Incident Report Investigation Scheme with about 500–600 reports made each year, of which 37 per cent potentially could cause injury or death (Australian Council for Safety and Quality in Health Care 2004a: 94).

Areas of patient management: Certain areas of patient management involve a higher risk, such as poor communication at patient hand-over, mistakes in procedures, wrong patient/site surgery, poor hand hygiene, and blood clots arising from immobility. A hospital patient usually is cared for by many staff in regular changes of shift and poor staff communication is a common cause of adverse events. Poor communication is a frequently cited root cause of sentinel events (Joint Commission 2008), and a common cause of adverse events associated with clinical handover of patients (Wong et al. 2008). The World Health Organization thus urges better communication during patient hand-over as one of its nine patient safety solutions (World Health Organization 2007).

Types of Incidents: Things that go Wrong for Patients

Adverse events can also be classified in terms of harmful outcomes for patients, such as pressure ulcers, health care associated infections, medication errors, and patient falls (Australian Council for Safety and Quality in Health Care 2004b: 19). These are areas where substantial improvements can be made by implementing evidence-based solutions that reduce the risk of adverse events. Table 2.3 summarizes the main studies on types of adverse events. Estimates are indicative rather than precise because different definitions of adverse events produce different numbers (also the proportions of patients sum to greater than 100 per cent since multiple things can go wrong with one patient).

Table 2.3 Studies of types of adverse events

Type	Study	Sample size	Adverse event rate
Pressure ulcers	Pressure Ulcer Point Prevalence Study (PUPPS)	87 acute and sub-acute Victorian hospitals and nursing homes 2003 and 2004	20–27% patients, most ulcers preventable, 4.6% had severe ulcers, 17.9% acquired ulcer in hospital
Hospital acquired infections	McLaws et al. 1988	National 1984 survey of 28,643 patients in Australian hospitals	6.3% patients, many infections preventable 4.6% infections contribute to death
Hospital acquired infections	Collignon 2005	Survey of S. aureus in 17 Australian hospitals	0.15% patients 36% preventable (half cases arose in community)
Medication errors	Day 1995	QAHCS (14,655 admissions in 28 acute hospitals NSW and SA)	2–3% hospital patients, 43% preventable errors
Medication errors	Bates 1995	2 North American hospitals	6.7% hospital patients
Patient falls	Rigby et al. 1999	Australian Incident Monitoring System (AIMS) data	38% of admissions (2–5% in acute hospitals, 46% sub-acute) 60% preventable
Surgical errors	Western Australia Audit of Surgical Mortality (WAASM)	From 2001, 85% surgeons in WA contribute data	0.017% surgical deaths due to adverse events, adverse events caused 3% surgical deaths and contributed to death in18%
Surgical Errors	Leape et al. 1991 Thomas et al. 2000	Harvard Medical Practice Study, 51 NY State hospitals in 1984; Utah and Colorado 15,000 acute hospitals discharges	Up to two-thirds adverse events in surgical care, More than half preventable
Surgical Errors	McGuire, Horsley, Salter and Sobel 1992	44,603 surgical procedures in a US hospital 1977–90	6.3% complication rate 3.1% preventable adverse events 8.4% preventable events result in death

Pressure ulcers

Pressure ulcers (decubitus ulcers) can cause substantial tissue damage and can lead to death when infection occurs, and mostly are preventable since the risk factors include immobility and friction. Pressure ulcers ('bed sores') occur as a result of friction causing injury to the skin, or from unrelieved pressure preventing blood flow and causing the skin and underlying tissue to break down and die, and are graded in four stages of severity, their most severe leading to life-threatening infection (Australian Wound Management Association 2001). The financial cost for the health system in managing a stage two ulcer (dressings and nursing time) was estimated at A$586 per month per patient (Australian Council for Safety and Quality in Health Care 2004a).

Estimates of prevalence range from 10.1 per cent to 14.8 per cent among hospital patients in developed countries (World Health Organization 2007: 7). A Victorian survey in 2003 in 87 hospitals and nursing homes, the Pressure Ulcer Point Prevalence Survey (PUPPS), found higher rates, however, with 26.5 per cent of hospital patients showing signs of a pressure ulcer, 4.6 per cent had severe ulcers, and 17.9 per cent had acquired the ulcer during a hospital stay (Australian Council for Safety and Quality in Health Care 2005b). Pressure sores can also develop among ambulatory patients where there is unrelieved friction on the skin. For example, an 82-year-old nursing home resident who fractured her arm developed a pressure sore under the plaster that became infected with antibiotic-resistant staph, causing her death a month later in hospital (Clinical Liaison Service 2007b).

Health care associated infections

Hospitals treat large numbers of sick people in close proximity and so offer opportunities for pathogenic organisms to spread. Hospital-acquired infections afflict at least 10 per cent of patients in European hospitals and are a major and growing problem in modern hospitals (National Audit Office 2000; Taylor et al. 2001). In Australia, an estimated 6 per cent of hospital patients acquire an infection, most commonly catheter-associated urinary tract infections, infections related to intravenous cannulas, and surgical wound infections (Spelman 2002). Prevalence is high in units such as intensive care, burns, neonatal care and units treating immune-suppressed patients (Ayliffe et al. 1999).

The adoption of aseptic and antiseptic techniques in the late nineteenth century and the later invention of antibiotics led many to think that the battle against hospital-acquired infection had been won, but rates of hospital-acquired infections were rising by the end of the twentieth century (Swartz 1995). First, susceptibility to infection rises with age and patients admitted to hospital are older, reflecting aging populations, as well as the increased scope for intervention in older patients who might previously have been deemed unfit for more aggressive treatment. Second, procedures have become more extensive with longer operation times and greater use of implants. Third, more patients are on immunosuppressive treatments. Fourth, the risks are increasing of blood-borne viral infections, such as hepatitis B and C and HIV. Finally, antibiotic-resistant micro-organisms have expanded dramatically with the profligate use of antibiotics.

The rise in multi-drug resistant strains of bacteria is a big problem (McKee et al. 2002). Bacteria are capable of rapid evolutionary change, and many types of bacteria exhibit increasing rates of antibiotic resistance, such as *Staphylococcus aureus*, which many individuals carry without any problem. New strains have evolved, such as methicillin-resistant *S. aureus* (MRSA), which are resistant to almost all antibiotics. Bacteremia responded to a short course of penicillin five decades ago but is now difficult to treat and can kill 20–30 per cent of those infected within a month. An Australian study in 17 hospitals found that 1.5 per 1000 hospital admissions had *S. aureus* bacteremia, which extrapolated nationally means 6900 cases of which 2500 are preventable with about 1700 deaths (Collignon et al. 2005).

Rates of *Clostridium difficile* infections in hospitals throughout the world also have risen including highly virulent strains. The *C. difficile* bacterium sometimes occurs in the gut of healthy children and adults without causing problems, such as diarrhoea, unless the balance in the gut is disturbed. It forms spores that can be spread in the air and survive for long periods in the environment, such as on floors around toilets. Rigorous cleaning of hands and hospital environments is the most effective means of removing spores. The best form of prevention of all hospital-acquired infections still is old-fashioned hand-hygiene (these days with hand gel) before touching a patient.

Medication errors

Medication errors involving misuse, underuse, and overuse of medication mostly are preventable. The causes of medication error have been exhaustively studied and many solutions proposed. Medication errors can occur at many steps in the medication pathway: unclear labelling, storage and packaging, undecipherable prescriptions, incorrect medication, incorrect strength or dosage, medicine administered to the wrong patient, and harmful medicine interaction. Two examples illustrate the serious repercussions from medication errors. A vincristine medication alert was issued in several countries after cases of inadvertent intrathecal injection, including a 28-year-old man who was paralysed and died in a New South Wales hospital when vincristine mistakenly was injected into his spinal cord rather than into a vein (Australian Council for Safety and Quality in Health Care 2005a). The incorrect administration of drugs to a woman during labour that resulted in the death of the baby caused the Victorian Coroner to recommend that drugs not be drawn up until they are needed, that different drugs be placed in different dishes, and that ampoules be re-checked before being administered (Clinical Liaison Service 2006).

More medication means more opportunities for errors. Studies in several countries found rates of medication error ranging from 2–7 per cent of patient admissions (Kaushal and Bates 2001). For example, serious or potentially serious medication errors were found in the care of 6.7 per cent of patients in two leading

North American hospitals (Bates et al. 1995). According to recent estimates, 7.5 per cent to 10.4 per cent of hospital patients in high-income countries experience an adverse drug event (World Health Organization 2007: 3). In Australia, drug therapy errors have been found in 5–20 per cent of drugs administered in hospital (Australian Council for Safety and Quality in Health Care 2002), and the number of reports have continued to rise (Roughead 2005; Roughead and Lexchin 2006), as have adverse drug reactions as found in age-standardized hospital stays for people aged 60 years and over in West Australian hospitals (Burgess et al. 2005).

Patient falls

A fall in an elderly person is a high-risk event with possibly severe consequences, such as hip fracture or head injuries. Falls account for substantial trauma especially among people aged 65 years and over, resulting in increased lengths of stays in hospital and higher health costs. For example, an 84-year-old woman taken to a Victorian hospital emergency department, after falling at home and hitting her head, was discharged after a few hours when her vital signs appeared normal, but was readmitted next day when her condition deteriorated and died later that day. A CT scan showed a subdural haematoma. The hospital changed its procedure and now routinely scans patients with a head injury over the age of 60 years and also those on anticoagulants (Clinical Liaison Service 2007a). Estimates on the incidence of falls range from 2–5 per cent of patients in acute care hospitals (Bakarich et al. 1997), to up to 46 per cent of patients in sub-acute and rehabilitation settings (Tutuarima et al. 1997). Patient falls are the most common injury reported to the adverse event reporting system for England and Wales (National Patient Safety Agency 2007). An analysis of South Australian adverse events data found that falls accounted for 38 per cent of reported adverse events in public hospitals (Rigby et al. 1999), while in 2001–02 in Victoria, 514 fall-related injuries resulting in death occurred in a health service setting or residential aged care facility (Ranson and Emmett 2003).

Surgical errors

One-half to two-thirds of adverse events in US hospitals involve surgical patients and more than half of these events are preventable (Gawande et al. 1992; Leape 1994; Thomas et al. 2000a). Studies in high-income countries show a perioperative death rate from inpatient surgery of 0.4–0.8 per cent and a rate of major complications of 3–17 per cent (Haynes et al. 2009). The Western Australia Audit of Surgical Mortality (WAASM) indicated that around 0.17 per cent of patients die from adverse events associated with surgery (Australian Council for Safety and Quality in Health Care 2004a: 79). Some types of errors should not happen if protocols are followed, such as swab and instrument counts. For example, a woman endured great pain from a pair of 17 cm surgical scissors left inside her for 18 months after colon surgery (Australian Broadcasting Corporation 2004). Another type of error that should never occur is surgery or other procedures performed on the wrong patient or wrong site, with evidence accumulating that such errors are more frequent than originally thought (Australian Institute of Health and Welfare and the Australian Commission on Safety and Quality in Health Care 2007).

Blood safety
Unsafe blood and blood products are a major problem in developing countries in the absence of established quality systems (World Health Organization 2007: 5). Blood safety became a higher priority with the advent of HIV/AIDS and increasing rates of hepatitis. In Australia, blood, blood components, plasma derivatives, tissue and cellular products, and tissue and cell based derivatives are regulated under the *Therapeutic Goods Act* 1989 (Cth). In high-income countries, the risks revolve mostly around procedures that take from, or give blood to, patients. The risky stages for patients include: sample collection (miscollecting and labelling errors), the decision to transfuse (whether appropriate), and administration of blood (wrong blood type or wrong patient). For example, a 90-year-old woman died of haemolysis and multi-organ failure after she received an incorrect transfusion of type A– blood instead of O+. The staff had failed to comply with the protocol that two nurses check the label on the blood unit against the patient's identity band, and also verbally, if possible, ascertain the patient's name and date of birth (South Australian Coroner 2005). Rates of adverse events involving blood safety among hospital patients are not well documented, but a significant proportion of blood transfusions are said to be unnecessary and to unnecessarily increase patient risk.

Conclusion

This chapter has shown, first, that patient safety is a significant problem that warrants regulatory action. Second, it is possible to map the contours of safety and quality and identify the quality heights and safety chasms as well as the risky parts of the terrain – at least in a snapshot if not a moving picture. The benchmark, based on retrospective studies of patient records in several countries, is that around 10 per cent of hospital patients are harmed by an adverse event, about 2 per cent of patients suffer serious consequences including death, and around one-third to one-half of adverse events are judged to be avoidable. A one in ten chance of being inadvertently harmed during one's hospital treatment does not inspire confidence. The scale of medical errors, along with attendant miseries and costs for patients and health care providers, constitutes a powerful 'business case' for health systems to invest in improving patient safety.

The rationale for identifying, measuring and monitoring patient safety is first, to better understand problems in order to craft preventive strategies, and second, to establish benchmarks in order to assess progress. The main conclusion from decades of debate is that multiple rather than single metrics are necessary since one method cannot capture all aspects of complex issues. The two main measurement strategies are special data collections and routine data collections and as each has advantages and disadvantages these strategies often are combined. If the aim is to draw population-level and trend conclusions then valid and reliable data are needed, but if the aim is to change clinical behaviour and clinical systems then the data do not have to be highly accurate.

Since large-scale reviews of patient medical records have not been repeated, these decade-old studies still provide the best estimate of adverse events. Given the lack of valid and reliable time series data, no one is sure whether the surge in regulatory effort has significantly improved safety and quality outcomes for patients. Some researchers argue that such surveys should be repeated at regular intervals in order to track progress (Wilson and Van Der Weyden 2005) (Leape and Berwick 2005). Adverse event reporting is used more as a learning tool that alerts us to problems and possible solutions. The second strategy, improving routine data collections, aims to track progress in specific areas more amenable to existing data collections, such as hospital classifications of patient outcomes.

While there has been a considerable investment in measurement, does remedial action follow? Donald Berwick of the US Institute for Healthcare Improvement warns that 'while measurement sets the stage for action, it shouldn't be confused with action itself'. Safety and quality experts urge governments to drive the agenda, to set explicit goals and monitor progress. Effective government action depends upon four preconditions: political will, careful design and organizational capacity, commitment of resources, and explicit priorities (Leatherman and Sutherland 2004: E290). Although few countries exhibit those four preconditions for government action, many have embarked upon varied regulatory interventions. The next chapter analyses the dramatic expansion of regulatory actors in countries around the world.

References

Auerbach A (2001), 'Beta-blockers and reduction of post-operative cardiac events'. In Shojania K, Duncan B, McDonald K, et al. *Making Health Care Safer: A Critical Analysis of Patient Safety Practices*. (Rockville, MD: Agency for Healthcare Research and Quality).

Australian Broadcasting Corporation, The 7.30 Report: Patient fights for justice after surgical nightmare, (13 August 2007 13 August 2007) http://www.abc.net.au/7.30/content/2004/s1090620.htm

Australian Council for Safety and Quality in Health Care (2002), *Second National Report on Patient Safety: Improving Medication Safety*. (Canberra: Commonwealth of Australia).

Australian Council for Safety and Quality in Health Care (2004a), *Charting the Safety and Quality of Health Care in Australia*. (Canberra: Australian Council for Safety and Quality in Health Care).

Australian Council for Safety and Quality in Health Care (2004b), *Maximising National Effectiveness to Reduce Harm and Improve Care: Fifth Report to the*

Australian Health Ministers' Conference. (Canberra: Australian Council for Safety and Quality in Health Care).

Australian Council for Safety and Quality in Health Care (2005a), Medication Alert 2:Vincristine can be fatal if administered by the intrathecal route. (Canberra: Australian Council for Safety and Quality in Health Care).

Australian Council for Safety and Quality in Health Care (2005b), *State and Territory Highlights: Improving Patient Safety: A Report on Achievements and Action for Safety and Quality Improvements in Australian States and Territories*. (Canberra: Commonwealth of Australia).

Australian Institute of Health and Welfare (2007), *Older Australia At A Glance*. (Canberra: AIHW).

Australian Institute of Health and Welfare and the Australian Commission on Safety and Quality in Health Care (2007), *Sentinel Events in Australian Public Hospitals 2004–05*. (Canberra: AIHW).

Australian Wound Management Association (2001), *Clinical Practice Guidelines for the Prediction and Prevention of Pressure Ulcers*. (West Leederville WA: Cambridge Publishing).

Ayliffe G, et al. (1999), *Hospital-acquired Infection: Principles and Prevention*. (Oxford: Butterworth-Heinemann).

Bakarich A, et al. (1997), 'The effect of nursing intervention on the incidence of older patient falls.' *Australian Journal of Advanced Nursing* 15: 26–31.

Baker G, et al. (2004), 'The Canadian Adverse Events Study: the incidence of adverse events among hospital patients in Canada.' *Canadian Medical Association Journal* 170(11): 1678–1686.

Bates D, et al. (1995), 'Incidence of adverse drug events and potential drug events: implications for prevention.' *Journal of the American Medical Association* 274(1): 1–98.

Boettcher B (1998), 'Personal views: fatal episodes in medical history.' *British Medical Journal* 317(7172): 1599.

Braithwaite J (2002), *Restorative Justice and Responsive Regulation*. (Oxford. New York: Oxford University Press).

Brennan T, et al. (1991), 'The incidence of adverse events and negligence in hospitalized patients: results of the Harvard Medical Practice Study 1.' *New England Journal of Medicine*(324): 370–376.

Britt H, et al. (2008), *General Practice Activity in Australia 2007–08*. (Canberra: Australian Institute of Health and Welfare).

Britt H, et al. (2003), *General Practice Activity in Australia 2002–03*. (Canberra: Australian Institute of Health and Welfare).

Brown P, et al. (2002), 'Cost of medical injury in New Zealand: a retrospective cohort study.' *Journal Health Services Research and Policy* 7(1 Supplement): S29–34.

Burgess C, et al. (2005), 'Adverse drug reactions in older Australians, 1981–2002.' *Medical Journal of Australia* 182(6): 267–270.

Care Quality Commission, CQC reaction to Alberti and Colin-Thome reviews on Mid Staffordshire NHS foundation trust, (1 May 2009 1 May 2009) www.cqc.org.uk

Care Quality Commission, Heart Surgery in the United Kingdom, (8 February 2010 8 February 2010) http://heartsurgery.cqc.org.uk/

Cartwright S (1988), *The Report of the Committee of Inquiry into Allegations Concerning the Treatment of Cervical Cancer at National Women's Hospital and into other Related Matters*. (Auckland: Government Printing Office).

Chief Medical Officer (2006), *Good Doctors: Safer Patients: Proposals to strengthen the system to assure and improve the performance of doctors and to protect the safety of patients*. (London: Department of Health).

Choudhry N, et al. (2005), 'Systematic review: The relationship between clinical experience and quality of health care.' *Annals of Internal Medicine* 142(4): 260–273.

Clark RB (2004), *Health Care and Notions of Risk*. (North Melbourne: Therapeutic Guidelines Ltd).

Clinical Liaison Service (2006), 'Medications: double checking at the bedside?' *Coronial Communique* 4(4): 4.

Clinical Liaison Service (2007a), 'Head injuries in the anticoagulated elderly.' *Coronial Communique* 5(2): 3.

Clinical Liaison Service (2007b), 'Recently closed cases.' *Coronial Communique* 5(2): 3.

Collignon P, et al. (2005), 'Staphylococcus aureus bacteremia, Australia.' *Emerging Infectious Diseases* 11(4): 554–561.

Davies Report (2005), *Queensland Public Hospitals Commission of Inquiry Report*. (Brisbane: State of Queensland).

Davis P, et al. (2002), 'Adverse events in New Zealand public hospitals I: occurrence and impact.' *New Zealand Medical Journal* 115(1167): U271.

Davis P, et al. (2003a), 'Adverse events in New Zealand public hospitals II: preventability and clinical context.' *New Zealand Medical Journal* 116(1183): U623.

Davis P, et al. (2003b), 'Preventable in-hospital medical injury under the 'no fault' system in New Zealand.' *Quality and Safety in Health Care* 12(4): 240–241.

de Vries E, et al. (2008), 'The incidence and nature of in-hospital adverse events: a systematic review.' *Quality and Safety in Health Care* 17: 216–223.

Donaldson Report (2000), *An Organisation With A Memory*. (London: Stationery Office).

Douglas N, et al. (2001), *Inquiry into Obstetrics and Gynaecology Services at the King Edward Memorial Hospital 1990–2001*. (Perth: Department of Premier and Cabinet).

Dunbar JA, et al. (2007), 'In the wake of hospital inquiries: impact on staff and safety.' *Medical Journal of Australia* 186(2): 80–83.

Dyer O (2002), 'Shipman murdered more than 200 patients, inquiry finds.' *British Medical Journal* 325: 181.

Eagar K (2004), 'The weakest link?' *Australian Health Review* 28(1): 7–12.

Ehsani J, et al. (2006), 'The incidence and cost of adverse events in Victorian hospitals 2003–04.' *Medical Journal of Australia* 184(11): 551–555.

Faunce T and Bolsin S (2004), 'Three Australian whistle-blowing sagas: lessons for internal and external regulation.' *Medical Journal of Australia* 18(1): 44–47.

Frankel S, et al. (2000), 'Mortality variations as a measure of general practitioner performance: implications of the Shipman case.' *British Medical Journal* 320: 489.

Frankum B, et al. (2004), 'Be very afraid.' *Medical Journal of Australia* 180: 362–363.

Garling Report (2009), *Final Report of the Special Commission of Inquiry: Acute Care Services in NSW Public Hospitals*. (Sydney: State of New South Wales).

Gawande A (2002), *Complications: A Surgeon's Notes on an Imperfect Science*. (New York: Metropolitan Books, Henry Holt and Company).

Gawande A, et al. (1992), 'The incidence and nature of surgical adverse events in Colorado and Utah in 1992.' *Surgery* 126: 66–75.

Gawande A, et al. (2003), 'Analysis of errors reported by surgeons at three teaching hospitals.' *Surgery* 133(6): 614–621.

Gray A (2003), Adverse Events and the National Health Services: An Economic Perspective: A Report to the National Patient Safety Agency. (London: National Patient Safety Agency).

Grol R and Jeremy G (2003), 'From best evidence to best practice: effective implementation of change in patient's care.' *Lancet* 362: 1225–1230.

Harley M, et al. (2005), 'Was Rodney Ledward a statistical outlier? Retrospective analysis using routine hospital data to indentify gynaecologists' performance.' *British Medical Journal* 330: 929–932.

Hart C and Parnell S (2005), Dr Death inquiry scuttled over bias, *The Australian*, 2 September.

Haynes A, et al. (2009), 'A surgical safety checklist to reduce morbidity and mortality in a global population.' *New England Journal of Medicine* 360: 491–499.

Health Services Commissioner Victoria (2002), *Royal Melbourne Hospital Inquiry Report*. (Melbourne: Health Services Commissioner).

Healy J and McKee M, eds. (2004), *Accessing Health Care: Responding to Diversity*. (Oxford: Oxford University Press).

Hindle D, et al. (2006), *Patient Safety: A Comparative Analysis of Eight Inquiries in Six Countries*. (Sydney: UNSW Centre for Clinical Governance Research, and Clinical Excellence Commission).

Hovenga E (2002), 'Queensland: the Health Rights Commission'. In Thomas D. *Medicine Called to Account: Health Care Complaints Mechanisms in Australasia*. (Sydney: University of New South Wales): 55–65.

Institute of Medicine (2000), *To Err is Human: Building a Safer Health System*. (Washington, DC: Institute of Medicine, National Academy Press).

Institute of Medicine (2001), *Crossing the Quality Chasm: A New Health System for the 21st century*. (Washington, DC: National Academy Press).

Joint Commission, Sentinel events, (9 October 2006) http://www.jointcommission.org/SentinelEvents/PolicyandProcedures/

Joint Commission, National Patient Safety Goals 2008, (22 February 2009) http://www.jointcommission.org/PatientSafety/NationalPatientSafetyGoals/

Kaushal R and Bates D (2001), 'Chapter 7: The clinical pharmacist's role in preventing adverse drug events'. In Shojania K, Duncan B, McDonald K, et al. *Making Health Care Safer: A Critical Analysis of Patient Safety Practices*. (Rockville MD: Agency for Healthcare Research and Quality): 71–78.

Lamb R (2004), 'Open disclosure: the only approach to medical error.' *Quality and Safety in Health Care* 13: 3–5.

Leape L (1994), 'Error in medicine.' *Journal of the American Medical Association* 272: 1851–7.

Leape L and Berwick D (2005), 'Five years after *To Err is Human*: what have we learned.' *Journal of the American Medical Association* 293(19): 2384–2390.

Leatherman S and Sutherland K (2004), 'Quality of care in the NHS of England.' *British Medical Journal* 328: 288–290.

Little J (1994), *Inside 60 Minutes: the Story behind the Stories*. (Sydney: Allen & Unwin).

Mangione-Smith R, et al. (2007), 'The quality of ambulatory care delivered to children in the United States.' *New England Journal of Medicine* 357(15): 1515–1523.

Masso M (2004), 'Peer review of adverse events - a perspective on Macarthur.' *Australian Health Review* 28(1): 26–33.

Masso M and Eagar K (2009), 'Do public inquiries improve health care?'in Healy J and Dugdale P. *Patient Safety First: Responsive Regulation in Health Care*. (Crows Nest NSW: Allen & Unwin): 318–340.

McGlynn E, et al. (2003), 'The quality of health care delivered to adults in the United States.' *New England Journal of Medicine* 348(26): 2635–2645.

McKee M and Healy J (2002), 'The significance of hospitals: an introduction'. In Mckee M and Healy J. *Hospitals in a Changing Europe*. (Buckingham. Philadelphia: Open University Press): 3–13.

McKee M, et al. (2002), 'Pressures for change'. In McKee M and Healy J. *Hospitals in a Changing Europe*. (Buckingham. Philadelphia: Open University Press): 36–58.

McLean J and Walsh M (2003), 'Lessons from the Inquiry into Obstetrics and Gynecology Services at King Edward Memorial Hospital 1990–2000.' *Australian Health Review* 26(1): 12–23.

Merry A and McCall Smith A (2001), *Errors, Medicine and the Law*. (Cambridge: Cambridge University Press).

Millenson M (2002), 'Pushing the profession: how the news media turned patient safety into a priority.' *Quality and Safety in Health Care* 11: 57–63.

Miller G, et al. (2006), 'Adverse drug events in general practice patients in Australia.' *Medical Journal of Australia* 184(7): 321–324.

Moynihan R (1998), *Too Much Medicine?* (Sydney: ABC Books).

Moynihan R and Cassels A (2005), *Selling Sickness: How Drug Companies Are Turning Us All Into Patients*. (St Leonards NSW: Allen and Unwin).

Nason D and Fraser A, On the trail of Doctor Death, *The Australian*, 21 April 2005.

National Audit Office (2000), *The Management and Control of Hospital Acquired Infection in Acute NHS Trusts in England*. (London: The Stationery Office).

National Patient Safety Agency (2007), *Slips, Trips and Falls in Hospital*. (London: National Patient Safety Agency).

Nimmo G and Looke D (2001), 'Non-multiresistant methicillin-resistant Staphylococcus aureus in the community: next chapter in the story of stahphylococcal sepsis?' *Medical Journal of Australia* 174: 617–618.

O'Neill A, et al. (1993), 'Physician reporting compared with medical-record review to identify adverse medical events.' *Annals of Internal Medicine* 119: 370–376.

Ovretveit J (2009), *Does Improving Quality Save Money? A Review of Evidence of which Improvements to Quality Reduce Costs to Health Service Providers*. (London: The Health Foundation).

Parnell S, Dr Death review chief ruins appeal prospects, The Australian, 12 September 2005

Paul C (2000), 'Internal and external morality of medicine: lessons from New Zealand.' *British Medical Journal* 320: 499–503.

Pizzi L, et al. (2001), 'Chapter 40: Promoting a culture of safety'. In Shojania K, Duncan B, McDonald K, et al. *Making Health Care Safer: A Critical Analysis of Patient Safety Practices*. (Rockville MD: Agency for Healthcare Research and Quality): 447–457.

Plowman R, et al. (1999), *The Socioeconomic Burden of Hospital Acquired Infection*. (London: Central Public Health Laboratory).

Porter R (1997), *The Greatest Benefit to Mankind: A Medical History of Humanity from Antiquity to the Present*. (London: HarperCollins).

Porter R (2001), *Bodies Politic: Disease, Death and Doctors in Britain, 1650–1900*. (London: Reaktion Books).

Raleigh V and Foot C (2010), *Getting The Measure of Quality: Opportunities and Challenges*. (London: The King's Fund).

Ranson D and Emmett S (2003), 'Falls and fall-related injuries: far-reaching implications.' *Journal of Law and Medicine* 11: 16–17.

Reason J (1990), *Human Error*. (New York: Cambridge University Press).

Reason J (1995), 'Understanding adverse events: human factors'. In Vincent C. *Clinical Risk Management*. (London: BMJ Publications).

Rigby K, et al. (1999), 'Adverse events in health care: setting priorities based on economic evaluation.' *Journal of Quality Clinical Practice* 19(1): 7–12.

Roughead E (2005), 'Managing adverse drug reactions: time to get serious.' *Medical Journal of Australia* 182(6): 264–265.

Roughead E and Lexchin J (2006), 'Editorials: Adverse drug events: counting is not enough, action is needed.' *Medical Journal of Australia* 184(7): 315–316.

Runciman WB, et al. (2007), *Safety and Ethics in Healthcare: A Guide to Getting it Right*. (Aldershot: Ashgate).

Runciman W, et al. (2002), 'Setting priorities for patient safety.' *Quality and Safety in Health Care* 11: 224–229.

Runciman W and Moller J (2001), *Iatrogenic Injury in Australia*. (Adelaide: Australian Patient Safety Foundation).

Runciman W, et al. (2000), 'A comparison of iatrogenic injury studies in Australia and the USA. II: reviewer behaviour and quality of care.' *International Journal of Quality in Health Care* 12(5): 379–388.

Sari A, et al. (2007), 'Sensitivity of routine system for reporting patient safety incidents in an NHS hospital: retrospective patient case note review.' *British Medical Journal* 334: 79.

Schioler T, et al. (2001), 'Danish Adverse Event Study. Incidence of adverse events in hospitals. A retrospective study of medical records.' *Ugeskr laeger* 163(39): 5370–5378.

Schoen C, et al. (2007), 'Towards higher-performance health systems: adults' health care experiences in seven countries, 2007.' *Health Affairs* 26(6): w717–w734.

Schoen C, et al. (2005), 'Taking the pulse of health care systems: experiences of patients with health problems in six countries.' *Health Affairs* Web exclusive 3 November 2005: W5 509–525.

Shipman Inquiry (2004), *Fifth Report: Safeguarding Patients: Lessons from the Past - Proposals for the Future*. (London: The Stationery Office).

Smith R (1998), 'All changed, changed utterly.' *British Medical Journal* 316: 1917–1918.

South Australian Coroner (2005), Finding of inquest Number 21/2004: Dorothy Alberta Squires. (Adelaide: South Australian Coroner).

Spelman D (2002), 'Hospital-acquired infections.' *Medical Journal of Australia* 176: 286–291.

Swartz M (1995), 'Hospital-acquired infections: diseases with increasingly limited therapies'. In Roizman B. *Infectious Diseases in an Age of Change: The Impact of Human Ecology and Behaviour on Disease Transmission*. (Washington, DC: National Academy Press).

Taylor K, et al. (2001), *The Challenge of Hospital-Acquired Infection*. (London: Stationery Office).

The Bristol Royal Infirmary Inquiry (2001), *The Report of the Public Inquiry into Children's Heart Surgery at the Bristol Royal Infirmary 1984–1995: Learning from Bristol*. (London: The Bristol Royal Infirmary Inquiry).

Thomas D (2002), 'Introductory overview'. In Thomas D. *Medicine Called to Account: Health Care Complaints Mechanisms in Australasia*. (Sydney: University of New South Wales): 1–14.

Thomas D (2006), 'Peer review as an outmoded model for health practitioner regulation'. In Freckleton I. *Regulating Health Practitioners*. (Annandale, NSW: The Federation Press).

Thomas E, et al. (2000a), 'Incidence and types of adverse events and negligent care in Utah and Colorado.' *Medical Care* 38: 247–249.

Thomas EJ, et al. (2000b), 'A comparison of iatrogenic injury studies in Australia and the USA: context, methods, casemix, population, patient and hospital characteristics.' *International Journal for Quality in Health Care* 12(5): 371–378.

Thomas H (2007), *Sick to Death*. (St Leonards NSW: Allen & Unwin).

Tutuarima J, et al. (1997), 'Risk factors for falls of hospitalised stroke patients.' *Stroke* 28: 297–301.

Van Der Weyden M (2004), 'The "Cam affair": an isolated incident or destined to be repeated?' *Medical Journal of Australia* 180(3): 100–101.

Van Der Weyden M (2005), 'The Bundaberg Hospital scandal: the need for reform in Queensland and beyond.' *Medical Journal of Australia* 183(6): 284–285.

Van Der Weyden M (2009), 'In the wake of the Garling inquiry into New South Wales public hospitals: a change of cultures?' *Medical Journal of Australia* 190: 51–52.

Vincent C (2004), 'Analysis of clinical incidents: a window on the system not a search for root causes.' *Quality and Safety in Health Care* 13: 242–243.

Vincent C, et al. (2001), 'Adverse events in British hospitals: preliminary retrospective record review.' *British Medical Journal* 322: 517–519.

Vincent CA, et al. (2008), 'Is health care getting safer?' *British Medical Journal* 337: 1205–1207.

Walshe K (2003), *Regulating Healthcare: A Prescription For Improvement?* (Maidenhead. Philadelphia: Open University Press).

Walshe K and Shortell S (2004), 'When things go wrong: how healthcare organizations deal with major failures.' *Health Affairs* 23: 103–111.

Whitehead M and Hanratty B (2004), 'Health care for rich and poor alike'. In Healy J and McKee M. *Accessing Health Care: Responding to Diversity*. (Oxford: Oxford University Press).

Wilson B (2004a), *Does shaming, naming and blaming improve the quality of our health services? Adversarial versus conciliatory approached to investigating health complaints*. 10th Conference of the Australian Bioethics Association, (University of New South Wales.

Wilson LL (2004b), 'What's wrong with our hospitals?' *Australian Health Review* 28(1): 20–25.

Wilson RM, et al. (1995), 'The quality in Australian health care study.' *Medical Journal of Australia* 163: 458–471.

Wilson RM and Van Der Weyden M (2005), 'The safety of Australian healthcare: 10 years after QAHCS.' *Medical Journal of Australia* 182(6): 260–261.

Wong M, et al. (2008), Clinical Handover Literature Review. (Hobart: eHealth Services Research Group, University of Tasmania).

World Health Organization, World Alliance for Patient Safety: Patient Safety Solutions, (2 May 2008 2 May 2008) http://www.who.int/patientsafety/solutions/en/

World Health Organization (2009a), *World Alliance for Patient Safety: The Conceptual Framework for the International Classification for Patient Safety: Final Technical Report: Chapter 2 The Conceptual Framework for the International Classification for Patient Safety*. (Geneva: World Health Organization).

World Health Organization (2009b), *World Alliance for Patient Safety: The Conceptual Framework for the International Classification for Patient Safety: Final Technical Report: Technical Annex 2: Glossary of Patient Safety Concepts and References*. (Geneva: World Health Organization).

Yu X, et al. (2004), 'Estimating regional variation in cancer survival: a tool for improving cancer care.' *Cancer Causes Control* 15(6): 611–6118.

Chapter 3
Regulatory Actors: Who Governs Health Care?

Regulatory Constellations

The architecture of health sector regulatory fields is being redrawn with the entry of new actors into existing regulatory arenas. While some regulators date from the nineteenth century, such as medical registration boards, by the beginning of the twenty-first century new bodies were being set up to improve health care. The array of health sector regulatory bodies can be characterized as an *institutional constellation*, which concept highlights the dynamic nature of a regulatory field and suggests how ideas, relationships and rules are constructed:

> We conceive [institutional constellations] as entire sets of formal institutions and interconnected rules that shape public decision-making in a given regulatory arena, including shared interpretive structures, affecting the patterns of interaction by decision-makers within the sector. (Jordana and Sancho 2004: 298)

The bodies in these constellations are scattered, however, since there are, as yet, few shared formal rules and few shared interpretative structures. To continue the metaphor, it is early days for these constellations. The bodies have had little time to develop links and the gravitational field is not strong enough to attract and keep them in a fixed orbit, at least in those constellations that lack a dominant body such as a national regulator. Regulatory constellations are in the process of forming in many countries, however, and this chapter examines the old and the new regulatory bodies and the emergence of networked governance.

Networked and Nodal Governance

The diffusion of power in modern economies means that the state must mobilize networks of power to get things done (Braithwaite and Drahos 2000). 'Governance today is characterized by a plurality of actors … forming more or less interconnected governance networks' (Burris et al. 2005: 31). *Networked governance* occurs when events are steered through a web of linked actors across many organizations (Braithwaite et al. 2005: 58). This concept is particularly apt in the health sector given its multitude of stakeholders and extensive flows of information, and since one actor does not possess all the knowledge and influence necessary to implement change. The growth of the network society, with its more fluid and complex flows of power, makes governance more challenging than in earlier eras, since governance can no longer be managed solely through older structures such as government departments (Castells 2000). Further, governments cannot necessarily announce a policy and expect compliance, as in a command and control strategy, but must consider other actors and negotiate a generally acceptable plan of action.

A *node of governance* can be defined as a place where resources, ideas, capacity and leadership converge. Nodal governance works by recruiting key actors who control different strands of governance, and who collectively have the capacity to tie these strands together into an effective web of influence. But even though each strand in the network may be weak, yet, if the right strand is pulled at the right time, the entire web can tighten to become quite strong. Learning how to pull the right strand at the right time can be accomplished by deliberation at nodes of governance (Braithwaite et al. 2005: 10). Regulators may decide to concentrate on a few strategic strands in order to exert maximum pulling power. Four characteristics are said to be essential for forming a node of governance that has the capacity to steer the flow of events (Burris et al. 2005: 37–38):

- a way of thinking about the matters that the node has emerged to govern (mentalities);
- a set of methods for exerting influence over the course of events at issue (technologies);
- funds and people to support the operation of the node and the exertion of influence (resources);
- a structure that enables the directed mobilization of resources, mentalities and technologies over time (institutions).

Successful networked governance requires the actors to engage in *regulatory conversations* to arrive at a shared way of thinking about principles and processes. Julia Black contends that since regulation is in large part a communicative process aimed at changing the behaviour of individuals, it is important to encourage respectful dialogue between all involved in 'the regulatory space' (Black 2002b). People are more likely to engage in conversations framed in terms of their interests, however; for example, doctors want to retain public trust, payers want value for money, and consumers want assurances. A cultural strength of the health professions in engaging in such conversations is that ethical principles generally unite rather than divide them. Health professionals are described as a group of 'moral acquaintances': a cross between Englehardt's classification of a community of moral friends and a society of moral strangers (Kerridge et al. 2005). In discussing regulatory action, health professionals all affirm that patient safety is a core principle.

Many countries are seeking to connect health sector actors into an effective regulatory network. National regulatory bodies (new bodies or restructured bodies) have been set up in the anglophone countries of the United Kingdom, United States,

Australia, Canada and New Zealand as well as in many other countries. These regulatory networks are developing shared ideas and trying different methods, but most have limited resources, and many do not exert direct power over service providers but must work through other bodies.

The concepts of networked governance and nodal governance highlight the interconnected nature of regulatory actors and their actions and offer a way of thinking about possibilities for strategic action. Strategic action in the health sector usually involves *co-regulation*, that is, a regulatory partnership between government and other regulatory actors in civil society and the market. Co-regulation increasingly is used to 'steer the flow of events' in the governance of professionals and organizations.

Decentred Regulation

The concept of *decentred regulation* is illuminating as it makes clear that regulation in the health sector does not revolve around one single body: the planets in these regulatory constellations do not necessarily orbit around one sun. A health sector exemplifies decentred regulation, with the concept, as proposed by Julia Black, defined by five characteristics: fragmentation, complexity, interdependencies, overlapping public and private spheres, and ungovernability (Black 2002a). The health field is fragmented with power and knowledge dispersed across public and private spheres so that no one actor possesses all the capacity required to understand an issue and implement a policy. It is complex since the many regulators and myriad of regulatees make it difficult to trace cause and effect. There are interdependencies since responding to a problem requires action by several actors. There is considerable overlap across levels of government and across public and private sectors. Finally, the health field is widely regarded as ungovernable given perennial tensions, for example, between managers and clinicians, doctors and nurses.

The decentred nature of health sector regulation is particularly apparent in the United States, where long-standing health reform failures prompted stakeholders to bypass traditional vested interests and set up new forums to tackle issues such as rising costs and inconsistent quality (Trubek 2004). Trubek argues that three sets of actors have emerged as active collaborators in health sector governance: the retooled doctor, the concerned payer, and the active consumer. Retooled doctors have become adept leaders and managers in the United States given their experience in dealing with managed care insurers and providers; UK doctors have years of experience in the quasi-market National Health Service; whereas Australian general practitioners have not retooled to the same extent. Concerned payers want better value for money and have linked pay to performance in the United States and United Kingdom. Active consumers are vocal on patient safety issues in the United States but less so in the United Kingdom and Australia. The Trubek triumvirate leaves out government as an active regulator, except in its role as payer, which makes sense in the context of the United States, but government is a key regulatory actor in many other countries and not just in its role as payer.

Attributes of a Formal Regulator

A regulator in a decentred field does not necessarily possess all the attributes of a formal regulator and must deploy strategies that rely on persuasion more than coercion. The four key attributes of a formal regulator are said to be authority, centralized oversight, neutrality, and acting in the public interest (Walshe 2003b: 20–21). A formal regulator possesses authority acknowledged by other stakeholders. Oversight is centralized on behalf of other stakeholders who cede power. The regulator is a neutral third-party to transactions. Finally, the regulator takes action in the public interest, such as protecting the public. But in a decentred health field, a regulator may not possess authority and other actors may be unwilling to cede oversight power. The limited scope of authority leaves gaps in the available options and may lop the use (or threat) of enforcement off the top of the regulatory pyramid. This is problematic since a responsive regulator can rely more upon persuasion when there is the capacity to escalate upwards in regulatory strength if necessary. Many regulatory actors are not external bodies (third party regulators) but rather internal or quasi-external regulators, such as health departments and medical colleges. All health sector regulators, however, claim to take action in the public interest.

The responsive regulation model rejects the bipolar distinction between persuasion and coercion in favour of a nuanced and graduated regulatory response. But characterizing the two styles at either end of a regulatory continuum does make the differences clearer. Two types of regulators have been broadly distinguished: deterrence and compliance regulators (Walshe 2003b: 34–41). *Deterrence regulators* are more likely to use enforcement strategies since they see people as 'amoral calculators' out to get what they can and conforming to rules only when forced. Such regulators tend to have formal and adversarial relationships with those they regulate and to make extensive use of sanctions. A deterrence approach is more likely where regulators have limited contact with a multitude of regulatees and where the sector is heterogeneous. This hypothesis suggests that a deterrence approach in the health sector is more likely to be pursued by payers, such as insurance funds, in relation to a multitude of pathology laboratories and doctors. *Compliance regulators* see people as fundamentally ethical and well-intentioned and who do their best to comply with rules. This fits the responsive regulation model view of the world. These regulators maintain respectful relationships and use penalties only as a last resort. Compliance regulation is more likely in homogeneous sectors, where the regulator oversees fewer organizations and people, and where there is a strong professional ethic. The compliance model is by far the more common approach in the health sector. It is also a key strategy in many sectors of the economy including in globalized business sectors (Braithwaite and Drahos 2000).

Eras in Safety and Quality Regulation

The regulatory field of patient safety is expanding rapidly as new regulatory bodies and new strategies are added to long-established ways of working. Five chronological eras of regulation can be discerned whose accretions gradually build up regulatory frameworks.

Self-regulation: Self-regulation by professional and industry groups has been the dominant approach for centuries dating from the medical guilds in the Middle Ages in Europe. The medical profession achieved state protection over its title and field of practice with the 1858 *Medical Reform Act* in England and this approach remains the prototype for many countries. Professional boards guard entry to the health professions, set standards, provide guidance, and take disciplinary action in egregious cases.

Information strategies: Health professionals deal with information on an every-day basis so that information dissemination is a well-accepted regulatory strategy that basically depends upon a voluntary take-up by professionals and organizations. The medical world has seen a dramatic expansion in knowledge in the last few decades and evidence-based advocates aim to improve the take-up of evidence into policies and practice. All countries promote normative standards and guidelines and run training programmes. The health consumer movement also seeks to provide information to empower patients.

Clinical leadership: The medical profession traditionally has looked for transformational leaders to provide visionary leadership and energize others in achieving change (Spurgeon and Latham 2003). Regulatory bodies set up by government need medical leaders who can influence professional and organizational policies and practices. The patient safety movement always seeks to engage clinical leaders.

Legal and financial strategies: Legal frameworks for safety and quality are being constructed although countries vary in their use of legal and financial strategies. While health sector attention in the 1990s focused on improving efficiency (Ham 1998), in the 2000s it also is directed at improving quality. A supply side approach uses financial incentives to obtain better value for money, for example, funding hospitals through Diagnostic Related Groups (DRGs), and is adopting 'pay for performance' for doctors. The continuing rise in health care expenditure as well the high cost of adverse events will focus more attention on patient safety.

Meta-regulation: The twenty-first century has seen a shift from internal regulation to more external regulation. Meta-regulators (the state or its agents) seek to regulate the regulators, that is, to ensure that regulatory mechanisms are in place and are working. Health departments have stepped up performance monitoring, accreditation agencies have adopted mandatory criteria, and professional registration boards are being made more accountable. As patient safety has become an international issue in a globalizing world, supranational actors now add impetus to national regulatory efforts.

Supranational Regulatory Actors

Supranational organizations have emerged to 'steer the flow of events' in safety and quality. These include an international tier of long-established organizations that accredit the national-level accreditors (see Chapter 7), while recent entrants to patient safety regulation include the World Health Organization, the European Union, and the Organisation for Economic Cooperation and Development (OECD).

An NGO established in 1947 to develop standards in engineering and manufacturing, the *International Organization for Standardization (ISO)* is a world-wide federation with members and associates in over 140 countries. The procedure is for an applicant to conduct a self-audit against ISO standards, either for a whole organization, a component such as a laboratory or particular technical procedure, and then apply for a certificate of compliance from an ISO-recognized certification body. While originally applied to the manufacture of pharmaceuticals and medical devices, ISO health sector standards (ISO 9000 series) have been developed for technical components, such as radiology and pathology, and to quality assurance systems in units and whole hospitals.

The *International Society for Quality in Health Care* (ISQua), an international NGO with members in over 70 countries, accredits the accreditation agencies. Its developmental model encourages a self-assessment of strengths and limitations against the ISQua International Principles for Healthcare Standards. ISQua publishes the *International Journal for Quality in Health Care*, offers extensive information materials, and runs an annual conference.

The *Joint Accreditation System of Australia and New Zealand* (JAS–NZ) is a quasi-government organization set up under a trans-Tasman trade treaty with a governing board appointed by the Australian Government and the New Zealand Government. It uses international standards and guidelines from ISO and others and accredits bodies that certify management systems, products and personnel, and some health services.

The *World Alliance for Patient Safety* was launched by the *World Health Organization* in 2004, in response to a resolution by the 55th World Health Assembly that called upon member states to take action on patient safety. The aims are to sustain international political momentum and to strengthen the commitment of countries to the issue of patient safety (World Health Organization 2004). The WHO has set up a patient safety programme that publishes extensive material, runs workshops, mounts pilot programmes, funds action research, and promotes evidence-based and/or best practice patient safety solutions (World Health Organization 2005).

The *European Commission* does not have a treaty basis to mandate a single approach to health care across member states, but it funds research projects and promotes progress on quality improvement (Legido-Quigley et al. 2008b). The Committee of Ministers of the Council of Europe adopted recommendations on patient safety in 2006 that called for governments to 'ensure that patient safety is the cornerstone of all relevant health policies' (Council of Europe 2006). The European Commission ensures the 'four freedoms' in the common market: the free movement of people, goods, services, and capital. Member countries are subject to the EU legal framework, the Aquis Communautaire, an accumulated body of European legislation (treaties, regulations, directives, decisions, opinions, recommendations) that take precedence over national laws. The European Commission expects member states (27 in 2007) to converge in their levels of economic and social well-being, which implies some harmonizing of health care policies and practices, the rationale being that citizens should be able to expect good health care across all EU member countries.

The *Organisation for Economic Co-operation and Development* (OECD) has a long-standing interest in regulatory reform (Organisation for Economic Co-operation and Development 2002). The OECD notes that regulatory initiatives by policy-makers on the quality of medical care represent a paradigm shift, since the state previously took for granted that the institutions of professional self-regulation would ensure satisfactory health care. The OECD promotes performance indicators as a key regulatory strategy; for example, its Health Care Quality Indicators Project reports on quality of care in OECD countries in five areas: cardiac care, diabetes, primary care and prevention, mental health, and patient safety (Mattke et al. 2006).

Mapping Regulatory Styles

Health sector regulatory styles can be mapped against the four quadrants of society that undertake regulatory activities: government, professions, civil society, and the market. *Governments* pass legislation, set up government or statutory authorities, and have considerable financial leverage; for example, median government expenditure as a proportion of total health expenditure was around 76 per cent in the 28-country OECD in 2005 (Australian Institute of Health and Welfare 2008: 528). *Professions* regulate health care through their councils, associations and colleges, and through their unions on industrial matters. *Civil society* includes NGOs and interest groups such as consumer groups and peak bodies for health providers. *Market* actors include industry associations for hospitals, laboratories, pharmaceuticals, and health insurance, as well as purchasers and consumers.

Countries can be mapped against a regulatory constellation of four quadrants (Figure 3.1) that indicates how regulatory styles are shaped by context and culture. Regulatory styles also are shaped by a country's legal system (Evetts 1998; Dubois et al. 2006). The institutional tradition of civil law systems emphasizes the codification of rules, making countries such as France and Germany reluctant to establish regulatory agencies that are independent of government. In contrast, common law countries, such as the United Kingdom, United States and Australia, emphasize judicial discretion as opposed to codification, and the protection of individual rights against government encroachment, and so are more prepared to set up quasi-government regulators. Government regulatory action also is more constrained in federal systems where levels of government must agree (Australia, Canada, Germany, Spain, United States) compared to unitary systems (England, France, New Zealand).

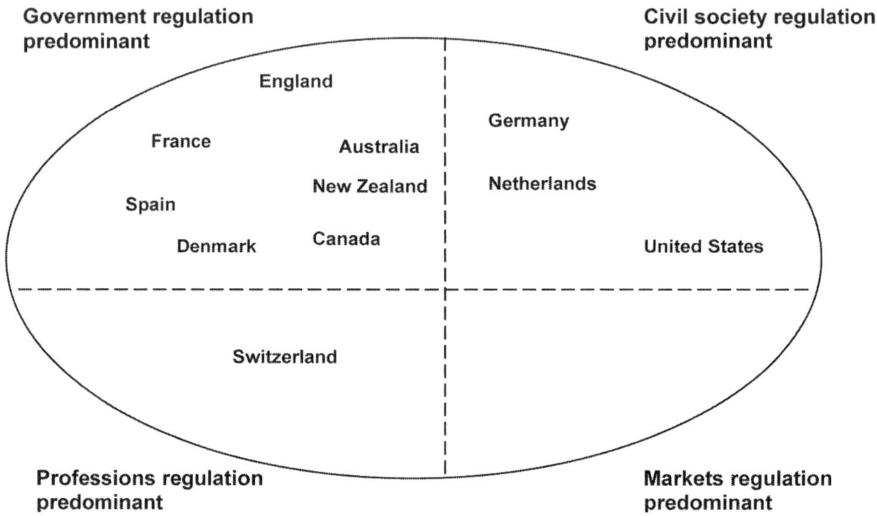

Figure 3.1 Health sector regulatory constellation by country

To give some examples, the United States illustrates a 'nightwatchman' stance with its regulatory style located near civil society and market quadrants, and is also more litigious and less trusting than other countries. The United Kingdom (more precisely England) retains a welfare state and Keynesian approach to regulation in a government-dominated regulatory model. Australia can be located in the government quadrant but close to the professions. Germany illustrates a stakeholder governance model in its corporatized health system (Busse and Riesberg 2004). The Netherlands has set up government agencies to regulate competition in its managed market and has active NGOs (Enthoven and Van de Ven 2007). Denmark has patient safety legislation, government regulators and active NGOs (Lehmann Knudsen 2009). *S*witzerland leaves the regulation of quality to its cantons and professional associations (Minder et al. 2000). Spain undertakes safety and quality programmes through its national and regional governments.

The anglophone countries (United Kingdom, United States, Canada, New Zealand and Australia) are sufficiently similar in their institutions and populations to allow meaningful cross-national comparisons. The Commonwealth Fund conducts regular surveys on health policy issues in these countries (Schoen et al. 2004). The following sections discuss these five countries.

United States

The US health sector is more fragmented and privatized than in other OECD countries (Walshe 2003a; Harrison 2004). Health sector governance works through a stakeholder model to engage public and private actors mainly through information and market strategies, although at the sharp end of the regulatory pyramid, federal and state governments enact an array of legislation. Regulators are motivated by the democratic belief that patients are entitled to information, and by the market model belief that well-informed purchasers will compel providers to compete on the basis of cost and quality. Patient safety became a hot topic after well-publicized reports of safety failures and a rise in litigation by patients. But despite new regulatory actors, an apparent lack of progress is attributed to the lack of national leadership (Leatherman and Sutherland 2004:E290). Health spending reached 17.3 per cent of GDP in 2009 (the most expensive health system in the world) and was projected to rise to 19.3 per cent by 2019. The Obama administration in 2010 signed long-awaited legislation on health insurance reform that should improve the plight of the uninsured population.

Government

The national quality agenda dates back to a commission appointed by President Clinton to recommend strategies to improve health care (President's Advisory Commission on Consumer Protection and Quality in the Health Care Industry 1998). Congress has passed legislation in relation to federal programmes, and some of the 53 states and territories have legislation mandating reporting on adverse incidents and performance indicators. The Agency for Healthcare Research and Quality (AHRQ) as the lead government agency on safety and quality funds research, disseminates information, provides training, develops standards, and tracks and compares quality indicators. The AHRQ has published biennial national quality reports since 2003 that track progress in 57 areas of performance (Agency for Healthcare Research and Quality 2003), and also offers on-line data on how each state measures up on 14 quality standards.

The federal government exerts financial leverage over quality standards through its health insurance programmes: Medicare covers 42 million people aged 65 years and over, and Medicaid covers 53 million poor people (The Commonwealth Fund 7 March 2005). The Centers for Medicare and Medicaid Services contract directly with health providers, set performance standards, and contract with Quality Improvement Organizations in each state that undertake peer review against specified quality standards. The Veterans Health Administration (VHA) also is an influential federal agency via its 150 hospitals, 850 clinics and purchasing arrangements with thousands of private physicians. VHA Offices develop practice guidelines, investigate complaints, evaluate programmes, and measure performance outcomes. The VHA Patient Safety Centre has reduced medical errors in VHA hospitals and is an international leader on patient safety (Bagian et al. 2001).

Professions

The Institute of Medicine, under the National Academy of Sciences, advises the federal government on matters pertaining to the health of the public. Its influential report, *To Err is Human* (Institute of Medicine 2000) galvanized US policy makers into action and was followed by a series of reports: quality (Institute of Medicine 2001), improving quality (Institute of Medicine 2002), patient safety (Institute of Medicine 2004b), and the work environment (Institute of Medicine 2004a). The American Board of Medical Specialties defines competencies and runs certification programmes for practising doctors; the National Board of Medical Examiners accredits medical schools; and the Accreditation Council on Graduate Medical Education accredits specialist training. The Federation of State Medical Boards maintains a database of disciplinary information on doctors, assesses applicants for re-registration after removal of licence, and runs a credential verification service.

Civil society

The US regulatory field has influential NGOs that conduct research and promote quality programmes. The Joint Commission, the main accreditation agency for hospitals, is a national and international leader on safety and quality. The Commonwealth Fund supports independent research on health and social issues and campaigns for US health sector reform. It undertakes regular cross-national surveys, identifies practices that lead to improved performance, and issues scorecards that show that 'the state you live in affects the health care you receive'(The Commonwealth Fund 2007).

NGOs publish reports that increase the pressure for quality improvements. The National Quality Forum publishes performance measures including on the quality of physician care in outpatient settings (National Quality Forum 2005). The National Committee for Quality Assurance publishes quality measures on the care received by patients enrolled in managed care plans and on the performance of health plans and individual physicians (National Committee for Quality Assurance 2004). The National Patient Safety Foundation brings together leaders and runs regular conferences (National Patient Safety Foundation 2005). The Institute for Healthcare Improvement sponsors collaborative projects with participating hospitals and runs campaigns to reduce deaths from adverse events.

Market

Market actors promote public reporting and pay-for-performance to improve health care. With the growth of 'managed care', private health insurance funds use provider payment mechanisms such as quality incentives and some refuse to cover the cost of medical errors (Institute of Medicine 2000). The Leapfrog Group, made up of over 170 companies that buy health insurance plans for their employees, publishes hospital ratings on safety and quality (Leapfrog Group 2005). Health insurance funds, such as Blue Cross and Blue Shield, use a pay-for-performance formula that rewards high-quality health providers and penalizes poor performers. The media are important players in publicizing medical scandals and their revelations have prompted significant reforms.

United Kingdom

The United Kingdom has gone further than many countries in strengthening state regulation in the context of its (previously) unitary form of government, a national health service, a series of high profile public inquiries, and the high priority the public attaches to health care. Government is the dominant regulatory actor and implements strong national programmes on quality and safety (McLoughlin et al. 2001). The National Health Service (NHS) has undergone over a decade of restructuring that shows no signs of abating. At least seven national regulators have been established since 1999 and others restructured. Four national government agencies constitute a grouping of meta-regulators: the Council for Healthcare Regulatory Excellence, the National Institute for Clinical Excellence, the National Patient Safety Agency, and the Care Quality Commission. Regulatory policy aims to strengthen networked governance and extend its regulatory reach, reduce overload and duplication, and harmonize regulatory principles and practices. The Darzi Review endorsed quality monitoring but also called for less top-down regulation and more clinician engagement (Darzi 2009). The global financial crisis that blew up at the end of 2008 has put huge pressure on UK public finances with reductions likely of 2.3 per cent a year up to 2017. NHS spending has grown, on average, by 6.6 per cent since 2000 (bringing it in line with European Union levels) so that zero growth, let alone spending cuts will have a serious impact (Hawkes 2009). With the advent of regional governments, health care governance differs somewhat between England, Wales, and Scotland, and much of the following review refers to England.

Government

The Government embarked upon a reform agenda in the late 1990s as part of a 'modernization' drive to place 'quality at the heart of the NHS' (Department of Health 1998). For example, clinical governance was introduced in order to make NHS agencies more accountable for delivering quality care (Scally and Donaldson 1998). England's Chief Medical Officer published several reports on safety and quality, including *An Organization with a Memory*, which recommended that the NHS should set up an adverse event reporting system, encourage a more open culture, design a systems approach to preventing, analysing and learning from errors, and monitor whether hospitals put changes in place (Donaldson Report 2000). The Department of Health since the mid 1990s has published NHS performance data including on each hospital (Department of Health 1999).

The National Institute for Clinical Excellence (NICE) was set up as a government authority in 1999 to advise on evidence-based assessments of existing and new treatments, technology and pharmaceuticals, including their cost-effectiveness. Recommendations against making treatments or drugs free on the NHS can be controversial, as in the case of Viagra (the anti-impotence drug), and drugs for influenza (zanamivir, Relenza). NICE develops clinical guidelines on specific treatments that set out an optimal package of care for particular conditions, such as the management of cardiovascular disease. These guidelines are based on systematic reviews of evidence on overall management, spanning prevention, treatment and rehabilitation, against which progress can be measured. NICE has developed audit methods to assess the take-up of guidelines, and maintains mortality registers such as on perioperative deaths.

The Commission for Health Improvement was set up as a statutory authority in 1999 (later the Healthcare Commission now the Care Quality Commission). It was charged with conducting rolling reviews of the 2,000 NHS facilities in England and Wales through the collection of data and site visits with particular reference to progress with clinical governance.

The National Patient Safety Agency was created in 2001 as an NHS Special Authority charged with setting up a National Reporting and Learning System on adverse events. NHS staff were urged to report an incident or a 'near miss' to their local manager or directly to the agency website and the Agency analyses this data in order to promote system-wide learning from adverse events.

The National Clinical Assessment Authority was set up in 2001 with a mandate to detect and correct underperforming or incompetent doctors, and to refer cases for disciplinary proceedings to the General Medical Council (Dyer 2001). Now a division of the National Patient Safety Agency, it has developed methods for assessing and improving competence among doctors and dentists.

The Council for Healthcare Regulatory Excellence was set up in 2003 as a meta-regulator to harmonize regulation in the health sector and to maintain oversight of the nine statutory regulators responsible for the performance of health professionals and their registration, re-registration and disciplinary activities.

The Healthcare Commission was established in 2004 to review quality of care in England and Wales within the NHS and the private sector. The Department of Health sets standard but delegated monitoring and enforcement to the Commission. It replaced the Commission for Health Improvement, took over the inspection functions of the National Care Standards Commission for private and non-profit health care, and some work of the Audit Commission on health care cost-effectiveness. It undertook regular on-site audits of organizations, conducted an 'annual health check' of performance ratings, and published results on each organization against two criteria: quality of services and use of resources. The Commission from April 2009 was reorganized as the Care Quality Commission in a merger with the Commission for Social Care Inspection and the Mental Health Commission, making it a mega-regulator of health and social care, with additional powers under the *Health and Social Care Act 2008*. The majority of NHS trusts are accountable through regional health authorities to the Secretary of State for Health. Foundation trusts are more autonomous and quasi-market organizations, with 52 established by late 2007, accountable to an independent regulator, Monitor, established in 2004, which licenses new foundation trusts and monitors their performance.

Professions

Health profession regulation is UK-wide unlike the regulation of health care organizations. The model of self-regulation by the health professions has been overtaken by co-regulation involving the Government and the public (Chief Medical Officer 2006: 127), and medical governance has undergone highly contested reforms (Secretary of State for Health 2007). Although the General Medical Council tightened its governance of the medical profession after several medical scandals, these efforts were regarded by its critics as too little and too late (Walshe and Benson 2005: 1505). In major reforms of medical governance, the General Medical Council has been over-hauled to ensure stronger regulation of the performance of doctors, who now must demonstrate 'fitness to practise' for re-registration (Chief Medical Officer 2006).

Civil society

While less prominent than in the United States, several UK NGOs are active on patient safety and quality. The Nuffield Trust has assessed the government's quality agenda as the most ambitious and comprehensive of any country, and reported progress in several domains (access, effectiveness, system capacity, patient centredness), but drew attention to the lack of 'validated, standardized, and longitudinal data' upon which to base conclusions (Leatherman and Sutherland 2004: E289). While the Government said that the report showed the NHS was improving, the editor of the *British Medical Journal* was less complimentary, saying that given the extra billions and a modernization plan, the lack of sufficient evidence to reliably answer the question of whether the NHS was improving was in itself an indictment, since the NHS was awash with bodies auditing and inspecting it (Smith 2003). The Health Foundation undertakes research on what works to improve quality and performance and publishes systematic reviews on quality enhancing interventions. The King's Fund is a long-established foundation that carries out research, policy analysis and development activities especially in London. The Picker Institute Europe is a research and development institute that has been influential in advocating patient-centred health care.

Market

The United Kingdom has a small private health sector, principally a few private hospitals, so that market players are not prominent. The conservative Government in the 1990s introduced a quasi-market into the NHS that involved major restructuring and procedural changes (Robinson and Dixon 1999). Many of these policies continued under Labour governments including patient choice in order to promote competition between hospitals on the basis of quality, fund-holding by groups of general practitioners, and pay-for-performance.

brief!

Canada

Canada has a federal system of government and mixed public and private health care. The *Constitutional Act 1867* made provincial governments (13 provinces and territories) responsible for health care and health care policy now involves ongoing funding negotiations between the federal government and provinces. The *Canada Health Act 1984* set out several principles: needs-based health care, public administration, accessibility, universality, comprehensiveness, and portability. The national health insurance scheme, Medicare, covers medically necessary consultations with medical practitioners and hospital care. Provincial health care systems were restructured in the 1990s and some provinces created regional health authorities. Provincial governments are responsible for the administration of public sector health services and for regulating provider organizations, while medical practitioners mostly are governed by their specialist colleges. Ontario notably has established a common framework for the registration of all health professions.

The Romanow Commission in 2002 concluded that Canadians supported the pan-Canadian principle but called for an end to intergovernmental blame-shifting. The Prime Minister and the premiers subsequently agreed to reform primary health care, improve access for rural and remote communities, and improve poor health outcomes among the Indigenous population. Debate continues about the public-private funding balance (about 70 per cent public) and respective service delivery responsibilities. Health ministers meet regularly to decide a collaborative health agenda. For example, the 2004 meeting rejected fundamental structural change but agreed on a larger and more targeted transfer of health funds (Marchildon 2005).

Canada has had its share of medical scandals. For example, a long-running inquest into the deaths of 12 patients in 1994 treated at the Winnipeg Paediatric Cardiovascular Surgery Program concluded that the surgeon in question did not have the experience to undertake the complex cases he took on, and that a province the small size of Manitoba should not be running a paediatric cardiac programme (Sibbald 1998; Davies 2001). The Canadian Government in 2002 announced funds for patient safety initiatives, including the creation of the Canadian Patient Safety Institute. This independent not-for-profit corporation was set up in 2003 as an advisory body to the national and provincial health ministers, based upon a stakeholder governance model (Baker et al. 2004). It undertakes programmes that promote policy dialogue, support demonstration studies and disseminate information. The Canadian Health Services Research Foundation also is an important NGO in the quality field that promotes the use of evidence in strengthening the delivery of health services. The Foundation funds research, provides training, promotes knowledge transfer and exchange (Lomas 2000), and promotes the translation of research into policy and programmes. For example, its *Mythbusters* series offers a concise synthesis of evidence on health system issues. Canada publishes *Quality of Healthcare in Canada: a Chartbook* that provides data on the quality and performance of healthcare and draws comparisons with other countries.

New Zealand

New Zealand has a unitary form of government, a 'mixed member proportional' voting system that often produces coalition governments, and its health care system has undergone major phases of restructuring. Governments during the 1990s introduced market model practices but the subsequent Labour/Alliance Government elected in 1999 drew back from competition and a rigid purchaser/provider split. The health system is funded mainly through general taxation, health services are administered by 21 district health boards set up under the *Public Health and Disability Act 2000*, and services are delivered by a mix of public and private providers (French et al. 2001). Government is the main regulatory actor and its efforts include a legal strategy on safety and quality.

New Zealand has a no-fault accident insurance system that also covers outcomes of adverse events for patients. The *Accident Rehabilitation and Compensation Insurance Act 1992* covers medical costs, compensation and rehabilitation. This government-funded scheme essentially bars medical malpractice litigation and so replaces the tort-based system for compensating medical injuries. Amendments in 2005 improved the rights of patients by expanding their eligibility for compensation for treatment injuries (Bismark and Paterson 2006).

Health care regulation was stepped up in response to public outrage following the 1988 Cartwright Inquiry into unethical research and treatment of women with cervical cancer. The *Health and Disability Commissioner Act 1994* established an independent Commissioner to respond to patient complaints and alleged breaches of consumer rights. The Code of Health and Disability Consumers' Rights published in 1996 sets out 10 legally enforceable rights of consumers and corresponding duties of providers (Paterson 2002). Protection of patients was strengthened by the *Medical Practitioners Act 1995* that requires medical practitioners to demonstrate their continuing competence to practise medicine, and protects the confidentiality of quality assurance activities (Paterson 2001). The *Health Professionals Competency Assurance Act 2003* replaced 11 statutes for the separate health professions, established a common framework for registration and disciplinary proceedings, and set up an independent Health Practitioners Disciplinary Tribunal. The *Health and Disability (Safety) Act* 2001 requires health provider organizations, such as hospitals, to demonstrate compliance with standards in order to gain certification with the Ministry of Health. National health plans set quality improvement goals and nationally consistent standards. The Ministry of Health reorganized a statutory Quality Improvement Committee in 2007 to provide independent advice to government and several national quality improvement programmes are underway.

European Union Countries

European Commission law and directives are beginning to bear upon health sector aspects of the common market, such as the licensing of new health technologies, cross-border recognition of professional qualifications, and access to health care across member countries after European Court of Justice rulings on cross-border treatment (Bertinato et al. 2005). Health care performance is the responsibility of the member states of the European Union, however, so that the European Commission recommends rather than requires quality standards. While safety and quality is an increasing concern throughout the European Union, the member states vary considerably in their structures and strategies. Several countries have established national bodies to ensure quality and safety (Denmark, Germany, Spain, the Netherlands and England), with England, Denmark and the Netherlands recognized as early leaders in the field (SIMPATIE 2007). A survey by the MARQUIS project of 68 experts in 24 EU countries classified countries into three groups on quality strategies: well-established, recent adopters, and slow starters. Countries with well-established strategies were Austria, Belgium, Denmark, England, France, Finland, Germany, Italy, the Netherlands, Spain and Sweden. A larger group of recent adopters were the process of developing strategies (such as hospital accreditation and clinical guidelines), but the biggest group were slow starters who lacked a coherent quality and safety programme (Legido-Quigley et al. 2008a).

Health Sector Governance in Australia

The history of health policy in Australia is a story of increasing involvement by the national government in an area historically left to the states and the professions. Australia has a federal system of government with nine jurisdictions (the Australian Government and six states and two territories – hereafter called the states). In general, the national government funds rather than provides health services; the states are autonomous jurisdictions that fund, administer and provide public sector health services, in particular public hospitals; private medical practitioners provide most community-based medical care; and the large private sector includes hospitals, health insurance schemes and diagnostic services. Regulation in the Australian health sector is decentred reflecting its public and private mix of services and federal system of government (Healy et al. 2006).

A complex division of fiscal and functional responsibilities has emerged for constitutional and historical reasons that involves overlaps (for example, public hospital funding), duplicated activities (for example, nursing home inspections), and happenstance and historical divisions of responsibility (for example, the national government checks people's hearing, state governments check their teeth). Divided fiscal and functional powers in Australia's federal system of government cause tensions about who, if anyone, runs the health care system (Duckett 2007). Although the Australian health care system is of a high standard and comparable to other high-income countries (Healy et al. 2006), a report on health reform found increasing tensions (National Health and Hospital Reform Commission 2009). Hospital policy problems included a 'blame game' between levels of government, rising hospital costs (10 per cent each year) beyond the capacity of state budgets, and variable efficiency across the public hospital system.

The Council of Australian Governments (except Western Australia) in April 2010 after considerable debate signed the National Health and Hospitals Network Agreement and a reform plan later emerged (Australian Government 2010). The 762 public hospitals across the country would form groups of three to four hospitals, to create around 200 Local Hospital Networks, with each statutory authority run by a hospital board and CEO. The Australian Government will fund Local Hospital Networks (partly by withholding GST revenue from the states) on a case mix basis for 60 per cent of the 'efficient cost' of every public patient admission, as well as 60 per cent of the costs of training and capital costs, and national standards would be set to improve quality. The Australian Government will take over full policy and funding responsibility for general practitioner services (which it mostly does anyway) and other primary care services, the aim being to reduce 9.3 per cent unnecessary hospital admissions. Critics pointed to the lack of immediate extra funds, the small size of the networks, the extra level of bureaucracy, and a lack of management expertise.

Government health sector regulation in Australia is reviewed below in terms of five forms of authority. In terms of legislative authority, parliaments can pass laws that relate to health care safety and quality. In terms of financial authority, governments possess the 'power of the purse' since they allocate funds. In terms of administrative authority, governments administer or deliver many public sector health services and are a major employer of health professionals. Health departments possess professional authority through their employees, and acquire representative authority by appointing stakeholders to advisory committees.

Legislative Authority

Government regulatory bodies, unlike other regulatory actors, possess legislative means for achieving their policy ends. Legal instruments include legislation, regulations under an act, rules, directives, common law and contracts. A review of patient safety legal instruments in several countries (Australia, Denmark, New Zealand, United States, the United Kingdom) identified a shift to legal frameworks of oversight that displace or supplement the legal frameworks that traditionally conferred a significant degree of autonomy on organizations and professionals (Downie et al. 2006: iv). Some countries, such as the United States, emphasize the law as a key strategy for regulating health care while others assign it a more limited role. Australia has recently begun to strengthen its legislative framework for health care governance.

The 1901 Constitution granted health powers to the Australian Government only on quarantine matters in order to prevent diseases entering the country. The national government began to play a significant role in health matters after World War II as a continuation of its strong role during the war years, and in line with international developments in post-war welfare states (Kewley 1973). The

Australian Government over the years has assumed health policy-making powers through amendments to the Constitution, and through broader interpretations of the responsibilities of a national government for the health of its population. The 1946 amendment to section 51 (xxiiia) of the Constitution enables the Australian Government to make laws on pensions and benefits; section 81 allows it to allocate funds 'for the purposes of the Commonwealth' under the appropriate legislation; and section 96 allows grants to the states for specific purposes.

While this section concentrates upon national laws since the 1940s, legislation in each state frames responsibilities through omnibus health sector legislation as well as other legislation (see Chapter 8). Each state has an array of similar legislation relevant to health care safety and quality through broad powers on public health services, licensing of health facilities, coronial powers, professional standards, patients' complaints, professional liability, and registration of health professionals. In relation to the latter, the Australian Government and the states from 2008 embarked upon reforms to professional registration (see Chapter 4).

Proposals by the national Labor Government (1941–49) to introduce national health insurance met strong resistance to so-called 'socialized medicine' from doctors, conservative political parties, and private insurance funds. Further, a short-lived *Pharmaceuticals Benefits Act* 1945 (Cth) was challenged by the Australian branch of the British Medical Association in the High Court of Australia, which found that Parliament had exceeded its constitutional power. The Australian Government then successfully put the issue to the voters in the 1946 referendum, and introduced subsidized pharmaceuticals in the *Pharmaceutical Benefits Act* 1950 (Cth).

The 1946 amendment to section 51 (xxiiia) of the Constitution enabled the Australian Government to make laws with respect to pensions and benefits as well as medical and dental services. The addendum on civil conscription in Section 51 (xxiiia), however, has been used to enshrine the fee-for-service model for paying doctors, the addendum reading as follows: 'The provision of maternity allowances, widows' pensions, child endowment, unemployment, pharmaceutical, sickness and hospital benefits, medical and dental services (but not so as to authorize any form of civil conscription), benefits to students and family allowances.' The medical profession has argued that the civil conscription clause protects medical practitioners essentially as self-employed and unable to be compelled to work for government, nor be required to provide medical services for a prescribed fee. This contested clause has implications, therefore, for how the government might use financial levers to regulate the clinical performance of doctors.

Under the *Hospital Benefits Act* 1946 (Cth) the Australian Government entered into agreements with the states to subsidize public hospital beds, on condition that patients in public beds were not charged, the intention being to remove financial barriers to hospital access by patients. This is the basis of intergovernmental hospital financing agreements. The states historically are responsible for administering public hospitals and for licensing private hospitals.

The Australian Government entered the field of residential care for older people under the *Aged Persons Homes Act* 1954 (Cth) that enabled grants to eligible organizations towards the capital cost of building or purchasing sheltered housing. The *Aged Care Act* 1997 (Cth) enables fee subsidies and empowers government to require participating aged care homes to meet certain standards. Responsibility is divided, however, since the states license premises in relation to building and physical requirements, while the Australian Government sets the standards and regulates the performance of the homes.

The *National Health Act* 1953 (Cth) consolidated the four main pillars of the Australian post-war health care system: the Pharmaceuticals Benefits Scheme, the Hospital Benefits scheme (Commonwealth funding for public hospitals), Pensioner Medical Services enacted in 1951 (health care subsidies for pensioners), and the Medical Benefits Scheme (medical cost subsidies for members of non-profit health insurance schemes, later transformed into Medicare). Therapeutic products, including complementary and alternative medicines and dietary supplements, are regulated under the *Therapeutic Goods Act* 1989 (Cth).

Australia's national health insurance scheme, Medicare, is administered by Medicare Australia (previously the Health Insurance Commission). The battle over national health insurance was resumed by a Labor Government (1972–75) and legislation finally was passed after dissolution of both Houses of Parliament and a new election. Medibank commenced in 1975 administered by a Commonwealth authority, the Health Insurance Commission, providing universal health insurance funded from taxation including a 1 per cent mandatory levy on income. The Liberal-Coalition Government (1975–83) allowed individuals to opt out of Medibank and to purchase private health insurance or pay a levy of 2.5 per cent of taxable income to remain in the scheme. Labor governments (1983–96) re-established the universal, tax-funded health insurance system, Medicare, and raised the mandatory levy on taxable income to 1.5 per cent. The Liberal Howard Government (1996–2007) offered various financial incentives to people (including a 30 per cent tax rebate) to take out additional private health insurance cover.

Financial Authority

Economists argue that regulation is most effective when based on explicit economic incentives and disincentives. Health care is funded from various sources: directly by government, by third party payers such as insurance funds and employers, and by consumers. Since health sectors in many countries have substantial public funding, governments have considerable regulatory leverage if they so choose. For example, the percentage of total health expenditure from public sources in 2005 was 87 per cent in the United Kingdom, 77 per cent in New Zealand, 70 per cent in Canada, 67 per cent in Australia, and 45 per cent in the United States (World Health Organization 2008).

The Australian Government has 'the power of the purse' as in 2005–06 it accounted for 43 per cent of total health expenditure, the states 25 per cent, with the remaining 32 per cent from non-government sources (Australian Institute of Health and Welfare 2008: 400). The Australian Government funds the states mainly through general purpose revenue, specific purpose grants, and revenue from the Goods and Services Tax (GST). Wrangling over the distribution of funds is a regular feature of intergovernmental forums. The health portfolio is very important in fiscal terms to the states (at least one-third of recurrent state budgets of which hospitals take about half), while in political terms the health portfolio, and particularly public hospitals, often are major issues in state elections.

The Australian Government subsidizes health care through the national health insurance scheme (Medicare), subsidizes pharmaceuticals, funds population health activities, and funds public hospitals. The Medicare Benefits Schedule sets out fee subsidies for patient consultations with medical practitioners and for laboratory tests, and the Pharmaceutical Benefits Schedule sets subsidies for drug purchases; The Australian Government negotiates funding agreements with the states for population health activities, and funds NGOs for some health services, such as disability-related services. Public hospitals have been funded through intergovernmental Australian Health Care Agreements. As noted above, the Australian Government in 2010 announced it would become the majority funder of public hospitals, and set up a National Health and Hospitals Network Fund (but not a standards meta-regulator).

The Australian Government could exert more financial leverage over the performance of medical practitioners, if it so chooses, via Medicare Australia. It sets the schedule of Medicare fees, that is, the subsidies paid for consultations, procedures and laboratory tests. General practitioners, for example, can bill patients who then claim the schedule fee from Medicare, or else a doctor can bill Medicare directly for patients (bulk billing) provided that the doctor accepts the schedule fee as full payment. The Medicare fees schedule and bulk-billing can apply downward pressure upon doctors' fees. The Medicare subsidy is based upon fee-for-service, however, a method of payment criticized as encouraging over-servicing by doctors.

Administrative Authority

While the state (government) generally now seeks to steer rather than row the economy (Osborne and Gaebler 1992), governments in some countries directly provide health care. For example, a hospital may be directly run by government, by a government-appointed board, or as an autonomous non-profit enterprise. A health department generally retains an oversight regulatory role and may be viewed as an internal or quasi-external regulator. Some third party regulatory bodies do not directly administer sanctions but rather act through another agency. For example, an accreditation agency may recommend that a health department revoke the licence of a hospital, or a coroner may recommend a medical board revoke the licence of a doctor.

Privatization did not proceed far in Australia since there was already a large private health sector. Market model practices introduced into the public sector from the 1980s included some purchaser/providers splits and the contracting out of some functions. The devolution trend partly was reversed in the early 2000s, however, in order to tighten ministerial control and several states abolished the boards of previously autonomous public hospitals. Following reviews of state health departments, many returned to centralized authority structures and centralized some administrative and policy functions such as workforce strategies, clinical services, and quality and safety (Dwyer 2004; Rix et al. 2005).

Professional Authority

Regulatory bodies exercise professional authority through the expertise of their professional staff, though appointees to boards, and through a penumbra of committees of experts who offer advice and impart legitimacy to pronouncements. Professional authority is crucial when governments seek to formulate health care policies. State health departments are major employers of health professionals and so exert professional authority through their staff. Health departments appoint advisory committees in order to tap professional expertise and to engage stakeholders in policy formulation. This is strategically important since resistance by the medical profession to government intervention is a continuing ideological theme in health policy debates (Sax 1984). Historically, governance of the professions has taken place at state level through registration boards and state chapters of professional associations, but this is about to change (see Chapter 4).

Representative Authority

A regulatory body draws authority from members of its council and committees who represent stakeholders, such as professional and industry bodies, and also through its wider network of connections. In market terms, a regulator is strategically located if its members represent the whole market. For example, an accreditation agency derives regulatory authority through its members when it accredits most or all hospitals in the country even under a voluntary accreditation scheme.

Regulatory Actors in the Australian Health Sector

Actors who regulate health care in Australia can be placed within four quadrants of a constellation (government, professions, civil society, and the market) and within concentric spheres (employers, states, national, inter-governmental, supranational (see earlier Figure 1.2). The boundaries are porous since a regulatory agency may be composed of actors from various quadrants and spheres. These actors are reviewed below beginning with government agencies.

Intergovernmental Agencies

The proliferation of intergovernmental organizations in Australia constitutes a 'fourth branch' of government (Weller 2000). Intergovernmental relations in Australia's federal system of government in areas that spill over state jurisdictions are underpinned by a large network of organizations linked by both formal and informal relationships. Key intergovernmental bodies are set up to provide a forum to agree on national policy and its implementation. But despite decades of discussions, the nine governments have been slow to take effective action on many urgent national issues. Australia's federal system of government is criticized for not keeping pace with the requirements of a modern national economy let alone a globalizing world (Steketee 2006). It is not surprising, therefore, that the health sector finds it difficult to implement a national approach to patient safety.

The Council of Australian Governments (COAG) was established in 1992 to address gaps and overlaps in functional responsibilities, such as energy, water and regional development. Chaired by the Prime Minister, the Council has representation from the Australian Government and each of the states and discusses intergovernmental fiscal and functional responsibilities at regular meetings. COAG initiatives in recent years include changes to health professional registration and to public hospital funding.

The Australian Health Ministers' Conference is the intergovernmental health sector forum, comprising health ministers from each state and the Australian Government (and the New Zealand Health Minister). While decisions are not binding, the expectation is that health ministers will take an endorsed policy back to their states to be implemented. The associated Australian Health Ministers' Advisory Council (AHMAC) consists of senior national and state health officials (and the New Zealand Health Ministry CEO), who consider health matters referred by the Conference or any of the health ministers, and who report back to the Conference. AHMAC is a key body in health sector governance since senior health officials propose policy and translate policy into action.

National Government Bodies

The two national agencies most relevant to the safety and quality of health care are the Department of Health and Ageing and the Australian Commission for Safety and Quality in Health Care, while other agencies are involved in particular health sector aspects.

Australian Department of Health and Ageing

The department formulates national health policies, administers health funds to the states, and manages national programmes, but has little authority over health care performance. The department is divided into 16 divisions (as at June 2009) many of which have regulatory responsibilities. The Therapeutic Goods Administration, for example, examines the safety and efficacy of products, diagnostic treatment devices and pharmaceuticals. The Regulatory Policy and Governance Division interacts with the Therapeutic Goods Administration, the National Health and Medical Research Council, the Office of the Gene Technology Regulator, the Australian Radiation Protection and Nuclear Safety Agency, the National Blood Authority, Food Standards Australia New Zealand, and the Australian Commission on Safety and Quality in Health Care. In addition, Ministerial advisory committees include the Pharmaceutical Benefits Advisory Committee (PBAC) that advises on the efficacy and cost-effectiveness of drugs listed on the Pharmaceutical Benefits Scheme, and the Medical Services Advisory Committee (MSAC) that advises on procedures subsidized by Medicare. The Minister and department also commission research and policy reports from government-run task forces. For example, the National Health and Hospitals Reform Commission made 123 recommendations in its 2009 report on 'a long-term health reform plan for a modern Australia' (National Health and Hospital Reform Commission 2009).

Australian Commission on Safety and Quality in Health Care

The Commission was announced in 2005 by the Australian Health Ministers. Commencing in January 2006 (replacing the Australian Council for Safety and Quality in Health Care), it has a board of twelve members appointed by the Ministers, a chief executive officer, an annual budget of about $10 million (half each from the Australian Government and the states), about 30 staff, and its programme of work is approved each year by the Health Ministers. There are three committees: an inter-jurisdictional committee (officials from all health departments), a primary care committee, and a private hospital sector committee. The Commission's mandate is to lead and coordinate safety and quality improvements in the public and the private sector, identify policy directions, and recommend priorities for action, which roles emphasize information and consultation strategies. It reports publicly on safety and quality indicators, funds research, recommends national data sets, recommends national standards, promotes safety and quality programmes, and publishes regular reports on solutions and progress.

The Commission has some financial capacity and professional expertise but no legislative authority, and no administrative authority except via the Australian Health Ministers Advisory Committee and the Australian Health Ministers' Conference. In terms of a node of governance, the Commission engages many (but not all) the key stakeholders; its members do not necessarily share the same way of thinking; it tries many methods to influence the flow of events; it has resources in the shape of funds and staff; but has a limited enabling structure to implement initiatives and must work through its members, such as health departments, professional associations and industry groups. The National Health and Hospitals Reform Commission in its 2009 report recommended that the Commission be made a statutory agency and legislation to this effect was introduced in Parliament in June 2010.

Other regulatory agencies

Nursing homes are regulated by the Aged Care Standards and Accreditation Agency (ACSAA), a national company set up by the Australian Government in 1998 as the sole accreditation agency for residential aged care. In contrast, the United Kingdom and the United States retained direct government-run regulation of nursing homes. While the intention was to distance the Australian Government from inspections, in practice the Minister is still blamed for scandals involving poor quality homes. In a dual regulatory model, ACSAA inspects the homes and recommends any serious sanctions to the Department of Health and Ageing as the enforcement agency.

The National Health and Medical Research Council (NHMRC), the major health research funding body, became a statutory authority in 2006 (previously it was under the Australian Department of Health and Ageing). Its statutory obligations include raising health standards, fostering research and training, and promoting debate on ethical issues. It funds research on improving quality and publishes guidelines on health issues.

The National Institute of Clinical Studies (NICS), under the NHMRC since 2006, was established in 2000 with the aim of improving the take-up of evidence into clinical practice. NICS commissions and disseminates evidence-based clinical guidelines and monitors their take up. It aims to close the gap between evidence and practice, regulates through persuasion (its strategies mainly are located at the voluntary base of the regulatory pyramid), and has no enforcement powers. Since NICS does not authorize but rather disseminates clinical protocols, it avoids conflict with professional groups and drug companies.

Medicare Australia, Australia's national health insurance fund (previously the Health Insurance Commission), was restructured in 2005 as a agency under the Department of Human Services, the rationale being that an authority responsible for such a large amount of tax-payers' money should be under closer Ministerial control. The Health Insurance Commission was established as a statutory agency in 1974 to administer the national health insurance scheme, principally the Medicare Benefits Scheme and the Pharmaceutical Benefits Scheme. It can apply enforcement powers from the top of the regulatory pyramid, and as the major health insurance fund, potentially could influence health care quality, as insurance funds do in other countries.

The National E-Health Transition Authority (NEHTA) was established in 2005 as a company owned by the Commonwealth and the states and reports to the Australian Health Ministers Advisory Council. It takes a national approach to delivering better health care through electronic information technology. The aims are to set standards, specifications and infrastructure requirements for secure, interoperable electronic health information systems. It negotiates with health departments and hospitals on developing unique identifiers and standardizing electronic documents, such as referrals and discharge summaries. The expected benefits are better quality and safer health services (due to more accessible, accurate and complete patient information), streamlined care (seamless handovers), and improved efficiency (unique identifiers and standardized information in electronic systems).

The Australian Institute of Health and Welfare provides information on Australia's health and welfare, through statistics and data that inform discussion and decisions on policy and services. It works with the Australian Government and the states in collecting, analysing and disseminating data on patterns of health, housing and community services.

Two new authorities were established in 2009 in relation to the health care workforce (see Chapter 4). The Australian Health Practitioner Regulation Agency is to oversee 10 national-level registration boards for the health professions, and Health Workforce Australia will manage and oversee reforms to the workforce.

State Government Regulatory Actors

Much health sector governance takes place at state-level in Australia. State health departments (six states and two territories) are internal regulatory actors and also are the largest employers of health professionals in their jurisdictions. They administer and most also provide public sector health services, principally hospitals, as well as community health services (for example, early child development), and population health services (for example, cancer screening). Other areas of health-related public services include rehabilitation, mental health, drug and alcohol, dental health, disability, home and community care, environmental health, and occupational health and safety. Health departments formulate health policies and plan programmes, review programmes and budgets, negotiate industrial and personnel matters, set performance standards, inspect and license private premises, and undertake major capital works.

State health departments undergo regular reviews and restructuring, particularly when a new government is elected. During the 1970s, some states amalgamated separate administrations for hospitals, community health, and mental health into health commissions; in the early 1980s health and community functions were separated; and in the early 1990s super departments were created that brought together most aspects of health and community services under a single bureaucracy ('human services' being a popular label); while in recent years most states have reinstituted separate health departments. Health sectors have developed a little differently in each state (although are characterized more by commonality than diversity), with variations in policies, organizational structures, and per capita health expenditure, given different political and bureaucratic histories and the impact of events such as public inquiries.

State health departments also differ in administrative arrangements and styles in response to their environmental context, such as population size and geographic area. Populations range from over 6 million in New South Wales down to under a quarter-million in the Northern Territory, and from 2.5 million square kilometres in Western Australia to less than 2,000 square kilometres in the Australian Capital Territory (Australian Bureau of Statistics 2007). Public sector cultures also differ.

Table 3.1 Safety and quality governance bodies, states and territories 2009

States	State dept	Dept S & Q unit	S & Q Council	Health Complaints Commission	Coroner	Professional registration boards*
NSW	Health	S&Q Branch, area advisers	Clinical Excellence Commission 2004	Health Complaints Commissioner 1993	yes	Multiple boards, legislation under review
Vic	Health	Health System Performance Division	Victorian Quality Council 2000	Health Services Commissioner 1987	yes	Multiple boards, common legislation
Qld	Health	Innovation & Workforce Reform Directorate	Safety & Quality Board 2005 (restructured 2007)	Health Quality & Complaints Commissioner 2006	yes	Multiple boards
WA	Health	Office of Safety and Quality	Safety & Quality Council 2002	Office of Health Review	yes	Multiple boards
SA	Health	Director of Clinical Services	Safety & Quality Council 2000 (restructured 2007)	Health Quality & Complaints Commissioner 2004	yes	Multiple boards
Tas	Health & Human Services	Hospital quality committees	Quality Council 2003	Health Complaints Commissioner	yes	Multiple boards
ACT	Health & Community Services	S&Q unit	Quality & Safety Forum 2000	Health Services Commissioner	yes	Several boards
NT	Health & Community Services	S&Q officers	Council on Safety & Quality in Health Care 2004	Health & Community Services Complaints Commissioner 1998	yes	Multiple boards, Health Professions Licensing Authority

* *Note*: State professional boards were replaced by national boards in 2010

For example, New South Wales has a more adversarial style of governance, Queensland a hierarchical administrative style, while Victoria stresses consultation. Convergence in their quality programmes has been evident since the Australian Government from 1998 began to allocate funds for quality initiatives (Department of Health and Ageing 2004), and in response to leadership from the national safety and quality council/commission. Table 3.1 lists the main safety and quality governance bodies in the states that are discussed in the following sections.

State departments of health

In New South Wales, the Department of Health (NSW Health) reduced 17 area health boards to eight in 2005 that also took over public hospitals. The Quality and Safety Branch sets standards, publishes information, offers training programmes, and runs the adverse incident reporting system. In the wake of public inquiries into the state's hospitals, the 'inspectorial' powers of the Clinical Excellence Commission CEC were expanded, legal requirements were tightened that bear upon the regulation of doctors, and the powers of the Health Care Complaints Commissioner were strengthened (Iedema et al. 2005). The administration of public hospitals by NSW Health was scathingly criticized in a recent public inquiry (Garling Report 2009).

In Victoria, health and community services were merged in the Department of Human Services in 1996 but were separated again in 2009. Hospital boards were abolished in the mid 1990s and hospitals were grouped into administrative networks each with a management board in order to facilitate regional management, and some small hospitals were merged or closed. Victoria has a large array of complaints and review bodies and the health department engages with a wide range of stakeholders.

In Queensland, the health department has undergone several administrative reorganizations over the last decade and has decentralized administration to 38 districts. The state has many small rural hospitals with consequent problems in quality and staff recruitment. The inquiry into Bundaberg and other hospitals recommended major reforms to the health department (Davies Report 2005), described as 'a gigantic dysfunctional conglomerate' by the editor of the *Medical Journal of Australia* (Van Der Weyden 2005: 285). The government in the 2006 election announced extra funds for a 'health action plan' to recruit more doctors, invest in hospitals, reorganize the department, and promote a patient safety culture. Queensland Health now takes an active approach to quality and safety (Duckett 2009).

In Western Australia, the health department was reorganized after a 2004 review, one of the aims being to improve safety and quality.

In South Australia, health and human services departments were separated in 2004, hospital boards abolished, and administrative boundaries redrawn. Departmental safety and quality advisers stress improving safety in hospitals through training programmes and incident reporting.

In Tasmania, the Department of Health and Human Services has several quality assurance committees. Tasmania as a small state with limited capacity generally is slower to implement national recommendations.

The Australian Capital Territory also is a small jurisdiction and ACT Health takes a consultative approach that involves professionals and other stakeholders on committees and reviews that address specific quality and safety issues.

In the Northern Territory, the Department of Health and Community Services administers services for people across a vast geographic area (1.3 million square kilometres). Programmes concentrate upon overcoming distance issues, improving basic services and improving health services for Indigenous people. Given limited resources and large health challenges, the Territory often has different priorities to those 'down south'.

State safety and quality councils

All states and territories from 2000 onwards set up safety and quality councils mostly as internal advisory bodies to departments of health. The NSW Clinical Excellence Commission is unique among the states as a statutory commission with powers of review that advises on systemic safety and quality issues, monitors self-assessment by health organizations, analyses data, and conducts reviews as required by the minister or department. The Victorian Safety and Quality Council is an advisory body with a large consultative council (over 30 members) and supports action-research programmes. The Queensland Patient Safety and Quality Board replaced an internal advisory group, but the Complaints Commission is regarded as the key body. The WA Council for Safety and Quality in Health Care is an advisory body that works with the department on patient safety initiatives. The SA Safety and Quality Council, initially an internal advisory body with a focus on public hospital care, was reorganized in 2007. The Tasmanian Quality Council is mainly an internal information and advisory forum. The ACT Quality and Safety Forum is an advisory body to the department. The NT Council on Safety and Quality in Health Care is a departmental advisory body.

These councils do not possess the attributes for nodal governance: a network, ideas, methods, resources, and an enabling structure (Burris et al. 2005). In terms of their place in a regulatory constellation, most are an internal advisory body to a health department rather than a governance node of stakeholders. Since state health departments mainly focus on their public hospitals the councils have few links to other regulators such as registration boards, professional colleges, coroners, complaints commissioners, and accreditation agencies. The councils are in the process of developing shared ideas among their members, but few (except New South Wales and Victoria) control budgetary resources, and have a weak grasp on strands of governance since they work through health departments for their enabling structure.

The councils can be located against four quadrants (government, civil society, professions and market) in terms of their models of representational authority (Figure 3.2). The New South Wales council (the council with the most authority) can be classified as a stakeholder governance model, as can the Victorian and Western Australian councils; Queensland, Tasmania and the Northern Territory are government dominant models; South Australia and the Australian Capital Territory fit a combined government and professional model. None of the councils exhibit a consumer model although most have at least one consumer representative.

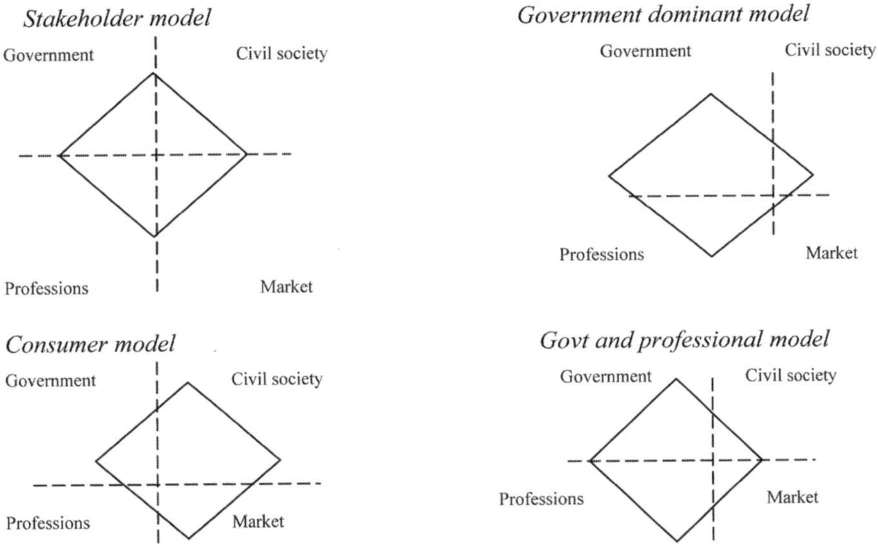

Figure 3.2 Models of networked governance

Coroners

Each Australian state has a coroner with functions under respective *Coroner's Acts* that vary somewhat in terms of powers and responsibilities and most have updated their legislation over the last decade. The function of a coroner is to investigate 'reportable deaths' (the definition varies) usually notified by a police officer or a medical practitioner, to conduct an autopsy if necessary, and in some circumstances, such as suspected homicide, to conduct a court hearing termed an inquest. The coronial process in Australia is a medico-legal process led by legally trained practitioners assisted by medically trained practitioners, in contrast to a medical examiner system that operates in some parts of the United States and Canada (Bugeja and Ranson 2005). The striking motto of the Victorian Coroner's Office is 'We speak for the dead to protect the living'.

Health care complaints commissioners

Democratic societies offer their citizens a variety of grievance procedures and the ombudsman is a key societal actor in a 'national integrity system' for ensuring accountability and for safeguarding civil liberty (Transparency International 2009).

Many countries from the 1980s onwards set up an ombudsman as an independent and external authority to mediate between public sector institutions and citizens (Swingdau 2000). In addition to public sector ombudsmen nationally and in each state, Australia also established health complaints commissioners from the 1980s onwards. The 'Australasian solution' of an independent 'health ombudsman' is internationally unusual apart from in Sweden and a few US states (Newby 2002).

The impetus was dissatisfaction with the responses of medical boards to complaints about medical practitioners, the lack of external avenues for complaints about hospitals, and a demand for greater accountability after several 'medical scandals'. State branches of the Australian Medical Association mostly opposed the establishment of commissioners as threatening medical autonomy (Thomas 2002). The Australian Health Care Agreement was a further impetus since the amended *Medicare Agreements Act 1992* (Cth) required the states to establish independent complaints bodies.

The two functions of health ombudsmen are, first, to act as 'a public watchdog' on health care standards, and second, to resolve patients' complaints about public and private health services through conciliation, investigation or prosecution. The role, function and structure of the commissions vary somewhat, including the balance they strike between public watchdog and complaints resolution, and their relationships with professional registration boards. Ombudsmen generally refer malpractice complaints (about all health professionals, not just doctors) to the relevant professional registration board so that they respond to complaints mostly about hospitals. The powers of most commissioners are restricted to reacting to consumer complaints and to ministerial requests for reviews, except in New South Wales and Queensland whose commissioners have greater powers. The NSW Commissioner investigates and prosecutes complaints against doctors, and has the final say on which cases should be referred to the Medical Tribunal (Thomas 2006). Queensland set up an independent Health Quality and Complaints Commissioner in 2006 with proactive powers to initiate reviews of public sector organizations.

Civil Society

While the Australian health sector has many non-government organizations, they mostly focus on specific health conditions, in contrast to other countries with influential safety and quality NGOs, notably the United States. Accreditation agencies are the exception (see Chapter 7). The Consumers' Health Forum of Australia is the national voice for health consumers through its over 75-member organizations. Formed in 1987, its funds come from membership fees and the Australian Department of Health and Ageing. It lobbies governments to include consumer representatives in decision-making and provides consumer representatives to over 200 committees. It advocates on health issues, runs training programmes for consumer representatives, and provides information and resources to its members. Its priorities are effective health care for people with chronic conditions, affordable health care, safe and affordable use of medicines, and safety and quality although it has not so far mounted a major campaign on patient safety.

Market

The Australian Competition and Consumer Commission (ACCC) is an independent statutory authority set up in 1995 by the Australian Parliament as a successor to the Trade Practices Commission to enforce national competition policy across the market. The ACCC goal is to protect the rights of consumers and rights of business by encouraging vigorous competition in the market place, and by enforcing consumer protection and fair trading. The ACCC operates under the *Trade Practices Act 1974* (Cth), other legislation, such as the *Competition Policy Reform Act 1995* (Cth), and equivalent Fair Trading Acts in the states. Amendments in 1995 extended the law to all areas of business including the health professions. Problems arising from the commercialization of medicine previously had largely been ignored by policy makers. These include 'kick backs' between doctors for referring patients, fee-splitting, exclusionary practices by specialists against others (for example, withholding hospital practice privileges), and conflicts of interest, such as doctors ordering tests for patients from laboratories they owned or had shares in, or referring patients for admission to hospitals they owned or had shares in (Walton 1998: chapter 3).

Professions

The professions quadrant is very important in all countries in the regulation of safety and quality. In Australia, many professional bodies exert regulatory influence over practitioners, including registration boards for the professions, the Australian Medical Council, professional associations, and the specialist medical colleges. These bodies are discussed in Chapter 4.

Conclusion

Networked governance is essential in health sectors to produce better health care since no one actor understands all the issues or holds all the strands of governance. Constellations of regulatory actors have expanded rapidly and these actors are engaging in regulatory conversation on principles and mechanisms so that networked governance in relation to safety and quality began to emerge in the early 2000s. But effective nodal governance takes time as this requires the capacity to engage people, share ideas, apply effective methods of governance, command resources, and build a structure to mobilize action (Burris et al. 2005). Much of the regulatory attention so far has concentrated on the architecture of regulatory systems: the establishment of national regulatory agencies and governance networks. The impact of these agencies and networks is much harder to discern. In reviewing efforts to improve health care in the United Kingdom and the United States, Ferlie and Shortell conclude that each country should consider trade-offs: the United Kingdom should balance its centralized approach with a more bottom-up approach that involves health professionals, while the United States should balance its decentralized and pluralistic approach with national efforts to set standards and require accountability (Ferlie and Shortell 2001).

Health governance is a globalized area in its movement of experts and knowledge and each country picks up ideas from other countries and in turn influences their policies (McLoughlin et al. 2001). Australia might consider governance ideas from other countries. The United States has considerable experience with stakeholder forums and collaborative approaches, and is the world leader on measuring safety and quality and public reporting. The United Kingdom has strong and coherent national policies on safety and quality, its national regulatory agencies take a meta-regulation approach, and performance indicators are publicly reported. Leaders on safety and quality among European Union member countries, such as Denmark and the Netherlands, stress 'quality improvement' and avoid the term 'regulation', have strengthened established agencies, and are active meta-regulators in monitoring performance indicators.

In Australia, and in other federal forms of government, networked governance is important at state-level, particularly where states/regions primarily are responsible for health care. In Australia, some states, notably New South Wales and Queensland, increasingly take a meta-regulatory approach in monitoring actions and outcomes and draw on legislative, funding, administrative, professional and representational sources of authority. But Australia has no national-level and independent health meta-regulator with review and enforcement powers.

Safety and quality advocates in Australia are impatient with what they see as a glacial rate of change, however, with a proliferation of governance bodies and plenty of discussion, but a failure of political will to take effective enforcement action (Wilson and Van Der Weyden 2005). Similarly in the United States, while Leape and Berwick acknowledge that regulatory agencies have improved patient safety at the margins, such as better infection control in hospitals, they argue that any overall impact is hard to see in national statistics and call for commitment to a national strategy:

> Five years ago, the Institute of Medicine (IOM) called for a national effort to make health care safe. Although progress since then has been slow, the IOM report truly 'changed the conversation' to a focus on changing systems, stimulated a broad array of stakeholders to engage in patient safety, and motivated hospitals to adopt new safe practices. But improvement of the magnitude envisioned by the IOM requires a national commitment to strict, ambitious, quantitative, and well-tracked goals. (Leape and Berwick 2005: 2384)

Many countries are in the process of strengthening regulatory agencies, developing a national strategy, and pushing the implementation of evidence-based safety reforms. The challenges are to identify the regulatory approaches most likely to ensure that promising patient safety practices are put in place and to commit to and monitor 'well-tracked goals'. The following chapters analyse the strategies being pursued by range of regulatory actors around the world, beginning with the health professions.

Main focus Australia.

References

Agency for Healthcare Research and Quality (2003), *National Healthcare Quality Report*. (Rockville MD: Agency for Healthcare Research and Quality).

Australian Bureau of Statistics, Australia at a Glance, 1309.0, (21 June 2007) http://www.abs.gov.au/AUSSTATS

Australian Government (2010), A National Health and Hospitals Network for Australia's Future: Delivering the Reforms. (Canberra.

Australian Institute of Health and Welfare (2008), *Australia's Health 2008*. (Canberra: AIHW).

Bagian J, et al. (2001), 'Developing and deploying a patient safety program in a large health care delivery system: you can't fix up what you don't know about.' *Joint Commission Journal on Quality Improvement* 27(10): 522–532.

Baker G, et al. (2004), 'The Canadian Adverse Events Study: the incidence of adverse events among hospital patients in Canada.' *Canadian Medical Association Journal* 170(11): 1678–1686.

Bertinato L, et al. (2005), *Policy Brief: Cross-Border Health Care in Europe*. (Brussels: World Health Organization and European Observatory on Health Systems and Policies).

Bismark M and Paterson R (2006), 'No-fault compensation in New Zealand: harmonizing injury compensation, provider accountability, and patient safety.' *Health Affairs* 25(1): 278–283.

Black J (2002a), 'Critical reflections on regulation.' *Australian Journal of Legal Philosophy* 27: 1–35.

Black J (2002b), 'Regulatory conversations.' *Journal of Law and Society* 29(1): 163–196.

Braithwaite J and Drahos P (2000), *Global Business Regulation*. (Cambridge: Cambridge University Press).

Braithwaite J, et al. (2005), *The Governance of Health Care Safety and Quality*. (Canberra: Commonwealth of Australia).

Bugeja L and Ranson D (2005), 'Coroners' recommendations: a lost opportunity.' *Journal of Law and Medicine* 13(2): 173–175.

Burris S, et al. (2005), 'Nodal governance.' *Australian Journal of Legal Philosophy* 30: 30–58.

Busse R and Riesberg A (2004), *Health care systems in transition: Germany*. (Copenhagen: European Observatory on Health Care Systems and Policies).

Castells M (2000), *The Rise of the Network Society*. (Malden, MA. Oxford. Carlton, Australia: Blackwell Publishing).

Chief Medical Officer (2006), Good Doctors: Safer Patients: Proposals to strengthen the system to assure and improve the performance of doctors and to protect the safety of patients. (London: Department of Health).

Council of Europe, Recommendation 2006(7) of the Committee of Ministers to the Member States on Management of Patient Safety and Prevention of Adverse Events in Health Care, (29 January 2009) https://wcd.coe.int/ViewDoc.jsp?id=1005439&BackColorInternet=9999CC&BackColorIntranet=FFBB55&BackColorLogged=FFAC75

Darzi A (2009), High Quality Care For All: NHS Next Stage Review Final Report. (London: Department of Health).

Davies J (2001), 'Painful inquiries: lessons from Winnipeg.' *Canadian Medical Association Journal* 165: 1502–1504.

Davies Report (2005), *Queensland Public Hospitals Commission of Inquiry Report*. (Brisbane: State of Queensland).

Department of Health (1998), *A First Class Service: Quality in the New NHS*. (London: Stationery Office).

Department of Health (1999), *The NHS Performance Assessment Framework*. (London: Department of Health).

Department of Health and Ageing (2004), *Australian Health Care Agreements Performance Report 1998–99 to 2002–03*. (Canberra: Commonwealth of Australia).

Donaldson Report (2000), *An Organisation With A Memory*. (London: Stationery Office).

Downie J, et al. (2006), *Patient Safety Law: From Silos to Systems: Final Report*. (Halifax, Nova Scotia: Health Law Institute, Dalhousie University).

Dubois C-A, et al. (2006), 'Analysing trends, opportunities and challenges'. In Dubois C-A, McKee M and Nolte E. *Human Resources for Health in Europe*. (Maidenhead, Berkshire: Open University Press): 15–40.

Duckett S (2007), *The Australian Health Care System*. (South Melbourne: Oxford University Press).

Duckett S (2009), 'Transforming clinical governance in Queensland health'. In Healy J and Dugdale P. *Patient Safety First: Responsive Regulation in Health Care*. (Crows Nest NSW: Allen & Unwin): 124–143.

Dwyer JM (2004), 'Australian health system restructuring - what problem is being solved?' *Australia and New Zealand Health Policy* 1(6): 1–6.

Dyer C (2001), 'New agency set up to identify incompetent doctors.' *British Medical Journal* 322: 67.

Enthoven A and Van de Ven W (2007), 'Going Dutch: managed competition health insurance in the Netherlands.' *New England Journal of Medicine* 357: 2421–2423.

Evetts J (1998), 'Professions beyond the nation-state: international systems of professional regulation in Europe.' *International Journal of Sociology and Social Policy* 18(11/12): 47–64.

Ferlie E and Shortell S (2001), 'Improving the quality of health care in the United Kingdom and the United States: a framework for change.' *Milbank Quarterly* 79(2): 281–315.

French S, et al. (2001), *Health Care Systems in Transition: New Zealand.* (Copenhagen: European Observatory on Health Care Systems).

Garling Report (2009), Final Report of the Special Commission of Inquiry: Acute Care Services in NSW Public Hospitals. (Sydney: State of New South Wales).

Ham C, ed. (1998), *Health Care Reform.* (Buckingham. Philadelphia: Open University Press).

Harrison MI (2004), Implementing Change in Health Systems: Market Reforms in the United Kingdom, Sweden & the Netherlands. (London. Thousand Oaks. New Delhi: Sage Publications).

Hawkes N (2009), 'Body politic: That sinking feeling.' *British Medical Journal* 339: 370.

Healy J, et al. (2006), 'Australia: Health system review.' *Health Systems in Transition* 8(5): 1–155.

Iedema R, et al. (2005), 'Clinical governance: complexities and promises'. In Stanton P, Willis E and Young S. *Workplace Reform in the Healthcare Industry: The Australian Experience.* (Basingstoke, New York: Palgrave Macmillan): 253–278.

Institute of Medicine (2000), *To Err is Human: Building a Safer Health System.* (Washington, DC: Institute of Medicine, National Academy Press).

Institute of Medicine (2001), *Crossing the Quality Chasm: A New Health System for the 21st century.* (Washington, DC: National Academy Press).

Institute of Medicine (2002), Leadership by Example: Coordinating Government Roles in Improving Health Care Quality. (Washington DC: The National Academies Press).

Institute of Medicine (2004a), *Keeping Patients Safe: Transforming the Work Environment of Nurses.* (Washington DC: The National Academies Press).

Institute of Medicine (2004b), *Patient Safety: Achieving a New Standard of Care.* (Washington DC: Institute of Medicine, The National Academies Press).

Jordana J and Sancho D (2004), 'Regulatory designs, institutional constellations and the study of the regulatory state'. In Jordana J and Levi-Faur D. *The Politics of Regulation: Institutions and Regulatory Reforms for the Age of Governance.* (Cheltenham. Northampton: Edward Elgar).

Kerridge I, et al. (2005), *Ethics and Law for the Health Professions.* (Annandale, NSW: Federation Press).

Kewley T (1973), *Social Security in Australia: 1900–1972.* (Sydney: Sydney University Press).

Leape L and Berwick D (2005), 'Five years after *To Err is Human*: what have we learned.' *Journal of the American Medical Association* 293(19): 2384–2390.
Leapfrog Group, Home page, (11 August 2005 11 August 2005) www.leapfroggroup.org
Leatherman S and Sutherland K (2004), 'Quality of care in the NHS of England.' *British Medical Journal* 328: 288–290.
Legido-Quigley H, et al. (2008a), *Assuring the Quality of Health Care in the European Union: A Case for Action*. (Brussels: World Health Organization and European Observatory on Health Systems and Policies).
Legido-Quigley H, et al. (2008b), 'How can quality of health care be safeguarded across the European Union?' *British Medical Journal* 336: 920–923.
Lehmann Knudsen J (2009), *From professional to regulatory driven quality improvement in Danish Healthcare*. International Society for Quality in Health Care, (Dublin: ISQua).
Lomas J (2000), 'Using 'linkage and exchange' to move research into policy at a Canadian foundation.' *Health Affairs* 19(3): 236–240.
Marchildon G (2005), 'Canadian health system reforms: lessons for Australia?' *Australian Health Review* 29(1): 105–120.
Mattke S, et al. (2006), 'The OECD Health Care Quality Indicators Project: history and background.' *International Journal for Quality in Health Care* September (Special issue): 1–4.
McLoughlin V, et al. (2001), 'Improving performance using indicators: recent experience in the United States, the United Kingdom, and Australia.' *International Journal for Quality in Health Care* 13(6): 455–462.
Minder A, et al. (2000), *Health Care Systems in Transition: Switzerland*. (Copenhagen: European Observatory on Health Systems and Policies).
National Committee for Quality Assurance (2004), *The State of Health Care Quality 2004*. (Washington DC: National Committee for Quality Assurance).
National Health and Hospital Reform Commission (2009), *A Healthier Future for all Australians: Final Report June 2009*. (Canberra: Australian Government).
National Patient Safety Foundation (2005), About the Foundation.
National Quality Forum, Home page, (9 August 2005) www.qualityforum.org
Newby L (2002), 'Concluding commentary'. In Thomas D. *Medicine Called to Account: Health Care Complaints Mechanisms in Australasia*. (Sydney: University of New South Wales): 111–118.
Organisation for Economic Co-operation and Development (2002), Regulatory Policies in OECD Countries: From Interventionism to Regulatory Governance. (Paris: OECD).
Osborne D and Gaebler T (1992), Reinventing Government: How the Entrepreneurial Spirit is Transforming the Public Sector. (Boston: Addison-Wesley).
Paterson R (2001), Patients' rights in New Zealand: Lessons for Ontario? (Auckland, NZ: Office of the Health and Disability Commissioner).

Paterson R (2002), 'The patients' complaints system in New Zealand.' *Health Affairs* 21(3): 70–79.

President's Advisory Commission on Consumer Protection and Quality in the Health Care Industry (1998), *Quality First: Better Health Care for All Americans*. (Silver Spring MD: Agency for Healthcare Research and Quality).

Rix M, et al. (2005), '(Re)form with substance? Restructuring and governance in the Australian health system 2004–05.' *Australia and New Zealand Health Policy* 2(19): 1–8.

Robinson R and Dixon A (1999), *Health Care Systems in Transition: United Kingdom*. (Copenhagen: European Observatory on Health Care Systems).

Sax S (1984), A Strife of Interests: Politics and Policies in Australian Health Services. (Sydney: Allen and Unwin).

Scally G and Donaldson L (1998), 'Clinical governance and the drive for quality improvement in the new NHS in England.' *British Medical Journal* 317: 61–65.

Schoen C, et al. (2004), 2003 Commonwealth Fund International Health Policy Survey of Hosapital Executives. (New York: The Commonwealth Fund).

Secretary of State for Health (2007), Trust, Assurance and Safety - The Regulation of Health Professionals in the 21stcentury. (London: The Stationery Office).

Sibbald B (1998), 'Why did 12 infants die? Winnipeg's endless inquest seeks answers.' *Canadian Medical Association Journal* 158: 883–789.

SIMPATIE (2007), Final Report of the Mapping Exercise. (Utrecht: CBO).

Smith R (2003), 'Is the NHS getting better or worse?' *British Medical Journal* 327: 1239–1241.

Spurgeon P and Latham L (2003), 'Pursuing clinical governance through effective leadership'. In Dopson S and Mark A. *Leading Health Care Organizations*. (Basingstoke: Palgrave Macmillan): 51–62.

Steketee M 2006, Hardly a system for this century, *The Weekend Australian*, 28–29 October.

Swingdau O (2000), 'The ombudsman: mediating on behalf of patients.' *Hospital: Official Journal of the European Association of Hospital Managers* 2(1): 14–15.

The Commonwealth Fund (7 March 2005), Washington Health Policy Week in Review: amazing Medicaid facts. (New York: The Commonwealth Fund).

The Commonwealth Fund, State scorecard on a high performing health system, (18 June 2007) http://www.commonwealthfund.org/aboutus

Thomas D (2002), 'Introductory overview'. In Thomas D. *Medicine Called to Account: Health Care Complaints Mechanisms in Australasia*. (Sydney: University of New South Wales): 1–14.

Thomas D (2006), 'Peer review as an outmoded model for health practitioner regulation'. In Freckleton I. *Regulating Health Practitioners*. (Annandale, NSW: The Federation Press).

Transparency International, National integrity system, (5 January 2009) http://www.transparency.org/policy_research/nis

Trubek L (2004), *New governance practices in US health care*. Workshop on New Governance and Constitutionalism, (Cambridge UK: Cambridge University).

Van Der Weyden M (2005), 'The Bundaberg Hospital scandal: the need for reform in Queensland and beyond.' *Medical Journal of Australia* 183(6): 284–285.

Walshe K (2003a), 'International comparisons of the quality of health care: what do they tell us?' *Quality and Safety in Health Care* 12: 4–5.

Walshe K (2003b), *Regulating Healthcare: A Prescription For Improvement?* (Maidenhead. Philadelphia: Open University Press).

Walshe K and Benson L (2005), 'GMC and the future of revalidation: time for radical reform.' *British Medical Journal* 330(7506): 1504–1506.

Walton M (1998), The Trouble with Medicine: Preserving the Trust between Patients and Doctors. (St Leonards NSW: Allen & Unwin).

Weller P (2000), 'Introduction: the institutions of governance'. In Keating P, Wanna J and Weller P. *Institutions on the Edge: Capacity for Governance*. (St Leonards, NSW: Allen & Unwin).

Wilson RM and Van Der Weyden M (2005), 'The safety of Australian healthcare: 10 years after QAHCS.' *Medical Journal of Australia* 182(6): 260–261.

World Health Organization, Media release: Global leaders join the World Health Organization to announce accelerated efforts to improve patient safety, (2 November 2004 2 November 2004) www.who.int/mediacentre/news/releases/2004/pr74/en/print.html

World Health Organization (2008), *World Health Statistics 2008*. (Geneva: World Health Organization).

World Health Organization WAfPS (2005), *Global Patient Safety Challenge 2005–2006: Clean Care is Safer Care*. (Geneva: World Health Organization).

Bit chaotic – too much

Chapter 4
Regulating the Health Professions

Rethinking Medical Governance

The health care portrayed in the TV programme 'Dr Finlay's Casebook', following a GP in rural Scotland in the late 1920s, is a world away from the high-technology urban setting of 'ER' and other contemporary TV hospital dramas. The hospital of a century ago is nearly unrecognizable from the hospital of today although the framework of the original building may remain (McKee and Healy 2002). Medical governance until recently, however, continued within its century-old traditions. This chapter discusses the changes to self-regulation by the professions, the emergence of new regulatory bodies, and the debates surrounding the licensing, developing and disciplining of health professionals.

Self-regulation by the medical profession has its origins in a state mandate to practise as the profession of medicine. This mandate is seen as a triumph by the medical profession in protecting the public from charlatans (a good guys interpretation), or alternatively as the medical profession protecting its monopoly practice (a greedy guys interpretation). Willis, for example, sees the licensing of a profession as the legal protection of monopoly: 'Licensing is a form of legal protection for the occupational territories of various health occupations from competitors' (Willis 1989: 29). Osborne, drawing upon Foucault's governmentality concept of decentralized power, argues that a state mandate was not conferred in the nineteenth century because medical interests prevailed, but rather was a characteristically liberal response by the state to seek not to govern the medical profession but rather to ensure that medicine governed itself (Osborne 1993: 348). The contemporary neo-liberal preference also is that medical governance should be undertaken by civil society. The state was, and is, a reluctant regulator of the professions. If pushed to regulate, the state does not seek to 'command and control' the professions but prefers to engage in co-regulation.

The regulation of the health workforce now is being reformed in many countries (Dubois et al. 2006; Walshe 2009). The trend internationally is to move away from the 'unfettered self-regulation of health practitioners' (Freckelton 2006b: 500). A review of medical governance around the world concluded that external regulation is overtaking self-regulation by the medical profession, the number of regulatory bodies has increased, formal rules are being applied, and greater transparency is expected (Allsop and Jones 2006). Many countries have established a common framework for registering all the health professionals, implemented schemes to assess the continuing competence of doctors to practise ('fitness to practise'), set up systems to identify and remedy poor performers, made disciplinary tribunals independent from professional councils, and have tightened medical governance legislation.

The United Kingdom is a leader in medical governance reforms. Sir Donald Irvine, a former president of the General Medical Council, argues that the public has a right to expect that the medical profession is properly governed and meets patient-centred standards. He points out that while the vast majority of doctors are competent and trustworthy, below them are a layer of doctors whose practice is substandard (and who other doctors avoid when their own families are ill), and beyond them are a small number of outlier doctors who are potentially dangerous to patients and unfit to practise. While the 'new regulatory state' has strengthened the regulation of many social institutions (Majone 1994; Jordana and Levi-Faur 2004), the medical profession had escaped external scrutiny longer than other groups. But 'leaving it to the doctors' is no longer regarded as a regulatory option. Medical reformers in Europe and the United States are urging doctors to 'rethink medical professionalism' and instead to focus on 'patient-centred professionalism' (ABIM Foundation 2006a).

Patient-Centred Professionalism

Reverberations from Bristol and Shipman and inquiries in other countries (see Chapter 2), as well as revelations that medical authorities often fail miserably to ensure safe patient care, bolstered the political resolve of governments to usher in fundamental reforms. Public inquiries transformed the regulatory debate by making the protection of patients the fundamental issue. A series of governance reviews by the UK Department of Health argued that the primary aim of regulation should be to protect patients. The concept of patient-centred professionalism also has informed medical governance reforms:

> We all want good doctors. We want our doctor to be honest, properly skilled, fully up-to-date, to inform us, to take account of our preferences and to treat us with dignity and respect. Such a doctor we can trust. Equally we want to be confident that the medical profession is making sure that these standards of good practice are observed by all doctors, everywhere. This is the heart of patient-centred professionalism. (Picker Institute Europe 2007)

Medical governance in the United Kingdom has undergone highly contested reforms as laid out in the White Paper titled 'Trust, assurance and safety: the regulation of health professionals in the twenty-first century' (Secretary of State for Health 2007). First, the General Medical Council (GMC) was made more accountable to the state and the public (and changed its website slogan to 'Regulating doctors, ensuring good medical practice'). GMC members will be appointed by government rather than elected by the medical profession, disciplinary determinations have been moved to an independent tribunal with the burden of proof lowered to the civil standard of balance of probability, GMC local affiliates will investigate complaints about medical practitioners, and medical register information on practitioners will be made freely available to the public. Recertification (or revalidation) is the second key reform whereby medical practitioners are required to demonstrate their 'fitness to practise' every five years in order to gain re-registration (Secretary of State for Health 2007).

Changing the Medical Culture

Changes to medical governance call for cultural change within the medical profession and patient safety advocates see efforts to achieve cultural change as a key regulatory strategy. Understanding resistance to cultural change requires some understanding of medical history and traditions. For example, the Hippocratic Oath has gained more contemporary relevance with revelations that medical error is not a rare occurrence. The phrase *primum non nocere*, 'First, do no harm', is said to derive from *Epidemics*, in which Hippocrates wrote, 'As to diseases, make a habit of two things – to help, or at least to do no harm' (Markel 2004: 2026). This injunction implies that it was common in ancient times for harm to result from medical interventions. While physicians traditionally practised within self-imposed codes devised by their guild, there are early examples of the state imposing legal penalties for incompetence. For example, the legal code of Hammurabi in Babylon around 2000 BC inscribed 282 laws in stone, including draconian penalties for malpractice by physicians that included the amputation of the offending surgeon's hand or financial compensation:

> 218. If a physician make a large incision with the operating knife, and kill him, or open a tumour with the operating knife, and cut out the eye, his hands shall be cut off.
>
> 219. If a physician make a large incision in the slave of a freed man, and kill him, he shall replace the slave with another slave. (Wikipedia 2006)

The high status of the medical profession is a relatively recent historical phenomenon, dating mainly from the late nineteenth century with aseptic and antiseptic techniques, effective anaesthesia, greater medical and surgical knowledge and skills, and a revolution in technology (McGrew 1985). Patients in earlier times were fortunate if surgical and medical interventions, such as amputations, blood-letting, purging and potions, resulted in no harm. Doctors often were satirized as performing procedures that harmed or killed their patients. A painting by Thomas Rowlandson, titled 'Death and the Apothecary or the Quack Doctor', demonstrates the risks of medication when doctors prescribed, mixed and dispensed their own potions. Roy Porter, the pre-eminent historian of medicine, quotes part of a mock epic by Samuel Garth, titled *The Dispensary* (1699), penned as part of the ongoing rivalry between the College of Physicians and the Society of Apothecaries:

> While others meanly ask'd whole months to slay
> I oft dispatch'd the patient in a day: …
> Some fell by laudanum, and some by steel,
> And Death in ambush lay in every pill … (Porter 2001: 137)

Evan Willis in *Medical Dominance* applies a conflict analysis in explaining the long climb by medicine to dominance in the health sector division of labour. He analyses the production of medical dominance (how it was created originally); its reproduction (how defended and extended over time); its subordination of other groups (for example, midwives); its limitation of other groups (for example, dentists); and its exclusion of other groups (for example, chiropractors) (Willis 1989: 6). The history of professions is characterized as one of competition over jurisdictions, with relationships between occupations a contest for power that involves controlling an area of work and excluding others from practising in that area except as subordinates (Abbott 1988). A networked governance approach from a power relationships perspective involves 'a strife of interests' (Sax 1984).

Medicine is the cynosure of other aspiring professional groups. When an occupation achieves professional recognition it gains a number of advantages: the protection of a title, the ability to exclude others from a defined domain, public authority, social status, access to a good income, and control over subordinated occupations. The attributes of a profession are much debated in the sociological literature (Turner 1987; Freidson 1994), with medicine regarded as the 'gold standard' against which the claims of others are judged (Greenwood 1957; Etzioni 1969). The four attributes generally viewed as essential for an occupation to claim professional status are special knowledge, social significance, social acceptance, and autonomy.

First, the claim to special knowledge is based on a body of complex and esoteric knowledge acquired during a lengthy education. Second, the significance of an occupation to society refers to the essential service that it provides – and clearly the medical profession provides a quintessential service. The Hippocratic ideal calls for health professionals to be responsible, not only for their own patients, but also for the well-being of society. This can be expressed as the ethical principle of beneficence, defined as 'active well-doing, altruism, or conduct aimed at the good and well-being of others' (Kerridge et al. 2005: 52). Medicine has expanded its domain (and hence its significance) by greatly increasing its clientele, by medicalizing health issues, and by excluding other occupations from access to patients (Turner 1987). Third, public acceptance (cultural authority or public trust) is required in order for an occupation to be granted and to retain a legal mandate from the state. Medicine maintains its authority partly through its mystique of control over life or death and its unique mandate to 'invade the body' physically by surgery and chemically by drugs (Freidson 1970: 127).

Autonomy, the fourth attribute, is a much debated concept and particularly relevant to regulatory policy. One aspect refers to self-determination in the sense of freedom to practise, that is, clinical autonomy, meaning the freedom to use one's own judgement in decisions about patient care (Turner 1987). Absolutist views on 'clinical autonomy' have become outmoded given pressures to practise evidence-based medicine, to be more accountable for performance, and to acknowledge patients as partners in clinical decisions. But some doctors still equate calls for greater accountability with a de-professionalization conspiracy. Another aspect of autonomy refers to a profession's capacity to control its conditions of work, such as control over entry to the profession and over disciplinary decisions. Freidson argues that the formalization of professional control is a driving force in professionalization (Freidson 1984). The traditional view of medical autonomy is that doctors are accountable primarily to their peers, and that the doctor-patient relationship precludes the scrutiny of any third party. Medical leaders seek to protect professional control in negotiations with the state and with employers, while in their bid for professional status, other groups, such as nurses, seek to wrest their occupation away from medical control. The regulatory debate over medical governance must weigh up the claims of the medical profession to autonomy, the claims of the public for protection, and the claims of the state for greater accountability.

Donald Irvine, in asking why a profession with a strong public service ethos acts so defensively in opposing external scrutiny, ascribes this opposition to the lingering effects of a nineteenth-century cultural mindset of unfettered professional autonomy, and to excessive adherence to professional solidarity imbued during medical training (Irvine 2007: 257). The ethos of professional solidarity and the protection of 'secret doctors' business' are recurring themes in medical governance. As well as keeping patient information confidential, the Hippocratic Oath required an apprentice to keep secret the knowledge transmitted from the teacher. The echoes of trade secrets resonate today in a medical culture of solidarity and secrecy (Millenson 1997). Such a culture alongside a professional service ethos can throw up painful contradictions for a medical practitioner, such as whether to report malpractice by a colleague.

The Health Care Workforce

Severe shortages of health professionals in many countries make it all the more important to train and retain skilled health professionals (World Health Organization 2006). As health care is highly labour-intensive, achieving quality requires a substantial investment in human resources. The health workforce is a significant part of the total labour force (around 7 per cent) in high-income countries and salaries and related charges account for over 70 per cent of health budgets (Maynard 2006). Cost containment and budget cuts thus bear heavily on the health workforce.

The health workforce is undergoing rapid change. Future workforce needs are notoriously difficult to predict, however, given rapid changes in medical knowledge and technology, fluctuations in migration, temporary exits by women from the workforce, uncertainties inherent in the time lag between entry to training and graduation, as well as uncertainties in predicting demand for health services. It is difficult to inculcate the behavioural changes required to achieve a patient safety culture, however, among over-worked and stressed professionals. Many health professionals argue that the main strategy for improving health care should be investment in more and better-trained staff.

In Australia, changing demographics and structural workforce rigidities are a matter of concern. A Productivity Commission report noted that the health workforce was highly feminized (74 per cent female in 2001), part-time employment had grown (39 per cent worked part-time), the workforce was ageing rapidly, the number of specialities had increased, and there was heavy reliance upon overseas trained doctors – around 25 per cent of medical practitioners. The report called for more training places, nationally integrated governance of the professions, and major reforms to address fragmentation, inflexibility and entrenched workplace behaviours (Productivity Commission 2005: xvi).

The composition of the health workforce varies somewhat between countries although everywhere is increasingly diverse and specialized. There is no consensus on the 'best' structural composition, however, including the number of doctors and nurses for a population. The desirable ratio of nurses to every one doctor depends upon respective training and functions. For example, nurse practitioners in some countries undertake many tasks performed in other countries by doctors. In Australia, nurses make up more than half of the health workforce, doctors account for about 12 per cent, and allied health workers for 9 per cent (Productivity Commission 2005).

The Australian Government policy in the 1990s of limiting medical student numbers was reversed when medical practitioner shortages became evident (Australian Institute of Health and Welfare 2004: 271). The constraint policy dated from advice in the mid 1990s by the Australian Medical Workforce Advisory Committee, which had called for containing medical workforce growth by limiting entry to medical schools, limiting the immigration of doctors, and restricting the number of medical practitioners eligible to bill Medicare. The Australian Medical Association at the time wanted to restrict supply since the inflation-adjusted incomes for doctors had declined (Anderson 1998). The Australian Government has since expanded medical training places in universities, raised the cap on student entry numbers, and increased tertiary medical education funds. For example, medical degrees were offered by 19 universities in 2009 compared to the previous 15 universities.

Shortages of nurses were ascribed to a drop in the number of nurse trainees, trained nurses leaving the workforce, and a shift in skill mix to more highly-trained registered nurses rather than enrolled nurses. Nurse education in Australia had completed its move in the mid 1990s from hospital-based training for registered nurses to a three-year university degree, while enrolled nurses continue to receive mainly vocational training (Productivity Commission 2005: 60). Government initiatives intended to expand the number of nurses in the health workforce include increasing training places, offering financial assistance to non-practising nurses to resume their nursing careers, and offering scholarships to help cover transport, tuition and childcare costs involved in refresher training.

Australia: Regulatory Actors in the Health Professions

Governance of the professions mostly rests with statutory regulatory boards that perform four functions (although some countries split these functions between bodies): maintain a register of members of the profession, set and assure educational standards, investigate and deal with problems, and assure continuing competence to practise (Walshe 2009). Medical governance in anglophone countries mostly derives from the English model. Medical care in earlier centuries in England was organized in a hierarchical social structure of three separate groups practising 'the profession of physic', 'the craft of surgery', and 'the apothecary's trade' (Porter 1997). In the Middle Ages, these occupations largely were organized in guilds with a mandate under royal charter to govern their members. Medical groups did not possess a claim to a title, or a monopoly on practice in a defined jurisdiction, until legislation in 1838 that defined the qualifications of medical witnesses appearing before the courts. The *1858 Medical Reform Act* unified the three groups in the United Kingdom into a single occupation under one central governing body (now the General Medical Council), and required medical practitioners to be listed on a medical register (Porter 1997).

Australia has a constellation of regulatory bodies that have the capacity to influence the behaviour of health professionals (see Figure 1.2 in Chapter 1). First, this diagram takes a broad view of regulation as efforts to influence behaviour. Second, most bodies are located in the government and profession quadrants with few in civil society or market quadrants, although the location of governance bodies in other countries may differ; for example, the United States has influential civil society and market bodies. Third, regulatory bodies are moving to more co-regulation between the government, professions, civil society and the market. These bodies are discussed in the following sections.

Registration Boards

Medical practitioners in Australia set up medical registers from the early nineteenth century onwards and obtained a legislative mandate using as their model the UK *1858 Medical Reform Act*. A register of recognized doctors was important for public trust since doctors in colonial Australia were not necessarily held in high repute. The first medical register was set up in 1837 in Tasmania followed by New South Wales in 1838. The NSW register defined as 'qualified' a person who had a university degree, or was a member of the Apothecaries Society of London, or a member of the college of physicians or surgeons in the United Kingdom or Ireland, or had served as a doctor in the sea or land service (Willis 1989: 47). In Victoria, the Port Philip Medical Board was set up in 1844 and the later *Medical*

Registration Act 1862 (Vic) required practitioners to post their qualifications on the medical register. (Britain granted self-government to Australian colonies from the 1850s onwards, and the Commonwealth of Australia was formed as a federation of states in 1901).

While national professional boards belatedly are being established (see later) professional governance historically has been state-based. State boards differed somewhat in legislative frameworks, registration requirements, structures and procedures. Some moved towards common standards and mutual recognition across boundaries in the late nineteenth century, and after legislation on mutual recognition under the *Commonwealth Mutual Recognition Act 1992* (Cth), the *Mutual Recognition Agreement 1993* (Cth), and the *Trans Tasman Mutual Recognition Act 1997* (Cth). Professional legislation was updated in most states in the 1990s, particularly in relation to definitions of medical malpractice, such as the *Medical Practice Act 1992* (NSW), followed by another round of updating a decade later, such as the *Health Professionals Act 2004* (ACT).

Some states in the early 2000s moved to rationalize professional registration within their jurisdictions. Victoria, the Northern Territory and Queensland each set up a central office as a cost-effective way to support the multiple boards, and Victoria and the Northern Territory passed multi-profession registration legislation. For example, the *Health Professions Registration Act 2005* (Vic) repealed separate legislation for 12 registered health professions and set up a single regulatory framework with a consistent powers for each of the 12 boards and an independent disciplinary process through the Victorian Civil and Administrative Tribunal (VCAT).

While regulatory debate mostly focuses on medical boards, nursing boards regulate the largest health profession. The Nurses Board of Victoria, for example, is a statutory authority incorporated under the *Nurses Act 1993* (Vic), its statutory existence dating from 1923. (Under new legislation it will become a state committee of a national nursing board). The Board approves qualifications and requirements for a licence to practise including whether the applicant was 'a fit and proper person'. The Board also accredits education providers against standards set by the Australian Nursing and Midwifery Council, and approves training places and supervisors for nurse trainees. Nurses renew their registration each year and must demonstrate current practice and continuing competency. In 2007–08, the Board dealt with 190 complaints (out of 85,500 registered nurses) and its Professional Standards Panel held 22 formal hearings. The Board maintains a nurse register and the public can check its website on whether a particular nurse is registered, the ID number, the specialty division, the expiry date of registration, and whether restrictions have been placed on practice.

National registration and accreditation

Proposals for a national medical register have been around for years in Australia. In contrast in the United States, state medical boards set up a federation of boards a century ago in order to promote a national approach (Brennan 1998: 713).

Pressures for change in Australia built up with a series of malpractice scandals, while the limitations of multiple state boards and ineffective procedures for assessing credentials became glaringly obvious, for example, in the case of Dr Raad (see Box 4.1).

Box 4.1 Dr Raad

The career of Dr Raad is one of many examples where eight Australian medical boards enabled medical practitioners found to be incompetent in one region or country to set up unhindered practice elsewhere. Dr Maurice Raad, whose registration was fast-tracked by the Tasmanian Medical Board, was recruited from South Africa in 2001 by a private company that recruits and supervises doctors for rural areas. This was despite the South African Medical and Dental Council suspending him in 1982 and again in 1984 and revoking his licence in 1990. Dr Raad also previously was registered and worked briefly for general practices and hospitals in other Australian states leaving most without notice

Source: Shakespeare 2005.

The Australian Health Ministers Advisory Council set up a working party on nationally consistent medical registration in 2004 and the Australian Health Ministers' Conference endorsed the concept in 2006 (Carlton 2006: 35). The glacial pace of reform sped up following criticisms by the Productivity Commission of the sheer inefficiency of 90 health profession boards around the country (Productivity Commission 2005: chapter 7). The Council of Australian Governments proposed one national board to cover all health professions, but retreated after protests including from the Australian Medical Association that opposed doctors being rolled into a multi-profession board (Australian Medical Association 2007). The Council of Australian Governments in March 2008 signed an intergovernmental agreement on a national scheme for registering nine types of health professionals and for accrediting training programmes (Council of Australian Governments 2008), and legislation ensued after considerable consultation: the *Health Practitioner Regulation (Administrative Arrangements) National Law Act 2008*, and the *Health Practitioner Regulation National Law 2009*. Since the states have statutory responsibility for professional regulation, each state must enact prototype legislation to implement the national scheme. It remains to be seen how well this complex arrangement will work – some critics describe it as 'federation politics gone mad'.

The landscape of professional registration began to change in 2010. The national scheme comprises an advisory council, national boards for each of ten professions (medicine, nursing and midwifery, physiotherapy, dentistry, pharmacy, optometry, chiropractic, osteopathy, podiatry and psychology), boards in each state as a committee of their national board (based on existing state boards), and an administrative oversight body, the Australian Health Practitioners Regulation Agency (established July 2010). Three additional occupations are due to be regulated from mid 2012: Aboriginal and Torres Strait Islander Health Practice, Chinese Medicine, and Medical Radiation Practice.

The criticism made worldwide of medical boards (and other professional boards) is that they protect professionals first and protect the public second. The Australian national scheme addresses this concern in several ways. First, a 'fitness to practise' reform has several aspects: clarifies the definition of professional malpractice, professionals must be recertified regularly, criminal history and identity checks will be instituted, and professionals are required to report colleagues who place the public at risk. Second, a disciplinary reform recognizes professional standards panels but requires serious matters to be referred to an independent tribunal. Third, an accountability reform addresses the 'regulatory capture' concern about boards controlled by professionals, as administrative arrangements now require members of boards to be appointed by the Australian Health Workforce Ministerial Council, with not more than two-thirds practitioners and at least two community members. The Australian Health Workforce Ministerial Council (comprising all Health Ministers) and the Australian Health Practitioner Regulation Agency have meta-regulatory powers under the legislation to ensure that lower level regulators govern satisfactorily. Fourth, a harmonization reform aims for more commonality in standards and procedures across regions and professions. Finally, a transparency reform makes professional registers more accessible to the public and establishes the office of a public interest assessor.

Medical Colleges and Councils

Medical colleges provide specialist training, ensure applicants have the appropriate qualifications for entry to their specialty, offer programmes of continuing medical education, and represent the interests of their members. Their council members are elected and most colleges have state branches. While colleges have no legislative power they control membership and hence recognition as a specialist. Specialist training can take up to ten years of education, practical work under supervision, an exam to gain membership, followed by continuing professional development. The colleges prefer a light rather than heavy-handed regulatory approach and some have taken a voluntary approach to continuing professional education – but this is about to change in Australia under the new national legislation.

Registration boards require an assessment from the relevant college before registering a doctor for practice in his/her field of specialization. Colleges regulate the quality of specialists since they decide the content of training programmes, assessment of trainees, and entry to college membership. Colleges also control the supply of specialists as they approve training places and may restrict when governments wish to increase numbers. For example, the Royal College of Surgeons argued that its members were insufficiently resourced to train more specialists, although the Australian Competition and Consumer Commission (ACCC) suspected that specialists wanted restricted supply in order to maintain high demand and hence high incomes. Australia currently has 13 colleges (see Box

4.2), about 20 medical specialities and about 70 sub-specialties some with their own faculties within the colleges.

Box 4.2 Medical speciality colleges, Australia

Royal Australasian College of Physicians (RACP), which includes the Australasian Faculty of Public Health Medicine, Australasian Faculty of Rehabilitation Medicine, Australasian Faculty of Occupational Medicine;
Royal Australasian College of Surgeons;
Australian and New Zealand College of Anaesthetists (ANZCA), which includes the Australian College of Intensive Care Medicine;
Royal Australian College of General Practitioners;
Australasian College for Emergency Medicine (ACEM);
Australasian College of Dermatologists (ACD);
Royal Australian and New Zealand College of Obstetricians and Gynaecologists, (RANZCOG);
Royal Australian and New Zealand College of Ophthalmologists (RANZCO);
Royal College of Pathologists of Australasia (RCPA);
Royal Australian and New Zealand College of Psychiatrists (RANZP);
Royal Australian and New Zealand College of Radiologists (RANZCR), including the Faculty of Radiation Oncology;
Royal Australasian College of Medical Administrators (RACMA);
Australian College for Rural and Remote Medicine (ACRRM).

The Royal Australian College of General Practitioners (RACGP), for example, the college with the largest membership, was formed in 1958. The college is organized in state faculties and in 2009 had over 19,000 members including 6,000 in its National Rural Faculty. The Australian College for Rural and Remote Medicine (ACRRM), with 2500 members was established in 1997 by rural doctors dissatisfied with their status as a minority RACGP faculty, bills itself as the world's first college for rural and remote medicine.

Divisions of General Practice

Divisions of General Practice, comprising around 100–300 general practitioners in a geographic area, offer general practitioners a network for professional support, run professional development activities, fund and administer health promotion projects, and coordinate health care arrangements. Funded from 1992 onwards by the Australian Government as part of a national strategy to improve the quality of general practice, Divisions must identify local population needs, agree on outcomes, and identify professional activities (Department of Health and Ageing 2005). The Australian Divisions of General Practice was established as the peak body in 1998 and in 2009 represented 111 Divisions covering 94 per cent of GPs and eight state-level organizations. Now called the Australian General Practice Network, this GP-run body represents and supports rather than directs groups of GPs.

Australian Medical Council

The Australian Medical Council (AMC) is an independent national standards body for medical education and training with an elected Council and representatives from each state medical board. Unlike the UK General Medical Council, the AMC does not license and discipline doctors. It has three main functions: recognition of specialties, accreditation of training, and assessment of international medical graduates. First, the AMC recommends to the Minister of Health which fields of medical practice should be recognized as specialties for the purposes of the *Health Insurance Act 1973* (Cth). The AMC pronounces on claims of medical groups to become specialties and on specialty claims to become a college – originally a royal prerogative hence the quaint terminology (at least to Australian republican ears) of royal colleges.

Second, the AMC accredits medical schools in Australia and New Zealand, the training programmes of specialist colleges, and continuing medical education/ professional development programmes. The AMC from 2002 tightened its accreditation of training programmes to require these to test a trainees' knowledge, clinical skills, attitudes and expertise. Under the *Health Practitioner Regulation National Law 2009* existing accreditation bodies, such as the AMC and the Australian Pharmacy Council, will continue to make recommendations against agreed standards to the new national boards.

Third, the AMC administers the exam that international medical graduates must pass for full registration with a medical board. The exceptions are where the AMC already recognizes the qualification and where doctors are 'fast-tracked' through state registration boards for an 'area of need' (see later).

Professional Associations and Unions

Professional associations, such as the Australian Medical Association and the Australian Nursing Federation, are influential actors in health sector policy-making, as are health sector trade unions as these have retained their members despite falling union membership elsewhere in the economy (Willis et al. 2005). Major policy changes cannot be formulated, still less implemented, without involving these interest groups. The main function of associations and unions is to look after the interests of their members, however, and not necessarily the interests of patients.

The Australian Medical Association (AMA) has around 27,000 members (nearly half of practising doctors). Governments consult it on matters that affect the medical workforce, AMA representatives sit on government committees, and the AMA puts out frequent position statements and media releases. The AMA supports fee-for-service payments, patient choice of doctor, voluntary professional development, soft re-registration criteria, and internal quality activities such as peer review. The AMA argues that well-trained and well-paid professionals, not regulatory bodies or standard-setting, are the key to improving health care

(Australian Medical Association 2006: 3). The AMA argues that any blame for patient safety problems lies with the system not with professionals:

> We need to be clear that placing blame on medical practitioners, nurses, pharmacists and others, or asking them to try harder, will not solve this critical problem. Patients are needlessly suffering and dying as a result of a faulty system that undermines and profoundly marginalises clinicians' best efforts or does not help them succeed. (Australian Medical Association 2005)

The peak body for nurses, the Australian Nursing Federation (ANF) established in 1924, offers industrial and professional leadership, has 170,000 members employed in a wide range of areas. Australian nurses threw off their Florence Nightingale image in the 1980s when they went on strike to secure a better career structure (Gardner 1989). Trade unions are influential in nursing; for example, 60–70 per cent of nurses in some large hospitals are union members (Willis et al. 2005: 26). The ANF lobbies governments and employers, puts out regular media releases and position statements, represents nurses on government committees, and offers views on governance standards and professional codes of conduct.

The Australian Healthcare and Hospitals Association represents publicly funded and not-for-profit health care organizations. It acts as a lobby group for its members, provides information resources to members, and promotes debate on health system reforms. The AHA supports a national approach and more action on patient safety and quality. The Australasian Association for Quality in Health Care offers resources and information, promotes the employment of quality managers in hospitals, provides professional credentialing for those engaged in safety and quality improvement in the health industry, and promotes debate and research through its annual conferences attended by over 600 delegates each year.

Medical Defence Organizations

Medical indemnity cover in Australia is arranged through mutual associations of doctors known as Medical Defence Organizations (MDOs). Professional registration legislation requires doctors to possess indemnity insurance. MDOs defend their members in malpractice claims, seek to limit damage to professional reputations and finances, are not keen to publicize malpractice cases, and as many claims are settled out of court this limits wider learning from patient litigation. MDOs in Australia so far have not refused to defend members who do not follow patient safety protocols, although some US insurance funds have threatened to withdraw cover in such cases, but they apply their own risk management techniques such as premium loadings for high risk practitioners, restrictions on insurable practice, and supervision and training requirements.

MDOs now are regulated under general insurance legislation after a 2002 crisis left many doctors temporarily uninsured. The United Medical Protection (UMP), the major insurer of doctors (with 60 per cent of the market at its peak), applied for provisional liquidation after its re-insurer, HIH Insurance, went into liquidation. Contributing to the UMP collapse were an increase in litigation by patients wishing to claim before tort law reforms came into effect, under-pricing of premiums, and a failure to set aside funds against the possibility of claims arising from the past. The Australian Government assumed the UMP debt and liabilities thus allowing the insurer to recover from liquidation. The Medical Indemnity Industry Association of Australia was set up in 2003 as a peak group for medical indemnity insurers and to negotiate agreed industry standards (Rogers 2005).

Regulatory Mechanisms

Professional governance bodies in many countries, including Australia, are being pushed to strengthen their regulatory mechanisms and to harmonize principles and procedures. Regulatory mechanisms that bear upon quality and safety are discussed in the following sections in relation to three functions: registering/licensing professionals, developing professionals, and disciplining professionals.

Registering Health Professionals

The legislation of registration boards usually makes it an offence for unregistered persons to use the professional title reserved for that profession, a regulatory model known as 'protection of title'; while other boards make it an offence for unregistered persons to undertake practices reserved for that profession, known as 'protection of practice' (Carlton 2006: 21). A third and less common licensing model regulates the 'scope of practice' (reservation of practice) usually in relation to the specific activities that a professional can undertake, such as prescribing or surgical intervention (Walshe and Benson 2005: 1505). A fourth model defines the set of competencies that practitioners should be able to undertake for registration, which entails assessing whether they can do so, in other words, assessing their 'fitness to practise'.

The first step in registration procedures is to set an entry qualification to the profession, usually prescribed by the professional association, the assumption being that possession of a formal qualification indicates that the practitioner has a minimum acceptable level of competence. The next step is to assess an application since registration requirements might be more restrictive than the prescribed entry qualifications, for example, current practice may be required. One of several categories of registration may be granted, including general registration, provisional registration during a period of supervised training, or registration for a specific purpose or a specific length of time. A third step is to decide on the principles and procedures for re-registering practitioners.

Re-registering health professionals

Different terms carry somewhat different implications. Re-registration refers to a requirement that a professional must reapply to a registration authority to retain registration. Relicensing is a relatively routine procedure that usually requires completing an application statement and paying an annual fee. Recertification requires a declaration by a professional (or a recognized authority) that he/she has participated in continuing professional development and so has updated knowledge and skills. Revalidation involves some demonstration of continuing competence to practise and can take two main forms: a developmental process that lends itself to self-appraisal, or an external assessment that agreed standards of competence are met (Irvine 2004; Irvine 2007).

Professional boards in the Australian states (and most medical boards) generally operated a relicensing model whereby practitioners maintained 'a licence to practise', assuming no major disciplinary issues, through payment of an annual fee. As the legislation did not require them to keep up-to-date, in effect, this meant 'a licence for life', even if their training was 30 years or more in the past. The Australian national registration scheme from mid 2010 will apply a recertification model, whereby registered health practitioners are required to demonstrate that they have participated in a continuing professional development (CPD) programme approved by their national board. Australia has not adopted a revalidation model whereby a practitioner must demonstrate continuing competence through some sort of evaluation of 'fitness to practise'.

Many countries have moved towards recertification schemes that require some type of periodic assessment in order to retain practising certificates (Allsop and Jones 2006). The literature is not always clear, however, whether this involves continuing education, self-appraisal or an external assessment of competence. Specialists in the Netherlands are recertified every five years (Chief Medical Officer 2006: chapter 6), medical practitioners in Spain every three years (Duran et al. 2006: 114), and health insurers in Germany require their contracted physicians to be recertified regularly (Shaw 2006). In New Zealand, the *Medical Practitioners Act 1995* requires the NZ Medical Council to certify that a practitioner is competent to practise in their field before issuing an annual certificate, and the Council has powers to review doctors where there is reason to question their competence, to order retraining, place conditions on practice, grant provisional registration or refuse registration.

A revalidation model is now in place in the United Kingdom after fierce debates. In order to practise, doctors must obtain a licence every five years from the General Medical Council (GMC), which involves an assessment against standards set by the GMC, an annual appraisal of workplace practice, resolution of any issues regarding conduct or practice, and specialist recertification (Secretary of State for Health 2007). An earlier GMC proposal was dropped after criticism the GMC had watered it down to soft self-appraisal rather than an external judgement of a doctor's competence (Shipman Inquiry 2004). In the United States, while a voluntary process in legislative terms, in practice many bodies require physicians to be certified (see Box 4.3).

Box 4.3 Certification of American physicians

Certification in the United States is a voluntary process but in practice is endorsed or required by many medical associations, insurers, hospitals, quality and credentialing organizations as well as the federal government, so that around 85% of US physicians are recertified regularly (Brennan, Horwitz, Duffy et al. 2004). The American Board of Medical Specialties (ABMS), a not-for-profit organization comprising 24 medical specialty Member Boards, is the pre-eminent entity overseeing the certification of physician specialists in the United States. The primary function of ABMS is to assist its Member Boards in developing and implementing educational and professional standards to evaluate and certify physician specialists. Board certification demonstrates a physician's expertise in a particular specialty and/or subspecialty of medical practice. Certification by an ABMS Member Board involves a rigorous process of testing and peer evaluation that is designed and administered by specialists in the specific area of medicine. The ABMS in 2006 replaced periodic recertification (every six to 10 years) with a continuous Maintenance of Certification (MOC) programme for all specialties that covers six areas of competence: Patient Care, Medical Knowledge, Interpersonal and Communication Skills, Professionalism, Systems-based Practice, and Practice-based Learning and Improvement. The website asserts that: 'Patients experience fewer medical errors, better communication and quality clinical outcomes when they choose a board certified physician. Medical specialists who participate in MOC use the most current evidence-based guidelines and standards in their specialty and are widely recognized as leaders in the national movement for healthcare quality'. The ABMS urges consumers to check whether their physician is certified, and to check whether their physician has been awarded a Gold Star in recognition of consistent and superior clinical outcomes (American Board of Medical Specialties 2009).

Assessing international medical graduates

The regulation of international medical graduates in Australia has been found to be seriously deficient. When the shortage of doctors became evident in the late 1990s, state governments pushed the Australian Government to issue temporary visas to allow the employment of doctors from overseas in 'areas of need', that is, mainly public hospitals and rural areas, and also pushed for a 'fast track' assessment of international qualifications. Around 2,000 medical practitioners on four-year visas were working in Australia in 2004 plus another 1,500–2,000 on two-year visas (Birrell 2004: 635). Australia depends heavily on overseas trained doctors who comprise 25 per cent of the total medical workforce with a much higher percentage in rural areas (Productivity Commission 2005: 98).

The first problem for a sustainable medical workforce is the lack of predictability in relying on doctors from overseas. A second problem is public acceptability since over half those on temporary visas come from diverse countries with consequent issues arising from differences in language and culture, in addition to lack of familiarity with Australia's medical education and health care system (Birrell 2004: 635; Harvey and Faunce 2006). The third problem was that Australia had no national standard for checking the qualifications and practice competence of international medical graduates.

The Australian Medical Council offers four assessment pathways and has recently agreed national standards with the states and has tightened procedures: more English language proficiency tests, verification of medical qualifications by an International Credentials Service, and accredited authorities to undertake workplace-based assessments of international medical graduates. First, the Standard Pathway requires doctors trained in medical schools not recognized by the AMC to sit a multiple-choice exam and undertake a half-day clinical evaluation. These are tough requirements. For example, of 884 non-specialist applicants in 2001–02, only 56 per cent passed the exam and only 52 per cent passed the clinical assessment (Australian Institute of Health and Welfare 2004: 273). Second, the Competent Authority Pathway waives the AMC exam for non-specialists whose qualifications have been approved by a recognized authority. Third, the Standard Pathway (workplace-based assessment) requires them to sit the AMC written exam and also undertake a workplace-based assessment while working under supervision.

Fourth, the Specialist Assessment Pathway, offers conditional registration for a temporary resident doctor to work in positions designated as 'areas of need' by a state health department. This was set up in 2002 in response to state governments desperate to recruit doctors for their short-staffed health services and since AMC registration set a high hurdle. This pathway involved an employer finding a candidate and stating there was no local candidate for the job; an employer applying to a state health department to have the job classified as an 'area of need'; a state medical board assessing the candidate's qualifications and his/her knowledge and professional standing against the position description; and in the case of specialists an assessment was required by the relevant college. The procedure depended on state boards not the AMC and each state medical board prescribed its own standards with little systematic evaluation of medical knowledge or clinical skills, and most did not require an English language proficiency test (Birrell 2004). For example, the Queensland Medical Board was found to be negligent in the case of Dr Jayant Patel since it failed to check his credentials or to assess his qualifications and experience to practise surgery (Davies Report 2005: 377). The Board subsequently embarked on a state-wide audit of all 1,670 overseas-trained doctors. The media maintained that the problem was not confined to Queensland, however, and that most medical boards had 'rubber-stamped' registrations for area-of-need doctors.

International medical graduates are not treated fairly in Australia when they are abandoned to sink or swim rather than provided with satisfactory induction courses and supervision (McGrath 2004), and one of the consequences of negative publicity is that some international medical graduates are greeted with suspicion (Harvey and Faunce 2006). The President of the AMA, Dr Mukesh Haikerwal, in an address to the National Press Club pointed out that: 'Because of the Patel case, doctors with funny names, accents, coloured skin and different backgrounds are getting a hard time' (Haikerwal 2005).

Complementary and alternative medicine practitioners: partially regulated practice

There is considerable debate on whether, and how, to regulate complementary and alternative medicine (CAM) practitioners (Bodeker et al. 2005). Regulatory authorities have hesitated to come to grips with this amorphous area despite increasing pressure for some form of registration (Freckelton 2006b). CAM goods and services are big business in Australia. Total expenditure was estimated at A$810 million in 2004 (MacLennan et al. 2006). Many people also consult CAM practitioners, nearly 4 per cent of the adult population, compared to 23 per cent who consulted a doctor in the two weeks prior to the 2004–05 National Health Survey (Australian Institute of Health and Welfare 2006: 394, 342). CAM goods are used increasingly, such as homeopathic, herbal and nutritional preparations. For example, 40 per cent of people with arthritis and/or osteoporosis used vitamins, minerals and/or herbal treatments according to the National Health Survey (Australian Institute of Health and Welfare 2006: 359), while a South Australian survey estimated that around half the adult population use alternative medicines (Australian Institute of Health and Welfare 2006: 359). CAM goods are better regulated than CAM practitioners since any therapeutic good in Australia must be entered on the Australian Register of Therapeutic Goods and undergo a scientific evaluation for quality, safety and efficacy (von Tigerstrom and Ellena 2006). The CAM industry received a major regulatory shock in 2003 when the Therapeutic Goods Administration suspended the licence to manufacture of Pan Pharmaceuticals, which company accounted for 40 per cent of the complementary and alternative medicine market.

The public is not well protected, given the patchy nature of CAM practitioner regulation (Weir 2006). Most CAM practitioners are unregistered with variation across the states. Chiropractors and osteopaths had state registration boards and each has a national board under the *Health Practitioner Regulation National Law 2009*. Chinese medicine practitioners are registered in Victoria and are due for national registration in 2012. Australia also has financial regulatory levers in relation to some CAM procedures, such as Medicare rebates for acupuncture performed by a medical practitioner, and private health insurance funds cover some services provided by chiropractors, osteopaths, acupuncturists and naturopaths. New Zealand has a more comprehensive regulatory model with most CAM services covered under its *Health Practitioners Competence Assurance Act 2003*: registered health practitioners who use CAM methods; registered CAM practitioners who use only registered CAM methods; and non-registered CAM providers who offer a range of CAM methods (von Tigerstrom and Ellena 2006).

Protection of the public is the main rationale for regulating practitioners and/or procedures, the argument being that some CAM activities present significant health risks. The 'reservation of practice' registration offers a possible CAM regulatory model. A particular procedure with significant risks could be defined, such as spinal manipulation, and the procedure limited to certain practitioners (Weir 2006). The second rationale, consumer protection, argues that consumers need better information to make informed choices. Opponents of registration express conflicting views. Some oppose the statutory regulation of CAM practitioners and procedures as ineffectual, while others oppose registration on the grounds this would confer recognition on dangerous practitioners and practices (Weir 2006: 177). Others see the case for CAM regulation as a trade-off between consumer safety and provider accountability, versus protection of providers from disproportionate regulation (von Tigerstrom and Ellena 2006: 202).

Cosmetic surgery: unregulated clinical practice

Cosmetic surgery lies outside the traditional boundary of medicine. It poses an ethical challenge for the medical profession in being part of the beauty industry rather than a service that meets 'medical need' (Ring 2002). A NSW Committee of Inquiry in the late 1990s, in calling for stronger regulation, defined cosmetic surgery as 'a procedure performed to reshape normal structures of the body, or to adorn the body, with the aim of improving the consumer's appearance and self-esteem' (Committee of Inquiry into Cosmetic Surgery 1999: v). In contrast, reconstructive plastic surgery is performed for narrower therapeutic reasons in order to correct variously caused abnormalities (for example, birth defects, injuries). Cosmetic surgery is becoming increasingly common. For example, 7 per cent of women aged 45–50 years in a longitudinal Australian women's health survey reported that they had undergone cosmetic surgery at some time (Hussain et al. 2002). The public is bombarded by promotional material and media stories that present cosmetic surgery as normal, safe and highly successful; one example being the 'Extreme Makeover' US TV programme. Cosmetic surgery and cosmetic procedures, however, remain mostly unregulated in Australia. In New South Wales, some practices are outlawed under the *Medical Practice Amendment (Advertising) Regulation 2008* (NSW) such as manipulated 'before and after' photographs, while the NSW Medical Board has tightened its guidelines to doctors on cosmetic surgery. Victoria has restricted the procedures that can be carried out in unregulated clinics or premises (Wilson 2006). The regulation of cosmetic surgery also has been strengthened in the United Kingdom (see Box 4.4).

Box 4.4 Cosmetic surgery regulation in the United Kingdom

In the United Kingdom, the Care Quality Commission registers and inspects all independent clinics and hospitals that provide cosmetic surgery, or treatments that use lasers and intense pulsed light. This includes the following procedures: face, neck or brow lifts; liposuction; tummy tucks and other types of body lift; nose or ear reshaping; weight loss surgery; breast surgery; any other type of cosmetic surgery involving full or local anaesthetic; treatments that use lasers, such as refractive eye surgery; treatments that use intense pulsed lights, such as cosmetic hair removal; and laser lipolysis (such as Smart Lipo) (Care Quality Commission 2009). The Commission also provides information to consumers on how to go about selecting a safe practitioner, safe premises and safe procedure. In addition, the General Medical Council requires cosmetic surgeons to apply for registration on a specialist register.

There are two main arguments against regulating cosmetic surgery and other procedures. The first is that the state should not intervene in a transaction between buyer and seller and that the onus is upon the consumer to choose carefully. The second argument is that tax-payer money is not involved since these procedures are not covered by Medicare or by private health insurance funds. Cosmetic surgery certainly can be expensive for the consumer, for example, an eyelid tuck costs A$6,000 in Sydney, according to an audience member on the SBS *Insight* programme in March 2005. The main argument for regulation is that the state has a responsibility to protect the public. Cosmetic surgery involves risks, as do non-surgical procedures but to much lesser extent; for example, a Botox injection could permanently paralyse facial muscles. But while some instances of harm are known, there are no systematic data on adverse outcomes. Four regulatory options are reviewed below: regulate practitioners, procedures, places, and publicity.

Regulate practitioners: The 1999 NSW report recommended unsuccessfully that a Cosmetic Surgery Credentialing Council be established to verify qualifications and training for all registered providers of cosmetic surgery (Committee of Inquiry into Cosmetic Surgery 1999). Such a 'protection of title' model would apply to the many types of medical and dental practitioners who perform cosmetic surgery, including plastic surgeons, cosmetic surgeons, cosmetic physicians, general practitioners, dermatologists, opthalmologists, otolarynologists and dentists. Many occupations also perform non-surgical procedures including doctors, nurses and beauty therapists. The problem is that it is difficult for the public to know who is qualified to do what. In relation to cosmetic surgery, no legislation (except in Queensland) prevents doctors (since they hold a Bachelor of Medicine and Bachelor of Surgery) from calling themselves cosmetic physicians or cosmetic surgeons. Although over a dozen specialist colleges and professional associations claim to represent doctors performing cosmetic surgery, the main turf war is between two professional groups. The gold standard for surgery is Fellowship of the Royal Australasian College of Surgeons (FRACS), which includes those who hold a plastic surgery diploma, but while other FRACS members cannot call themselves plastic surgeons they can call themselves cosmetic surgeons. The second body, the Australasian College of Cosmetic Surgery, formed in 1999 (motto 'artistry, integrity, excellence') has applied for accreditation with the Australian Medical Council.

Regulate procedures: The 'reservation of practice' regulatory model requires defining the scope of practice of the various practitioners and so would be a large undertaking. The most popular cosmetic surgical procedures are liposuction, breast surgery, rhinoplasty (nose surgery), and facelifts, while other types of surgical procedures include eyelid tucks, abdominoplasty (stomach tuck), thigh lifts, sclerotherapy to treat varicose veins, phalloplasty (penis extensions), cosmetic muscle enhancement, and hair transplants. The many cosmetic non-surgical procedures include laser resurfacing for vaporizing skin layers, and remodelling techniques that use cells (for example, injections of Botox, a protein produced by the bacterium *Clostridium botulinium)*, collagen (fat), tissue (skin fillers) or synthetic products, while the many procedures claimed to rejuvenate the face include chemical facial peels and dermabrasion.

Regulate places: The NSW 1999 Inquiry recommended that facilities performing medical procedures using local anaesthetic and sedation should be licensed (Committee of Inquiry into Cosmetic Surgery 1999). Advances in technology, sedation and anaesthesia, mean that many cosmetic surgery procedures now are done in doctors' rooms that previously were done in a licensed hospital. Many new clinics, such as skin care clinics, offer procedures, such as laser treatment and inject substances such as the proprietary drug Botox. Private hospitals and day procedures centres are required under legislation in all states to be licensed by departments of health, but licensing procedures concentrate more upon building design and qualifications of the principals to run such centres. Further, many clinics escape regulation in that they are not defined as day procedure centres. Accreditation of facilities is to be addressed in the proposed national accreditation scheme (see Chapter 7).

Regulate publicity: The NSW 1999 Inquiry recommended that regulators should enforce the law with regard to misleading claims made in cosmetic surgery promotions, that statistics be published annually on cosmetic surgery, and that information about providers and procedures should be provided to the public (Committee of Inquiry into Cosmetic Surgery 1999). The Australian Competition and Consumer Commission (ACCC) has the power to ensure that advertising and other promotional activity complies with the *Trade Practices Act 1974* (Cth), specifically section 52 that prohibits conduct by businesses that is false, misleading or deceptive, or which is likely to mislead or deceive. Promotional material, including in the Australian Cosmetic Surgery Magazine, also uses ageist and hence discriminatory language, such as 'turkey neck', 'crepey' and 'withered' (Ring 2002).

Regulating relationships with the pharmaceutical industry

The pharmaceutical industry exerts a pervasive influence over the prescribing behaviour of doctors and over medical education (Tattersall and Kerridge 2006). The industry gives away many 'freebies' to doctors, while some claim it is possible to earn all 130 RACGP professional development points by attending lavish drug company-funded events. The Australian Competition and Consumer Commission (ACCC) now requires professional activities to disclose industry support, and a Federal Court Tribunal in 2007 upheld the ACCC requirement that Medicines Australia, the peak body representing pharmaceutical companies, publish reports on its website every six months listing their sponsorship of meetings and symposia of health professionals.

Close links between the medical profession and the pharmaceutical industry do not necessarily benefit patients. The criticism is that doctors collude with drug companies by prescribing drugs for healthy people and by over-prescribing for sick people (Moynihan 1998; Moynihan and Cassels 2005). Proper relations between doctors and the pharmaceutical industry have mostly depended upon voluntary ethical behaviour by doctors. The AMA states that: 'Practising doctors should not accept, nor allow their prescribing habits to be influenced by, personal gifts from the pharmaceutical industry or similar bodies' (Australian Medical Association 2002). In the United States, however, the federal government no longer accepts the medical profession's claim to effective self-regulation of relationships with the pharmaceutical industry in light of revelations of kick-backs to doctors from drug companies (Studdert et al. 2004). The Office of the Inspector General of the US Department of Health and Human Services issued new guidelines in 2003, Medicare and Medicaid have new regulations, federal law dealing with 'fraud and abuse' are being applied to offending drug companies and physicians, and professional organizations have strengthened their guidelines regarding physicians' interactions with drug companies.

Developing Health Professionals

Ongoing professional education/development in the information age can be regarded as one of the attributes of modern professionalism. Rapid advances in knowledge, techniques and drugs mean that doctors can no longer rely upon their medical education of decades ago.

Good professionals continually learn from their own practice and from the practice of their peers. A good professional engages in critical self-reflection, during and after the performance of their work, in a way that combines knowledge with experience. For example, Donald Schon's concept of 'reflective practice' urges practitioners to 'think what they are doing while they are doing it' (Schon 1983). Also termed 'mindful practice' (Epstein 1999), this influential approach stresses experiential professional learning. Voluntary regulation, that is, encouraging an individual to do the right thing, sits at the base of the responsive regulation pyramid as the most common and desirable regulatory strategy.

Moving upwards on the regulatory pyramid from voluntarism to self-regulation by the professions, professional association promulgate codes of ethics, and while not legally enforceable, such guidelines do indicate the standard of behaviour expected of individual professionals. Medical registration boards, specialist colleges and professional associations, such as the Australian Medical Association, issue codes of ethics. A resurgence of interest over the last decade has produced a new generation of professional codes: the UK General Medical Council has published a set of standards in 'Good medical practice', the ABIM Foundation (the American Board of Internal Medicine) published a Physicians' Charter, and the British Medical Association produced an updated version of the Hippocratic Oath (Irvine 2007: 258). The Hippocratic Oath, in various versions, is particularly popular in the United States where it is much recited in medical graduation ceremonies (Markel 2004).

Continuing professional development programmes

Health professional registration in many countries increasingly requires professionals to engage in some form of professional education/development in order to maintain registration. While the medical profession holds that practitioners have a personal responsibility to update their knowledge and skills, this was not mandatory until recently under Australian practitioner legislation. In contrast, the American Board of Medical Specialties and the American Board of Internal Medicine have long required continuing professional development (ABIM Foundation 2006b). Under the *Health Practitioner Regulation National Law 2009*, the nine national boards in Australia will make re-registration dependent upon completing approved programmes. The state now has adopted 'command and control' via legislation rather than leaving continuing education to voluntary action by professionals and to self-regulation by professional boards and colleges. While many colleges had promoted continuing education, only a few had made it compulsory in order to maintain college membership, namely the Royal Australian and New Zealand College of Obstetricians and Gynaecologists, and the Royal Australian College of General Practitioners.

The history of general practice (GP) training in Australia illustrates the regulatory debates that surround basic training and continuing education/development. General practice was established as a specialty in Australia in 1989. The Australian Government in 1996 applied a powerful financial incentive by requiring doctors to complete GP specialist training before granting them a Medicare provider number. The Royal Australian College of General Practitioners (RACGP) previously had run GP training but a new organization was established in 2001 after lobbying from several groups (Dwan and Boyce 2003). Australian General Practice Training (AGPT) is an incorporated body with a board appointed by the Minister and funded by the Australian Government. AGPT purchases three-year full-time equivalent training programmes from regional providers (usually coalitions of medical schools, divisions of general practice, and hospitals) that it accredits against standards set by the RACGP and also the Australian College for Rural and Remote Medicine (ACCRM). GP training involves a complex arrangement where a college (RACGP or ACRRM) sets the curriculum and standards, AGPT approves and purchases programmes from regional providers, regional consortia deliver the training, and graduates apply for membership with respective colleges (Department of Health and Ageing 2005: 290).

Continuing professional development (CPD) is run by the Royal Australian College of General Practitioners through many accredited providers with about 24,000 GPs participating in 2009. To maintain RACGP membership, a GP must accumulate a minimum of 130 points over three years by undertaking approved activities. The programme has moved its emphasis from education to include development and GPs can choose from a range of activities, such as attending talks and conferences, peer audit, and personal learning plans. The RACGP came in for media criticism in 2005 after approving a seminar titled 'GP Wealth Creation 05' for 30 points that included sessions on investing and asset protection. A newspaper editorial protested that professional development should be about health creation not wealth creation and that GPs were doing just fine on an average income of $212,000 per year (Editorial 2005). The RACGP said the seminar was about practice management not personal finance. Letters to the paper claimed that some courses were a farce and an income earning venture for the RACGP, while others said this was an insult to GPs who did not 'rort the CPD system'. Quality of training is a long-running issue with stories of doctors signing up for conference points in a desirable tourist site and then disappearing for a day of golf, fishing or skiing. As professional development is compulsory for college membership these criticisms raise quality and integrity issues (Cresswell 2005). Accreditation of training programmes in future will involve oversight by the National Registration and Accreditation Scheme.

Peer review

Peer review is a long-established method of self-regulation within the medical profession, defined in the Medical Dictionary Online as: 'an organized procedure carried out by a select committee of professionals in evaluating the performance of other professionals in meeting the standards of their specialty'. A performance review of a health professional may be conducted for a developmental purpose (clinical peer review), or for a disciplinary purpose (disciplinary peer review). The rationale is that peers are best able to evaluate professional performance, but critics argue that peer review bodies are too tolerant of sub-optimal and unprofessional behaviour (Freckelton 2006b: 500). Clinical performance is examined against standards that may be based upon the 'best practice' consensus of peers, practice guidelines of professional groups, or evidence-based systematic reviews. The effectiveness of clinical peer review depends on the validity of the standards and the care taken in the review procedure.

Clinical peer review is primarily a developmental and quality assurance tool. 'The Clinician's Toolkit' published by the NSW health department urges clinicians to engage in peer review meetings at least four times a year and sets out principles and procedures for such meetings, including injunctions not to attach blame to staff involved in sub-optimal performance or adverse events (NSW Health 2001: 10–11). While doctors in Australian hospitals complain that their workload allows little time for reflection and that public hospitals do not properly resource peer review, it nevertheless is an important element in the medical culture. Atul Gawande praises the weekly peer review meetings in US teaching hospitals, known as the Mortality and Morbidity Conference or M&M, whose confidentiality is legally protected in most states against malpractice claims by patients (similar to 'qualified privilege' legislation in Australia):

> Surgeons, in particular, take the M&M seriously. Here they can gather behind closed doors to review the mistakes, untoward events, and deaths that occurred on their watch, determine responsibility, and figure out what to do differently next time. (Gawande 2002: 58)

A disciplinary peer review may be set up by an employer or by a professional board in response to complaints made by patients. Peer review in relation to disciplinary matters is ' … a system under which health practitioners exercise the exclusive right to examine the practice standards and general conduct of fellow practitioners and to decide, where necessary, what corrective or disciplinary measures should be applied to those who fail to meet those standards' (Thomas 2006). Peer review is criticized as an out-dated model for underpinning formal disciplinary procedures. Members of the public do not trust a system where consumer complaints about health practitioners are resolved by their peers (Freckelton 2006b: 500). The trend internationally, therefore, is to separate peer review from disciplinary determinations at least in serious cases, as is the case in the 2009 Australian legislation on professional registration.

Disciplining Health Professionals

Concern about professional reputation has moved to a focus on professional conduct and now to professional performance. Medical boards in Australia historically did not concern themselves with poor clinical performance but rather with 'infamous conduct' based on nineteenth-century British legislation:

> If any registered medical practitioners shall be convicted in England or Ireland, of any felony or misdemeanour, or in Scotland of any crime or offence, or shall after due enquiry be judged by the General Council to have been guilty of infamous conduct in any professional respect, the General Council may, if they see fit, direct the registrar to erase the name of such a medical practitioner from the Register. (*Medical Act 1858* s29)

Medical practitioner legislation in the Australian states during the 1990s belatedly broadened the concept of 'infamous conduct' beyond the implication that only appalling cases warranted disciplinary attention (Thomas 2002; Thomas 2006). For example, section 36 of the *Medical Practice Act 1992* (NSW) changed the archaic wording of 'infamous conduct' to 'unsatisfactory professional conduct'. The *Health Practitioner Regulation National Law 2009* now defines 'unsatisfactory professional performance' as one or more instances that demonstrate that 'the knowledge, skill or judgement possessed, or care exercised by, the practitioner in the practice of the health profession is significantly below the standard reasonably expected of a practitioner of an equivalent level of training or experience'.

Most disciplinary attention to date has concentrated upon unprofessional conduct rather than incompetence. Unprofessional conduct may be personal, professional or financial. Health professional boards take firm disciplinary action in cases of sexual misconduct, and doctors in particular may incur charges of sexual assault under criminal law: 'Today doctors can expect a finding of sexual misconduct will result in de-registration, marital or relationship breakdown, severe financial loss, guilt and shame' (Walton 1998: 72–3). The media give more coverage to cases of sexual misconduct by doctors than other forms of misconduct and these cases sometimes result in a criminal conviction (see Box 4.5).

Box 4.5 Adelaide doctor jailed for taking intimate photographs of female patients

Dr Gurmit Singh Dhillon, 65 years, received a two-year jail sentence in 2007 with a non-parole period of 14 months, after pleading guilty to 15 charges of indecent behaviour and a further two counts of indecent assault involving nine female patients between September 2004 and October 2005. Reprimanded by the South Australian Medical Board in September 2005, Dhillon had continued to see and assault patients until his name was removed from the register of doctors a month later. The South Australian Medical Professional Conduct Tribunal in 2008 ruled that he be banned from practice because of the humiliation and distress caused to his victims – the victims later had to identify photographs for the court case. During consultations he unnecessarily asked patients to remove their underpants and secretly took photographs with a digital camera and put these photographs onto a laptop or computer hard drive.

The Australian media have regularly run stories of 'rogue doctors' who appear to (mal)practice with impunity undeterred by the medical boards. The Melbourne county court in 2008 jailed a dermatologist, Dr Tong, for eight years on seven counts of rape and seven of indecent assault for conducting vaginal examinations of patients for conditions such as skin rashes, and noted that the Victorian Medical Board had dismissed complaints by two patients. According to the newspaper, the case 'adds to the current climate of patient distrust in the state medical boards across the country' (Brown 2008). In New South Wales in 2008, police investigated a doctor said to have botched procedures on hundreds of women and to have sexually assaulted others at several hospitals in 2002 and

2003. Despite the NSW Medical Board in 1997 ordering him to cease practising obstetrics, Dr Graeme Reeves was employed in public hospitals and not struck off the medical register until 2004 (Ramachandran 2008). A public inquiry found that the 'calculated dishonesty' of Dr Graeme Reeves allowed his appointment with NSW Southern Area Health Service, which had failed to examine his credentials or his standing with the NSW Medical Board that in 1997 had banned him from practising obstetrics (Garling Report 2009). Criminal charges were brought against Reeves by the Director of Public Prosecutions on nine counts of aggravated sexual assault, six counts of indecent assault, and a count of female genital mutilation and of maliciously inflicting grievous bodily harm.

Professional performance refers to a satisfactory level of skill, knowledge and judgement. In principle, a 'professional performance' concept allows the registration boards to investigate the capacity or competence to practise on the part of a health practitioner (Freckelton 2006a). But in the absence of re-registration procedures that require evidence of 'fitness to practise' the detection of poor performance in Australia relies mostly on complaints from the public. Different countries apply different models for detecting, and hopefully correcting, poor performance on the part of medical practitioners: complaint investigation model (Australia, New Zealand); performance assessment model (Canada, United Kingdom); and a surveillance model (United States) (Allsop and Jones 2006).

Complaint investigation model

Complaints by patients to professional boards are one way to detect professionals who perform poorly, but a very unreliable way given the low number of complaints, the varied nature of complaints, and because it is hard for patients to assess whether a practitioner is competent. Complaints to medical boards in the Australian states have increased over the past decade although the actual number of complaints lodged remains quite low. As the Victorian board pointed out, 690 complaints is not many given nearly 18,000 registered doctors and many millions of consultations (Medical Practitioners Board of Victoria 2005). This begs the question whether Australian doctors are an exemplary lot or whether patients seldom complain. Medical boards receive around 2–4 complaints per 100 registered doctors annually but it is not possible to identify trends since complaints, procedures and outcomes are categorized differently.

The pathway for a patient's complaint to a state medical board in Australia depended upon whether the complaint is serious and its nature. It may have involved no further action by a board, an assessment of the complaint, an informal or formal hearing by a professional standards panel or a health panel, an investigation of the doctor's performance or health, a decision by a board, or a referral to an independent tribunal. The *Health Practitioner Regulation National Law 2009* promises to make complaints procedures more standard, systematic and transparent. Patients have not been happy with board responses to their complaints about practitioners.

Box 4.6 Dr Stuart Mauro

The South Australian Coroner found in June 2005 that the treatment of a patient by an Adelaide doctor, Stuart Mauro, was seriously inadequate. The Coroner found no evidence that the doctor was to blame for the death of a patient discharged from hospital in July 2002 with pain killers for gastro-enteritis, who collapsed and died from a bowel obstruction 16 hours later. The doctor at the time smoked ten cones of cannabis a day and was later sacked from the hospital for stealing valium. The Medical Board of South Australia had not investigated despite a complaint about Dr Mauro in 2000 and a letter from his psychiatrist in 2002 concerned about his drug use. The Health Minister requested an urgent report from the Board. Dr Mauro was later de-registered.

For example, over half of complainants were not satisfied with the handling of complaints by five Victorian practitioner registration boards (Newby et al. 2004). The case of Dr Mauro (Box 4.6) illustrates the criticism that medical boards can be slow to act on complaints.Boards can choose among a range of disciplinary options that escalate upwards in strength: a warning, counselling, an undertaking to improve behaviour, a requirement to undertake further education, a requirement to undertake a treatment programme (for example, for alcoholism), a formal reprimand, a fine, limits placed on practice, supervision requirements, suspension for periods of time, and de-registration for periods of time or permanently. Few complaints to medical boards proceed to a formal disciplinary hearing (3.5 per cent in Victoria in 2004–05), and very few doctors are struck off the medical register. A search of medical board annual reports for 2004–05 found eight doctors were de-registered in New South Wales, two de-registered and six suspended in Victoria, three de-registered and two relinquished registration in Queensland, and one doctor de-registered in South Australia.

Separation of powers: The regulatory criticism is that professional boards, medical boards in particular, are 'soft on doctors'. The legal argument is that investigative and judicial powers should be separate (a police and courts model). Criticism by the Shipman Inquiry of a poor separation of powers within the UK General Medical Council prompted the Secretary of State to divert serious cases to an independent tribunal (Secretary of State for Health 2007). Victoria also transferred disciplinary matters in 2005 from the professional boards to the independent Victorian Civil Administration Tribunal (VCAT), which comprises a legal practitioner (chair) and two health professionals from the relevant professional board, while less serious charges are heard by a VCAT Professional Standards Panel. The *Health Practitioner Regulation National Law 2009* has adopted the separation model and also sets up an independent 'public interest assessor' based in the Australian Health Practitioner Regulation Agency (and in each state) to ensure that the public interest is upheld in disciplinary decisions. A sporting analogy makes the separation of power issue clear in the criticism made by a sports journalist of the Australian Football League panels that deal with code infractions by players:

> One problem is obvious. Both panels are manned by former players and umpires. This was to bring sense, feel and understanding to the decision-making. Instead, it has introduced locker-room law that is unacceptable to the broader community. Justice is now so gentle and without rigor that the players are enchanted by the tribunal system. (Smith 2006: 32)

Mandatory reporting by professionals: Despite exhortations in the AMA Code of Ethics and in state legislation that professionals should report concerns about unprofessional conduct by a colleague to the appropriate peer review body, public inquiries have found that few do so (Dunbar et al. 2007). New South Wales amended practitioner legislation in 2009 to include a reporting requirement, dubbed 'dob in a doctor' by the press. The *Health Practitioner Regulation National Law 2009* now imposes a legal obligation on all registered health practitioners to report to the relevant board any registered health practitioner whose impaired health (physical, mental or practising under the influence of drugs or alcohol) places the public at risk, or who is practising incompetently or unethically. Failure to report may make them liable to disciplinary action by their board. It remains to be seen whether more professionals report, especially doctors, given a culture of professional solidarity and fears of being sued for slander by an aggrieved colleague.

Performance assessment model

Systematic detection and correction of poor performance depends upon professional boards undertaking some form of competency assessment. Although this requirement is not easy, it is undertaken in several countries. In the United States, the American Board of Medical Specialties certifies whether physicians are competent to practise, and the United Kingdom has several assessment bodies. Under the *Medical (Professional Performance) Act 1995*, the General Medical Council (GMC) can undertake a performance assessment of an allegedly poorly performing medical practitioner, and require remedial training or suspend or revoke registration. The National Clinical Assessment Authority (now under the Patient Safety Agency) was set up in 2001 to detect and correct underperforming or incompetent NHS health professionals, and in the case of doctors, refer these to the General Medical Council (Dyer 2001). Substandard performance by medical practitioners will be systematically detected under the five-yearly revalidation procedure for GMC re-registration. The Council for Healthcare Regulatory Excellence established in 2003 can review individual 'fitness to practise' decisions under s115 of the *Health and Social Care Act 2008* and has referred several GMC decisions to the Appeals Court on grounds of undue leniency. Prior to the new registration procedure, the GMC conducted about 80 assessments of doctors each year triggered by any of the following concerns:

- a tendency to use inappropriate or outdated techniques;
- a basic lack of knowledge/poor judgement;
- a lack of familiarity with basic clinical/administrative procedures;

- poor record keeping or failure to keep up-to-date records;
- inadequate practice arrangements;
- concerns over referral rates;
- inadequate hygiene arrangements; and
- poor prescribing (Freckelton 2006a: 152).

In Australia, the *Health Practitioner Regulation National Law 2009* does not include a 'fitness to practise' competency assessment although applicants for re-registration are required to engage in professional development programmes. Professional boards have procedures to assess practitioner competence in response to complaints. It remains to be seen whether the Australian Health Practitioners Regulation Agency will act as a meta-regulator in monitoring competency assessment methods by the boards and whether it will push for a systematic procedure for assessing practitioner performance.

England's Chief Medical Officer concludes that unsafe performance by health professionals occurs for a variety of reasons including 'inadequate education and training, poor motivation, physical or psychiatric ill health, behavioural misconduct, an excessively stressful working environment or poor relationships within the clinical team' (Chief Medical Officer 2006: 96). It is not known what proportion of doctors perform so poorly that they pose an unacceptable risk of harm to patients – since estimates range from 0.5 per cent to 10 per cent of doctors in different countries. For example, the annual referral rate for poor performance to the UK National Clinical Assessment Service is 0.5 per cent (one in 200) of all NHS doctors (Chief Medical Officer 2006: 77–78).

Non-disciplinary pathways

Medical regulation authorities around the world are introducing non-disciplinary programmes intended to correct poor clinical performance (Schattner et al. 2004; Reid 2006a), whereby complaints can be diverted from a disciplinary pathway to a 'health pathway', in other words, a 'therapeutic jurisprudence' approach (Freckelton 2009). The medical community historically has been unwilling to face up to problems with colleagues and may be more willing to act if remediation programmes are available (Rosenthal 1995) (Lens and Van der Wal 1997). 'Impaired doctors' are those whose ability to practise medicine safely is believed to be affected by health problems, such as cognitive impairment, mental illness, or drugs or alcohol. The rationale for a health pathway is three-fold. First, the aim is to correct and rehabilitate rather than drive doctors out of the medical profession and waste a very expensive human resource. Second, poorly performing doctors may be sick or over-stressed not bad and do not deserve punishment. Third, some poorly performing doctors are suffering from health impairments that with help are remediable. The important proviso is that a non-disciplinary pathway is only appropriate if a doctor's remediation does not put his/her patients at risk.

Estimates on the proportion of health impaired doctors vary considerably. Studies in the United States suggest that 30–40 per cent of medical practitioners will have a health-related problem at some time during their career that will impair their ability to practise medicine safely, including 15 per cent with impairment due to drugs or alcohol (Leape 2006). Lower estimates are given in the United Kingdom as a British Medical Association working group estimated that nearly 7 per cent of doctors are affected by drug or alcohol dependence at some point in their career (Chief Medical Officer 2006: 95). Rates of health problems among Australian doctors are not known although small surveys and anecdotal reports indicate similar concerns.

In Australia, state medical boards, such as New South Wales and Victoria, have a health pathway outside the disciplinary framework administered by a health committee (or similar name) that undertakes an assessment where a doctor's ability to practise medicine safely is believed to be affected by health problems. According to 2004–05 annual reports, 98 doctors were enrolled in health programmes in Victoria and 131 in New South Wales.

The NSW Board may appoint peer assessors to investigate the practitioner's professional practice and write an assessment report, and if the Performance Review Panel finds that performance is unsatisfactory, they may direct that conditions be placed on the practitioner's registration, order a specified educational course, order supervision, order the practitioner to regularly report on his/her medical practice, order the practitioner to seek and take advice from specified persons, or recommend disciplinary action. About 100 performance assessments were conducted in New South Wales between 2000 and 2005. The assessors note that most doctors did not realize that their performance was substandard and displayed a profound lack of insight into their deficiencies (Reid 2006b).

Surveillance model

A surveillance model for detecting poor performance is less common. But the increasing use of clinical performance indicators means that it is becoming technically possible to monitor the performance of individual practitioners (see Chapter 8). Some countries (United States, United Kingdom) already monitor the surgical mortality outcomes of individual surgeons. The United States also has considerable surveillance capability through its Medicare and Medicaid datasets (Allsop and Jones 2006). Medicare Australia electronically monitors 'over-servicing' through its claims datasets but otherwise Australia has not applied a surveillance model to clinical performance.

Conclusion

The health professions are being pressed to strengthen their internal governance, embed patient-centred standards, and engage in partnerships with external regulators. Reliance upon self-regulation by the health professions is no longer acceptable and is giving way to co-regulation, meta-regulation to ensure that professional bodies regulate their members satisfactorily, and command and control intervention by the state in strengthening the legislation governing health professionals.

Registering Professionals

Registration aims to protect the public by ensuring that only qualified health practitioners can claim a title to practise. The example of unregulated cosmetic procedures suggests that charlatans still prey on a gullible public. In Australia, the new National Registration and Accreditation scheme seeks to make governance of the professions more effective, transparent and responsive to patients, but requires recertification upon evidence of continuing professional development, rather than revalidation of competence to practise. In contrast, re-registration in the United Kingdom and some other countries requires an assessment of 'fitness to practise'. The research challenges are to find valid and feasible methods for assessing competence, and to examine the impact of certification and revalidation in making health care better and safer for patients.

Developing Professionals

The public had assumed erroneously that medical boards and colleges require professionals to maintain their knowledge and skills. Re-registration requirements in Australia for the ten health professions from 2010, however, will require evidence of continuing professional development. Evidence is accumulating that doctors who engage in continuing professional development provide better health care to their patients. A systematic review of 62 studies, for example, reported that over half found an inverse relationship between the number of years that a doctor had been in practice and the quality of care provided (Choudhry et al. 2005). Two explanations were suggested: an ageing effect as older doctors had not sufficiently updated their knowledge; and a cohort effect as older doctors had not been trained in evidence-based medicine. While early reviews (Oxman et al. 1995; Cantillon and Jones 1999) found that educational activities, such as attending workshops, produced little improvement in clinical performance, a Cochrane review on the efficacy of educational techniques concluded that interactive workshops, as opposed to didactic lectures, produce moderately large changes in professional practice (O'Brien et al. 2003). Another systematic review concluded that continuing medical education (CME) does improve clinical performance if provided in the following ways: (a) based upon an assessment of the practitioners' learning needs; (b) encourages interactive learning and provides opportunities to practise skills; and (c) is sequenced and multifaceted: 'To achieve its greatest potential, CME must be truly continuing, not casual or sporadic or opportunistic' (Mazmanian and Davis 2002).

Disciplining Professionals

The responsive regulation argument is that regulators should first try persuasion but have available a range of supports and sanctions. The limited use of stern disciplinary sanctions by medical boards can be interpreted in three ways. First, most patients' complaints may be on minor matters that do not warrant a stern response to doctors; second, the boards apply a responsive approach that aims to remediate, rather than punish doctors; or third, the medical boards are 'soft on doctors'. The registration boards rightly aim to correct rather than cull poorly performing health professionals, have developed a hierarchy of options to respond proportionately to complaints, and can direct practitioners down a 'health pathway' as well as a 'disciplinary pathway'. While revoking the licences of doctors who engage in gross infractions clearly is necessary, some argue that there is no evidence that culling a few bad apples acts as a deterrent and so improves the general quality of medical care (Brennan 1998: 713). As medical boards have been reluctant regulators except in egregious cases, the public suspect they are more concerned to protect professionals than to protect patients. The state in many countries has strengthened legislation on professional governance to improve accountability and transparency and has separated the investigation of complaints from a disciplinary determination. This new disciplinary framework for the health professions has yet to be researched or evaluated for its impact upon the safety and quality of patient care.

References

Abbott A (1988), *The System of Professions: An Essay on the Division of Expert Labour*. (Chicago. London: University of Chicago Press).

ABIM Foundation, Medical professionalism in the new millenium: a physician charter, (10 January 2007) http://www.abimfoundation.org/professionalism/charter.shtm

Allsop J and Jones K (2006), *Quality Assurance in Medical Regulation in an International Context: Report for the Department of Health England*. (London: University of Lincoln).

American Board of Medical Specialties, About board certification (3 August 2009) http://www.abms.org/About_Board_Certification/

Anderson G (1998), *Multinational Comparisons of Health Care, Expenditures, Coverage and Outcomes*. (New York: The Commonwealth Fund).

Australian Institute of Health and Welfare (2004), *Australia's Health 2004*. (Canberra: Australian Institute of Health and Welfare).

Australian Institute of Health and Welfare (2006), *Australia's Health 2006*. (Canberra: AIHW).

Australian Medical Association, AMA Position Statement: Doctors' Relationship with the Pharmaceutical Industry, (13 March 2007 13 March 2007) http://www.ama.com.au/web.nsf/doc/WEEN-5GJ7MH

Australian Medical Association (2005), AMA submission to the review of future governance arrangements for safety and quality in health care. (Canberra: AMA).

Australian Medical Association, Position Statement: Quality and Safety in Public Hospitals, (14 December 2006) http://www.ama.com.au/web.nsf/doc/WEEN-6WE5C2

Australian Medical Association (2007), Media Release: COAG must adopt Abbott plan for national registration of health professionals. (Canberra: AMA).

Birrell RJ (2004), 'Australian policy on overseas-trained doctors.' *Medical Journal of Australia* 181(11/12): 635–639.

Bodeker G, et al. (2005), *WHO Global Atlas of Traditional, Complementary and Alternative Medicine*. (Kobe: WHO Kobe Centre).

Brennan T (1998), 'The role of regulation in quality improvement.' Milbank Quarterly 76: 709–731.

Brennan T, Horwitz R, Duffy D, et al. (2004), 'The role of physician specialty certification process in the quality movement'. *Journal of the American Medical Association* 292(4): 1038–1042.

Brown R (2008), The World Today: Medical board queried after doctor jailed over sex offences, 2 April http://www.abc.net.au/worldtoday/content/2008/s2189674.htm

Cantillon P and Jones R (1999), 'Does continuing medical education in general practice make a difference?' *British Medical Journal* 318: 1276–1279.

Care Quality Commission Cosmetic Surgery (3 August 2009) http://www.cqc.org.uk/usingcareservices/healthcare/makingdecisionsaboutindependenthealthcare/cosmeticprocedures/cosmeticsurgery.cfm

Carlton A (2006), 'National models for regulation of the health professions'. In Freckelton I. *Regulating Health Practitioners*. (Leichhardt NSW: The Federation Press).

Chief Medical Officer (2006), *Good Doctors: Safer Patients: Proposals to strengthen the system to assure and improve the performance of doctors and to protect the safety of patients*. (London: Department of Health).

Choudhry N, et al. (2005), 'Systematic review: The relationship between clinical experience and quality of health care.' *Annals of Internal Medicine* 142(4): 260–273.

Committee of Inquiry into Cosmetic Surgery (1999), *The Cosmetic Surgery Report: Report to the NSW Minister for Health*. (Sydney: Health Care Complaints Commission).

Council of Australian Governments (2008), Council of Australian Governments Meeting Communique 26 March 2008. (Adelaide: COAG).

Cresswell A (2005), Flunking the test, *The Weekend Australian*, 17–18 September.

Davies Report (2005), *Queensland Public Hospitals Commission of Inquiry Report*. (Brisbane: State of Queensland).

Department of Health and Ageing (2005), *General Practice in Australia: 2004*. (Canberra: Commonwealth of Australia).

Dubois C-A, et al. (2006), 'Reshaping the regulation of the workforce in European health care systems'. In Dubois C-A, McKee M and Nolte E. *Human Resources for Health in Europe*. (Maidenhead, Berkshire: Open University Press): 173–192.

Dunbar JA, et al. (2007), 'In the wake of hospital inquiries: impact on staff and safety.' *Medical Journal of Australia* 186(2): 80–83.

Duran A, et al. (2006), 'Spain: Health system review.' *Health Systems in Transition* 8(4): 1–208.

Dwan K and Boyce R (2003), 'Competition policy and intra-professional conflict: re-regulating general practice'. *International Journal of Public Sector Management* 16(2): 141–152.

Dyer C (2001), 'New agency set up to identify incompetent doctors.' *British Medical Journal* 322: 67.

Editorial (2005), Healthy business, *The Australian*, 13 September 2005.

Epstein R (1999), 'Mindful practice.' *Journal of the American Medical Association* 282(9): 833–839.

Etzioni A, ed. (1969), *The Semi-Professions and Their Organization: Teachers, Nurses, Social Workers*. (New York: Free Press).

Freckelton I (2006a), 'The margins of professional regulation: disjunctions, dilemmas and deterrence'. In Freckleton I. *Regulating Health Practitioners*. (Annandale, NSW: The Federation Press).

Freckelton I (2006b), 'Regulation of health practitioners'. In Freckelton I and Petersen K. *Disputes and Dilemmas in Health Law*. (Leichhardt NSW: The Federation Press).

Freckelton I (2009), 'Non-disciplinary pathways in practitioner regulation'. In Healy J and Dugdale P. *Patient Safety First: Strategies for Regulating Health Care*. (Crows Nest NSW: Allen & Unwin): 167–191.

Freidson E (1970), *Professional Dominance: The Social Structure of Medical Care*. (Chicago: Aldine).

Freidson E (1984), 'The changing nature of professional control.' *Annual Review of Sociology* 10: 1–20S.

Freidson E (1994), *Professionalism Reborn: Theory, Prophecy and Policy*. (Chicago: Polity Press).

Gardner H (1989), 'Emerging militiancy? The politicisation of Australian allied health professionals'. In Gardner H. *The Politics of Health*. (Melbourne: Churchill Livingstone).

Garling Report (2009), *Final Report of the Special Commission of Inquiry: Acute Care Services in NSW Public Hospitals*. (Sydney: State of New South Wales).

Gawande A (2002), *Complications: A Surgeon's Notes on an Imperfect Science*. (New York: Metropolitan Books, Henry Holt and Company).

Greenwood E (1957), 'Attributes of a profession.' *Social Work* 2(3): 45–55.

Haikerwal M (2005), Speech to the National Press Club, AMA President 20 July 2005 – Observations From an Overseas Trained Doctor, (11 January 2007) http://www.ama.com.au/web.nsf/doc/WEEN-6EG7CN

Harvey K and Faunce T (2006), 'A critical analysis of overseas-trained doctor (OTD) factors in the Bundaberg Base Hospital surgical inquiry'. In Freckleton I. *Regulating Health Practitioners*. (Annandale, NSW: The Federation Press).

Hussain R, et al. (2002), 'Cosmetic surgery history and health service use in midlife: Women's Health Australia.' *Medical Journal of Australia* 176: 576–579.

Irvine D (2004), 'Time for hard decisions on patient-centred professionalism.' *Medical Journal of Australia* 181(5): 271–274.

Irvine D (2007), 'Everyone is entitled to a good doctor.' *Medical Journal of Australia* 186(5): 256–261.

Jordana J and Levi-Faur D, eds. (2004), *The Politics of Regulation: Institutions and Regulatory Reforms for the Age of Governance*. (Cheltenham. Northampton: Edward Elgar).

Kerridge I, et al. (2005), *Ethics and Law for the Health Professions*. (Annandale, NSW: Federation Press).

Leape L (2006), *Problem doctors*. 4th Australasian Conference on Safety and Quality in Health Care, (Melbourne: AAQHC).

Lens P and Van der Wal G, eds. (1997), *Problem Doctors: A Conspiracy of Silence*. (Amsterdam: IOS Press).

MacLennan A, et al. (2006), 'The continuing use of complementary and alternative medicine in South Australia: costs and benefits in 2004.' *Medical Journal of Australia* 184(1): 27–31.

Majone G (1994), 'The rise of the regulatory state in Europe.' *West European Politics* 17: 77–101.

Markel H (2004), ''I swear by Apollo' – on taking the hippocratic oath.' *New England Journal of Medicine* 350(20): 2026–2029.

Maynard A (2006), 'Incentives in healthcare: the shift in emphasis from the implicit to the explicit'. In Dubois C-A, McKee M and Nolte E. *Human Resources for Health in Europe*. (Maidenhead, Berkshire: Open University Press): 140–154.

Mazmanian P and Davis D (2002), 'Continuing medical education and the physician as a learner: guide to the evidence.' *Journal of the American Medical Association* 288: 1057–1060.

McGrath BP (2004), 'Integration of overseas-trained doctors into the Australian medical workforce.' *Medical Journal of Australia* 181(11/12): 640–642.

McGrew RE (1985), *Encyclopaedia of Medical History*. (London: Macmillan).

McKee M and Healy J, eds. (2002), *Hospitals in a Changing Europe*. (Buckingham. Philadelphia: Open University Press).

Medical Practitioners Board of Victoria (2005), *Annual Report 2005*. (Melbourne: Medical Practitioners Board of Victoria).

Millenson M (1997), *Demanding Medical Excellence: Doctors and Accountability in the Information Age*. (Chicago: University of Chicago Press).

Moynihan R (1998), *Too Much Medicine*? (Sydney: ABC Books).

Moynihan R and Cassels A (2005), *Selling Sickness: How Drug Companies Are Turning Us All Into Patients*. (St Leonards NSW: Allen & Unwin).

Newby L, et al. (2004), *Bringing in the Consumer Perspective: Final Report*. (Melbourne: Health Issues Centre).

NSW Health (2001), *The Clinician's Toolkit – For Improving Patient Care*. (Sydney: NSW Department of Health).

O'Brien T, et al. (2003), 'Continuing eductaion meetings and workshops: effects on professional practice and health care outcomes'. In Review C. *The Cochrane Report Issue* 2. (Oxford: Cochrane Collaboration).

Osborne T (1993), 'On liberalism, neo-liberalism and the liberal profession of medicine.' *Economy and Society* 22(3): 345–356.

Oxman A, et al. (1995), 'No magic bullets: a systematic review of 102 trials on interventions to improve professional practice.' *Canadian Medical Association Journal* 153: 1423–1431.

Picker Institute Europe (2007), Patient Centred Professionalism, 10 January http://www.pickereurope.org/page.php?id=9

Porter R (1997), *The Greatest Benefit to Mankind: A Medical History of Humanity from Antiquity to the Present*. (London: HarperCollins).

Porter R (2001), *Bodies Politic: Disease, Death and Doctors in Britain, 1650–1900*. (London: Reaktion Books).

Productivity Commission (2005), *Australia's Health Workforce*. (Canberra: Commonwealth of Australia).

Ramachandran A (2008), Strike force probes 'mutilation' doctor, 5 March http://www.smh.com.au/articles/2008/02/27/1203788403639.html

Reid A (2006a), 'Medicare regulation through Professional Services Review – lessons learned'. In Freckleton I. *Regulating Health Practitioner*s. (Annandale, NSW: The Federation Press).

Reid A (2006b), 'To discipline or not to discipline? Managing poorly performing doctors'. In Freckleton I. *Regulating Health Practitioner*s. (Annandale, NSW: The Federation Press).

Ring A (2002), 'Using "anti-ageing" to market cosmetic suregry: just good business, or another wrinkle on the face of medical practice.' *Medical Journal of Australia* 176: 597–599.

Rogers G (2005), *Review of Competititve Neutrality in the Medical Indemnity Insurance Industry*. (Canberra: Commonwealth of Australia).

Rosenthal M (1995), *The Incompetent Doctor: Behind Closed Door*s. (Philadephia: Open University Press).

Sax S (1984), *A Strife of Interests: Politics and Policies in Australian Health Service*s. (Sydney: Allen & Unwin).

Schattner P, et al. (2004), 'Editorial: Doctors' health and wellbeing: taking up the challenge in Australia.' Medical Journal of Australia 181(7): 348–349.

Schon D (1983), *The Reflective Practitione*r. (New York: Basic Books).

Secretary of State for Health (2007), *Trust, Assurance and Safety - The Regulation of Health Professionals in the 21st Century*. (London: The Stationery Office).

Shakespeare N (2005), 'Oh my god, he's done it again'. *The Monthly Essays* (June): 31–36.

Shaw C (2006), 'Managing the performance of health professionals'. In Dubois C-A, McKee M and Nolte E. *Human Resources for Health in Europe*. (Maidenhead, Berkshire: Open University Press).

Shipman Inquiry (2004), *Fifth Report: Safeguarding Patients: Lessons from the Past – Proposals for the Future*. (London: The Stationery Office).

Smith P, Round ball excitement hides problems on oval ball home front, *The Australian*, 22 June

Studdert D, et al. (2004), 'Financial conflicts of interest in physicians' relationships with the pharmaceutical industry – self-regulation in the shadow of federal prosecution.' *New England Journal of Medicine* 351(18): 1891–1900.

Tattersall M and Kerridge I (2006), 'Editorials: Doctors behaving badly.' *Medical Journal of Australia* 185.

Thomas D (2002), 'Introductory overview'. In Thomas D. *Medicine Called to Account: Health Care Complaints Mechanisms in Australasia*. (Sydney: University of New South Wales): 1–14.

Thomas D (2006), 'Peer review as an outmoded model for health practitioner regulation'. In Freckleton I. *Regulating Health Practitioners*. (Annandale, NSW: The Federation Press).

Turner B (1987), *Medical Power and Social Knowledge*. (London: Sage Publications).

von Tigerstrom B and Ellena K (2006), 'Regulation of complementary and alternative medicine: a trans-Tasman perspective'. In Freckleton I. *Regulating Health Practitioners*. (Annandale, NSW: The Federation Press).

Walshe K (2009), 'Regulating health professionals'. In Healy J and Dugdale P. *Patient Safety First: Responsive Regulation in Health Care*. (Crows Nest NSW: Allen & Unwin): 144–166.

Walshe K and Benson L (2005), 'GMC and the future of revalidation: time for radical reform.' *British Medical Journal* 330(7506): 1504–1506.

Weir M (2006), 'Regulation of complementary and alternative medicine practitioners'. In Freckleton I. *Regulating Health Practitioners*. (Annandale, NSW: The Federation Press).

Wikipedia, Code of Hammurabi, (21 February 2006 21 February 2006) http://en.wikipedia.org/wiki/The_Code_of_Hammurabi *The_complete_set_of_known_Laws*

Willis E (1989), *Medical Dominance: The Division of Labour in Australian Health Care*. (Sydney: George Allen & Unwin).

Willis E, et al. (2005), 'Health sector and industrial reform in Australia'. In Stanton P, Willis E and Young S. *Workplace Reform in the Healthcare Industry: The Australian Experience*. (Basingstoke. New York: Palgrave Macmillan): 13–29.

Wilson B (2006), 'Health systems, quality control and corporatisation: New challenges for accountability'. In Freckelton I and Petersen K. *Disputes and Dilemmas in Health Law*. (Leichhardt NSW: The Federation Press).

World Health Organization (2006), *The World Health Report 2006: Working Together for Health*. (Geneva: WHO).

Chapter 5
Safety Cultures and Safety Systems

Designing for Fallibility

High-risk industries assume both human fallibility and system fallibility but the health sector has been reluctant until recently to acknowledge that professionals can make mistakes and that systems can fail. This is paradoxical since the health professions value learning from failures as well as successes. This chapter examines regulatory efforts to inculcate a safety culture and to design safer systems. This is a challenge since the medical profession, in particular, as shown in the previous chapter, has been reluctant to overcome its complacency, to put patients first, and to comply with interventions to improve safety and quality. Contemporary medical culture in this regard has been likened to the culture of mediaeval knights:

> Some knights feel that the trials and tests required to obtain knighthood guarantee lifelong performance, and there is uneasiness about a knight criticizing another … like the knights of Camelot, medicine has its own all-pervading culture, occupationally centred, exclusive to the initiated and tending to the traditional, which can inhibit doctors' participation in quality improvement. The medical Camelot needs to be deconstructed. (Jorm and Kam 2004: 248, 251)

A Safety Culture

The safety management literature stresses the importance of promoting cultural change throughout industries and organizations (Helmreich and Merritt 1998). The term ***safety culture*** refers to 'a constant commitment to safety as a top-level priority, which permeates the entire organization' (Pizzi et al. 2001: 452). A patient safety culture proceeds from the premise that health care involves risk, the potential for error cannot be totally eliminated since people and systems are fallible, and therefore we must learn from the 'things that go wrong' in order to prevent future incidents. But efforts to learn from error will not flourish unless there is a culture of safety where people can discuss adverse events without incurring recriminations, disciplinary proceedings and legal consequences (Wellington 2004). One of the lessons the UK Government drew from public inquiries into hospital scandals was that staff are afraid to report safety concerns in a blame culture. The National Patient Safety Agency therefore made 'building a safety culture' the first step in its seven-step guide to patient safety for NHS staff (National Patient Safety Agency 2004). A 'no blame' culture means that people are confident they will not be punished for reporting adverse events that involved them. Since public inquiries into medical scandals look to fix blame upon individuals, front line staff suspect that in an adverse event inquiry the management hierarchy will look to blame them. Clinicians themselves also are inclined attribute adverse incidents to personal failure:

> The surgeons believe that mistakes only happen to bad surgeons. But lawyers point out that the surgeons they represent usually are not bad surgeons. They are good surgeons and of high repute. The surgeon in New South Wales who removed the wrong breast was well respected. (State safety and quality coordinator)

But the public may be unhappy if no blame is attached to things that go wrong. The victims of corporate crime, for example, are not happy to learn that the institutional philosophy is that no one is to blame (Fisse and Braithwaite 1993). The NSW Minister for Health rejected the 'no blame' approach of the Health Care Complaints Commissioner in her inquiry into the Campden and Campbelltown hospitals (Thomas 2006). In dismissing the Commissioner, the Health Minister commented 'But for an investigation that took 13 months to complete, the HCCC doesn't go far enough in terms of finding anyone responsible for these failures' (Van Der Weyden 2004). A 'no blame' culture should not mean a 'no accountability' culture. Accountability by health authorities entails a commitment to investigating the systemic and human factors that contribute to adverse events, and to providing support both to staff and patients (Wellington 2004). Regulators should not immediately react by blaming and shaming, however, since this kills off a culture of active responsibility (Braithwaite 2002). Moving beyond a culture of blame means moving from passive responsibility that holds someone responsible for something that happened in the past, to active responsibility where people take responsibility for putting things right in the future.

Attributes of a patient safety culture

How does a hospital go about becoming a high-performing organization that incorporates a patient safety culture? The characteristics common to such organizations are the sort of things that create a positive working environment, in other words, a place where people like their work and feel valued, including attributes of interpersonal responsibility; person-centredness; co-workers helpful and supportive of one another; friendly, open and sensitive personal relations; creativity; achievement of goals and strong feelings of credibility; strong feelings of interpersonal trust; and resiliency (Roberts 1993). While such desirable attributes may describe an aspirational rather than actual workplace, this is the sort of place where a safety culture flourishes and where taking active responsibility is rewarded. This is important in a hospital environment where patients' lives are at stake.

A structured review of organizational attributes that promote a patient safety culture (Kirk et al. 2006) covers a range of areas (see Box 5.1). The question is whether the factors that characterize high-performing organizations with a patient safety culture can be exported to less successful organizations (National Institute of Clinical Studies 2003). While there are no clear guidelines on how managers might go about embedding such desirable attitudes and practices, especially since these are likely to require systematic and continued effort in a 'whole of organization' approach, some strategies are discussed later in this chapter in relation to patient safety.

Box 5.1 Characteristics of a positive patient safety culture

- Communication founded on mutual trust and openness
- Good information flow and processing
- Shared perceptions of the importance of safety
- Recognition of the inevitability of error
- Confidence in the efficacy of preventative (safety) measures
- Proactive identification of the latent threats to safety
- Organizational learning
- Committed leadership and executive responsibility
- A 'no blame, non-punitive' approach to incident reporting and analysis.

Source: Kirk, Marshall, Claridge et al. 2006: 174

In organizational research that focuses on nurses (since nurses are the largest occupational group in the health sector), studies of hospitals regarded as providing good nursing care have identified common enabling characteristics (McClure et al. 1983) (Hayhurst et al. 2005). These enabling characteristics are particularly evident in the case of *'magnet hospitals'*, so termed because their organizational attributes make them successful in recruiting and retaining professional (registered) nurses. Compared to other hospitals, magnet hospital offer greater nurse autonomy, more nurse control over the practice setting, and better working relationships with doctors. Notably, positive patient outcomes were associated with magnet hospitals compared to control hospitals (Aiken and Sloane 2002). In other words, happy nurses make for better patients. The American Nursing Association took up the magnet hospital concept in assessing hospitals against 14 criteria, with 'magnet' credential status awarded to about 60 hospitals each year that promote excellence in nursing. The magnet hospital concept is influential as most hospitals are looking for ways to recruit and retain trained nurses.

A converse research theme seeks to identify the characteristics displayed by 'failing' hospitals, whether financial, governance, or clinical performance failures. There are plenty of candidates to study. Such hospitals are said to display 'the vulnerable systems syndrome' that makes them more liable to adverse events: blaming front line individuals, denying the existence of systemic weaknesses, and the blinkered pursuit of production and financial targets (Reason et al. 2001). Common themes emerged in a study of major hospital failures in several countries:

problems were longstanding; problems were well-known in the organization but not handled; and the organizations lacked adequate management systems for quality review, incident reporting and performance management (Walshe and Shortell 2004). Identifying candidates for remedial intervention before poor performance sinks into outright failure is difficult, however, and health authorities typically intervene only after a crisis.

Changing organizational and professional cultures

Culture is defined as 'a complex framework of national, organizational, and professional attitudes and values within which groups and individuals function' (Helmreich and Merritt 1998). *Organizational culture* refers to the shared norms, values and beliefs of the people who work in the organization (Westrum 2004). Culture is difficult to change particularly since it is an amorphous concept and there are few guide books. Building a hospital environment with patient safety at the forefront requires wide-ranging efforts to both change systems and change behaviour. Jeffrey Braithwaite's formulation for cultural change is for clinical leaders to embed patient safety practices as 'the way we do things around here' (Braithwaite et al. 2006). This is helpful since it focuses on concrete pieces of practice and links systemic change with cultural change. Some hospital managers said that cultural change depends mostly on generational change. Junior doctors are trained in evidence-based medicine, are familiar with new technology, and are more open to quality and safety practices than senior consultants:

> Some people are more willing to embrace change than others and to reflect on their practice and the evidence for change. I think it is age related. If you engage with the younger people, they get this a lot quicker and embrace it a lot quicker. They have been trained differently (Hospital CEO).

Patient safety guidelines call for standardizing practices and this can be problematic to implement since occupational groups hold different views. For example, a study of 26 hospitals in four countries (Australia, England, Wales and New Zealand) in surveying five professional groups (nurse clinicians, nurse managers, lay managers, medical managers, and medical clinicians) found that doctors took a more individualistic view than nurses, held more negative views about systematization, and generally rejected many aspects of hospital reform (Degeling et al. 2003; Degeling and Carr 2004). Entrenched differences between professional groups are well known and medicine itself is said to be organized around tribal groups with the biggest division between surgeons and physicians (Finn and Waring 2006). Hospital leaders therefore must take account of different views to get across a safety message:

> You have to talk the right talk to your audience. If you are talking to doctors and surgeons you need to give them statistics to support your argument. If you are talking to an administrator you have to get across a financial message.

> Another way is to talk about the adverse events that have happened in your own organisation. That brings the message home. (Hospital safety and quality coordinator)

In inculcating a 'patient safety culture', the medical culture is regarded as the most challenging to change. A 'culture of silence' within the medical profession impedes reporting and learning from adverse events: a silence of word in failing to report and to discuss medical errors, and a silence of deed in that medical leaders fail to respond with corrective action (Millenson 1997). A culture of silence undermines the public interest ethic when professional interests are placed before patient interests (Bolsin et al. 2005b). For example, although 40 per cent of medical students were able to identify (in a questionnaire and focus group discussion) ethically correct behaviour, only 13 per cent would 'blow the whistle' on a serious medical error involving their peers and this proportion declined during training (Rennie and Crosby 2002). While medical students aspire to the impossible goal of error-free practice since teachers present themselves as role models who never make mistakes, even experienced doctors perpetuate a medical culture of infallibility in preferring not to discuss their mistakes when participating in training programmes (Wilf-Miron et al. 2003: 36). When error is regarded as personal failure and so better not admitted this impedes learning from mistakes:

> One result is that physicians, not unlike test pilots, come to view an error as a failure of character – you weren't careful enough, you didn't try hard enough. This kind of thinking lies behind a common reaction by physicians: 'How can there be an error without negligence?'(Runciman and Moller 2001: 71).

Such values help explain under-reporting by doctors to adverse event reporting systems, and why investigations find that although doctors had been aware of the problem for years they had not reported their concerns about a colleague. Changing a culture of silence to a patient safety culture, therefore, calls for introducing patient safety training into the medical curriculum and into professional development programmes (Walton and Elliott 2006). Since waiting for cultural and generational change can take years, regulators must change the system to force behavioural change and embed new ways of working as 'the way we do things around here'.

Safety Systems

The term high reliability organization was coined to describe organizations where, since the risk of error involves dire consequences, considerable effort goes into developing safety systems that produce exemplary safety track records (Pizzi et al. 2001: 451). A *high-reliability organization* is defined as an organization that succeeds in avoiding catastrophes in an environment where accidents can be expected due to risk factors and complexity (Weick and Sutcliffe 2001). High-reliability organizations can be located in industries, such as aviation, air traffic control, shipping, mining, nuclear power production, and chemical manufacturing. The following five cultural characteristics underlie the 'mindfulness' that keeps them working well when facing unexpected situations: preoccupation with failure; reluctance to simplify interpretations, sensitivity to operations; commitment to resilience; and deference to expertise (Weick and Sutcliffe 2001: 10–17).

There are two schools of thought as to the better strategy to prevent accidents: high-reliability theory or normal accident theory (Pizzi et al. 2001). *High-reliability theory* holds that accidents can be prevented through better organizational design and management, such as detailed specification of work practices. *Normal accident theory*, on the other hand, holds that since near misses and accidents are to be expected, staff must have the ability and flexibility to respond quickly in a crisis. Staff cannot respond rapidly enough to the threat of an accident if they rely too heavily upon the 'tight coupling' of work processes (Perrow 1999). For example, in an analysis of the near melt-down in 1979 at the Three Mile Island nuclear reactor, Joseph Rees argued that nuclear plant operators had become rule-following automatons rather than strategic thinkers, and when something went wrong that was not covered by a rule, they lacked the risk analysis intelligence to think about what needed to be done (Rees 1994). In response to this near disaster, the US nuclear regulation industry changed to being less about government inspectors checking compliance with rules, and more about the regulatory scrutiny of risk management systems, so that the safety record as measured by the safety-related automatic shut-downs of nuclear plants thereafter fell dramatically (Braithwaite and Drahos 2000: 302). The two perspectives of normal accident theory and high reliability theory can complement rather than contradict each other, however, as argued in an analysis of the Challenger spacecraft launch decision (Vaughan 1997; Weick 1997).

A hospital can be regarded as a form of high reliability organization: health care is complex, the risk of adverse events is high and outcomes can be catastrophic for patients, and the organization must have the capacity to meet periods of high demand. Staff must function at a high level of alertness and mostly do succeed in managing emergencies. Hospitals should apply perspectives from both high reliability theory and normal accident theory. They need professionals with the experience and autonomy to respond rapidly to patients in a great variety of life-threatening situations as surgeons and emergency room physicians do on a daily basis. They also need better design and procedures to prevent accidents in areas of known and recurring risk. A hospital should combine safety mechanisms from normal accident theory (for example, discretionary decisions by highly trained professionals) and from high reliability theory (for example, clinical protocols).

A systems perspective also highlights the many factors within a hospital environment that influence clinical practice: organizational and management factors, work environment, team factors, task factors and patient characteristics (Vincent et al. 1998). Donabedian's classic SPO model (structure, process and outcome) applied systems design thinking to how outcomes for patients are shaped by an organization and its patient management processes (Donabedian

1966). Systems thinking draws on many perspectives: for example, studying patient management within a hospital from a systems engineering perspective can identify factors involved in improving safety mechanisms (Carayon et al. 2006). Research on failures in high-reliability organizations reveals organizational and technical failures related to system performance as well as failures related to human behaviour (Van Vuuren 1999). Attributing adverse events to systems (organizational and technical failures), not just to people, makes safety initiatives more acceptable to the health professions. The US Institute of Medicine adopted a systems perspective in arguing that a blame culture is counter-productive:

> The common initial reaction when an error occurs is to find and blame someone. However, even apparently single events or errors are due most often to the convergence of multiple contributing factors. Blaming an individual does not change these factors and the same error is likely to recur. Preventing errors and improving safety for patients requires a systems approach in order to modify the conditions that contribute to errors. People working in health care are among the most educated and dedicated workforce in any industry. The problem is not bad people; the problem is that the system needs to be made safer. (Institute of Medicine 2000: 49)

Patient safety thinking has been greatly influenced by the work of James Reason who holds that human error usually involves system failure rather than being solely the failure of an individual (Reason 1990; Reason 2000). A high-reliability organization, such as a hospital, should engineer a series of barriers and safeguards to guard against a confluence of factors that allows an error to occur (Reason 1997). This is because accidents typically have multiple, not single, causes. For example, a medication error may occur because the prescribing doctor writes an illegible prescription, the pharmacist is busy and does not check the pharmacopeia, and the junior nurse is too in awe of the consultant to query the dosage before administering the drug to the patient. The 'Swiss cheese' model of how accidents can occur (Reason 2000) shows that an adverse incident can result from a confluence of mistakes that singly might not matter but together can be fatal (see Figure 5.1). A high-reliability organization has several defensive layers that in an ideal world are intact, but in reality are more like slices of Swiss cheese with many holes, and these holes can momentarily line up to permit a trajectory of accident opportunity that results in harm to a patient. Holes in the defences may arise from the proximal human propensity for active failures and/or in more distal factors or in latent conditions that hitherto had lain dormant within a system. Mistakes can occur despite apparent fail-safe procedures.

> We had one actual event that shook people up. It got through all the safety layers. There was potentially a whole heap of stop signs that could have alerted people, but didn't, which is why that lesson was quite instructive. It showed that even with all those potential fail-safes, mistakes can happen. (Hospital CEO)

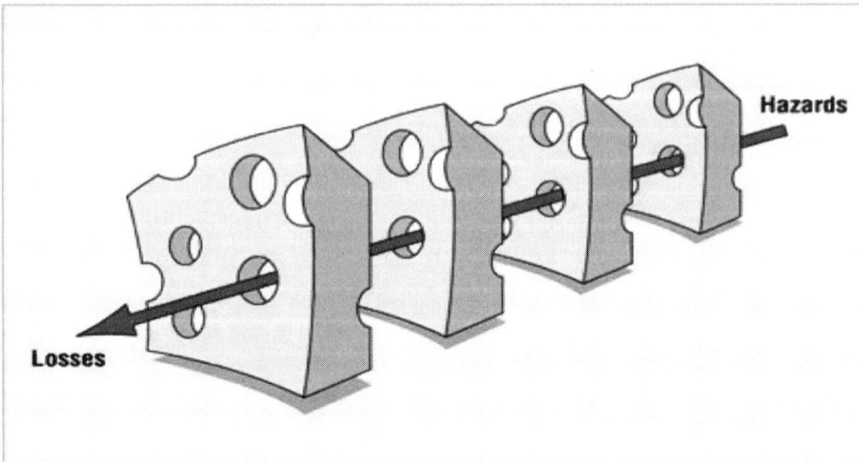

Figure 5.1 The Swiss cheese model of an accident trajectory. Source: Reason 2000

Regulatory Mechanisms

Adopt a Learning Model Strategy

Since a near miss or adverse event typically has multiple causes that are sometimes hard to unravel, it makes sense to enlist those involved in the incident in identifying the causes and proposing a solution. An adverse event presents a learning opportunity. A regulatory framework must support the creativity of professionals in solving their own safety and quality problems in their own organizations and encourage solutions that arise from 'bottom-up' practice rather than always imposing 'top-down' solutions. This is a crucial regulatory approach in the health care sector. A learning model approach is a regulatory strategy that aligns well with the health professions' bases in a body of knowledge, with a commitment to continuing professional development, and with the voluntarist preference of individual professionals. Runciman and colleagues draw upon a learning model approach and concepts of reflective practice in offering 10 tips for clinicians to help them provide high quality and safe care for their patients (see Box 5.2).

The concept of *triple-loop learning* suggests ways to spread learning beyond the voluntary take up of information by individuals (Parker 2002). The goal is to disseminate a successful innovation throughout a health sector. Triple-loop learning is based on the premise that good practice often arises from high-performing front-line professionals who are reflective and innovative in their practice. The first loop occurs when a good self-regulatory innovator monitors his/her effectiveness at improving an outcome. This is the essence of reflective practice. One example is

Box 5.2 Ten tips for clinicians in delivering safer patient care

1. Know your patients, listen, assess and reassess. Appoint a case manager
2. Know your limits, do not overstretch
3. Simplify and standardize
4. Teach, train, learn and get involved
5. Communicate and document
6. Be a champion for safety, high quality care and ethical behaviour
7. Practise graded assertiveness
8. Find and use the fixers
9. Learn from your mistakes and system failures
10. Follow through

Source: Runciman, Merry and Walton 2007: 231

the use of programmed handheld computing devices, personal digital assistants (PDAs), which accustoms practitioners to recording their own adverse events and near misses and so enables a culture of self audit or reflective practice (Bolsin 2003). The crucial contribution of PDAs to cultural change is that trainees (in this case anaesthesia registrars) become used to examining and discussing their own performance (Bolsin 2003; Bolsin et al. 2005a; Bolsin et al. 2005b). Another example is the simulation training programmes run by teaching hospitals that encourage reflective practice:

> We are working on simulation exercises that will allow us to look at procedures. It's about worst-case scenario planning and how you deal with those kinds of situations. We have a simulation set up here in the hospital and the anaesthetists use it a lot. You do a scenario and simulate an emergency situation where people are anxious and rushing from one patient to another. You play out a script so that, for example, 'time out' in the operating theatre gets missed and something bad happens. You use that as an opportunity to debrief and then re-run the script and say how could we do that better? (Hospital risk manager)

A second learning loop occurs when managers take a successful innovation from one unit within a hospital and apply it throughout the organization. For example, hospital managers might require staff on each ward to identify and discuss their biggest safety problem and then to design one improvement project and measure its outcomes. If one ward devises a simple way of improving infection control, or reducing medication error, managers can spread the success story to all wards of the hospital. A third learning loop occurs when a regulator spreads the news of a successful innovation in one hospital throughout the hospital sector. For example, the 2009 Victorian Public Healthcare Awards selected 52 finalists and announced category winners in a public ceremony. The regulatory argument is that leaders lift the laggards and so raise standards in the whole industry – the economic aphorism being 'a rising tide lifts all boats'. A fourth loop of learning might be conceived as an international organization publicizes the conclusions from a published study of a patient safety innovation. For example, the WHO World Alliance for Patient Safety Alliance is promoting the safe surgery protocol that was trialled in a large demonstration project in several countries (Haynes et al. 2009).

The following sections discuss five widely used learning model mechanisms for improving the take-up by health professionals of patient safety practices: knowledge networks, clinical practice guidelines, health alerts, action-research collaboratives, and patient safety campaigns.

Develop knowledge networks

Regulators have a responsibility to manage and disseminate knowledge in a way that is readily accessible to practitioners, rather than just berate busy practitioners for slow take-up of knowledge into practice. Health professionals need help to become reflective practitioners able to translate experience and evidence into practice. They are expected to consult electronic databases on evidence-based health care and make informed decisions, and need to stay well-informed since their patients can and do trawl the Internet for information (and misinformation) that they expect to discuss with their doctor. The evidence-practice gap in the low and slow take-up of clinical practice guidelines by medical practitioners has long been remarked, such as the time-lag of several years in prescribing anti-thrombolytic drugs in the treatment of post-heart attack patients (Freemantle 2002), while only around half of patients receive the care recommended in evidence-based clinical guidelines (McGlynn et al. 2003).

Knowledge networks have emerged in the information age, therefore, composed of groups of experts who assemble knowledge in specialized fields and present this in accessible forms to practitioners and policy makers (World Health Organization 2004: 140). State-of-the-art reviews on particular conditions are published by professional journals, such as on-line Clinical Evidence by the *British Medical Journal*, and Cochrane Collaboration groups undertake systematic reviews on precisely defined research questions.

Knowledge portals are internet sites that offer synthesized information in user-friendly forms and an increasing number address patient safety issues. The United States, for example, places a high priority on information as a regulatory strategy. The Agency for Healthcare Research and Quality (AHRQ) commissions reviews of the scientific literature and produces evidence reports and technology assessments including an influential analysis of patient safety practices (Shojania et al. 2001), and the Joint Commission website offers an online resource on quality and safety practices. The Institute of Health Improvement has developed an extremely useful 'improvement map' for managers and practitioners to consult that addresses 'whether to' and 'how to' questions by rating interventions on four attributes: cost to implement, time to implement, level of evidence, and difficulty to implement (Institute for Health Improvement 2009).

Issue clinical practice guidelines or directives

Guidelines are a well-established mechanism for informing clinical decision-making and their number has expanded exponentially since the first guidelines in the 1930s issued by the American College of Surgeons (Weisz et al. 2007). *Clinical practice guidelines* are defined as 'systematically developed statements to assist practitioner and patient decisions about appropriate health care for specific clinical conditions' (Field and Lohr 1990). A guideline is a compilation of evidence on the overall management of a particular condition, such as asthma, and may cover prevention, treatment and rehabilitation, while others set out steps in a particular procedure, such as patient handover. Clinical protocols and care pathways are more prescriptive in setting out recommended steps in the management of a patient's condition. Some experts argue that clinical guidelines generated by groups of expert clinicians on priority conditions should be made standards, and that these standards should be enforced unless there is a good reason why treatment should diverge from the standard in some cases (Runciman and Lumby 2009). Moving from guidelines to directives, however, usually provokes a battle within the medical profession. For example, the clinical protocols issued by the UK Department of Health were resented by many clinicians as reducing their professional autonomy (Claridge et al. 2006), while some clinicians persist in rejecting 'cookbook medicine'. One medical leader commented he had given up on 'the medical dinosaurs' but that younger doctors readily consulted guidelines. Clinical guidelines, however, are not intended to be applied inflexibly and to improve acceptability their voluntary nature often is emphasized:

> Clinical practice guidelines are not intended to replace clinical judgement, nor can they. They are not prescriptive, but serve to guide practitioners in making relevant clinical interventions. Used correctly, they can assist more informed and meaningful patient participation in treatment decisions. They can enhance and maintain professional standards and quality assurance programmes. By reducing unnecessary variations in practice they may encourage cost-effective healthcare. (Dwyer 1998: 292)

But do clinical guidelines have legal implications? A practice guideline sets a standard against which clinical performance can be assessed. If a doctor does not follow a clinical guideline and an adverse event occurs followed by litigation, would a court find him/her negligent? Under the application in tort law of the 'Bolam judgement', it is up to the court to determine the standard demanded by the law in the practice of medicine. The duty of care exercised by a practitioner may be regarded as less than reasonable should clinical practice guidelines not be followed, unless a departure can be justified on clinical grounds (Dwyer 1998). For example, while judges in the Netherlands refer to clinical guidelines in judicial decision-making, they are not regarded as legal rules that necessarily constrain clinical autonomy, although if a patient sues for malpractice a clinician may need to defend any deviation from the guideline (Buijsen 2000).

As clinical guidelines and alerts are produced by a bewildering range of agencies efforts are underway to coordinate these missives. In the United Kingdom, the National Institute for Clinical Excellence (NICE) produces clinical guidelines, and the National Patient Safety Agency has set up a national portal for issuing medical alerts. The Darzi Report recommended that one NHS web-based portal be set up to offer authoritative information on clinical and non-clinical evidence and best practice (Darzi 2009). In the United States, the Agency for Healthcare Research and Quality issues 'evidence reviews' rather than 'guidelines', since Congress in the mid 1990s debated cutting AHRQ funds after it issued guidelines on the treatment of back pain that infuriated spine surgeons (The Commonwealth Fund 27 June 2005). In Australia, the National Institute for Clinical Studies (NICS) has set up a 'one-stop shop' portal for clinical practice guidelines, undertakes campaigns to persuade clinicians to follow guidelines, and monitors their take up (National Institute of Clinical Studies 2005). Persuading clinicians to follow patient safety guidelines can take multiple and ongoing efforts:

> It is really important to have strong clinical leadership, because if clinicians don't buy a protocol they're not going to do it. Endorsement from a professional body also is important, but it has to be the right professional body. But in the end there is nothing like a big fright. (Hospital medical director)

Issue medical alerts

Medical alerts are produced by professional associations, industry groups, employer organizations, health departments and research centres. Well-publicized medical alerts have been issued, for example, on concentrated potassium chloride and on vincristine. Many countries took up the World Health Organization issue of Alert No. 115 on the use of vincristine, a widely used chemotherapeutic agent, warning of over 50 known deaths around the world from administering vincristine via a spinal route rather than intravenously (see Box 5.3). Specialty areas also issue alerts. For example, in Australia, the Adverse Drugs Reaction Advisory Committee to the Therapeutic Drug Administration (TGA) puts out regular bulletins on adverse drug reactions and the TGA has the capacity to order drug recalls.

Conduct clinical research collaboratives

Clinicians enrol in trialling ways to improve their own practice through *clinical research collaboratives*, a method that draws upon the principles of action research. The idea of such collaboratives is to involve a number of participants both in testing new ideas and in implementing action for change (Reason and Bradbury 2001). Multiple sites usually are sought so that a significant improvement across many sites indicates a robust intervention. Participants engage in a research process over a cycle of change that involves monitoring and evaluating the effects of their own actions. The process is similar to the Plan-Do-Study-Act (PDSA) cycle introduced in the industry sector by WE Deming and now widely applied in the health sector. The main principles are, first, the participating groups are involved in deciding

Box 5.3 Medication alert: Vincristine can be fatal if administered by the intrathecal route

Vincristine, a medicine commonly used in the treatment of leukaemias and lymphomas, is neurotoxic and must only be administered intravenously. Sentinel events associated with the inadvertent intrathecal administration of vincristine have been reported repeatedly. This error results in a fatal outcome in 85% of cases with devastating neurological effects in the few survivors. At least 55 cases of inadvertent intrathecal injection have been reported internationally since 1968. For example, in 2003 a 28-year-old Australian man was slowly paralyzed, and died, as a result of intrathecal administration of vincristine.

One common error: Vincristine, prepared in a syringe for intravenous administration, is mistaken as an injection to be given intrathecally. As a result, it is administered into the cerebrospinal fluid instead of, or in addition to, other medicines.

Incidents have a number of common contributing factors:

- Same time – prescription of intravenous vincristine in treatment protocols that require other medicines to be administered intrathecally on the same day or at the same time.
- Same place – transport, storage and administration of intravenous vincristine in the same location as medicines required to be administered intrathecally.
- Inadequate checking of medicine labels against treatment orders when selecting medicines from storage and immediately prior to administration.
- Staff with insufficient knowledge or experience delegated to manage chemotherapy.

Recommendations to reduce the risk of error with vincristine:

1. Vincristine should be administered in a minibag, not a syringe to 'design out the error' by preventing connection to a spinal needle.
2. All vincristine products, including outer wraps, should be labelled with a prominent warning label stating: 'FOR INTRAVENOUS USE ONLY – Fatal if given by other routes'.
3. The timing and location of vincristine preparation, delivery and administration should be separate from all medicines intended for intrathecal administration.
4. Vincristine, and other intravenous medicines, must be packaged, transported and stored in specifically designated containers. Separate packaging and different containers must be used for medicines to be administered intrathecally.
5. All medicines for intrathecal administration should be labelled with a prominent warning label, on the syringe and the outer wrap, stating 'For intrathecal use'.
6. Only staff specifically trained and experienced in cancer treatments should be designated to prescribe, prepare, dispense, deliver, receive or administer injectable chemotherapy. This includes registrars, consultants, pharmacists and nurses.
7. Staff administering intrathecal medicines must use formal checking procedures. This should include a 'time out' involving at least two health professionals. The patient identifiers, drug, dose, volume, route and rate should be verified against the medication order immediately prior to administration. Both health professionals should then sign the order.

Source: Australian Council for Safety and Quality in Health Care 2005

upon the intervention, and second, measurable outcomes are sought against a predetermined target. For example, a project on achieving better cardiac care may enrol multiple hospitals in managing patients who present with chest pain and measure improvements in service delivery outcomes, such as greater use of aspirin and beta blockers upon discharge from hospital. Action-research collaboratives are particularly popular in the health sector when project money is on offer. In Australia, research collaboratives have been trialled in several areas of patient safety concern, including medication, blood safety, pressure ulcers, hospital-acquired infections, and falls.

Medication is an area where adverse events are common and preventable with many points in the medication cycle where improvements can be made, including eliminating look-alike, sound-alike medication names, and assuring medication accuracy at transitions in care (World Health Organization 2007). The huge variety of drugs increase the risk of prescribing errors by doctors, dispensing errors by pharmacists, and administration errors by nurses. The Medication Safety Breakthrough Collaborative engaged nearly 100 teams around Australia with each team given A$15,000 to run their projects, ran workshops and sequential learning sessions (on how to research the issues and run and evaluate small intervention programmes), and organized a final presentation of team results (Australian Council for Safety and Quality in Health Care 2005a).

Blood safety is another risk area for patients and state health departments have run several research collaboratives. For example, nurse consultants in South Australia assisted participating hospitals with three risky focal points for patients: patient sample collection (miscollecting and labelling errors), the decision to transfuse (whether appropriate), and administration of blood (wrong blood type or wrong patient) (Australian Council for Safety and Quality in Health Care 2004).

Pressure ulcers are a large and preventable category of adverse events and several action research projects have been run. The Pressure Ulcer Point Prevalence Survey (PUPPS), which trained clinical staff in Victorian hospitals and nursing homes to survey and prevent ulcers, achieved an over 20 per cent reduction in ulcers prevalence over one year (Australian Council for Safety and Quality in Health Care 2005b). The Victorian health department has since bought static pressure reduction foam mattresses to reduce the high prevalence of ulcers, thereby opting for system redesign, rather than relying solely on changing staff behaviour.

Healthcare-associated infections are largely preventable through appropriate infection control practices (Australian Infection Control Association Expert Working Group 2001). Hospital infection control teams include staff with special expertise: microbiologist, infectious disease physicians, and infection control practitioners. In Australia, a national approach is urged using a National Infection Control Guideline, a National Surveillance System, and by funding infection control campaigns and interventions. Poor hand hygiene by staff is a prime cause of infections in hospitals (see later).

Patient falls are much studied and systematic reviews have found their reduction requires multi-faceted interventions. The National Patient Safety Agency in England has made patient falls a priority area and recommendations for improvement include risk assessment, safer environments and safer technology (National Patient Safety Agency 2007).

Mount patient safety campaigns

Saving lives rivets the attention more than reducing adverse incidents. The '100,000 Lives Campaign' launched by the US Institute for Healthcare Improvement in 2004 captured attention, rapidly enlisted over 2000 hospitals, and met its target of preventing unnecessary deaths from adverse events (Institute for Healthcare Improvement 2005). Although the impact of the campaign was hard to separate from parallel patient safety interventions in participating hospitals (Poteliakhoff 2006), campaigns are not designed as rigorous research interventions but rather indicate possibilities for effective interventions. It demonstrated the power of a campaign with a catchy title and a clear goal. This was followed by the 'Protecting Five Million Lives From Harm' campaign, that is, preventing adverse events rather than necessarily saving lives. Donald Berwick estimated that 230 lives per year could be saved in a 500-bed hospital by making six types of improvements shown by research to be feasible and effective (The Commonwealth Fund 2 May 2005). The six interventions are as follows:

- create rapid response teams that quickly mobilize to provide care when a patient's condition unexpectedly deteriorates;
- follow proven procedures for treating heart attack patients;
- use validated processes to prevent ventilator-acquired pneumonia;
- prevent blood-stream infections through the proper use of central venous catheters;
- prevent infections in surgery patients through the use of antibiotics;
- prevent dangerous drug interactions.

As its first global patient safety campaign, the WHO embarked on 'clean care is safer care' in promoting hand hygiene in health care facilities (World Health Organization 2005). Poor hand hygiene among healthcare workers (not washing hands or using disinfectants before touching patients) is known to be a major factor in healthcare associated infections (Doebbeling et al. 1992). Interventions to increase hand hygiene achieve some success and usually then falter despite numerous studies showing the benefits. Australia promoted the WHO campaign and audited the results across 182 public and private hospitals, finding hand hygiene compliance rates of nearly 64 per cent on average, the goal being to achieve and maintain rates above 70 per cent (Australian Commission on Safety and Quality in Health Care 2009b: 12). Some health departments, notably, New South Wales, now propose to make hand hygiene a mandatory directive and impose sanctions for non-compliance.

Design Safer Systems

Industries, such as mining, aviation and transport, pay great attention to designing safe physical environments and equipment and installing fail-safe procedures. But patient safety as the key principle of hospital design has been neglected although 'if we truly want safer care we will have to design safer care systems' (Berwick and Leape 1999). The Institute of Medicine argues that safer health care will not come from exhorting health professionals to try harder but rather from changing systems of care:

> Health care has safety and quality problems because it relies on outmoded systems of work. Poor design set the workforce up to fail, regardless of how hard they try. If we want safer, higher-quality care, we will need to have redesigned systems of care, including the use of information technology to support clinical and administrative processes. (Institute of Medicine 2001: 4)

Health policy makers are slow to embark upon a patient safety design overhaul for three reasons. First, the view is that health professionals are trained not to make mistakes. Cost is the second reason. Even though a cost-benefit analysis may indicate that the benefits of better design outweigh the costs, it is difficult to prise capital funds for physical redesign from government budgets, and a systems redesign of patient management involves time-consuming negotiations with health professionals. Politics is the third reason since politicians and the public have been more intent upon fixing blame than fixing hospitals:

> Perhaps inevitably, critics have pushed back against viewing safety as a problem of science – of system design. Public support for improving patient safety often turns instead on fixing blame. Despite the widely disseminated message from the IOM [Institute of Medicine] that systems failures cause most injuries, most individuals still believe that the major cause of bad care is bad physicians, and that if miscreant clinicians were removed everything would be all right. (Leape and Berwick 2005: 2384)

Redesign environments and equipment

Hospital design changes with changing ideas on what type of architecture is acceptable to society, responsive to new technology, functional for staff, and therapeutic for patients (Francis et al. 1999). For example, Florence Nightingale advocated airy wards in line with the miasma theory of infection: the right idea although the wrong reason. Hospitals today often inhabit old buildings that present basic safety and quality barriers, such as not enough electric plugs for proliferating appliances. Even relatively modern buildings may be poorly designed with consequent increased risk of adverse events, for example, air-conditioning systems that spread infections such as *Legionella* bacteria (Healy and McKee 2002). Poorly designed hospitals create hazards when staff and patients must traverse long corridors between treatment sites; slippery and hard floors cause injuries from falls; non-standardized equipment confuses staff; and cumbersome information systems record and retrieve misinformation about patients. A new era of hospital design now is underway with architects paying attention to designing safer facilities, as shown in the journal *Healthcare Design*. The Australian Resource Centre for Healthcare Innovations (ARCHI) also promotes better hospital and equipment design, and better patient management systems. A review of the literature identified nearly 700 rigorous studies on how the architecture of acute care hospitals affects the health of patients and staff, including considerable research that shows that better design of the physical environment can improve the safety of health care for patients (Ulrich 2006).

The regulatory literature uses the term 'architecture' to mean the environment built around an object of regulation that acts to physically constrain it. Prisons are the archetypal regulatory building and psychiatric hospitals also have a long history of physical design intended to regulate the inmates (Scull 1979). Jeremy Bentham proposed a panopticon design for prisons so that warders could watch the prisoners, and hospital wards also were designed on panopticon or cruciform principles. Hospital-like nursing homes took up this idea with wards radiating out from a nursing station surveillance point that made later efforts to create a more home-like atmosphere difficult (Braithwaite et al. 2007). Modern hospital design has rejected wards with long rows of beds reminiscent of the Crimean War in favour of smaller rooms that offer patients more privacy, although these now pose safety problems for monitoring their condition. Contemporary panoptic mechanisms, such as closed-circuit television cameras and biomedical monitoring devices, also present a conflict between patient privacy and patient safety. Single room occupancy, however, is desirable since it significantly reduces the risk of hospital-acquired infection compared to multi-bed rooms (Ulrich 2006).

Medical technologies are defined as 'all the drugs, devices and medical and surgical procedures and the organizational and support systems used to provide them' (Rosen 2002: 240). Technologies that hold out promise for improving patient safety include less invasive diagnostic and treatment technologies (MRI scans, laparoscopic surgery), assistive technologies (electric wheelchairs, speech devices), surveillance and monitoring technologies (personal alarms, heart monitoring devices), and information technology (the Internet, electronic patient records). Medical devices are poorly designed from a human factors perspective, however, when designers do not sufficiently consider the people and circumstances in which the equipment is used (Lin et al. 2001). Some design changes have made notable improvements to dangerous equipment and procedures. For example, anaesthesia has been made much safer by adding pulse oximetry to anaesthetic machines to monitor the amount of oxygen being given to anesthetized patients (Gawande 2002). Design improvements could significantly reduce adverse events in hospitals: standardized drug trolleys instead of different trolleys with drugs jumbled up in different drawers; purchasing dilute rather than concentrated electrolyte solutions; using alarms against accidental breathing circuit disconnections; insisting manufacturers fix faulty equipment design; laying out surgical instruments in a standardized way in operating theatres; and clear labelling and colour-coded packaging of drugs (Runciman and Moller 2001). Medication administration errors could be reduced by having syringes already filled with the correct medication, labelled and colour-coded by the pharmacy, and laid out in a tray in the correct order in the operating theatre.

In the United Kingdom, a scoping study on patient safety design in hospitals concluded that the NHS was seriously behind modern thinking and practice (Design Council and Department of Health 2003). The report noted that the design of many products, processes and services did not take into account the system into which they are placed, the needs of the people who use them, and the 'hot spots' in which errors occur. The report called for an authoritative body to drive improved safety design and also noted that manufacturers would respond if the NHS was to demand safer, rather than just cheaper, products and devices.

Roll out information technology

The Institute of Medicine, in *Closing the Quality Chasm,* called for 'embedding technology' in order to produce higher quality and lower costs through technological fixes (Institute of Medicine 2002). Information technology aims to improve the management of patients in a variety of ways: electronic patient medical records, electronic prescribing, electronic support for clinical decisions, computerized pharmaceutical order entry by doctors, recording and transmitting test result, computerized reminders sent to patients, and standardized bar codes on drugs that reduce errors in prescribing and dispensing. Information technology also is promising from a regulatory perspective since medical practitioners are rapid adopters when offered financial incentives. But there is a long way to go in 'embedding technology'. A seven-country survey in 2006 found that the proportion of primary care doctors using information technology for seven or more functions ranged from a high of 87 per cent in New Zealand down to a low of 8 per cent in Canada (Schoen et al. 2006). The greater use of IT in some countries was ascribed to access to public funds: for example, in the United Kingdom to government investment in the NHS, in New Zealand and Australia to government financial incentives, and in the Netherlands to funds from professional associations. One regulatory strategy for embedding technological solutions for patient safety would be for regulators, such as licensing and accreditation agencies, to require or at least recommend, that health facilities have these in place. This, of course, would have cost implications for the funders of these facilities.

In Australia, the information technology push is vested in the National e-Health Transition Authority to set standards, specifications and infrastructure requirements for a national and interoperable electronic health information system. NEHTA is working on unique identifier numbers for providers and patients, software for standard patient clinical information, and message security and privacy. Work on health care communications aims to ensure that patient referrals are sent safely by electronic means, prescriptions are accurately and securely transmitted, pathology results are accurately identified, and hospital discharge summaries are sent promptly to GPs.

Technology advocates in the United States argue that an investment in putting IT systems into every hospital and physician's office would be paid back in a few years by increases in efficiency and decreases in costly adverse events. But the *Wired for Health Care Quality Act* (S 1418) stalled in Congress, doctors want money to install information technology (Casolino et al. 2003; Wang et al. 2003), and a large investment is necessary since only 9 per cent of US doctors use electronic patient medical records (Schoen et al. 2006). Managed care plans are using financial incentives to increase IT use among their physicians (Epstein et al. 2004). The Centers for Medicare and Medicaid Services is trialling an electronic health record system for use in doctors' offices that lists all treatments a patient has received, writes electronic drug prescriptions, and issues reminders to patients (The Commonwealth Fund 26 September 2005).

In the United Kingdom, the NHS 'Connecting for Health Programme' is backing information technology, by installing more computers in hospitals, establishing information systems to connect hospitals and GPs, developing interoperable electronic systems, and rolling out access to centralized electronic patient medical records throughout the NHS (NHS Connecting for Health 2007).

Electronic patient medical records are an example of information technology that is expected to result in safer and better health care for patients (Bates and Gawande 2003). Modern hospitals maintain electronic records, although not necessarily as a single or comprehensive record, so that much patient management is still recorded in manila folders. A single electronic medical record for each person in a country, however, requires unique identifiers for each patient and each provider, information technology to be installed, and interoperable computer systems. Pilot programmes have been undertaken in several Australian states and NEHTA is working on specifications. An example of a patient safety use of information technology is to programme a 'forcing function' that does not allow access to the patient's operating theatre record until a safe surgery checks are done:

> We have full compliance now that we have a failsafe method. We have just got a new computer system with a new operating theatre module and 'time out' for a patient identification check is a compulsory field on the IT program. You cannot get up the patient information and go ahead with data entry until that is ticked. It prompts everybody, it is an automatic thing, and it has saved us several times from making an error. (Hospital safety and quality coordinator)

Electronic decision support systems are expected to improve the quality of care by providing up-to-date evidence-based information to health professionals in an accessible manner. Databases offer guidance on medical conditions, clinical protocols, diagnostic tests, drugs and dosages. Electronic support systems offer access to clinical protocols and decision trees to guide treatment decisions.

Personal digital assistants (PDAs) or hand-held computers can release a doctor from office-bound information by providing mobile access to decision support systems through computer technology. For example, PDAs are used in Australian and New Zealand College of Anaesthetists training programmes for anaesthetic registrars. The aims are to inculcate a safety culture, provide electronic support for decisions, and promote learning from reflective practice. A personal monitoring programme encourages trainees to record their own medical errors and near misses and discuss their performance with their supervisor. Since reporting compliance is high, mobile computing technology also could be used to report critical incidents (Bolsin 2004; Faunce and Bolsin 2004; Freestone et al. 2006).

Electronic medication prescribing is a rules-based computer system that indicates the best drug and dosage for particular patients with particular conditions and also warns the clinician of any prescribing errors (Bates and Gawande 2003). This technology promises to reduce medication errors as most occur at the prescribing stage of the medication pathway (Bates et al. 1995). Electronic systems for prescribing with decision support result in an increased use of tests and treatments known to improve patient outcomes, and reductions in inappropriate drugs and treatments and in adverse events (Epstein et al. 2004; Roughead and Lexchin 2006). Other studies have reported problems, however, with poorly designed and implemented prescribing systems (Koppel et al. 2005). Medication administration errors are not thereby reduced, however, since a study in one hospital found administration errors in over half of electronic medication orders (FitzHenry et al. 2007). Another study found electronic prescribing difficult to introduce into the hospital's existing computer system, staff had low IT access, and there were differing stakeholder views (Bomba and Land 2006). This study highlights the difficulty in introducing new technology into hospitals given old IT systems and rusted-on ways of working. Electronic prescribing is not yet widely used in hospitals.

Interoperable electronic systems in hospitals and in doctors' offices, that is, systems that are compatible and can talk to each other, is still a long way off. In the United States, the US Government does not want to set up a central database of medical records but rather to ensure that standards are in place for interoperable systems. The Department of Health and Human Services is devising rules to advance interoperable information technology, the model being the banking information infrastructure with its network of users. For example, health care providers would have to demonstrate compliance with interoperability standards when purchasing e-health systems. The intention is to fund demonstration projects run by local and regional stakeholders that will devise local standards and procedures and calm fears of excessive data collection in Washington (Trubek 2004).

Standardize procedures

Greater standardization in the health sector would improve predictability in line with practice in other high-risk industries. The health sector is a long way from standardization, however, since procedures and forms vary even within one hospital. A senior hospital clinician traditionally runs his/her own domain so that the introduction by hospital managers of a standard form or procedure often is fraught. First, it is not always possible to design a form or procedure to fit all situations. Second, senior clinicians oppose perceived threats to their autonomy in patient management. Third, busy health professionals are not very receptive to change since they are already overwhelmed by forms and procedures. Getting agreement on a standard approach in one hospital (in this case a safe surgery protocol) let alone across many hospitals can be difficult:

> State-wide we should all be doing the same thing but even in the hospital we do different things. I say to the surgeons, 'It's okay for you, you are a small department, but I've got lots of nurses. I can't say, no, ortho and general surgery do mark the site, but plastics and ENT and neuro don't mark'. Everyone needs to do the same otherwise people get confused and that's when we might make a mistake. We have to have one rule in a big place like this otherwise it is too hard. (Nurse manager, operating theatres)

A standard patient identification protocol is one of the current nine global patient safety solutions (World Health Organization 2007), and in Australia has been endorsed by the Australian Commission for Safety and Quality in Health Care but with variable take up so far by state health departments. A large hospital on any one day treats hundreds of people and must match them with the correct documentation, test results and procedures. This requires an unambiguous verbal identification protocol 'Can you tell me your full name, and your date of birth?' Incident reports of patient misidentification errors in outpatient clinics are not uncommon: 'People wait in outpatient clinics for procedures and think they heard their name called and go and have a procedure that wasn't intended for them'. Other patient identification solutions include a standard patient wrist band and electronic bar codes – if super markets can manage the technology, why not hospitals? The speed and volume of patient treatment increases the risk of identification errors:

> Something like 70 per cent of our surgery comes in only an hour or few hours before. We have patients who are having quite major operations who don't go to the ward before, but come straight into the admissions unit and go straight to the theatre. The idea of coming in the night before is long gone. So everything is sped up. That's why you need better checks. (Director of Surgery)

The following sections discuss efforts to ensure correct patient identification through a standard surgery protocol, to reduce medication errors through a standard inpatient medication chart, and to reduce communication errors through a standard procedure for patient handover.

Patient identification

A 'correct patient, correct site, correct procedure' protocol aims to eliminate incidents where surgery or other procedures are performed on the wrong patient, wrong side or body part, or where the wrong procedure was used. The Australian Health Ministers Conference in 2004 endorsed a protocol that included checking forms and diagnostic images, marking the site, confirming identification with the patient if possible, and taking 'team time out' in the operating theatre to verbally confirm all is correct. The World Health Organization has now incorporated patient identification in its 19-step safe surgery protocol (World Health Organization 2008). While an apparently sensible, low-cost and low-intrusion intervention, and despite endorsement from professional associations, the safe surgery identification protocol required ongoing regulatory mechanisms by external and internal regulators to improve compliance in operating theatres in Australian hospitals (Healy 2008). Surgeons resent attempts to impose 'a rule' and believe that they will not make mistakes – although they cite errors made by others. The protocol provoked power battles between managers and clinicians over medical governance, between doctors and nurses over medical dominance, and between specialties over professional procedures. While surgeons interpret a protocol as discretionary, nurses interpret it as a rule. The protocol was more readily adopted when championed by clinical leaders:

> To me it's good practice to stop talking about the footy scores, stop talking about what you did on the weekend, or the bottle of wine you drank last night, or stop even worrying about how I am going to do the operation. Just stand, take a deep breath, it takes about five seconds 'Are we all agreed this is the correct patient having the correct operation on the correct site?' (Orthopaedic surgeon)

Standard inpatient medication chart

A standard chart is an obvious patient safety solution to replace differently designed charts in each hospital that give rise to error from different documentation conventions, ambiguous abbreviations, and illegible entries. Medication error is a common category of adverse event in hospitals (Bates et al. 1995). The Australian Health Ministers endorsed a National Inpatient Medication Chart in 2004 but take-up by public hospitals was variable and many modified the chart so defeating the standardization purpose; implementation has been stepped up from 2006 onwards and manuals and audit tools developed (Australian Commission on Safety and Quality in Health Care 2008: chapter 4).

Safe patient handover

A communication breakdown at 'handover' points, when staff change shifts or when patients are transferred to another consultant or unit, is a major factor in adverse events. Continuity of patient information is more difficult to ensure with increasing numbers of staff caring for hospital patients including part-time and locum staff. Australian public hospitals generally have not used standard procedures for handover (Bomba and Prakash 2005). Better communication between staff at patient handover is one of the WHO nine priority patient safety solutions (World Health Organization 2007). Guides to practitioners on safe clinical handover include the AMA guide (Australian Medical Association 2006), and the 'OSSIE Guide to Clinical Handover Improvement' (Australian Commission on Safety and Quality in Health Care 2009a).

Conclusion

Is There Evidence That a Learning Strategy Improves Safety and Quality?

The responsive regulation model argues that single interventions each have their strengths and weaknesses but a combination of complementary mechanisms strengthens the overall web of controls (Gunningham and Grabosky 1998; Braithwaite 2002). The multiple intervention theory is borne out by studies on the take-up of evidence-based medicine by medical practitioners, the conclusion being that multiple interventions are more successful than single interventions (NHS Centre for Reviews and Dissemination 1999) (Freemantle 2002; Grimshaw et al. 2004). The main messages from over a decade of research are, first, clinical guidelines improve patient care, and second, guidelines do not implement themselves but need sustained implementation programmes.

A systematic review of the take-up of clinical practice guidelines in family medicine in the Netherlands concluded that a multi-faceted approach worked well since guidelines were followed in 67 per cent of treatment decisions (Grol and Buchan 2006). A systematic review of 59 guidelines studies found clear improvements in care processes in 55 studies and some improvements in patient outcomes (Grimshaw and Russell 1993). A later systematic review found that well-designed clinical guidelines achieve a moderate impact in terms of an 8–10 per cent improvement in patient care (Grimshaw et al. 2004). A structured literature review on the impact of patient safety guidelines concluded that despite a scarcity of studies there was 'convincing but by no means overwhelming evidence' that guidelines improve the use of safety procedures, and to a lesser extent care outcomes, but their take-up depends on the manner of implementation (Trowbridge and Weingarten 2001). Since patient safety guidelines have only been promulgated since the early 2000s, it is early days in research terms.

As evidence-based guidelines are expensive to develop and disseminate, producers should pay more attention to user needs if take-up rates are to improve (Grol and Buchan 2006). It is time for a more organized approach to clinical guidelines and for more support from government (Buchan et al. 2009: 92). While research shows that evidence-based clinical guidelines improve patient care, the question for regulatory research is how to ensure that guidelines are followed. Regulators mostly apply an information strategy by distributing guidelines through various methods and hoping for voluntary compliance from clinicians. A second approach is to offer clinicians incentives to follow guidelines and to apply disincentives for ignoring them. A third approach is for regulators to move higher up the regulatory pyramid and enforce their use, such as re-registration conditions that require clinicians to show evidence of guideline use, and to issue practice standards that carry more legal force (Runciman and Lumby 2009).

Action-research collaboratives are another learning model approach that produces improvements. But the benefit may lie more in training people than providing irrefutable evidence of an impact. The first caveat is that their participative nature across many hospitals means that the studies are seldom based on tight research designs, so that it is hard to know which one or more actions produced the improvement. Second, while participants usually report success, there is little evidence of sustained improvements after the project ends. Third, it remains to be tested whether a successful intervention in one organization can translate to another given the complexity and variability of hospital systems.

Is There Evidence that a Safety Culture Improves Safety and Quality?

Health reformers put enormous emphasis upon promoting a safety culture as the way to go in producing better patient outcomes (Institute of Medicine 2000). A systematic literature review has concluded, however, that while there are persuasive reasons for an organization to inculcate a safety culture, in the absence of robust studies there is little evidence so far that this reduces adverse events (Pizzi et al. 2001). Other industries can demonstrate a safety impact, however, such as a systematic review of occupational health and safety initiatives in 229 facilities across several industries, which found comprehensive initiatives reduced at-risk behaviours among employees and reduced accidents (Krause et al. 1999). The US Veterans Health Administration claims that a multi-faceted patient safety programme throughout its hospitals produced cultural change and improved safety for patients (Weeks and Bagian 2000). Research on 'magnet hospitals' also suggests that a supportive work culture has a positive impact upon patient outcomes, as a comparison of 39 magnet hospitals with five matched hospitals each (N=234) found significantly lower case mix-adjusted patient mortality (Aiken et al. 2002; Aiken and Sloane 2002).

Is There Evidence that Better Systems Design Improves Safety and Quality?

The evidence from other industries is that good physical design reduces both the risk and the impact of accidents, but the hospital sector has been less attentive to designing for patient safety. More effort has gone into occupational health and safety for staff in response to union vigilance, than safety for patients in the absence of strong consumer groups. Recent research studies, however, show good results from better physical design (Ulrich 2006). A structured review of research on better designed physical equipment, devices and procedures found a positive impact upon patient safety (Shojania et al. 2001). For example, the incidence of central venous catheter-associated infections among patients is reduced by donning sterile clothing and coating catheters with antibacterial agents (Saint 2001). Another example is the prevention of falls among hospital and nursing home patients as many studies point to poor physical design and unsafe procedures. Solutions include better physical design, such as softer flooring, and hip protectors for vulnerable people although the reviewers question the ethics of preventing adverse consequences rather than preventing falls (Agostini et al. 2001).

Information technology is said to hold enormous promise for making health care safer for patients (Institute of Medicine 2001). Installing information technology is of course expensive. Information technology also is driving efforts to standardize clinical information, such as medication charts. Standardized electronic forms improve care procedures such as clearer information transfers among health care providers (Murff and Bates 2001). The strongest evidence so far for a positive impact on patient safety comes from electronic prescribing where a structured literature review found that computerised physician order entry and clinical decision support systems reduced the frequency of adverse drug events (Kaushal and Bates 2001).

References

Agostini J, et al. (2001), 'Chapter 26: Prevention of falls in hospitalized and institutionalized older people'. In Shojania K, Duncan B, McDonald K, et al. *Making Health Care Safer: A Critical Analysis of Patient Safety Practices*. (Rockville MD: Agency for Healthcare Research and Quality): 281–295.

Aiken L, et al. (2002), 'Hospital staffing, organizational support, and quality of care: cross-national findings.' *International Journal for Quality in Health Care* 14(1): 5–13.

Aiken L and Sloane D (2002), 'Hospital organization and culture'. In McKee M and Healy J. *Hospitals in a Changing Europe*. (Buckingham. Philadelphia: Open University Press).

Australian Commission on Safety and Quality in Health Care (2008), *Windows into Safety and Quality in Health Care 2008*. (Sydney: ACSQHC).

Australian Commission on Safety and Quality in Health Care, Clinical Handover, (2 February 2010 2 February 2010) http://www.safetyandquality.gov.au/internet/safety/publishing.nsf/content/PriorityProgram-05#Tools

Australian Commission on Safety and Quality in Health Care (2009b), *Windows into Safety and Quality in Health Care 2009*. (Sydney: ACSQHC).

Australian Council for Safety and Quality in Health Care (2004), *State and Territory Action to Improve Patient Safety: A Report on Achievements and Activity for Safety and Quality Improvement in Australian States and Territories*. (Canberra: Commonwealth of Australia).

Australian Council for Safety and Quality in Health Care (2005), Medical Alert 2: Vincristine can be fatal when administered by the intrathecal route http://www.safetyandquality.gov.au/internet/safety/publishing.nsf/Content/F22384CCE74A9F01CA257483000D845E/$File/valert.pdf

Australian Council for Safety and Quality in Health Care (2005a), *Medication Safety Breakthrough Collaborative: Project Chronicle*. (Canberra: Commonwealth of Australia).

Australian Council for Safety and Quality in Health Care (2005b), *State and Territory Highlights: Improving Patient Safety: A Report on Achievements and Action for Safety and Quality Improvements in Australian States and Territories*. (Canberra: Commonwealth of Australia).

Australian Infection Control Association Expert Working Group (2001), National Surveillance of Healthcare Associated Infection in Australia. (Canberra: Commonwealth Department of Health and Aged Care).

Australian Medical Association (2006), Safe Handover: Safe Patients. Guidance on Clinical Handover for Clinicians and Managers. (Kingston ACT: AMA).

Bates D, et al. (1995), 'Incidence of adverse drug events and potential drug events: implications for prevention.' *Journal of the American Medical Association* 274(1): 1–98.

Bates D and Gawande A (2003), 'Improving safety with information technology.' *New England Journal of Medicine* 348: 2526–34.

Berwick D and Leape L (1999), 'Reducing errors in medicine.' *British Medical Journal* 319: 136–137.

Bolsin S (2003), 'Whistle-blowing.' *Medical Education* 37: 294–296.

Bolsin S (2004), 'Electronic incident reporting and professional monitoring transforms culture (letter).' *British Medical Journal* 329: 51–52.

Bolsin S, et al. (2005a), 'Using portable digital technology for clinical care and critical incidents: a new model.' *Australian Health Review* 29(3): 297–305.

Bolsin S, et al. (2005b), 'New technology to enable personal monitoring and incident reporting can transform professional culture: the potential to favourably impact upon the future of health care.' *Journal of Evaluation in Clinical Practice* 11(5): 499–506.

Bomba D and Land T (2006), 'The feasibility of implementing an electronic prescribing decision support system: a case study of an Australian public hospital.' *Australian Health Review* 30(3): 380–388.

Bomba D and Prakash R (2005), 'A description of handover processes in an Australian public hospital.' *Australian Health Review* 29: 68–79.

Braithwaite J (2002), *Restorative Justice and Responsive Regulation*. (Oxford. New York: Oxford University Press).

Braithwaite J and Drahos P (2000), *Global Business Regulation*. (Cambridge: Cambridge University Press).

Braithwaite J, et al. (2007), *Regulating Aged Care: Ritualism and the New Pyramid*. (Cheltenham. Northampton MA: Edward Elgar).

Braithwaite J, et al. (2006), 'Does restructuring hospitals result in greater efficiency? An empirical test using diachronic data.' *Health Services Management Research* 19(1): 1–2.

Buchan H, et al. (2009), 'Voluntary initiatives by clinicians'. In Healy J and Dugdale P. *Patient Safety First: Strategies for Regulating Health Care*. (Crows Nest NSW: Allen & Unwin): 71–97.

Buijsen M (2000), 'The legal significance of clinical guidelines in The Netherlands.' *Medicine and Law* 19(2): 181–188.

Carayon P, et al. (2006), 'Work system design for patient safety: the SEIPS model.' *Quality and Safety in Health Care* 15: i50-i58.

Casolino L, et al. (2003), 'External incentives, information technology, and organized processes to improve health care quality for patients with chronic diseases.' *Journal of the American Medical Association* 289: 434–431.

Claridge T, et al. (2006), 'Pathways to patient safety: the use of rules and guidelines in health care'. In Walshe K and Boaden R. *Patient Safety: Research into Practice*. (Maidenhead, Berkshire: Open University Press): 41–65.

Darzi A (2009), *High Quality Care For All: NHS Next Stage Review Final Report*. (London: Department of Health).

Degeling P and Carr A (2004), 'Leadership for the systemization of health care: the unaddressed issue in health care reform.' *Journal of Health Organization and Management* 18(6): 399–414.

Degeling P, et al. (2003), 'Medicine, management, and modernisation: a "dance macabre"?' *British Medical Journal* 326: 649–652.

Design Council and Department of Health (2003), *Design for Patient Safety: A System-Wide Design-Led Approach to Tackling Patient Safety in the NHS*. (London: Department of Health).

Doebbeling B, et al. (1992), 'Comparative efficacy of alternative handwashing agents in reducing nosocomial infections in intensive care units.' *New England Journal of Medicine* 327. 88–93.

Donabedian A (1966), 'Evaluating the quality of medical care.' *Milbank Memorial Fund Quarterly* 40: 166–206.

Dwyer P (1998), 'Legal implications of clinical practice guidelines.' *Medical Journal of Australia* 169: 292–293.

Epstein A, et al. (2004), 'Paying physicians for high-quality care.' *New England Journal of Medicine* 350: 406–410.

Faunce T and Bolsin S (2004), 'Three Australian whistle-blowing sagas: lessons for internal and external regulation.' *Medical Journal of Australia* 18(1): 44–47.

Field M and Lohr K, eds. (1990), *Clinical Practice Guidelines: Directions for a New Program*. (Washington, DC: Institute of Medicine, National Academy Press).

Finn R and Waring J (2006), 'Ethnographic methods in patient safety'. In Walshe K and Boaden R. *Patient Safety: Research into Practice*. (Maidenhead, Berkshire: Open University Press): 161–172.

Fisse B and Braithwaite J (1993), *Corporations, Crime and Accountability*. (Cambridge: Cambridge University Press).

FitzHenry F, et al. (2007), 'Medication administration discrepancies persist despite electronic ordering.' *J Am Med Inform Assoc* 14(6): 756–764.

Francis S, et al. (1999), *50 Years of Ideas in Health Care Buildings*. (London: The Nuffield Trust).

Freemantle N (2002), 'Optimizing clinical performance'. In McKee M and Healy J. *Hospitals in a Changing Europe*. (Buckingham. Philadelphia: Open University Press).

Freestone L, et al. (2006), 'Voluntary incident reporting by anaesthetic trainees in an Australian hospital.' *International Journal for Quality in Health Care* 18(6): 452–457.

Gawande A (2002), *Complications: A Surgeon's Notes on an Imperfect Science*. (New York: Metropolitan Books, Henry Holt and Company).

Grimshaw J and Russell I (1993), 'Effect of clinical guidelines on medical practice: a systematic review of rigorous evaluations.' *Lancet* 342: 1317–1322.

Grimshaw J, et al. (2004), 'Effectiveness and efficiency of guideline dissemination and implementation strategies.' *Health Technology Assessment* 8(6): 1–72.

Grol R and Buchan H (2006), 'Clinical guidelines: what can we do to increase their use?' *Medical Journal of Australia* 185(6): 301–302.

Gunningham N and Grabosky P (1998), *Smart Regulation: Designing Environmental Policy*. (Oxford: Clarendon Press).

Hayhurst A, et al. (2005), 'Work environmental factors and retention of nurses.' *Journal of Nursing Care Quality* 20(3): 283–288.

Haynes A, et al. (2009), 'A surgical safety checklist to reduce morbidity and mortality in a global population.' *New England Journal of Medicine* 360: 491–499.

Healy J (2008), Safe surgery in Australian hospitals: implementation of the correct patient, correct site, correct procedure protocol. *Occasional Paper 13*. (Canberra: Regulatory Institutions Network, Australian National University).

Healy J and McKee M (2002), 'Improving performance within the hospital'. In McKee M and Healy J. *Hospitals in a Changing Europe*. (Buckingham. Philadelphia: Open University Press).

Helmreich R and Merritt A (1998), *Culture at Work in Aviation and Medicine: National, Organizational and Professional Influences*. (Aldershot, UK: Ashgate Publishing).

Institute for Health Improvement (2010), IHI Improvement Map, 2 February http://www.ihi.org/IHI/Programs/ImprovementMap

Institute for Healthcare Improvement(2005), Home page, 9 August www.ihi.org

Institute of Medicine (2000), *To Err is Human: Building a Safer Health System*. (Washington, DC: Institute of Medicine, National Academy Press).

Institute of Medicine (2001), *Crossing the Quality Chasm: A New Health System for the 21st century*. (Washington, DC: National Academy Press).

Institute of Medicine (2002), *Fostering Rapid Advances in Health Care*. (Washington, DC: The National Academies Press).

Jorm C and Kam P (2004), 'Does medical culture limit doctors adoption of quality improvements? Lessons from Camelot.' *Journal of Health Services Research and Policy* 9(4): 248–251.

Kaushal R and Bates D (2001), 'Chapter 6: Computerized physician order entry (CPOE) with clinical decision support systems (CDSSs)'. In Shojania K, Duncan B, McDonald K, et al. *Making Health Care Safer: A Critical Analysis of Patient Safety Practices*. (Rockville MD: Agency for Healthcare Research and Quality): 59–70.

Kirk S, Marshall M, Claridge T, et al. (2006), 'Evaluating a patient safety culture'. In Walshe K and Boaden R. *Patient Safety: Research into Practice*. (Maidenhead: Open University Press): 173–184.

Koppel R, et al. (2005), 'Role of computerized physician order entry systems in facilitating medication errors.' *Journal of the American Medical Association* 293(10): 1197–1203.

Krause T, et al. (1999), 'Long-term evaluation of a behaviour-based method for improving safety peformance: a meta-analysis of 73 interrupted time-series replications.' *Safety Science* 32: 1–18.

Leape L and Berwick D (2005), 'Five years after *To Err is Human*: what have we learned.' *Journal of the American Medical Association* 293(19): 2384–2390.

Lin L, et al. (2001), 'Patient safety, potential adverse drug events, and medical device design: a human factors engineering approach.' *Journal of Biomedical Informatics* 34(4): 274–284.

McClure M, et al. (1983), *Magnet Hospitals: Attraction and Retention of Professional Nurses*. (Kansas City, MO: American Nurses Association).

McGlynn E, et al. (2003), 'The quality of health care delivered to adults in the United States.' *New England Journal of Medicine* 348(26): 2635–2645.

Millenson M (1997), *Demanding Medical Excellence. Doctors and Accountability in the Information Age*. (Chicago: University of Chicago Press).

Murff H and Bates D (2001), 'Chapter 42: Information transfer'. In Shojania K, Duncan B, McDonald K, et al. *Making Health Care Safer: A Critical Analysis of Patient Safety Practices*. (Rockville MD: Agency for Healthcare Research and Quality): 471–486.

National Institute of Clinical Studies (2003), *Factors Supporting High Performance in Health Care Organizations. Prepared by the Health Management Group at LaTrobe University*. (Melbourne: NICS).

National Institute of Clinical Studies (2005), *Evidence-Practice Gaps Report*. (Melbourne: NICS).

National Patient Safety Agency (2004), *Seven Steps to Patient Safety: An Overview Guide for NHS Staff*. (London: National Patient Safety Agency).

National Patient Safety Agency (2007), *Slips, Trips and Falls in Hospital*. (London: National Patient Safety Agency).

NHS Centre for Reviews and Dissemination (1999), 'Effective health care: getting evidence into practice.' *Bulletin on the Effectiveness of Health Service Interventions for Decision Makers* 5(1): 1–16.

NHS Connecting for Health (2007), NHS Connecting for Health Factsheet, 6 March http://www.coneectingfor health.nhs.uk

Parker C (2002), *The Open Corporation: Effective Self-Regulation and Democracy*. (Cambridge: Cambridge University Press).

Perrow C (1999), *Normal Accidents: Living with High-Risk Technologies*. (Princeton, NJ: Princeton University Press).

Pizzi L, et al. (2001), 'Chapter 40: Promoting a culture of safety'. In Shojania K, Duncan B, McDonald K, et al. *Making Health Care Safer: A Critical Analysis of Patient Safety Practices*. (Rockville MD: Agency for Healthcare Research and Quality): 447–457.

Poteliakhoff E (2006), Update on IHI's 100k Lives Campaign. *Health Policy Monitor*.

Reason J (1990), *Human Error*. (New York: Cambridge University Press).

Reason J (1997), *Managing the Risks of Organizational Accidents*. (Brookfield, VT: Ashgate Publishing Company).

Reason J (2000), 'Human error: models and management.' *British Medical Journal* 320(7237): 768–770.

Reason J, et al. (2001), 'Diagnosing 'vulnerable system syndrome': an essential prerequisite to effective risk management.' *Quality and Safety in Health Care* 10: 21–25.

Reason P and Bradbury H, eds. (2001), *Handbook of Action Research: Participative Inquiry and Practice*. (Thousand Oaks, CA: Sage).

Rees J (1994), *Hostages of Each Other: The Transformation of Nuclear Safety Since Three Mile Island*. (Chicago and London: University of Chicago Press).

Rennie S and Crosby J (2002), 'Students' perception of whistle-blowing: implications for self-regulation. A questionnaire and focus group survey.' *Medical Education* 36(2): 113–114.

Roberts K (1993), 'Cultural characteristics of reliability enhancing organisations.' *Journal of Managerial Issues* 5: 165–181.

Rosen R (2002), 'Introducing new technologies'. In McKee M and Healy J. *Hospitals in a Changing Europe*. (Buckingham, Philadelphia: Open University Press).

Roughead E and Lexchin J (2006), 'Editorials: Adverse drug events: counting is not enough, action is needed.' *Medical Journal of Australia* 184(7): 315–316.

Runciman WB, Merry A and Walton M (2007), *Safety and Ethics in Healthcare: A Guide to Getting it Right*. (Farnham: Ashgate).

Runciman W and Moller J (2001), *Iatrogenic Injury in Australia*. (Adelaide: Australian Patient Safety Foundation).

Runciman WB and Lumby J (2009), 'Regulating clinical practice'. In Healy J and Dugdale P. *Patient Safety First: Strategies for Regulating Health Care*. (Crows Nest NSW: Allen & Unwin): 192–220.

Saint S (2001), 'Chapter 16: Prevention of intravascular catheter-associated infections'. In Shojania K, Duncan B, McDonald K, et al. *Making Health Care Safer: A Critical Analysis of Patient Safety Practices*. (Rockville MD: Agency for Healthcare Research and Quality): 163–184.

Schoen C, et al. (2006), 'On the front lines of care: primary care doctors' office systems, experiences, and views in seven countries.' *Health Affairs* Web exclusive: W555-W571.

Scull A (1979), *Museums of Madness: The Social Organization of Insanity in Nineteenth Century England*. (London: Allen Lane).

Shojania K, et al. (2001), *Making Health Care Safer: A Critical Analysis of Patient Safety Practices*. (Rockville MD: Agency for Healthcare Research and Quality).

The Commonwealth Fund (2 May 2005), Washington Health Policy Week in Review: losing patience over losing patients. (New York: The Commonwealth Fund).

The Commonwealth Fund (26 September 2005), Washington Health Policy Week in Review: CMS releases test version of electronic health record for doctors' offices. (New York: The Commonwealth Fund).

The Commonwealth Fund (27 June 2005), Washington Health Policy Week in Review: AHRQ announces studies comparing effectiveness of treatments in Medicare. (New York: The Commonwealth Fund).

Thomas D (2006), 'Peer review as an outmoded model for health practitioner regulation'. In Freckleton I. *Regulating Health Practitioners*. (Annandale, NSW: The Federation Press).

Trowbridge R and Weingarten S (2001), 'Chapter 51: Practice guidelines'. In Shojania K, Duncan B, McDonald K, et al. *Making Health Care Safer: A Critical Analysis of Patient Safety Practices*. (Rockville MD: Agency for Healthcare Research and Quality): 575–580.

Trubek L (2004), *New governance practices in US health care*. Workshop on New Governance and Constitutionalism, (Cambridge UK: Cambridge University).

Ulrich R (2006), 'Essay: Evidence-based health-care architecture.' *The Lancet* 368: s38–s39.

Van Der Weyden M (2004), 'The "Cam affair": an isolated incident or destined to be repeated?' *Medical Journal of Australia* 180(3): 100–101.

Van Vuuren W (1999), 'Organizational failure: lessons from industry applied to the medical domain.' *Safety Science* 33: 14–29.

Vaughan D (1997), *The Challenger Launch Decision: Risky Technology, Culture and Deviance at NASA*. (Chicago, Ill: University of Chicago Press).

Vincent C, et al. (1998), 'Framework for analysing risk and safety in clinical medicine.' *British Medical Journal* 316: 1154–1157.

Walshe K and Shortell S (2004), 'When things go wrong: how healthcare organizations deal with major failures.' *Health Affairs* 23: 103–111.

Walton M and Elliott SL (2006), 'Improving safety and quality: how can education help?' *Medical Journal of Australia* 184(10): S60-S64.

Wang S, et al. (2003), 'A cost-benefit analysis of electronic medical records in primary care.' *American Journal of Medicine* 114: 397–403.

Weeks W and Bagian J (2000), 'Developing a culture of safety in the Veterans Affairs Administration.' *Effective Clinical Practice* 3: 270–276.

Weick K (1997), 'The Challenger launch decision: risky technology, culture, and deviance at NASA.' *Administrative Science Quarterly* 42: 395–401.

Weick KE and Sutcliffe KM (2001), *Managing the Unexpected: Assuring High Performance in an Age of Complexity*. (San Francisco: Jossey-Bass).

Weisz G, et al. (2007), 'The emergence of clinical practice guidelines.' *Millbank Quarterly* 85(4): 691–727.

Wellington H (2004), Governance, accountability and a 'just culture'. (Canberra: Paper prepared for the Australian Council for Safety and Quality in Health Care).

Westrum R (2004), 'A typology of organizational cultures.' *Quality and Safety in Health Care* 13 (Suppl II): ii122–127.

Wilf-Miron R, et al. (2003), 'From aviation to medicine: applying concepts of aviation safety to risk management in ambulatory care.' *Quality and safety in Health Care* 12: 35–39.

World Health Organization (2004), *World Report on Knowledge for Better Health: Strengthening Health Systems*. (Geneva: World Health Organization).

World Health Organization(2008), World Alliance for Patient Safety: Patient Safety Solutions, 2 May http://www.who.int/patientsafety/solutions/en/

World Health Organization (2008), Implementation Manual Surgical Safety Checklist (First Edition): Safe Surgery Saves Lives. (Geneva: World Health Organization).

World Health Organization WAfPS (2005), *Global Patient Safety Challenge 2005–2006: Clean Care is Safer Care*. (Geneva: World Health Organization).

Chapter 6
Regulating Staff: Internal Management

Making the Managers Manage

A classic book by Chester Barnard, a management guru of the 1930s, summarized the key functions of an executive as formulating the goals of the organization, securing essential resources, and ensuring good internal communications (Barnard 1938). While these basic concerns still occupy hospital CEOs today, they are also expected to be 'miracle managers' across many fronts. Hospitals must comply with a huge number of regulatory requirements including building regulations, financial audits, environmental regulations, fire safety, food safety, drug storage, and occupational health and safety. As well as these myriad of responsibilities managers must deal with the unexpected crises that regularly erupt. Some observers semi-facetiously claim that hospital managers have a shorter tenure than football coaches: a hospital scandal or a bad team loss respectively can end their appointment. Hospital managers (the coaches) also must share control with clinical leaders (the team captains) since the players won't take a step without the captain's approval. In addition, hospital managers have external regulators (health departments, commissions, accreditation agencies) looking over their shoulder: these meta-regulators require hospital managers as the internal regulators to put quality mechanisms in place and to report back on the outcomes.

Hospitals are dynamic not static organizations that undergo frequent changes. External pressures upon hospitals include demand-side factors such as changes in demographics, patterns of diseases and public expectations, and supply-side pressures such as advances in technology and knowledge, an ageing workforce, and financial constraints (McKee et al. 2002). Hospitals have undergone radical transformations since the 1980s: structural reorganizations with hospital mergers and closures, changes in public and private forms of ownership, internal restructuring of units and staffing, and redesigns in the delivery of patient care. Coping with change is a way of life for hospital staff so that restructuring fatigue is said to be common in the British NHS (Fulop et al. 2002). In a sample of 20 Australian teaching hospitals, 12 had undergone restructuring once over six years and four had been restructured twice (Braithwaite et al. 2006b). Efforts to introduce quality and safety reforms therefore often encounter jaded managers and cynical staff.

Hospital quality staff interviewed by this author said that in this rapidly changing environment hospital managers have a short attention span and want 'a quick fix' with a few one-off projects, rather than engaging in the continuous and systematic action required to consolidate a culture of safety within the hospital.

Their view was that the quality and safety of patient care was not the top concern of management although they conceded it was accorded more attention than in the past. This appears to be true internationally. For example, a survey of a nationally representative sample of chairs of boards of 1,000 US hospitals found that less than half rated quality of care as one of their two top priorities (Jha and Epstein 2010).

This chapter focuses on the internal regulation of safety and quality within hospitals by managers and clinical leaders. The distinctive nature of hospital governance is discussed as hospitals are organizations that present unique management challenges. Internal hospital governance is analysed in relation to three functions: regulating the hospital environment, regulating staff, and regulating procedures. The focus is upon activities that bear upon the safety and quality of patient care.

Hospital Governance

Models of hospital governance, replete with management theories and consultant nostrums, come and go without much systematic evaluation. Patterns of governance continue to change in response to the changing nature of hospital ownership, including whether hospitals are public or private entities or a type of public/private partnership. Public hospitals also go through cycles of being run by boards or health departments. During the 1990s, the United Kingdom transformed their centrally controlled NHS hospitals into semi-autonomous 'trusts' (Robinson and Dixon 1999), and central and eastern European countries also devolved centrally controlled hospitals to autonomous boards (Jakab et al. 2002). Australia in the early 2000s abolished hospital boards and brought autonomous public hospitals back under the direct control of health departments and ministers (in most states except Victoria). The national policy in 2010, however, is to return to hospital boards that will cover a network of local hospitals with health professionals included on the boards (Australian Government 2010). Hospitals have gone through a variety of governance arrangements although there is no empirical evidence on whether boards are more effective governors of clinical services than appointed departmental administrators (Wellington and Dugdale 2009: 115).

Who Runs Hospitals?

Hospitals are distinctive organizations in having highly professional employees who are more powerful than employees in other forms of organizations. Mintzberg classifies hospitals in his five types of organizations as 'professional bureaucracies' that rely on the skills and knowledge of professional staff in order to function (Henry 1989). Hospital management structures at the upper level are collegial rather than hierarchical although this does not mean a cosy management style. Hospitals have a long history of contested power relationships within the triumvirate of hospital manager, medical director and nurse director. Under the 'new public management' model of the 1980s ways of working in the public sector were profoundly changed, as power shifted away from professionals and into the hands of a new cadre of technocratic managers. The managerialist culture aimed to transform spenders into managers, make managers more accountable in flatter management structures, engineer competition in order to produce greater efficiency, link resources to results, and install performance indicators to assess productivity (Healy et al. 1999: 87). Hospital managers became preoccupied with whether the hospital was heading for a budget deficit, and more interested in the financial implications of a plan to increase elective surgery (more customers) than a plan to decrease hospital acquired infections (in the absence of financial incentives to reduce length of hospital stays). Hospital managers focused more on inputs, throughputs and outputs than patient outcomes.

Clinical services in most public hospitals now are organized under clinical directorates as the intermediate governing arrangement between the executive and departments, displacing the earlier forms of authority based around particular specialities. Clinical directorates span the traditional divisions of units organized around body parts (the heart) or particular conditions (cancer). A clinical directorate, such as paediatric services or surgical services, is led by one or more senior clinicians with some administrative support, which gathers together related wards, units and departments and is staffed by people from varied professional backgrounds (Braithwaite et al. 2006a). Clinical directors take on budgetary responsibility and are part of a collaborative approach to governance.

Tension between managers and clinicians remains a constant theme, and indeed a central theme in a recent review of NSW hospitals (Garling Report 2009), since despite changing models of governance they have different views of their world. Clinicians tend to see themselves as independent practitioners working within a system, rather than as part of that system and with responsibility for its workings (Walshe and Boaden 2006: 4). This perspective is reinforced in the visiting medical officer (VMO) arrangement where senior consultants are private physicians or surgeons who have visiting privileges in public hospitals and private hospitals and so are not full-time and active participants in hospital affairs. The divide also can be framed in Foucault's terms as city-state versus shepherd-flock philosophies (Dugdale 2008: 129). A city-state relationship is based on a social contract that involves consent between the ruler and the ruled. The clinicians' view of this social contract is that hospital managers are there to run the 'hotel' aspects and support the work of clinicians, and should not intrude in the clinicians' shepherd-flock model of pastoral care and direct relationship with patients.

Hospitals also are distinctive organizations in relation to the concept of rules within organizations. Much literature on regulation addresses why people obey rules, how to ensure compliance and the reasons for non-compliance (Tyler 1990). Formal and informal rules proliferate within organizations to ensure that things run smoothly. Health care organizations are not typical bureaucracies, however, and differ in how rules are viewed, devised and followed (Walshe and Boaden 2006). Charles Perrow, perhaps facetiously, claims that complex organizations that employ professionals need fewer rules, since professionals come with rules built into them during their professional education (Perrow 1972). Conflict arises when the internal rules of professionals differ from the rules of the organization; for example, medical values may conflict with treatment cost criteria.

A cultural issue in any attempt at rule-based regulation, however, is that doctors (especially surgeons) do not like being told what to do. As a hospital medical director said: 'Surgeons do not like rules and regulations but they are coming to realize that life has changed'. One of the ways that life has changed is the increased standardization of hospital procedures. A survey of hospital staff across several countries found that doctors, in contrast to nurses, dislike the trend towards rules and standardization (Degeling and Carr 2004). A survey in an Australian teaching hospital found that doctors took a combative view of the hospital culture while nurses perceived it as constructive, and that nurses were more positive about the introduction of a mandatory computerized provider entry system than doctors (Callen et al. 2009). The other way that life has changed is the push within hospitals towards participative governance and a bottom-up rather than top-down approach to quality improvement. When consultation runs its course, however, managers may need to issue a directive:

> We spent 18 months fluffing around. Then the staff representatives said 'Everyone's just waiting while we muck around. You've just got to say you're going to do it'. So we issued a directive. The clinical directors announced that the 'correct site, correct patient, correct procedure' would be implemented and no procedure would occur in the operating theatres of this hospital unless that occurred. We did it the week before the new lot of interns came on board so if there was a load of shit in response we would have dealt with it. The directive made clear when the new staff began that this is the way we do business and it went like a dream. (Director of Surgery)

Corporate and Clinical Governance

The ethos of corporate governance is that 'the buck stops here': the executive body of a hospital is responsible for patient care within the hospital and is responsible for making the appropriate arrangements for ensuring safe and high quality care. This is so whether the executive answers to an independent board or to the director of the health department. As public inquiries into medical scandals have warned, the executive cannot claim ignorance as a defence for poor clinical performance, and cannot claim that clinical care is the business of doctors not the executive. The Australian Securities Exchange defines corporate governance as 'the framework of rules, relationships, systems and processes within and by which authority is exercised and controlled in corporations' (Wellington and Dugdale 2009: 98). Within this broad framework of corporate governance, health systems have adopted the concept of clinical governance in an effort to engage senior clinicians in the tasks of hospital governance.

Clinical governance explicitly enrols clinical leaders in improving hospital performance, the aim being to make clinical directors, as well as hospital administrators, accountable for achieving cost effective patient outcomes (Olsen and Neale 2005). The concept emerged in the late 1990s in the British National Health Service in a convergence of the previously parallel tracks of managerialism and quality improvement. Clinical governance was defined as 'a framework through which the NHS organizations are accountable for continuously improving the quality of their services and safeguarding high standards of care by creating an environment in which excellence in clinical care will flourish' (Department of Health 1998). The intention was that a hospital would integrate financial control, service performance, and clinical quality (Scally and Donaldson 1998). More concisely, clinical governance is defined as 'corporate accountability for clinical performance' (Walshe 2000). Clinical governance potentially covers many activities intended to make links between inputs (money, staff, patients), throughputs (patient management), and quality (patient outcomes).

Clinical governance is interpreted in different ways so giving rise to some confusion. First, the policy is fuzzy in practice and although it makes managers and clinical leaders responsible for quality (who and why), it does not prescribe how to achieve quality (how, when and where). Second, clinical governance often is seen as a synonym for corporate governance although its original incarnation focused upon improving quality. Third, there is a philosophical divide between those who see clinical governance as a collaborative and self-regulatory mechanism, and those who see it as a disciplinary and inspectorial mechanism (Iedema et al. 2005). Fourth, many clinicians view it as a way to restore the power of doctors within hospitals. For example, several nursing leaders said that clinical governance in Australian hospitals is 'doctors' business' and nurse managers are shut out even though clinical directors leave patient safety issues to the nurses:

> Patient safety is seen as mainly a nursing issue especially as we are the ones who usually report adverse events. But we need medical leadership from committed clinical directors who are engaged in clinical governance and who will manage safety and quality programs so that junior doctors take notice, rather than leaving patient safety at the margins to be managed by nurses and quality officers who are shut out of clinical governance. (Nurse manager)

Clinical governance has statutory force in England under the *Health Act 1999* that placed a 'duty of quality' on CEOs to set up clinical governance structures in NHS organizations and report on the results (Edwards and Packham 1999). A later review found that virtually all NHS trusts had clinical governance structures in place, but progress in implementing quality procedures was patchy and the trusts lacked robust means of assessing improvements in patient care (National Audit Office 2003). Clinical governance now is being reframed in the wake of the Darzi Review that called for more power to clinicians to enable 'NHS staff to lead and manage the organizations in which they work' (Darzi 2009).

In Australia, state health departments endorsed a clinical governance policy and set up central or regional units to advise on implementation and to offer training (Braithwaite and Travaglia 2008). For example, Queensland Health promotes clinical governance through leadership programmes, a code of conduct, and regular staff surveys, while regional units assist the 37 district managers with several activities: a clinical risk management plan, credentialing and privileging of staff, clinical review and audit, education and research, consumer complaint management, and managing staff performance (Duckett 2007; Duckett 2009). But it seems that several years of clinical governance in New South Wales have not bridged the divide between managers and clinicians. The Garling Report characterized the public hospital system as 'on the brink' of breakdown and with poor working relations between managers and clinicians (Garling Report 2009). For example, a survey of NSW public hospitals had found huge gaps in trust in that only 17 per cent of doctors and 33 per cent of nurses trusted their managers compared to a national workplace average of 70 per cent, while senior clinicians wanted a return to the local hospital boards that had been abolished in 2005 (Stewart and Dwyer 2009). While centrally imposed clinical governance does not appear spectacularly successful, there are many successful local examples of engagement by clinical governance directors in quality improvement activities.

Regulating the Hospital Environment

Managers seek to regulate the hospital environment in several ways in order to promote safety and quality, including training clinical leaders, managing risk, implementing quality improvement methods, and monitoring a patient safety culture.

Train Clinicians in Leadership

The medical profession traditionally enlists clinical leaders in changing clinical performance since medicine is a hierarchical profession so that change has to be endorsed by prestigious doctors. As one hospital CEO said: 'You can't underestimate the role of the clinical leader in putting the message into practice'. Champions for change are sought among the ranks of senior clinical leaders since 'people only listen to grey-haired male consultants'. Getting clinical leaders to engage in governance is not easy, however, as many senior clinicians are disenchanted with hospital management (Jorm et al. 2006). Further, clinicians have not been trained in management and leadership. State health departments now take clinical leadership seriously and some, such as Queensland Health, have embarked on extensive training programmes (see Box 6.1)

Box 6.1 Leadership training in Queensland Health

Queensland Health set up a Workplace Culture and Leadership Centre in 2006 that has embarked upon programmes to train managers and clinicians in leadership skills. Training involves two-day residential workshops in leadership qualities and activities and self-reflection on experiences in implementing leadership behaviours. Workplace culture surveys are to be undertaken every two years on staff attitudes and morale in order to track progress in cultural change. The intention is to train over 5,000 staff in leadership skills.

Source: Crethar, Phillips, Stafford et al. 2009

While an effective leadership style varies depending on the person and situation, for example, whether authoritarian, democratic, or laissez faire (Burns 1978), clinical leaders now are urged to be more participative. A health authority CEO maintained that authority in hospitals is becoming less hierarchical: 'It is a matter of delegating authority to the right person and empowering that person with back up from the head of the unit'. While clinical leaders adopt a collegial style with their professional peers, they are more authoritarian with junior doctors and other health professionals seen as subordinate. Different regulatory actions flow from different leadership styles. For example, some hospital managers said that they usually enlisted a clinical leader to have 'a little fireside chat' with a recalcitrant doctor, thus shifting regulatory action from line management enforcement to collegial peer pressure:

> My preference is not a sanctions approach but to go for gentle and gradual change. So if nine out of my ten surgeons follow the protocol and the tenth one does not, there is peer pressure on that person to do it. If one surgeon is not performing, then another will go and have a chat with him. (CEO, private hospital)

Manage Clinical Risk

Risk management is the process of identifying risk, assessing the extent of exposure to risk, and then developing strategies to manage that risk. Different types of risk management apply to different types of risk. For example, traditional risk management focuses on the risks to individuals/organizations and their insurers stemming from physical or legal causes (for example, accidents, lawsuits), while financial risk management focuses on risks that can be managed using financial instruments. Risk management usually applies a prioritization process whereby the risks with the greatest loss and the greatest probability of occurring are addressed first, and risks with a lower probability of occurrence and lower loss are addressed later. Hospitals also apply the concept of clinical risk management to reducing medical error to reduce the likelihood of the hospital and/or its staff being sued by an aggrieved patient (Vincent 2001).

> The biggest risk for our hospital is doing the wrong consent or getting the operating list wrong. It is very easy when you are writing orthopaedics consents all day to put right instead of left, and likewise for the surgeon's secretary to type left when she means right. You would be surprised at how many errors like that we find. This is a big problem if you do everything according to the documentation. (CEO, private hospital)

Australian governments now require their agencies, including public hospitals, to devise risk management plans that identify likely risks and set out ways to minimize these risks. The NSW Department for Health, for example, produced guidelines for health facilities to devise their clinical risk management strategy in three high risk areas: maternity services, neurosurgery, and rural general practice. State health departments also require their public hospitals to have a risk management strategy for coping with a sudden influx of patients. Such an emergency may be a virulent infection taking hold in a hospital, a disaster such as a bushfire or cyclone, a terrorist attack, or an epidemic or pandemic, such as recurrent waves of influenza.

Engage in Quality Improvement Techniques

Quality is 'a seductive and slippery concept of management' (Wilkinson and Willmott 1995). The task of the manager is to enable people at the front line to find ways to organize their work better, and then to test whether these changes produce improvements. Quality improvement techniques were developed in large-scale manufacturing industries from the 1950s onwards by quality management 'gurus' such as WE Deming. Japan's take on continual improvement (Kaizen) in the manufacturing sector was that it was easier and more effective to work within workplace cultural boundaries and to make small improvements rather than aim for major transformational change. Continuous improvement is a key concept in quality principles and practices. Quality models now used in health sectors that incorporate this idea include Total Quality Management (TQM) and Continuous Quality Improvement (CQI).

Continuous quality improvement (CQI) is a management process whereby products and services are constantly evaluated and improved in the light of agreed goals, such as efficiency, effectiveness and responsiveness to customers. The concept requires identifying what is meant by quality, deciding how best to achieve it, and then monitoring progress towards a high standard. Managers are enjoined to be facilitators and to encourage and praise rather than inspect and rebuke. This approach leaves people freer from procedural rules since the work unit decides how best to achieve the agreed quality of service and/or product. Outcomes must be monitored, however, since work practices must be continually adjusted ('re-engineering') to ensure ongoing improvements. CQI expects dynamic management and unceasing vigilance. Its main messages are that leadership is essential, change is ongoing, and scientific methods improve daily work processes (Blumenthal and Kilo 1998).

Quality techniques were imported into the health sector in the 1980s including its central and ambitious idea, continuous quality improvement (CQI), but these techniques do not offer a single prescription or neat set of tools. The tools adopted and adapted by health sectors include benchmarking, checklists, the Plan-Do-Study-Act cycle, statistical process control, and various flowcharts and diagrams (Boaden 2006: 41–65). Measuring their impact requires measures of clinical performance, such as clinical outcomes, rates of adverse events, and rates of patient satisfaction. More hospital managers now are using CQI techniques as quality has been pushed higher up the public agenda by public inquiries and public reporting. CQI is a good fit in the health sector in the sense that the model engages front line professionals in learning how to improve their own practice and in a way that encourages creativity and autonomy. While quality improvement remains a voluntary activity on the part of health care organizations in many countries, including Australia, legislation in some European countries requires hospitals to have quality improvement procedures in place. Accreditation agencies also recommend or require quality improvement procedures (see Chapter 7).

Some critics doubted that quality techniques designed for factory production lines could be applied in hospitals, apart from building maintenance, laundry and meals production. Budgetary pressures upon hospitals also mean that cost competes with quality, clinical governance goals notwithstanding. Some argue that hospital managers generally do not engage in the interminable pursuit of continuous quality improvement unless galvanized into action by a medical scandal:

> Don Berwick has said that before organizations can commit themselves fully to continuous improvements in the quality of their goods and services, they must first experience a forceful reminder of their own mortality: a brush with death … the fact is that very few health care providers have experienced a true brush with death; even fewer have exhausted the enticing menu of quick fixes. (Blumenthal and Kilo 1998: 638)

Monitor Patient Safety Attitudes and Practices

Several instruments have been developed to enable managers to measure the culture of patient safety within their hospital and the extent of patient safety practices (Colla et al. 2005). Measuring and monitoring an organization's patient safety culture helps identify areas that need improvement. Questionnaires administered to staff can be repeated at time intervals – although a repeat questionnaire risks a learned response. The US Agency for Healthcare Research and Quality (AHRQ) instrument asks respondents about 12 dimensions: overall perceptions of safety, frequency of events reported, supervisor/manager expectations and actions promoting safety, organizational learning/continuous improvement, teamwork within units, communication openness, feedback and communication about error, non-punitive response to error, safe staffing, management support for patient safety, teamwork across hospital units, and protocols for patient handoffs and transitions (Agency for Healthcare Research and Quality 2006). The AHRQ website provides scores on a pilot survey in 20 hospitals; for example, 77 per cent of respondents agreed that 'My supervisor/manager overlooks patient safety problems that happen over and over'. The website offers a database where hospitals can benchmark their results, compare scores with other hospitals, and track progress over future surveys.

The UK National Patient Safety Agency instrument enables an organization to assess its patient safety culture, compare with others, and track changes over time (National Patient Safety Agency 2004). A Canadian instrument, the Patient Safety Culture Tool, assesses organizational practices, systems and processes in relation to nine patient safety culture elements so that managers can identify areas that need improvement. The organization can then see where it might fit on a typology of a safety culture maturity model: a pathological organization has no safety systems in place; a reactive organization has some piecemeal systems; a calculative organization responds only to specific events; a proactive organization has a comprehensive evidence-based approach; and a generative organization has a positive and creative safety culture (Fleming and Wentzell 2008).

Regulating Staff

Health care is highly labour intensive and the quality of patient care depends upon individual health professionals. Hospital managers must pay careful attention, therefore, to selecting, deploying, and supporting staff. Hospitals have begun to formalize activities such as credentialing and privileging, performance agreements, safe staffing practices, and redesigning patient management under multidisciplinary teams.

Establishing a Credentials Procedure

Many hospitals have a credentialing committee that examines the qualifications and experience of a health professional applying for a particular position. Such committees usually follow a formal appointments procedure and inquire into competence as well as formal qualifications. Arising out of the competency movement, credentialing seeks to define competence in terms of specific tasks that a person is able to successfully undertake, not just whether they possess the appropriate formal qualification:

> Credentialing is a formal process used by employers to verify the qualifications, experience, professional standing and other relevant professional attributes of health practitioners, for the purpose of forming a view about their competence, performance and professional suitability to provide safe, high quality health care

> services within specific organizational environments. (Australian Council for Safety and Quality in Health Care 2004: 3)

A credentials committee should also examine the qualifications and experience of a specialist before he/she is given practising rights (privileges) to treat patients as a visiting medical officer. Problems can occur when an appointments committee functions in an ad hoc way and does not follow standard procedures. For example, there are anecdotes of specialists being offered hospital 'privileges' solely on the word of their hospital consultant golfing partner. Threatened or actual withdrawal of visiting or operating privileges is a powerful sanction.

> We have sanctions that we consider and potentially could apply. It might be withdrawal of a surgeon's operating privileges. It is tricky because these are owner surgeons. But if somebody is not performing it reflects badly on the others. Somebody might say 'I've heard bad things about X in your hospital'. The other surgeons don't like that. (CEO, private hospital)

The related procedure of clinical privileging involves an employer defining the scope of clinical practice of an individual for working within that organization, either as an employee or as a visiting specialist. An employer should check whether the person has the appropriate qualifications and experience and also define the tasks that the professional is employed to undertake. For example, registration with a medical board and membership of the Royal Australasian College of Surgeons does not mean that a surgeon is competent to carry out any type of surgery. Defining the scope of practice means defining what tasks an individual will be allowed to undertake in the organization as opposed to defining the qualification that is required for that position.

Public inquiries have revealed that employers do not always check the veracity of an applicant's qualifications or make a proper assessment of their competence. Given increasing medical workforce mobility, failures by registration boards to check qualifications, cases of fake doctors and nurses, and lack of mandatory requirements to update professional education, employers should check the qualifications and competence of prospective employees. A meta-regulator, such as a health department or accreditation agency, should require an organization to have formal credentialing and scope of practice procedures and should check whether these are used.

An Australian national standard for credentialing and defining the scope of practice of medical practitioners has been developed for use in public and private hospitals (Australian Council for Safety and Quality in Health Care 2004). Employers now pay more attention to credentialing and privileging because they cannot assume that the registration procedures of boards and colleges guarantee an individual's qualifications let alone their 'fitness to practise' in a particular position – although this situation will improve with the advent of a national registration and accreditation scheme. Formal credentialing procedures by employers currently are a better guarantee of the quality of services delivered by health practitioners than are formal professional registration procedures (Productivity Commission 2005: 110). NSW Health in 2005, for example, issued a suite of policies on the appointment of visiting practitioners and staff specialists, delineation of clinical privileges for visiting staff, and requirements for performance reviews of visiting medical officers. While a self-evidently sensible procedure for an employer to undertake before appointing a person, a competency focus tends to involve a tight definition of tasks, and may have a downside in cases where a narrow definition is not necessary. Narrow task demarcations run counter to the call for fewer demarcation disputes and greater flexibility in the health sector (Productivity Commission 2005).

Negotiate and Enforce Performance Agreements

Governments can regulate staff in public sector health agencies either directly as employers through budgetary control and management or indirectly through industrial relations agreements. In Australia, some industrial relations bargaining shifted from the central to the enterprise level under the *Workplace Relations Act 1996* (Cth), but much of the health workforce in public hospitals remain covered by occupation-specific and state-wide awards and enterprise agreements, often based on collective bargaining between unions and employers (Willis et al. 2005). Industrial relations awards and agreements focus on conditions of employment, such as pay, hours of work and leave entitlements, however, rather than prescribing how work should be done.

CEOs of public and private hospitals in Australia usually have fixed-term employment contracts that often include performance clauses that make them accountable for improving safety and quality. For example, the NSW health department has a clause in its agreements with CEOs that requires them to reduce the number of adverse events in their hospitals. Hospitals can set performance requirements in their staff employment contracts but are cautious about enforcement given the power of professional associations and unions. Patient safety advocates have proposed that hospital managers use performance agreements with clinicians as a mechanism for regulating safety and quality (Australian Council for Safety and Quality in Health Care 2005). Private sector managers have more leeway in invoking performance agreements but some prefer to use reputational pressure in their dealings with hospital CEOs:

> We don't issue central directives. We work in other ways. We give hospital CEOs the performance evidence and add a bit of peer pressure. So on adverse incidents, they get comparative reports on incidents across all hospitals plus their risk ratings. The CEO of a hospital says 'whoops'. A head office manager then might phone and say, 'Joanne, do you need any help from us?' It is always help and support. (Manager, private hospital chain)

Ensure Safe Staffing

Safe staffing refers to the relationship between clinical outcomes and human resource issues, such as long working hours, fatigue and heavy workloads (McDonald 2008). Long working hours are regarded as an occupational health and safety issue for staff and a quality and safety risk for patients (Institute of Medicine 2004). Further, professionals who perceive themselves as overworked and unsupported are unlikely to be receptive to exhortations to improve their performance. Working long hours remains the norm in the medical profession, however, and a rite of passage for junior doctors to demonstrate that they are made of 'the right stuff'. In other industries, such as aviation and trucking, working hours are circumscribed and monitored since fatigue is considered to compromise safety. In relation to occupational health and safety, employers have a legal responsibility, and a risk management responsibility (to avoid being sued by staff for corporate violations of working hours), to ensure safe working conditions for their staff. Fatigue is a major concern for health professionals who work long hours often on rotating shifts. Achieving safe staffing in the health sector is problematic, however, given shortages of health professionals and consequent heavy workloads and long working hours (Joyce et al. 2004; Productivity Commission 2005).

The hospital workplace can be a stressful environment that may impinge upon the physical and mental health of its staff. For example, a survey of staff in several hospitals in the United Kingdom and in Australia found that lay managers and nurses experienced higher levels of anxiety than other hospital staff and also the general population (Degeling and Carr 2004). Health professionals also believe that unsafe staffing causes adverse events. For example, surgeons interviewed about the causes of surgical adverse events said that excessive workload/inadequate staffing was a contributing factor in 22 per cent of incidents, lack of supervision in 21 per cent, and fatigue in 16 per cent (Gawande et al. 2003).

The main instruments used to regulate working hours in health systems include tort law, labour law, collective agreements (co-regulation), self-regulation by professional and industry bodies, and government regulation, but the main regulatory response is to seek to cap working hours although this is difficult to apply and to police (McDonald 2008). Self-regulation by professional and industry groups generally has proved ineffective (Gerrity 2001). Regulations promulgated in New York state in the late 1980s after the widely publicized death of a patient prohibited trainee doctors working more than 80 hours per week and more than 24 consecutive hours, but later inspections found that these regulations were widely flouted (DeBuono and Osten 1998). The European Commission in 1993 prescribed the Working Time Directive (Directive 93/104/EC) that states that a working week must not exceed 48 hours with no longer than eight hour shifts (so much stricter than the NY regulation), and was amended in 2000 to include trainee doctors who work notoriously long hours. The financial impact upon hospitals has been substantial and a transition period on trainee doctors was agreed as some countries estimated they would need 24 per cent more doctors (Baeten and Jorens 2006).

In Australia, hospitals would have trouble complying with an EU-type working time directive in terms of finding additional staff and salaries. No jurisdictions have passed legislation on safe working hours in hospitals and many professionals work longer than the hours stipulated in awards and work contracts (Australian Council for Safety and Quality in Health Care 2003). The Australian Medical Association (AMA) in 1999 proposed a code of practice on work hours for hospital doctors, but a 2001 survey found this was ignored as 78 per cent of junior doctors worked long hours, despite clinical studies showing impaired performance after 18 hours without sleep. The AMA President said that work rosters in many hospitals were unsafe, codes of practice were ignored, and statutory law may be the only way to enforce safe working hours. Conditions were only slightly better in 2006 as a survey found that 62 per cent of public hospital doctors were working unsafe hours with some averaging 78 hour weeks (Australian Medical Association 2006).

Workloads and nurse-patient ratios are a longstanding industrial issue for nursing unions who aim to tie pay awards to caps on workloads. Heavy workloads not only impact negatively upon nurses but also on their patients. In relation to patient safety, a structured review of the literature found worse measures of patient outcomes, including mortality, as nurse workloads increased (Seago 2001). An extensive study of nurse working conditions and patient outcomes in US hospitals found a 7 per cent risk of patient mortality for each additional patient added to a nurse's average workload (Aiken and al 2002). A four-year study of workload and patient outcomes in a UK intensive care unit found increases in mortality were explained partly by excess staff workloads (Tarnow-Mordi et al. 2000). Hospital overcrowding is a proxy measure for a heavy staff workload. An accumulating body of research shows that the number of adverse events increases with overcrowding, or access block, defined as a lack of available inpatient beds for emergency department patients (Miro et al. 1999).

Deploy Staff in Multidisciplinary Teams

Personnel are deployed in many ways in hospitals. From the late twentieth century, however, people increasingly have worked together in multidisciplinary teams. Line management was switched from the leader of an occupational group, such as the chief nurse, to the leader of the work team. Teamwork generally is regarded now as the norm in providing high quality care in a complex hospital environment. A hospital patient today is cared for by teams of people from different professions as well as other occupational groups such as technicians, porters, cleaners and cooks. Multidisciplinary teams also have expanded and become more complex with increasing specialization and now include far more than the traditional trio of doctor, nurse and social worker. New members include many types of medical and surgical specialists as well as physiotherapist, occupational therapist, nutritionist and pharmacist. Improving safety and quality requires agreements between different groups of professionals

> I keep saying 'surgery is a team sport'. The team in the operating theatre consists of an anaesthetist, a surgeon and a nurse, that's the team and the team have to agree. The other problem in running a surgical department is getting all the specialities to agree. (Director of Surgery)

Prompted in large part by efforts to improve cost-efficiency, the reorganization of hospital work in the United States in the 1990s was dubbed 're-engineering' since the approach drew upon industrial task design, involved redesigning job responsibilities, determining who does the work and where the work is located, and by what processes or patterns the work will be done (Champy 1996). The re-engineering concept was unpopular among nurses who regarded it as a disguise for downsizing and de-skilling nursing staff, and later evaluations in the context of worsening nurse-patient ratios showed little discernable benefits for patients in terms of better care and better health outcomes (Walston and Kimberley 1997). Re-engineering studies did endorse the management of hospital patients by multidisciplinary teams rather than by single consultants or single specialties, however, and this arrangement has endured despite its human relations difficulties.

Effective teamwork is a long-standing and often vexed issue in hospitals. A large research literature examines how effective multidisciplinary teamwork can be developed among health professionals given varying power relationships, professional philosophies, knowledge and expertise (Ovretveit et al. 1997). Barriers to good teamwork include hierarchical relations, different disciplinary cultures, and rigid task demarcations. Leaders and teams do not mesh if clinical directors cling to old-style authoritarian leadership when other professionals want a more democratic style of teamwork. Power relationships between doctors and nurses also are exacerbated by gender relationships since many male doctors, at least in the past, expected female nurses to do as they were told.

Lack of stability in team membership is another barrier to developing good team working relationships, especially in large teaching hospitals, given the regular turnover of trainees, high employment turnover among nurses, and regular shift changes of staff. One solution to discontinuity in patient care is to assign a 'named nurse' or 'primary nurse' to each patient, and another is to assign case managers to coordinate the care of patients with complex treatment needs (Leung et al. 2004).

Understanding power relationships between the different occupations and ranks is essential because the working relationship between leaders and their teams can have a direct impact upon patient safety. A British airline pilot has described how the aviation industry changed its culture when they recognized that teamwork, or the lack of it, was a key factor in air safety. The captains of the huge passenger jets, the 'Atlantic barons', were required to shift from autocrat to team player and to accept questioning from junior pilots, since the evidence was that mistakes occurred when captains did not listen to their crews. 'Pilots now accept that professional competence in CRM [crew resource management] is as important as their technical knowledge and flying ability' (Johnson 2001 563). An operating theatre presents similar teamwork issues in the willingness of a surgeon to listen to a nurse when she/he questions whether the surgeon is about to operate on the correct patient, site or procedure. The implementation of the correct patient/site protocol brought power relationship issues in operating teams to the fore:

> I think the nurses should not hand the surgeon a scalpel until time out is completed. But the nurses say, 'We are not responsible for the surgery and the surgeons will abuse us. We'll say 'team-timeout' and the surgeon will say, get lost, a lot of nonsense'. So if the nurse says, 'No, I can't give you the knife', the surgeon will say, 'Yes, give me the bloody knife'. So nurses are reluctant to do it because they are at the bottom of the pile. (Director of Surgery)

Multidisciplinary teams became the norm rather than the exception in large acute care general hospitals when the management of patient care around a single-specialty, such as cardiology, became out-dated given older and sicker hospital patients with more co-morbidities (Hillman 1999). The management of patients, including 'patient flow' through a hospital and its treatment modalities, has been reorganized radically given dramatic advances in diagnostics and in medical and surgical treatment, and much quicker throughput of patients. These changes include grouping patients in terms of care requirements rather than medical conditions and creating multidisciplinary teams with the capacity to provide holistic and better quality care. These teams manage their own internal regulatory procedures for monitoring the quality of their patient care processes and outcomes, such as peer review, case meetings, and performance indicators. The following are examples of hospital teams where studies have demonstrated that they generally achieve better quality patient care.

Elderly care teams have a long history in hospitals. Geriatricians helped pioneer the multidisciplinary team concept in order to better manage the complex health and social care needs of older patients, and these teams survive as geriatric consultation services in the mainstream hospital treatment of older patients as well as in specialist aged care wards (Healy et al. 1999). Systematic reviews have found that aged care multidisciplinary teams provide better quality patient care, although no robust studies have specifically examined their impact upon patient safety (Agostini et al. 2001).

Intensive care teams are an example of grouping patients with similar nursing needs. Patients with intensive care requirements, especially post-surgery, generally are managed in intensive care units that are regarded as improving patient outcomes (Rothschild 2001).

Rapid response teams, or medical emergency teams (METs) have been set up to respond rapidly to medical emergencies around a hospital, including patients whose conditions are deteriorating, with the results showing evidence of improved patient outcomes (Kerridge and Saul 2003). Criteria for call-out are being developed as are systemic changes to improve responses by hospital staff, including clearer observation charts and better patient monitoring procedures.

Such teams are cited as a mechanism for reducing adverse events among critically ill patients, for example, some studies have shown a 15 per cent decrease in cardiac arrests (Leape and Berwick 2005). Trauma teams are assembled in some hospitals when ambulances bring in severe trauma cases.

Infection control teams have been set up in many hospitals to counter the alarming increase in hospital-acquired infections. A UK report called for infection control teams to undertake systematic surveillance and intervention programmes in every NHS hospital, and to aim for a 15 per cent reduction in infection, pointing out that despite ample evidence that the simplest and oldest methods still work best, staff compliance with a handwashing protocol remained poor (National Audit Office 2000). The challenge for infection control teams is to put into practice well-known principles for reducing hospital acquired infections by using a variety of regulatory interventions to bring about behavioural and systemic change (Spelman 2002).

Regulating Procedures

Hospital managers and clinical leaders increasingly are required to implement mechanisms within the hospital to monitor the safety and quality of clinical performance. The main tools used are clinical audit, performance indicators, adverse event reporting and critical incident analysis.

Embed Clinical Audit

Clinical audit is a traditional quality tool within a hospital and a key activity under the rubric of clinical governance. An audit means 'an official examination of accounts' (Oxford Dictionary). The term implies that clinical audit as a review of clinical performance is institutionalized within a health sector, whether undertaken by internal or external auditors, and whether conducted as a regular review of patient cases or as a more quantitative procedure. A clinical audit cycle involves measuring aspects of the clinical process, comparing results to predefined standards, and making the necessary adjustments to practice and/or standards (Chief Medical Officer 2006: 14). Peer review is more an internal process and generally more informal and episodic, such as mortality and morbidity (M&M) meetings that review interesting cases. Inquiries into substandard hospitals generally find that they lack both a robust clinical audit procedure and a robust peer review procedure.

As an internal monitoring procedure, clinical audit aims to pick up poor quality or unsafe practice on the part of individuals and work units. It may involve collecting and analysing performance indicators and comparing performance over time and with units in other hospitals. Health professionals see clinical audit as a quality strategy not a disciplinary strategy and as a confidential not public process. Formal quality committees in some countries can apply for confidentiality protection under qualified privilege legislation, such as in Australia, although most peer review activities proceed without such protection. It is not clear to what extent formal clinical audit is undertaken as part of routine clinical governance practice in hospitals, but there is increasing pressure upon hospitals to institutionalize the practice. Clinical audit procedures generally are believed to be a powerful regulatory tool:

> One thing I find really potent with clinicians is to give them data about their own performance in relation to everyone else. That can drive personal responsibility and accountability. They see their outcomes next to a benchmark for another hospital or state. That gets them to engage. They say, 'oh that can't be right, blah-blah-blah'. But they start thinking about it. I see people looking at piles of notes in their room as to why their data is not better than other peoples. So I think benchmarking is a potent tool. (Hospital CEO)

Monitor Performance Indicators

Hospitals are being pushed to collect clinical performance data on hospital units and individuals. The area of performance indicators is a rapidly expanding regulatory strategy (see Chapter 8). Hospitals can no longer continue to work in complacent isolation and ignorance but increasingly have access to national and international clinical performance measures as a benchmark for comparing their own performance. Given access to industry performance metrics, hospitals can conduct a clinical audit against the overall standard on their high volume cases and track progress, such as on cases of patients with fractured neck of femur (Degeling and Carr 2004). The World Health Organization seeks to assist hospitals to regulate their own performance through the Performance Assessment Tool for Quality Improvement in Hospitals (PATH) now being piloted to identify which of 18 performance indicators are valid and reliable measures of quality (for example, caesarean section rate, readmission), and also are feasible for a hospital to collect and track (Groene et al. 2008). Hospital managers are well aware of the power of reputational pressure as a tool for managing clinicians:

> We started a blitz on safe surgery in late 2006. We began monitoring compliance with the protocol across all nine surgical units. These data tell unit heads what is really happening because they often think their staff are doing things when they are not. So if a unit was aberrant then it was obvious to their peers. The results have steadily improved with up to 98 per cent compliance now in some units. We will continue regular audits because if you don't people take things for granted. (Hospital medical director)

Report Adverse Events in Hospitals

Adverse event reporting has become a key regulatory strategy and many countries have an electronic adverse event reporting systems (see Chapter 8). Meta-regulators, such as health departments and accreditors, increasingly require hospitals to link to such a reporting system. A staff member can report an adverse event to an electronic database maintained by the hospital or directly to an external reporting system that feeds back regular analyses of incidents and trends to hospitals. In Australia, all public hospitals link to reporting systems run by state health departments, although the actual reporting of adverse events is voluntary on the part of staff, except arguably, in the case of serious adverse events. The Advanced Incident Management System (AIMS), developed by the Australian Patient Safety Foundation, is the most commonly used software. The usual procedure is for a staff member to enter information (either minimal or detailed) on the incident (an actual incident or near miss) electronically on a database or phone through the information to a central number. The type of incident covers a spectrum of activities, behaviours, equipment and factors in both acute and non-acute settings. The AIMS Analyser provides customized and standard reporting options. Confidential information on those involved in the incident can be protected under state quality assurance legislation. The software enables data to be aggregated in various ways and analysed so that units receive comparative information on their performance. A Severity Assessment Code (SAC) scoring matrix measures the consequences for patients of an incident (five categories) and the probability of recurrence (five categories).

Much effort goes into improving reporting rates by hospital staff. For example, a South Australian hospital increased reporting three-fold (nurses generated 87 per cent of reports) after reducing the report form to one page, running training programmes, and training managers on giving feedback to staff (Selim et al. 2005), and a NSW study also showed that training improves reporting rates (Braithwaite et al. 2010).

What then follows? Hospitals use adverse event reports mainly as a quality tool given the limitations of reporting as a measurement tool (see Chapter 8). The first step is to identify an incident; the second step is to analyse the causes; the third step is to fix the cause/s of the problem to prevent any future occurrences; and a fourth step is publicize the lessons learned so that others can avoid the same errors (Leape 2002). The Victorian health department stepped up its oversight after a review of hospitals found that some had poor systems for reporting, investigating and seeking to prevent future errors (Auditor General Victoria 2005: 3); New South Wales hospitals are said to make good use of the data as a management and quality tool (Braithwaite et al. 2006a). The key question for patient safety is what action follows an incident report? It is unclear to what extent hospitals act on the reports. This may require an incident or group of incidents to be investigated and an intervention plan developed using methods such as critical incident analysis.

Conduct Critical Incident Analysis

Critical incident analysis, including Root Cause Analysis (RCA), is a systematic method for learning from errors, the method originating in industrial psychology and human factors engineering. Some prefer the term systems analysis to 'root cause' since the procedure looks for systemic causes (for example, rostering practices) not just behavioural causes (for example, a tired surgeon). Root cause or critical incident analysis has been adopted as one of the main clinical governance tools for engaging clinicians in taking responsibility for redesigning systems in order to improve clinical practice (Iedema 2003). An incident analysis is an additional step in learning from a reported incident since the report alone usually does not provide sufficient information about likely causes and solutions. The goals of root cause analysis are to find out what happened, why it happened, and what to do to prevent it from happening again (National Center for Patient Safety 2007).

The US Joint Commission requires its accredited hospitals to undertake analyses of sentinel events and provides a guide on how to conduct an RCA, and the UK National Patient Safety Agency also has developed an RCA toolkit and training programme (National Patient Safety Agency 2006). Jim Bagian of the US Department of Veterans Affairs has trained many people in an RCA method of investigation (Bagian et al. 2001). Australian state health departments run RCA training programmes that mostly draw on Veterans Affairs material (NSW Department of Health 2004). New South Wales legislation requires an RCA investigation for all serious adverse events (a SAC1 code) and the RCA team is covered by statutory privilege.

As the consequences of an adverse event can be considerable for all concerned, a hospital should have clear procedures for looking after all the people involved (patient, family and staff) as well as taking action to prevent future recurrences (Runciman et al. 2007: chapter 8, 9). A critical incident analysis is done on more minor incidents and a full-blown RCA on serious incidents. Hospitals do not embark on an RCA if the incident is likely to involve disciplinary action. Although RCA teams apply for legal clinical privilege in order to protect confidentiality, investigations still remain constrained by staff fears that they will be 'named, blamed and shamed'. The intention of an RCA investigation, however, is to avoid blame, to focus upon system failure not people failure, and to suggest feasible solutions. An RCA procedure usually involves the appointment of a small team, three to five people, including the appropriate clinical staff. They meet at least three times, first, to establish the known facts and agree on questions and interviews, second, to pool gathered information, and third, to develop statements about causes and recommended action.

Since a large teaching hospital undertakes many RCAs each year, the procedure is a substantial investment in staff time. A root cause analysis is a potentially powerful regulatory activity, however, since it brings together key people in a strategic node of action who deliberate on the actions that were taken, or not taken, that produced the error, and who can draw upon considerable systemic wisdom on how to put things right. Such a case study can offer a vivid illustration of the things that go wrong and the various paths that can be taken to prevent future occurrences. There are no studies so far on the extent to which a hospital implements RCA recommendations but hospital managers believe that RCAs are influential in changing behaviour:

> These incidents become widely known around the place and everyone thinks, 'Oh god, that could easily have happened to me and it could have been a disaster'. Fortunately, it wasn't in this case. We did a root cause analysis to find out why it went wrong. It was all the things that are well documented in the literature as contributing to adverse events. There wasn't a registrar assisting, the operating list order had been changed, the patient was already anaesthetized before the surgeon examined her, the consent form was not clear, and the surgeon did not communicate very well with the operating team. (Hospital medical director)

Whistle-blowers: A Failure of Management

A motto of the advocacy group, Whistle-blowers Australia, quotes Edmund Burke: 'All that is needed for evil to prosper is for people of good will to do nothing'. Health professionals generally are people of good will and some have felt compelled to blow the whistle on their colleagues and/or hospital in order to protect patients. A whistle-blower is defined as 'a person who discloses wrongdoing to another person, whether within or outside the organization in which the wrongdoing has occurred' (MPConsulting 2004: 3). Whistle-blowing is accepted under law as a legitimate and necessary avenue for an employee to address wrongdoing, if their organization fails through its internal regulatory procedures to do so. Virtually all Australian jurisdictions over the last decade have enacted legislation that purportedly offers protection to whistle-blowers (Kerridge et al. 2005: 171). Variation in the extent to which whistle-blowers are protected, and in what circumstance, as well as the often punitive responses of their employers, has prompted calls for a national guideline that health care organizations can use in handling public disclosures by their employees (MPConsulting 2004). Whistle-blowers who disclose wrong-doing in public and private organizations generally are subjected to considerable negative pressure, including from their colleagues, as well as attempts to discredit them.

Whistle-blowers have instigated several public inquiries into hospital scandals by alerting the media after they failed to get a satisfactory response within their organization. The inquiry into the Bristol Royal Infirmary in the United Kingdom was triggered by an anaesthetist, Steve Bolsin, after his repeated attempts to alert the hospital to the high paediatric surgical death rate were rebuffed by management (Bolsin 1998; Smith 1998; Rennie and Crosby 2002; Bolsin 2003). The inquiry into the Bundaberg Hospital and Dr Jayant Patel was instigated by a nurse, Toni Hoffman (see Box 6.2), whose repeatedly expressed concerns about botched surgical procedures were ignored by hospital managers.

Box 6.2 Toni Hoffman: Australia's Local Hero 2006

'Toni Hoffman showed great courage and ethical conviction as an advocate for patient safety at the Bundaberg Hospital in Queensland. After studying nursing in Australia, Hoffman travelled to London to undertake further training in midwifery and intensive care. She worked in intensive care for two decades in both Australia and Saudi Arabia before being appointed Nursing Unit Manager of the Intensive Care Unit at Bundaberg Hospital. In 2002 she also completed a masters degree in bioethics. For two years Hoffman consistently raised concerns about the patient safety record of a surgeon at the hospital. She faced inaction and resistance and experienced considerable personal stress but held true to her convictions.

In 2005 she took her concerns to politician Rob Messenger, who raised the matter in the Queensland Parliament. The result was the Davies Commission into public hospitals in Queensland and criminal charges against the surgeon. In 2007 Hoffman was made a member of the Order of Australia'.

Source: Australian of the Year website

Whistle-blowing should be protected as a necessary avenue for addressing wrongs despite being 'an extremely unpleasant experience' for the whistle-blower (Bolsin 2003: 294) and a traumatic and costly method of righting a wrong (Johnstone 2004). It is an avenue of last resort, since an array of regulatory mechanisms in Australian hospitals appears to have failed, including hospital accreditation, peer review, adverse event reporting, mortality reviews, regular case audits, and risk-management strategies (Faunce and Bolsin 2004).

Conclusion

Better Quality Management

Hospital managers can choose among a large array of quality improvement techniques. Surveying staff on the extent of a patient safety culture within the organization raises consciousness on quality and safety issues and indicates the organizational attributes and practices that could be strengthened. Quality frameworks, including continuous quality improvement (CQI) techniques, are widely used by hospital managers although systematic reviews of the evidence have been equivocal (Shortell et al. 1995; Blumenthal and Kilo 1998; Counte and Meurer 2001). Among hundreds of projects, some peer-reviewed publications found better clinical care was produced but the evidence in most was anecdotal (Blumenthal and Kilo 1998: 645). The limited evidence of CQI impact on the quality of health services compared to dramatic improvements in product quality in other industries may be due to several factors: CQI has not been embraced by doctors (Walshe 2003: 7); lack of evidence has inhibited its acceptance (Shortell et al. 1995); and it is harder to show improvement in patient care compared to, say, improvement in car axles. The CQI movement consequently must undertake more empirical studies on impacts (Counte and Meurer 2001). This should be possible as research opportunities have expanded since some European countries now require health care organizations to undertake quality improvement activities, while a shift from a voluntary to mandatory strategy should strengthen implementation and hence impact.

Adverse event reporting systems are in place in many hospitals but their impact on patient safety is so far not known. Within hospitals, adverse event reports are used mainly as a quality tool. Critical incident analysis, including Root Cause Analysis, is used for learning from adverse events. Since RCA evaluations essentially are qualitative case studies there is little hard evidence of their impact, so that an analysis of RCA investigations concluded that general solutions cannot necessarily be derived from single incidents (Iedema et al. 2006: 1209). One of the better studies attributed a decrease in serious adverse events in a large Texas hospital to a no blame culture generated by root cause analysis (Rex et al. 2000), but the effect could be due to other causes, such as a drop in reporting, or greater care since the reporting period followed a highly publicized fatality from an adverse event at the hospital (Wald and Shojania 2001: 54). A structured literature review found little evidence so far of its direct impact upon patient safety outcomes but concluded that RCA is a promising mechanism 'as it lends a formal structure to efforts to learn from past mistakes' (Wald and Shojania 2001: 55).

One positive by-product from the multitude of CQI initiatives, however, has been 'the education of thousands of health workers in the techniques of quality improvement' (Blumenthal and Kilo 1998: 633). This is true also of RCA training and procedures: 'RCA is unique in how it brings staff together from across the health care organization, and involves them in thinking and talking about the organization of their and others' work' (Iedema et al. 2006: 1209). Rather than a by-product, quality improvement activities help inculcate a quality and safety culture among health workers, and this is surely an important outcome. It is so far unclear, however, whether there is a causal link between a positive safety culture and improved performance (Kirk et al. 2006); for example, whether a hospital with a high score on safety culture has fewer adverse incidents (Hoff et al. 2004). The research challenge is to examine this link.

Better Staff Working Conditions

Recent studies have found an association between hospital overcrowding (a proxy indicator of heavy staff workloads) and patient deaths. An examination of over 60,000 admissions to emergency departments in Perth hospitals between 2000 and 2003 estimated that 120 patient deaths were linked to overcrowding (Sprivulis et al. 2006), while a study at the Canberra Hospital found that 13 deaths per year between 2002 and 2004 were associated with overcrowding (Richardson 2006). These studies have important implications for patient safety, since overcrowding is endemic in many hospital emergency departments. A structured literature review of 230 papers on safe staffing concluded that while a relationship was evident between staffing and patient safety there were few well-designed studies, and variations across the studies defeated any attempt at a meta-analysis, although there was evidence to recommend reducing fatigue and stress factors among staff (Australian Resource Centre for Hospital Innovations 2003). Although the negative impact of fatigue upon health professionals themselves is clear, a structured literature review concluded that the negative impact of sleep deprived staff upon patient safety has not been conclusively demonstrated. The reviewers comment, however, that the burden of proof should lie with those who believe that such work practices are safe:

> Given that medical personnel, like all human beings, probably function suboptimally when fatigued, efforts to reduce fatigue and sleepiness should be undertaken, and the burden of proof should be in the hands of the current system to demonstrate that it is safe. (Ashish et al. 2001)

Better Patient Management

Promising results on quality of care have emerged from research on a variety of multidisciplinary teams. Improving the way that health professionals are deployed in delivering services seems a sensible strategy, given that quality depends upon the commitment and competence of health professionals. Several WHO 'patient safety solutions' based on evidence from empirical studies call for redesigning staffing arrangements and for improving communication among staff. For example, a structured research review found evidence of reduced adverse drug events when pharmacists are ward-based and especially when they join the team in ward rounds (Kaushal and Bates 2001). Much of the research on patient management practices within hospitals is conducted in the context of overburdened public hospital systems. These studies bear out the contention of many health professionals that a key strategy for improving quality in public hospitals is to increase resources, support and train staff, and find ways to reduce patient demand, such as expanding after-hours general practice. In this view, the safety of patients is captive to ongoing political tensions as to who is responsible for reforming health care systems.

References

Agency for Healthcare Research and Quality, Hospital Survey on Patient Safety Culture (2006), 10 October http://www.ahrq.gov/qual/hospculture/

Agostini J, et al. (2001), 'Chapter 29: Multidisciplinary geriatric consultation services'. In Shojana K, Duncan B, McDonald K, et al. *Making Health Care Safer: A Critical Analysis of Patient Safety Practices*. (Rockville MD: Agency for Healthcare Research and Quality): 313–322.

Aiken L, et al. (2002), 'Hospital nurse staffing and patient mortality, nurse burnout, and job satisfaction.' *Journal of the American Medical Association* 288(16): 1987–1993.

Ashish K, et al. (2001), 'Chapter 46: Fatigue, sleepiness, and medical errors'. In Shojania K, Duncan B, McDonald K, et al. *Making Health Care Safer: A Critical Analysis of Patient Safety Practices*. (Rockville MD: Agency for Healthcare Research and Quality): 519–533.

Auditor General Victoria (2005), Managing Patient Safety in Public Hospitals. (Melbourne: Government Printer).

Australian Council for Safety and Quality in Health Care (2003), *Safe Staffing: Discussion Paper*. (Canberra: Commonwealth of Australia).

Australian Council for Safety and Quality in Health Care (2004), *Standard for Credentialling and Defining the Scope of Clinical Practice*. (Canberra: Commonwealth of Australia).

Australian Council for Safety and Quality in Health Care (2005), *Achieving Safety and Quality Improvements in Health Care: Sixth Report to the Australian Health Ministers' Conference*. (Canberra: Commonwealth of Australia).

Australian Government (2010), *A National Health and Hospitals Network for Australia's Future: Delivering the Reforms*. (Canberra: Commonwealth of Australia).

Australian Medical Association (2006), Safe Hours = Safe Patients: AMA Safe Hours Audit 2006. (Canberra: AMA).

Australian Resource Centre for Hospital Innovations (2003), *Safe Staffing and Patient Safety Literature Review*. (Canberra: Commonwealth of Australia).

Baeten R and Jorens Y (2006), 'The impact of EU law and policy'. In Dubois C-A, McKee M and Nolte E. *Human Resources for Health in Europe*. (Maidenhead, Berkshire: Open University Press).

Bagian J, et al. (2001), 'Developing and deploying a patient safety program in a large health care delivery system: you can't fix up what you don't know about.' *Joint Commission Journal on Quality Improvement* 27(10): 522–532.

Barnard C (1938), *The Functions of the Executive*. (Cambridge Mass.: Harvard University Press).

Blumenthal D and Kilo C (1998), 'A report card on continuous quality improvement.' *The Milbank Quarterly* 76(4): 625–648.

Boaden R (2006), 'The contribution of quality management to patient safety'. In Walshe K and Boaden R. *Patient Safety: Research into Practice*. (Maidenhead: Open University Press): 41–65.

Bolsin S (1998), 'Professional misconduct.' *Medical Journal of Australia* 169: 369–372.

Bolsin S (2003), 'Whistle blowing.' *Medical Education* 37: 294–296.

Braithwaite J and Travaglia J (2008), 'An overview of clinical governance policies, practices and initiatives.' *Australian Health Review* 32: 10–22.

Braithwaite J, et al. (2006a), Incident Information Management System in NSW: Overview of Studies. (Sydney: University of New South Wales).

Braithwaite J, et al. (2006b), 'Does restructuring hospitals result in greater efficiency? An empirical test using diachronic data.' *Health Services Management Research* 19(1): 1–2.

Braithwaite J, et al. (2010), 'Cultural and associated enablers of, and barriers to, adverse incident reporting.' *Quality and Safety in Health Care* 19: 229–233.

Burns J (1978), *Leadership.* (New York: Harper and Row).

Callen J, et al. (2009), 'The importance of medical and nursing sub-cultures in the implementation of clinical information systems.' *Methods Informatics Medicine* 49 (n-n doi:10.3414/ME9212).

Champy J (1996), *Reengineering Management: The Mandate for New Leadership.* (New York: Harper Business).

Chief Medical Officer (2006), *Good Doctors: Safer Patients: Proposals to strengthen the system to assure and improve the performance of doctors and to protect the safety of patients.* (London: Department of Health).

Colla J, et al. (2005), 'Measuring patient safety climate: a review of the surveys.' *Quality and Safety in Health Care* 14: 364–366.

Counte M and Meurer S (2001), 'Issues in the assessment of continuous quality improvement implementation in health care organizations.' *International Journal for Quality in Health Care* 13(3): 197–207.

Crethar M. Phillips J, Stafford P, et al. (2009), 'Leadership transformation in Queensland Health'. *Australian Health Review* 33(3): 357–364.

Darzi A (2009), *High Quality Care For All: NHS Next Stage Review Final Report.* (London: Department of Health).

DeBuono B and Osten W (1998), 'The medical resident workload: the case of New York State.' *Journal of the American Medical Association* 280: 1882–1883.

Degeling P and Carr A (2004), 'Leadership for the systemization of health care: the unaddressed issue in health care reform.' *Journal of Health Organization and Management* 18(6): 399–414.

Department of Health (1998), *A First Class Service: Quality in the New NHS.* (London: Stationery Office).

Duckett S (2007), 'A new approach to clinical governance in Australia.' *Australian Health Review* 31(Supplement 1): S16–S19.

Duckett S (2009), 'Transforming clinical governance in Queensland health'. In Healy J and Dugdale P. *Patient Safety First: Responsive Regulation in Health Care.* (Crows Nest NSW: Allen & Unwin): 124–143.

Dugdale P (2008), *Doing Health Policy in Australia.* (Sydney: Allen & Unwin).

Edwards J and Packham R (1999), 'A model for the practical implementation of clinical governance.' *Journal of Clinical Excellence* 1: 13–18.

Faunce T and Bolsin S (2004), 'Three Australian whistleblowing sagas: lessons for internal and external regulation.' *Medical Journal of Australia* 18(1): 44–47.

Fleming M and Wentzell N (2008), 'Patient safety culture improvement tool: development and guidelines for use.' *Healthcare Quarterly* 11(Special issue): 10–15.

Fulop N, et al. (2002), 'Process and impact of mergers on NHS Trusts: Multicentre case study and management cost analysis.' *British Medical Journal* 325(7358): 249–249.

Garling Report (2009), *Final Report of the Special Commission of Inquiry: Acute Care Services in NSW Public Hospitals*. (Sydney: State of New South Wales).

Gawande A, et al. (2003), 'Analysis of errors reported by surgeons at three teaching hospitals.' *Surgery* 133(6): 614–621.

Gerrity M (2001), 'Interventions to improve physicians' well-being and patient care: a commentary.' *Social Science & Medicine* 52: 223–225.

Groene O, et al. (2008), 'The World Health Organization Performance Assessment Tool for quality improvement in Hospitals (PATH): An analysis of the pilot implementation in 37 hospitals.' *International Journal for Quality in Health Care* 20(3): 155–161.

Healy J, et al. (1999), *Coming Up For Care: Assessing the Post-Hospital Needs of Older Patients*. (London: Policy Studies Institute).

Henry M (1989), *Mintzberg on Management: Inside Our Strange World of Organizations*. (New York: Free Press).

Hillman K (1999), 'The changing role for acute care hospitals.' *Medical Journal of Australia* 170(7): 325–329.

Hoff T, et al. (2004), 'A review of the literature examining linkages between organizational factors, medical errors, and patient safety.' *Medical Care Research and Review* 6(1): 3–37.

Iedema R (2003), *Discourses of Post-Bureaucratic Organizations*. (Amsterdam. Philadelphia: John Benjamins).

Iedema R, et al. (2005), 'Clinical governance: complexities and promises'. In Stanton P, Willis E and Young S. *Workplace Reform in the Healthcare Industry: The Australian Experience*. (Basingstoke, New York: Palgrave Macmillan): 253–278.

Iedema R, et al. (2006), 'A root cause analysis of clinical error: confronting the disjunction between formal rules and situated clinical activity.' *Social Science & Medicine* 63: 1201–1212.

Institute of Medicine (2004), *Keeping Patients Safe: Transforming the Work Environment of Nurses*. (Washington DC: The National Academies Press).

Jakab M, et al. (2002), 'Linking organizational structure to the external environment: experiences from hospital reform in transition economies'. In M M and J H. *Hospitals in a Changing Europe*. (Buckingham. Philadephia: Open University Press).

Jha A and Epstein A (2010), 'Hospital governance and the quality of care.' *Health Affairs* 29(1): 182–187.

Johnson D (2001), 'How the Atlantic barons learned teamwork.' *British Medical Journal* 322: 563.

Johnstone M-J (2004), 'Patient safety ethics and whistleblowing: a nursing response to the events at the Campbelltown and Camden Hospitals.' *Australian Health Review* 28(1): 13–19.

Jorm C, et al. (2006), 'Why don't doctors engage with the system?' in Iedema R. *Hospital Communication: Tracing Complexities in Healthcare Organizations*. (Basingstoke: Palgrave Macmillan): 222–243.

Joyce C, et al. (2004), 'Time for a new approach to medical workforce planning.' *Medical Journal of Australia* 180(7): 343–346.

Kaushal R and Bates D (2001), 'Chapter 7: The clinical pharmacist's role in preventing adverse drug events'. In Shojania K, Duncan B, McDonald K, et al. *Making Health Care Safer: A Critical Analysis of Patient Safety Practices*. (Rockville MD: Agency for Healthcare Research and Quality): 71–78.

Kerridge I, et al. (2005), *Ethics and Law for the Health Professions*. (Annandale, NSW: Federation Press).

Kerridge R and Saul W (2003), 'The medical emergency team, evidence-based medicine and ethics.' *Medical Journal of Australia* 179: 313–315.

Kirk S, et al. (2006), 'Evaluating a patient safety culture'. In Walshe K and Boaden R. *Patient Safety: Research into Practice*. (Maidenhead: Open University Press): 173–184.

Leape L (2002), 'Reporting of adverse events.' *New England Journal of Medicine* 347(20): 1633–1639.

Leape L and Berwick D (2005), 'Five years after *To Err is Human*: what have we learned.' *Journal of the American Medical Association* 293(19): 2384–2390.

Leung A, et al. (2004), 'Reducing utilization of hospital services by case management: a randomized control trial.' *Australian Health Review* 28(1): 79–86.

McDonald F (2008), 'Working to death: the regulation of working hours in health care.' *Law & Policy* 30(1): 108–140.

McKee M, et al. (2002), 'Pressures for change'. In McKee M and Healy J. *Hospitals in a Changing Europe*. (Buckingham. Philadelphia: Open University Press): 36–58.

Miro O, et al. (1999), 'Decreased health care quality associated with emergency department overcrowding.' *European Journal of Emergency Medicine* 6: 105–107.

MPConsulting (2004), Discussion Paper on Whistleblowing Legislation and Health Care: Draft to the Australian Council for Safety and Quality In Health Care. (Canberra: ACSQHC).

National Audit Office (2000), *The Management and Control of Hospital Acquired Infection in Acute NHS Trusts in England*. (London: The Stationery Office).

National Audit Office (2003), *Achieving Improvements through Clinical Governance: A Progress Report on Implementation by NHS Trusts*. (London: The Stationery Office).

National Center for Patient Safety (2007), Root Cause Analysis (RCA), 15 March http://www.patientsafety.gov/rca.html

National Patient Safety Agency (2004), *Seven Steps to Patient Safety: An Overview Guide for NHS Staff*. (London: National Patient Safety Agency).

National Patient Safety Agency (2006), RCA Training and RCA Toolkit, 9 October http://www.npsa.nhs.uk/health/resources/root_cause_analysis

NSW Department of Health (2004), *Checklist Flip Chart for Root Cause Analysis Teams*. (North Sydney: NSW Department of Health).

Olsen S and Neale G (2005), 'Clinical leadership in the provision of hospital care.' *British Medical Journal* 330: 1219–1220.

Ovretveit J, et al., eds. (1997), *Interprofessional Working for Health and Social Care*. (Basingstoke: Macmillan).

Perrow C (1972), *Complex Organizations: A Critical Essay*. (Glenview, Illinois: Scott, Foresman and Company).

Productivity Commission (2005), *Australia's Health Workforce*. (Canberra: Commonwealth of Australia).

Rennie S and Crosby J (2002), 'Students' perception of whistle blowing: implications for self-regulation. A questionnaire and focus group survey.' *Medical Education* 36(2): 113–114.

Rex J, et al. (2000), 'Systematic root cause analysis of adverse drug events in a tertiary referral hospital.' *Joint Commission Journal on Quality Improvement* 26: 563–575.

Richardson D (2006), 'Increase in patient mortality at 10 days associated with emergency department overcrowding.' *Medical Journal of Australia* 184(5): 213–216.

Robinson R and Dixon A (1999), *Health Care Systems in Transition: United Kingdom*. (Copenhagen: European Observatory on Health Care Systems).

Rothschild J (2001), 'Chapter 38: 'Closed' intensive care units and other models of care for critically ill patients'. In Shojania K, Duncan B, McDonald K, et al. *Making Health Care Safer: A Critical Analysis of Patient Safety Practices*. (Rockville MD: Agency for Healthcare Research and Quality): 413–422.

Runciman WB, et al. (2007), *Safety and Ethics in Healthcare: A Guide to Getting it Right*. (Aldershot: Ashgate).

Scally G and Donaldson L (1998), 'Clinical governance and the drive for quality improvement in the new NHS in England.' *British Medical Journal* 317: 61–65.

Seago J (2001), 'Chapter 39: Nurse staffing, models of care delivery, and interventions'. In Shojania K, Duncan B, McDonald K, et al. *Making Health Care Safer: A Critical Analysis of Patient Safety Practices*. (Rockville MD: Agency for Healthcare Research and Quality): 423–446.

Selim P, et al. (2005), *Uptake of an incident reporting system in a public teaching hospital: evidence and outcomes for solutions*. Evolution or Revolution: 3rd Australasian Conference on Safety and Quality in Health Care, (Adelaide: AAQHC).

Shortell S, et al. (1995), 'Assessing the impact of continuous quality improvement/total quality management: concept versus implementation.' *Health Services Research* 30: 377–401.

Smith R (1998), 'All changed, changed utterly.' *British Medical Journal* 316: 1917–1918.

Spelman D (2002), 'Hospital-acquired infections.' *Medical Journal of Australia* 176: 286–291.

Sprivulis P, et al. (2006), 'The association between hospital overcrowding and mortality among patients admitted via Western Australian emergency departments.' *Medical Journal of Australia* 184(5): 208–212.

Stewart G and Dwyer J (2009), 'Implementation of the Garling recommendations can offer real hope for rescuing the New South Wales public hospital system.' *Medical Journal of Australia* 190(2): 80–82.

Tarnow-Mordi W, et al. (2000), 'Hospital mortality in relation to staff workload: a 4-year study in an adult intensive care unit.' *The Lancet* 356(9225): 185–189.

Tyler T (1990), *Why People Obey the Law*. (New Haven: Yale University Press).

Vincent C, ed. (2001), *Clinical Risk Management*. (London: BMJ Books).

Wald H and Shojania K (2001), 'Chapter 5: Root cause analysis'. In Shojania K, Duncan B, McDonald K, et al. *Making Health Care Safer: A Critical Analysis of Patient Safety Practices*. (Rockville MD: Agency for Healthcare Research and Quality): 51–56.

Walshe K (2000), *Clinical Governance: A Review of the Evidence*. (Birmingham: Health Services Management Centre, University of Birmingham).

Walshe K (2003), *Regulating Healthcare: A Prescription For Improvement?* (Maidenhead. Philadelphia: Open University Press).

Walshe K and Boaden R (2006), 'Introduction'. In Walshe K and Boaden R. *Patient Safety: Research into Practice*. (Maidenhead: Open University Press): 1–6.

Walston S and Kimberley J (1997), 'Re-engineering hospitals: experience and analysis from the field.' *Hospital and Health Service Administration* 42: 143–163.

Wellington H and Dugdale P (2009), 'Integrating corporate and clinical governance'. In Healy J and Dugdale P. *Patient Safety First: Strategies for Regulating Health Care*. (Crows Nest NSW: Allen & Unwin): 98–123.

Wilkinson A and Willmott H, eds. (1995), *Making Quality Crucial*. (London: Routledge).

Willis E, et al. (2005), 'Health sector and industrial reform in Australia'. In Stanton P, Willis E and Young S. *Workplace Reform in the Healthcare Industry: The Australian Experience*. (Basingstoke. New York: Palgrave Macmillan): 13–29.

Chapter 7
Regulating Organizations: External Reviews

Reviewing and Inspecting

External schemes for reviewing health care organizations have multiplied since the 1990s as revelations mounted on the unsafe and poor quality care that patients received in some hospitals. Such schemes do not necessarily eliminate hospital scandals since problems continue to occur even in countries with generally good hospitals and established review mechanisms, but external reviews at least ensure that poor quality care is not covered up as in the past. For example, an inquiry into the Mid Staffordshire NHS Foundation Trust in England strengthened the regulatory resolve of the government to move to an enforcement strategy through a registration system that includes a legal requirement from April 2010 for all NHS Trusts to meet government standards. A public inquiry had heard a litany of complaints from patients and families about their experiences in Staffordshire hospitals (for example, see Box 7.1)

Box 7.1 Family testimony on conditions in Stafford Hospital, England

Following a colostomy operation at Stafford Hospital the patient was treated on the Intensive Care Unit where the care was 'second to none' and he slowly began to recover. The patient was then transferred to Ward 6 earlier than his family felt appropriate. On the ward his fluid levels were not monitored, the buzzer was placed out of his reach and his colostomy bag leaked regularly. The patient required his chest to be suctioned regularly yet many nurses admitted they did not know how to carry out the procedure. His family tried to find out about his treatment but there was a lack of staff on the ward to ask and on one occasion a nurse refused to leave her office to speak to the family. After eight days on the ward the patient contracted MRSA and was returned to the Intensive Care Unit, where he deteriorated rapidly and died.

Source: Francis Report 2010: 15

The international trend is that the state is taking a stronger regulatory role in ensuring safe and satisfactory health care. Some countries have passed legislation requiring health care organizations to meet basic standards and to participate in quality improvement activities, so that professional and industry groups are no longer solely relied upon to self-regulate performance. Voluntarism is giving way to compulsion in the interests of public protection. Fragmentation is a growing problem, however, as the proliferating schemes include licensing, certification, accreditation, quality awards, external peer review, investigative reviews, and performance monitoring. The best of these systems are characterized by 'explicit, valid standards, by reliable assessment processes and by some complementary mechanisms for implementing improvement' (Shaw 2000: 167). Countries also vary on whether the main purpose is to ensure that health services meet minimum standards or whether it is to assure continuing quality improvement. Some countries take an inspectorial approach as in England, and others take a quality improvement approach as in Denmark.

While information is patchy on the characteristics of external review schemes around the world, the European Commission has sponsored several studies on member states of the European Union (Legido-Quigley et al. 2008: chapter 2). Four main models were identified in western European countries: accreditation, peer review, ISO standards, and quality assurance (Heaton 2000). These models take different perspectives: accreditation is about organizational development, peer review takes a professional perspective, ISO emerges from industrial process control, and quality assurance is a management model (Klazinga 2000).

Countries vary on whether they prefer a hard or soft regulatory approach to external review. The UK has set up several inspectorial bodies in the health and social care sectors, has charged the Care Quality Commission with undertaking regular inspections of NHS hospitals, and has introduced certification and mandatory basic standards. Australia has taken a softer approach in relying mainly on accreditation bodies to review health care facilities, although the Australian Health Ministers in 2010 endorsed mandatory national standards.

How an external review is framed depends basically upon its purpose: an 'inspection' backed up by regulatory sanctions to check that standards are being met; or a quality improvement activity aimed at professional development. Inspections are a long-standing regulatory mechanism that can be located towards the enforcement peak of the regulatory pyramid. Inspections are becoming more common in the hospital sector where governments until recently were not inclined to appoint inspectors of hospitals, in contrast to the long history of government inspectors of mines, factories, schools and nursing homes. Accreditation undertaken through site visits is the best known of the external review schemes and is the main strategy for improving quality in some countries, while in others it is one of several strategies within a broader quality assurance framework.

A tier of organizations at the international level accredits the national-level accreditors and certifiers, develops standards, devises assessment procedures, and promotes their own models. For example, the International Society for Quality in Health Care (ISQua) is an international NGO that assesses accreditation agencies against standards developed specifically for the health industry, while other peak bodies apply a more industrial model, such as the International Organization for Standardization (ISO).

This chapter explores external review schemes around the world as a regulatory strategy for ensuring that patients receive high quality care in hospitals, general practice clinics, and nursing homes. Table 7.1 sets out the main external review schemes and their characteristics including their purpose and degree of authority, which mechanisms range from soft to hard according to their regulatory strength. For example, a quality award can be construed as a soft mechanism, while an investigative review is a strong mechanism that usually results in powerful sanctions. These are not absolute positions along a soft to hard continuum, however, since a well-publicized award can be strong mechanism for improving performance, a peer review scheme can apply a hard sanction such as 'naming and shaming', and a performance indicator scheme may involve only weak rewards and sanctions.

Types of External Review Schemes

Regulatory conversations are hindered by lack of agreement on terminology thus making it difficult to arrive at shared understandings let alone shared practices (Weingart 2005; Runciman 2006). The different values, principles and terms used in setting standards and reviewing organizations can make it difficult to agree on meanings. Terms get confused or 'lost in translation'. For example, accreditation often is used as a generic term for an external recognition that an organization meets certain standards, whether it is licensed, certified or accredited.

Licensure

The state in many countries requires private hospitals, but not necessarily public hospitals, to obtain a license from an authority before being allowed to treat patients (also called registration). Licensure refers to the legal recognition of an organization or a practitioner. *Licensing* is defined as a 'process by which a government authority grants permission to an individual practitioner or health care organization to operate or to engage in an occupation or profession' (Shaw 2003b: 10). Licensing procedures usually concentrate upon basic standards in building design, occupational health and safety, and the qualifications of the principals to run such centres; the focus is more upon infrastructure and inputs than outputs and outcomes. A licence may or may not be time-limited and a licensing authority usually has the power to investigate in the event of problems and to impose sanctions including varying or revoking a license. Licensing is undertaken by inspectors employed by government or its agents, but a license does not necessarily involve an on-site inspection but rather may be issued on the basis of a self-assessment against set standards. Hospital licensure potentially is a strong regulatory mechanism as it is based in law and standards can be legally enforced. Licensure has been neglected as an old-style form of regulation concerned more with minimum standards than quality assurance and with its scope limited by one-off procedures and inflexible rules. For example, the administration of hospital licensure schemes, at least in the United States, is poorly resourced and lax (Blum 2008). Licensure schemes are in the process of being overhauled in some countries with more rigorous criteria and inspection procedures being instituted – thus moving towards a form of certification.

Table 7.1 Characteristics of external review schemes

	Softer ←→						Harder
	Quality award	**Peer review**	**Accredit**	**Monitor**	**Certify**	**License**	**Inquiry**
Purpose	develop	develop	develop	benchmark compare	ensure standard	ensure basic standard	investigate problem
Regulator	industry	profession	NGO	state	industry	state	state
Accountability	industry	peers	members	state public	industry	state	state
Authority	industry	profession	varies	law/state	industry	law	state
Compliance	voluntary	voluntary	voluntary	**mandatory**	voluntary	mandatory	mandatory
Transparency	yes	no	varies	yes	limited	limited	yes
Procedure	self-assess	review	review	indicator database	inspect	self-assess	inspect investigate
Leverage	reward	reward sanction	reward sanction	sanction reward	sanction	sanction	sanction

In the United States, licensure is administered by state health departments and is an important mechanism given the many private hospitals (for-profit and non-profit). In England, the *Health and Social Care Act 2008* requires public and private health facilities and adult social care facilities to 'register' with the Care Quality Commission, which has certification powers to undertake external reviews and to enforce standards. Licensure of health care organizations is common among European Union countries although there are as yet no EU-wide standards (Legido-Quigley et al. 2008: 26). Israel is an example of a systematic approach to licensure and certification as the Ministry of Health in 2005 instituted a periodic audit of all hospitals (Health Policy Monitor 2005).

In Australia, private health facilities must be licensed by state health departments according to legislation in each state, such as the *Private Health Facilities Act 2007* (NSW). Each state has somewhat different legislation in relation to what is licensed (the facility, the type of service, the procedure, the beds, the owners), the licensing procedure (documentation, on-site inspection), and relicensing requirements (one-off licence, renewal fee, an on-site inspection) (Berrill and Healy 2009: 278).

Certification

Certification refers to a guarantee by a certification body that an organization possesses the capacity or technology in a certain field and meets design standards. Certification schemes apply more to technical aspects of health care, such as equipment or a laboratory, and to a component of a hospital rather than the whole hospital, and may be voluntary or mandatory. Organizations that carry out a certification procedure are approved by other bodies, such as the International Organization for Standardization (ISO). Certification is a well-established procedure in the health sector for goods and technical services, which generally seek certification against standards with the process geared to certifying whether minimum technical and procedural criteria are met.

The International Organization for Standardization (ISO) has a world-wide federation of members and associates that use accredited auditors. The ISO 9,000 series of standards for health care facilities mostly is applied to components such as laboratories. ISO certification is widely used in the health industry; for example, private hospitals in Asian countries prominently advertise their ISO certification. Its critics argue that the model is not appropriate for hospitals, and that local variability undercuts the ISO claim to internationally comparable standards (Sweeney and Heaton 2000).

In Australia, the peak NGO for many certification bodies, Standards Australia, states that certification bodies assess an organization's conformity to standards in relation to products, processes, systems or persons. ISO certifiers and the National Association of Testing Authorities (NATA) certify components of hospitals and also free-standing technical services, such as pathology laboratories, radiology services, optometric services, breast cancer screening, and blood products. The Therapeutic Goods Administration (TGA) within the Australian Government Department of Health and Ageing has extensive procedures for approving pharmaceuticals and medical devices. The Joint Accreditation System of Australia and New Zealand (JAS-NZ), a quasi-government organization set up under a trade treaty, has a governing board appointed by Australian and New Zealand governments, follows ISO standards and accredits bodies that certify management systems, products and personnel and some health sector accreditors.

Accreditation

Accreditation is regarded around the world as a key method for improving the quality of care in health care organizations (Shaw 2003a). Accreditation is a procedure whereby an independent body evaluates the degree of compliance by an organization with previously determined standards and, if adequate, awards a certificate of compliance (Scrivens 1998). An authority (either the accreditor or another body) sets standards that are capable of being assessed, and the accreditor designs a procedure for assessing applicants against those standards. Some standards may be compulsory while others are viewed as desirable goals to be achieved over time. Those undertaking an accreditation procedure usually are called surveyors or reviewers and take a more educative and developmental approach than do inspectors/assessors in licensing and certification schemes. The following definition of *accreditation* emphasizes its two essential factors of an independent assessment and measurable standards:

> Accreditation is the status obtained by an organization after a successful third party external evaluation by a recognized body to assess whether an organization meets applicable pre-determined standards. (Australian Council on Healthcare Standards 2006)

The various accreditation models are based on one of two philosophical approaches. The *developmental approach* regards accreditation as a voluntary process, awards some level of accreditation to all organizations, and aims to produce continuous quality improvement. The *minimum standards approach* regards accreditation as an outcome of an assessment against basic standards that must be met (and preferably surpassed) and usually is a mandatory scheme. Shaw argues that accreditation, unlike licensure or certification, should focus on the achievement of optimal rather than minimum standards as this developmental principle is the key to accreditation (Shaw 2003b). The 'best' type of accreditation system remains a matter of debate.

The advantages of a *voluntary accreditation scheme* are that it is acceptable to the health industry, provides public and professional recognition to facilities that engage successfully in an accreditation process, and is educative in that it encourages continuous improvement. Since accreditation in a market model health system confers a competitive advantage in attracting patients, staff and funds, voluntary schemes usually have high levels of participation. In a public sector system, accreditation confers a reputational advantage that attracts staff and may offer other benefits such access to funds and recognition as a teaching and training organization.

The main advantage of *mandatory accreditation* combined with compulsory standards is that it offers an assurance of satisfactory performance. A mandatory system requires all facilities to seek accreditation and so moves accreditation higher up the regulatory pyramid and involves incentives for compliance and sanctions for non-compliance. Accreditation may be required of a health care organization by the state or its agents under legislation or under departmental rules, by insurance funds if an organization is to become an approved provider, or by industry bodies in order to maintain membership. Mandatory accreditation may also carry an entitlement to government or private funds.

The philosophy of accreditation has changed over the last few decades in several ways. First, clinical performance now is assessed as well as structures and procedures. There is less reliance on the view that an organization with good structures and procedures automatically produces high-quality clinical performance. Second, accreditation begins to shift from a developmental to a regulatory model when it requires compliance with some minimum standards. Third, accreditation schemes have begun to take a more 'patient-centred' approach that involves examining treatment experiences and outcomes for patients. These changes shift the emphasis from a 'well run organization' fit for professionals to work in to a hospital fit for patients to be treated in (Scrivens 1995: 13). While accreditation schemes have been slow to seek the views of patients, some patient-centred review methodologies are being developed. For example, the Australian Council on Healthcare Standards uses a 'patient journey review' as one of its on-site survey tools in order to assess the quality of care received by patients during a hospital admission. Fourth, patient safety standards are being introduced and made compulsory. Fifth, the state in many countries has set up external regulators to ensure that hospital leaders are made accountable for improving the quality of clinical performance in their hospitals.

The trend to compulsory standards and compulsory schemes raises the stakes for accreditation. There is more pressure on an accreditation agency to base a decision on valid and reliable measures and to establish a link between accreditation standards and quality outcomes, and more pressure on applicants to pass the assessment. Accreditation agencies also incur more accountability when they guarantee (at least in the eyes of the public) that a health care facility is performing to a satisfactory standard. They incur greater political risk, therefore, if they make 'the wrong call' in accreditation decisions.

Many accreditation bodies were set up as NGOs governed by professional and industry representatives. Organizations pay a membership fee to an NGO to participate in an accreditation procedure – a different status to being involuntarily inspected by an external authority. A big shift in principles is required, therefore, for an NGO to move from accountability to its members to accountability to the state and to the public, and from confidential reports to its members to making reports available to the public. An applicant also shifts from participation in a confidential and developmental process to being the object of an inspectorial and public process.

Quality award schemes

Quality improvement activities are promoted widely in Europe and North America and are reinforced through awards conferred by various bodies (regional, national and international). Management frameworks for quality improvement mostly have emerged from a 'business excellence' background and draw on the ideas of Total Quality Management (TQM) and continuous quality improvement (CQI). Quality awards usually are based on a self-assessment model that aims to encourage organizational development. The European Foundation for Quality Management (EFQM) has devised a widely used instrument as a generic framework that conceptualizes organizational excellence, can be used as a management tool, and sets out quality criteria for an aspiring organization (Nabitz et al. 2000). Many European countries offer prestigious national quality awards that confer public recognition on a high-performing organization. Health policy makers in Australia have paid less attention to rewards as a regulatory strategy as there are no high-profile national awards although state health departments support award schemes for specific projects.

External peer audit schemes

External peer audit or peer review is conducted through a formal procedure that assesses and compares clinical performance by medical specialties. Peer review as a form of self-regulation by the professions is a long-established method and many clinicians argue that it is an appropriate and sufficient method to ensure the quality of clinical performance (see Chapter 4). External peer review as a form of quality assurance was introduced into health sectors from the 1970s onwards, such as the Professional Standards Review Organizations (PRSOs) in the United States, and many professional associations have long-established peer review arrangements for accrediting specialist training places. Peer audit programmes are organized and administered by specialty associations in some European countries. For example, the 'visitatie' scheme developed by Dutch professional associations from 1989 onwards now involves around 27 medical specialties, its popularity being attributed to professional control and confidentiality (Lombarts and Klazinga 2001). The associations organize site visits by peers to hospital specialty units every three to five years who assess clinical performance and patient outcomes and suggest improvement in confidential reports. The scheme is regarded as a credible form of external peer audit and is said to be trusted by the public even though the results are not published. Based upon a learning model of reflective practice, it depends upon trust, since those being assessed must be prepared to expose their performance to the scrutiny of peers. External peer review schemes conducted by professional specialities are more clinically detailed than a hospital-wide review carried out under a general accreditation scheme.

Reviews using performance indicators

Quality of performance can be measured using a set of performance indicators. (Performance monitoring and reporting is discussed in Chapter 8). Performance indicators increasingly are used in relation to hospitals, where a regulator may require hospitals to contribute data on a set of defined indicators, the purpose being to benchmark and to compare performance over time and between hospitals. While some databases remain internal and confidential to the health sector, countries increasingly publish these results and identify the hospitals. Hospitals in Germany, under the *Health Care Reform Act 2000*, must participate in quality assurance activities and provide data for analysis by the Federal Office for Quality Assurance, and are named and compared against national averages (212 quality indicators with targets) with under-performing hospitals required to explain and to remedy poor performance. Surveys show that patients and referring physicians consult at least some of this information when choosing a hospital (Geraedts et al. 2007). The Dutch Healthcare Inspectorate (IGZ) publishes annual information on a set of performance indicators developed in cooperation with professional and industry associations. The Swedish National Board of Health and Welfare sets national guidelines, for example on cardiac care, and publishes data on 45 indicators at hospital, regional and national level. The Australian Commission on Safety and Quality in Health Care is developing performance indicators that will be used to monitor hospital performance (Australian Commission on Safety and Quality in Health Care 2009: chapters 8 and 9)

Investigative reviews
Special reviews are done in response to a crisis or as one-off reviews on a particular topic. Some countries have set up a meta-regulator to develop a systematic review procedure intended to identify and remedy failing hospitals before they collapse into crisis and provoke a hugely expensive public inquiry. Bodies with an investigative review capacity include the Care Quality Commission in England and the Healthcare Inspectorate in the Netherlands. In the Australian states, investigative reviews mostly are undertaken by statutory bodies, such as the Clinical Excellence Commission in New South Wales and the Health Quality and Complaints Commission in Queensland. The establishment of such review bodies, however, appears not to mute the call for occasional independent public inquiries.

Setting Standards

An external review scheme usually assesses an organization, activity or product against a standard, that is, an expected level of capacity or performance. A *standard* can be defined as 'a published document which sets out specifications and procedures designed to ensure that a material, product, method or service is fit for its purpose and consistently performs in the way it was intended' (Standards Australia 2006). A standard represents a view by a competent authority on an acceptable or an optimal level of performance. An authority usually consults widely in devising a standard, particularly on whether it can be measured validly and reliably and is an achievable and desirable goal. The standards approach to certification is well-established in many sectors of the economy, particularly in manufacturing. Standards in the health sector were originally developed and applied to drugs, medical devices and equipment, and to the physical environment, such as building safety, fire safety, hazardous chemicals storage, food standards, and safe handling of technical devices. In contrast, the delivery of a health service was regarded until recently as a confidential transaction between a doctor and a patient, best left to health professionals and not amenable to standard setting.

The history of hospital standards dates back the American College of Surgeons in the early twentieth century, which devised aspirational standards for high-quality hospitals. The assumption was that a well-run hospital would create an environment in which professional standards would flourish and where patients would receive good health care (Scrivens 1995: 90). The standards emphasized structures and procedures (inputs and throughputs), rather than outputs, or still less outcomes, such as patient health outcomes. The ISQua 'toolkit' initially concentrated on processes rather than outcomes but claimed that good procedures improved clinical effectiveness and thus patient care (Shaw 2003b: 13). Hospital accreditation schemes from the 1990s began to add outcome standards to structure and process standards. For example, the Joint Commission developed clinical indicators on patient outcomes, revised standards to encompass aspects of patient care, such as patients' rights, and added patient safety standards, such as rates of hospital acquired infections (Scrivens 1995: 96).

An example of a standard in the health sector is a compendium of measures published by the Council of Europe designed to ensure the safety, efficacy and quality of blood components, which is regarded as the 'gold standard' and forms the basis of national guidelines in Europe and elsewhere (Council of Europe 2005). A regulatory agency may choose to transform a guideline into a standard and may also go further and make compliance mandatory.

The health sector is engaged in setting performance standards against which an organization may be assessed, whether 'best practice', or normative standards against which to compare organizations (which requires sector-wide performance indicators), whether a minimum, an average, or an acceptable range. Devising standards in the health sector is more controversial than in the manufacturing sector, and some argue that standards in the health sector should be aspirational not compulsory, that is, goals to be pursued not rules to be enforced. Three types of arguments are mounted against mandatory standards: technical, political, and procedural.

The *technical issue* is what standards can be set and how can they be measured. The complex nature of health care makes it difficult to develop valid (sound), reliable (repeatable), and achievable standards. Should 'quality' be insisted upon and can it be defined in measurable terms? Review schemes vary on how an organization is measured against a set of standards. Assessors may assign a pass/fail for each standard, a grade based on a scale, or assign a numeric score. Scores may be added to produce a single number, grade or ranking, but aggregation is problematic in any multivariate scoring system (Scrivens 1995: 98). The basis on which different aspects of performance are weighted needs to be agreed, but arriving at a total score is problematic if a poor score on one standard can offset a good score on another.

The *political issue* is who sets standards although this usually requires agreement between stakeholders on what is reasonable and desirable. Key regulatory questions are whether standards should be aspirational or mandatory and whether standards should be enforced and by what authority. Standard-setting becomes politically controversial when stakeholders hold different views on what is minimal and what is optimal and whether standards should be enforced. Standards may be set at three levels: minimal standards achievable by virtually everyone, so-called best practice achievable by most, or optimal standards achievable by a few high-performing organizations (Australian Commission on Safety and Quality in Health Care 2006: 9). A reviewer may apply standards set by another authority, such as a professional association or an international accreditor, or set its own standards (a dual standard-setting and assessment role). Supporters of separation argue that a dual body is too 'soft' and seldom fails applicants, while opponents claim that separation sidelines the industry from standards development (Berrill and Healy 2009: 283).

The *procedural issue* is how to assess organizations against agreed standards. An inspection procedure requires an instrument that sets out measurable standards, as well as surveyors with the ability to measure performance reliably. 'Inter-surveyor reliability is the extent to which two surveyors operating independently assign the same value for the attribute they are measuring, and intra-surveyor reliability is the degree to which a single surveyor assigns the same value when measuring the same attribute at different times' (Australian Commission on Safety and Quality in Health Care 2006: 17). Surveyor reliability matters a great deal if serious sanctions follow for organizations. One problem with an inspection regime is that the means can become the end when people become preoccupied with the minutiae of assessing and meeting standards. John Braithwaite and colleagues argue that an inspection regime can too easily turn into 'regulatory ritualism' when the inspection procedure becomes the focus rather than a means to produce quality improvements and when creative professionals resort to 'gaming' to beat the inspectors (Braithwaite et al. 2007).

Accreditation Schemes around the World

Accreditation is a widespread and well-documented regulatory approach that has the capacity to apply leverage through a range of rewards and sanctions. Hospital accreditation has become well-established in many countries since its origins in the early twentieth century. A survey by the International Society for Quality in Health Care (ISQua) identified accreditation schemes in around 40 countries after rapid adoption during the 1990s (Shaw 2003b). The accreditation movement emerged from a voluntary tradition that fits well in countries with strong professional associations and large non-government sectors. The hospital accreditation model developed in North America and taken up in anglophone countries (Scrivens

1995: 14) has since spread via the international arms of accreditation NGOs in the United States, Canada and Australia. With the enlargement of the European Union from 2004 onwards, many new member states have set up various types of schemes often under the aegis of their national Ministries of Health (Legido-Quigley et al. 2008: 33). Asian countries that have adopted accreditation schemes include the Republic of Korea, Japan and Thailand, and many Asian hospitals seek certification with ISO (International Hospital Federation and World Health Organization 2007: 114–115).

Governments may require hospitals to seek accreditation or may encourage accreditation as a quality assurance strategy, and some insurance funds require their contracted hospitals to be accredited. Policy makers look to accreditation both to ensure a basic standard of hospital care and to promote quality. Accreditation differs according to the context and priorities of a country: an accreditation scheme may be run by government, its agents or an NGO, be national or regional, voluntary or compulsory, take a minimum or optimal quality approach, and standards and assessment procedures also differ. A toolkit developed to guide countries in designing their own accreditation systems noted that there is no 'right' system, since structures and procedures depend upon the context of a country and its health system (Shaw 2003b).

Hospital Accreditation in Selected Countries

Several conclusions can be drawn from well-established accreditation schemes in different countries (Table 7.2). Accreditation or certification is conducted by different types of regulators: a national government agency (England, France), regional governments (Italy, Spain), a quasi-government agency (the Netherlands), or an NGO (Australia, Canada, United States). An accreditation provider usually sets standards and conducts reviews although in some cases these two functions are separated. Accreditation may be voluntary (not required by law) or mandatory although in long-established voluntary schemes most hospitals seek accreditation. Some countries have both mandatory certification and voluntary accreditation schemes that combine compulsory minimum standards with quality improvement. Finally, accreditation agencies increasingly publish their assessment reports so making their procedures more transparent and accountable to the public.

Table 7.2 Hospital accreditation by country 2009

Country	Agency	Type of accreditor	Legislation	Accreditation model
Australia	Australian Council on Healthcare Standards	NGO	None	Main hospital accreditor Sets standards and accredits Developmental model includes minimum standards.
Canada	Accreditation Canada	QUANGO	None	Sole hospital accreditor Sets standards and accredits Most seek accreditation Minimum standards
Denmark	Institute for Quality and Accreditation in Healthcare (IKAS)	Govt	Patient Safety Act 2005	National programme Minimum standards and continuous quality improvement Awards 'star' ratings
England	Care Quality Commission; Monitor	CQC statutory; Monitor QUAGO	Care Standards Act 2000; Health & Social Care Act 2008	Sole public hospital assessor Sets standards and inspects Mandatory performance reviews Minimum standards Published results
France	Haute Autorité en Santé (HAS)	QUAGO	Hospital Act 1991; National Health Reform Act 2004	Sole accreditor National programme Mandatory certification with minimum standards Published reports
Germany	Federal Office for Quality Assurance (BQS); Certification bodies	Govt NGOs	Health Care Reform Act 1989 & 2000	BQS reviews performance against quality indicators; Voluntary certification/ accreditation schemes
Netherlands	Healthcare Accreditation; Health Care Inspectorate (IGZ)	NGO QAGO	Quality in Healthcare Organizations Act 1996	Voluntary accreditation National standards IGZ inspects hospitals
New Zealand	Quality Health NZ	NGO	Health & Disability Services (Safety) Act 2001	One hospital accreditor, several certification bodies Voluntary accreditation, mandatory certification. Minimum certification standards

(*Continued*)

Spain	17 regional health depts	Govt.	Varies	National standards Regions accredit
United States	Joint Commission	NGO	None	Main hospital accreditor, Sets standards and accredits Voluntary scheme but most hospitals seek accreditation

Source: Accreditation agency websites

Voluntary Hospital Accreditation Scheme

Countries with voluntary accreditation systems include Australia, Canada, Finland, Germany, the Netherlands, Portugal, New Zealand, Switzerland, and the United States. Several of the well-established voluntary accreditation schemes are reviewed below – although it should be noted that some countries also have mandatory certification schemes. (Australia is discussed later in this chapter).

United States

The 'hospital standardization programme' begun by the American College of Surgeons in 1917 aimed to improve widely varying hospital conditions, with their surveyors inspecting against a set of standards, such as whether a hospital maintained medical records on patients. Over the next few decades hospitals were transformed by scientific advances in medicine and by rising demand from middle class patients so that about half of US hospitals sought accreditation by the end of the 1940s in response to reputational and market pressures.

The Joint Commission (previously the Joint Commission on Accreditation of Healthcare Organizations) is an important and influential regulatory actor on the world stage and within the highly privatized US health care sector. Based on an industry self-regulation model and the main accreditor since the 1950s, it is an independent and non-profit body that accredits over 15,000 organizations (including about 80 per cent of all US hospitals), its stated mission being: 'To continuously improve the safety and quality of care provided to the public through the provision of health care accreditation and related services that support performance improvement in health care organizations'. The Joint Commission both sets standards and checks compliance in a three-year cycle of accreditation. It included compulsory patient safety requirements from 2001, such as procedures to prevent and respond to medical error, and introduced a tougher procedure in 2004 with more mandatory standards and unannounced surveys.

Joint Commission International (with regional offices in Dubai, France/ Switzerland, Milan and Singapore) runs safety and quality assurance activities and provides accreditation service around the world: in 2008 it had nearly 250 accredited organizations in 36 countries.

There are legislative and financial pressures upon US hospitals to seek accreditation that make it virtually compulsory in practice since most hospitals cannot survive or compete in the market unless accredited. For example, Medicare requires its hospitals to be accredited, some US states make a licence conditional upon accreditation, health insurance schemes and managed care organizations require accreditation, and large companies recommend accredited hospitals to their employees.

The Joint Commission is subject to pressures from two directions. Governments want stronger regulation after revelations of high rates of medical error in hospitals, but its members on whom it relies for funding want a lighter touch. The Joint Commission often is criticized as a 'regulatory captive' of the health care industry who dominates its board. For example, an article in the *Washington Post* criticized its conflicts of interest and lack of inspection rigour, pointing out that its thriving subsidiary charges hospitals thousands of dollars for coaching on how to achieve accreditation, and that 99 per cent of hospitals are awarded accreditation including several hospitals later revealed as seriously substandard in certain areas (Gaul 2005). The longstanding criticism is that very few hospitals are refused accreditation (Brennan 1998; Walshe 2003).

Voluntary accreditation in other countries

In *Canada*, the Canadian Council on Health Services Accreditation (now Accreditation Canada) was established in 1958 with some funding from the federal government. Although not required by law, most hospitals (95 per cent) seek accreditation (Caillet and Baillet 2000). It is the sole accreditor of health care organizations with over 1,000 'client organizations', has a dual role of setting and inspecting standards that include 31 required patient safety practices, and its surveys are carried out mainly by peer reviewers. Its international department promotes its accreditation scheme around the world.

Germany, under its *Health Care Reform Acts* in 1989 and 2000, made quality assurance a legal obligation for hospitals, and insurance funds in their contracts require hospitals to have quality procedures in place. Oversight is vested in the Federal Joint Committee (the main decision-making body in the German health system), which defines quality standards, while the Federal Office for Quality Assurance (BQS) collects and publishes performance data. Hospitals are encouraged to participate in voluntary accreditation and in certification procedures and the two major schemes combine self-assessment against a standard protocol with external assessment conducted in a site visit by assessors (Busse and Riesberg 2004).

In the *Netherlands*, the *Quality in Healthcare Organizations Act 1996* made providers responsible for ensuring quality care. The Netherlands Institute for Accreditation of Hospitals (now Healthcare Accreditation Netherlands) runs the voluntary accreditation scheme and about half of hospitals are accredited. The Health Care Inspectorate (IGZ), an independent public agency that reports to the Minister of Health, inspects hospitals against regulations, investigates complaints and adverse incidents, and monitors performance indicators. The Dutch Healthcare Authority (NZa) established in 2006 supervises the growing health care market of providers and insurers (Legido-Quigley et al. 2008: 150–156).

New Zealand requires all health care facilities to be certified under the *Health and Disability Services (Safety) Act 2001* by designated audit agencies against a set of core standards with certification issued for up to five years. In addition, organizations may choose to participate in accreditation (as do virtually all large hospitals), the major provider being a national NGO established in 1993, Quality Health New Zealand.

Mandatory Hospital Certification/Accreditation Schemes

Countries with mandatory accreditation/certification schemes include England, Denmark, France, Italy and Spain, and some of these are summarized below.

England

England did not set up a certification scheme until 1999 possibly because the Department of Health was not keen on an external assessment of NHS hospitals. The Audit Commission conducted occasional reviews and some NGOs, such as the King's Fund, offered voluntary accreditation schemes. The scene changed dramatically with the establishment of the Commission for Health Improvement that embarked on performance reviews of NHS hospitals in England and Wales. It was superseded in 2004 by the Healthcare Commission, which undertook on an annual 'health check' on the performance of each NHS facility, where the trusts assessed their own performance against standards and the Commission awarded an annual rating. The Commission conducted in-depth 'improvement reviews' of selected aspects of health care in all hospitals and conducted inspections where there were serious concerns. Superseded in 2009 by the Care Quality Commission, the new independent regulator of health, mental health and adult social care has considerable powers to enforce standards under the *Care Standards Act 2000* and the *Health and Social Care Act 2008*. The Commission registers, reviews and inspects health and adult social care services across England, publishes scores on each NHS trust including scores from consumer surveys, and undertakes special reviews and investigations into serious incidents.

Other countries

In *Denmark*, health care is delivered mainly by five regional authorities while the national government sets standards. The Danish Ministry of Health and the National Board of Health have pursued a national quality improvement strategy since the 1990s, set up mandatory reporting of adverse events, and established the Institute for Quality and Accreditation in Health Care (IKAS). The Danish Health Care Assessment Programme has developed accreditation standards and indicators with some compulsory standards as well as continuous quality improvement and awards 'star' ratings to hospitals. The *Patient Safety Act 2005* makes quality assurance mandatory for hospitals (Knudsen 2009).

France from 1996 introduced compulsory accreditation for all public and private hospitals in its centralized health care system; in 2006 there were

3000 accredited health care organizations (Legido-Quigley 2008: 112–115). The independent public agency funded by government, Agence Nationale d'Accreditation Santé, became part of the National Authority for Health (Haute Autorité en Santé) established in 2005 under the *National Health Reform Act 2004*. HAS undertakes health technology assessments, produces clinical practice guidelines, certifies professionals working in high-risk specialties, and accredits healthcare organizations. HAS inspects health facilities against standards set out in its accreditation manual (about 80 standards and 300 criteria) including continual quality improvement criteria, a process that involves self-assessment and a site visit, with 490 accreditation reports issued in 2007 and lodged on its website.

In *Spain*, regional authorities finance and provide most hospital care in the country's devolved health system (Legido-Quigley 2008: 173–177). The Ministry of Health and Consumer Affairs promotes quality, as set out in the National Quality Plan 2006, which each regional health department is expected to implement. Private health care organizations require an accreditation certificate from the relevant regional health authority, but not public organizations, although some regions, such as Andalucia, promote accreditation and certification programmes including the EFQM and ISO models. The Catalonia health department has run a mandatory hospital accreditation programme since the 1980s.

In *Ireland*, the Commission on Patient Safety and Quality proposed a mandatory licensing system for all public and private health care organizations, among the many recommendations in its comprehensive report in 2008, as well as a national mandatory reporting system for adverse events.

Accreditation in Australia

Australia embarked on a policy overhaul in the early 2000s in order to promote accreditation throughout the health sector, develop national standards, harmonize the multiplicity of arrangements, and improve the validity and reliability of procedures. Hospital accreditation introduced in the 1970s had become the norm in response to governance, financial and reputational pressures. State health departments initially 'endorsed' accreditation and now expect or require their public hospitals to seek accreditation. Private hospitals, and public hospitals that treat private inpatients, have a financial incentive to seek accreditation, since private health insurance funds contract with preferred providers and pay higher reimbursement rates to accredited facilities. There is also a reputational incentive as accreditation is expected of reputable hospitals.

The Australian Health Ministers requested the Australian Commission on Safety and Quality in Health Care in 2006 to review the reform options and propose 'an alternative model'. The Commission conducted extensive consultations and issued several discussion papers and a final report with the following recommendations being endorsed by the Health Ministers:

- national health standards to apply to all health services;
- quality principles to guide continuous quality improvement activities;
- extended accreditation coverage beginning with 'high risk' services;
- national data collection and reporting to measure performance and progress;
- mutual recognition in order to minimize the compliance burden;
- a 'national entity' (a new or existing body) to lead and coordinate reform;
- obligations to comply with accreditation requirements and consequences for non-compliance. (Australian Commission on Safety and Quality in Health Care 2008b: 81).

The Commission is developing national standards in areas where there is evidence that adverse outcomes for patients can be improved, including hand hygiene, health service acquired infections, patient identification, open disclosure, medication management, clinical handover and falls (Australian Commission on Safety and Quality in Health Care 2007: 6). In 2010, the Commission produced ten draft standards; had commenced a review of state licensing and legislative powers with a view to moving towards a legal obligations upon hospitals to comply with standards; and was examining the processes and costs involved in implementing the recommendations. It is not yet clear whether an independent national authority will be given the power to regularly inspect hospitals.

The Accreditation Field

The accreditation field in Australia has multiple providers with at least 30 bodies engaged in accreditation or certification and/or standards setting (Australian Commission on Safety and Quality in Health Care 2006). The field consists of several tiers: international organizations that accredit the accreditors; national-level accreditors who license agents or directly accredit service providers; and accreditors who provide accreditation services themselves or approve other accreditation providers. Many health facilities seek a stamp of approval from accreditation agencies. Designing appropriate standards and procedures is not easy since health services are provided in different facilities and locations including hospitals of varied size, day hospitals, general practice clinics, specialist clinics and consulting rooms, and community health centres, while some services are delivered through mobile clinics or are taken to people at home. Accreditation requirements and practices differ across health services (see Table 7.3). Most hospitals seek accreditation even under the voluntary scheme; accreditation is voluntary for general practices but over three-quarters participate partly in order to establish eligibility for funding programmes; and accreditation is compulsory for residential aged care homes in order to receive subsidies from the Australian Government – without which homes are not financially viable.

Table 7.3 Accreditation areas and accreditation providers, Australia 2008

Health service	Accreditation requirement	Coverage	Accreditation agency
Public hospitals	Mandatory some policies	Virtually all	ACHS
Private hospitals	Mandatory some policies	Virtually all	ACHS, ISO
General practices	Voluntary	Over 80%	AGPAL, GPA
Aged care homes	Mandatory	All	ACSAA
Community health services	Mostly voluntary	Unknown	ACHS, QIC
Dental practices	Mostly voluntary	Very few	
Laboratories & imaging services	Mandatory under Medicare	100%	NATA
Medical specialty rooms	Voluntary	Very few	Medical colleges
Mental health services	Mandatory some policies	Unknown	ACHS, QIC, ISO
Physiotherapy private practice	Voluntary	Very few	QIP
Optometry practice	Voluntary	Very few	QIP

Source: Australian Commission on Safety and Quality in Health Care 2008b: 78

Note: Best estimate as at 2008

There are large gaps, however, in the community-based health sector where an array of health services are not accredited, such as the consulting rooms/clinics of specialists, dentists, and allied health professionals, although these facilities may be licensed. While specialists are registered with a medical board, their private consulting rooms do not seek accreditation despite performing an increasing number of procedures. Accreditation is voluntary in some states for community health centres and for district nursing services but mandatory in others. Public mental health services must be 'assessed' in most states. Diagnostic laboratories must be accredited to be eligible for Medicare subsidies. Peak bodies for professional associations, such as physiotherapy, optometry and radiology, set standards that are voluntary with reviews carried out by accreditation providers. Accreditation arrangements and the main providers are outlined below for hospitals, general practice clinics and aged care homes.

Accreditation of hospitals

Australia had 1,290 hospitals in 2006 of which 736 were public acute hospitals (Australian Institute of Health and Welfare 2008: 347). All large public hospitals and all private hospitals are accredited, although some small public hospitals do not apply, possibly because they lack the funds and capacity to engage in an intensive accreditation process. Most state governments require day hospitals to be licensed and the 200-plus private free-standing day hospitals usually also seek accreditation in order to claim from private health insurers. A day hospital generally is defined as a day procedure facility where surgery is performed with anaesthetics or intravenous sedatives, where endoscopic treatments are performed, or where other types of treatments are performed, such as chemotherapy and renal dialysis.

The Australian Council on Healthcare Standards (ACHS) was established in 1974 as an independent and non-profit organization, is accredited by ISQua, and most revenue comes from member fees. It is by far the biggest accreditation provider for hospitals and day hospitals, and also accredits some community health services, community nursing agencies and mental health services. ACHS had over 1000 organizations in its programme in 2009 accounting for over 90 per cent of all hospital beds. The 30-plus member council comprises representatives of national health bodies, professional associations, government, peak industry groups, and the Consumer Health Forum. Over half its 350 surveyors are volunteers whose time is underwritten by their employers as ACHS member organizations. The ACHS sets and assesses standards and from 2002 shifted its traditional developmental approach to include some compulsory standards. A list of accredited organizations is publicly available on its website but generally not the full accreditation reports. The ACHS international arm accredits hospitals in countries including New Zealand, India, Hong Kong, Bahrain, Saudi Arabia and the United Arab Emirates.

The other main accreditor, the Quality Improvement Council, accredits mainly community service agencies, physiotherapy and optometry clinics, mental health services, community care agencies, and some rural hospitals. A national non-profit organization, it has a developmental model of continuous quality improvement, awards accreditation for three years, and has never refused accreditation. It assists services to implement and manage quality improvement activities through several licensed providers, with about 400 agencies enrolled in accreditation in 2007. A survey of members not surprisingly found that most preferred continuous progress towards quality goals rather than compulsory minimum standards (Swerissen et al. 2000). The International Organization for Standardization (ISO) also accredits some hospitals or components of hospitals through its affiliated certification bodies.

Accreditation of general practices

Accreditation schemes more recently have been developed for general practice clinics including international frameworks for physician practices, such as the European Practice Assessment Practice Management (EPA-PM) scheme so far piloted in nine European countries. This framework involves a site visit and a review of five domains: infrastructure, staffing, information, finance, and quality and safety (Engels et al. 2005). In the United Kingdom, the General Medical Services contract between government and general practitioners since 2003 has included a Quality and Outcomes Framework that offers financial incentives for good quality care and for well-organized practices. A Commonwealth Fund survey has examined the extent of 'best practice' in general practices in eleven OECD countries in relation to systems such as tracking laboratory results and sending follow-up care reminders to patients (Schoen et al. 2009).

In Australia, most general practices seek accreditation against standards developed by the Royal Australian College of General Practitioners, prompted mainly by financial incentives since practices must be accredited to be eligible for funding from the Australian Government Practice Incentives Programme (PIP). The accreditation schemes operate a three-year cycle of assessment with self-assessment against RACGP standards followed by a site visit by two or three surveyors. Australian General Practice Accreditation Ltd. (AGPAL), itself accredited by ISQua, accredits over 80 per cent of practices (about 5,000 practices). Accreditation was part of the Australian Government's General Practice Strategy of the early 1990s, when a steering committee, including the Royal Australian College of General Practitioners and the Australian Medical Association, argued strongly for an industry self-regulation model of voluntary accreditation (Dwan and Boyce 2003). AGPAL was incorporated in 1997 as an independent company with representatives on its board from general practices, the Health Minister and the Consumer Health Forum. AGPAL's developmental approach aims to assist all practices reach minimum standards and so does not 'weed out the bad apples' or provide the public with an assurance that minimum standards are met (Department of Health and Ageing 2005: 486). The AGPAL website offers an on-line search by suburb of accredited practices but gives no scores or ratings.

General Practice Australia (GPA), established in 1999 as a private company, has a smaller market share, and applies standards from the ISO 9000 series plus the quality framework of the Royal Australian College of General Practitioners. Accredited by JAS-ANZ and recognized by the Australian Government, it functions through a self-regulation industry model with an advisory board of general practitioners and some community representatives.

Accreditation of aged care homes

Governments generally are more involved in inspecting and accrediting nursing homes than hospitals, perhaps because governments trust doctors more than nursing home proprietors, and because the state must protect vulnerable people. As a US health regulator said to John Braithwaite, governments regulate nursing homes 'because people come out of hospitals vertical and out of nursing homes horizontal'. Aged care homes in Australia undergo a more rigorous and transparent accreditation procedure than do other health care facilities. The Australian Government subsidizes fees only in licensed and accredited aged care homes and so virtually all aged care homes apply for accreditation. The Department of Health and Ageing undertakes initial certification (awards a licence) that involves an on-site inspection of the physical quality of the facility in seven areas: fire safety; hazards; privacy; access, mobility and occupational health and safety; heating and cooling; lighting and ventilation; and security. Weighted scores are awarded for each area and a home must achieve an overall score of 60 out of 100, while complaints may trigger a recertification procedure (Australian Institute of Health and Welfare 2005: 194).

The Aged Care Standards and Accreditation Agency (ACSAA), a national quasi-government company set up in 1998, is the sole accreditor for residential aged care. Nearly 3,000 aged care homes (virtually all homes) have accreditation status. In a dual regulatory model, ACSAA inspects the homes, publishes the full accreditation reports, and recommends any serious sanctions such as revocation of accreditation status to the Department of Health and Ageing as the enforcement agency. Its CEO draws a distinction between accreditation and regulation: 'We are not a regulator. The department is a regulator. We are an accreditor. We're about promoting quality of care' (Braithwaite et al. 2007: 191).

The following summary draws on a study by John Braithwaite and colleagues of nursing home regulation in Australia, the United Kingdom and the United States (Braithwaite et al. 2007). The poor quality of care in some Australian nursing homes was exposed in the 1980s in several scandals and inquiries prompting the Australian Government, as the major funder of aged care homes, to take over regulation from the states in 1987. The Department of Health set standards and inspected compliance but attempts to enforce standards were opposed by industry lobby groups, so that in the first three years of the new regulatory regime government funding was withdrawn from only three nursing homes. The national government set up the Aged Care Standards and Accreditation Agency as a QUANGO (quasi non-government organization) in 1998 so distancing itself somewhat from the inspection of aged care homes. In contrast, the United Kingdom and the United States have retained government-run regulation of nursing homes. The regulatory regime in Australia was tightened in the late 1990s in response to the rapid growth of for-profit nursing homes and media exposure of scandals (Gibson 1998). Periodic criticisms of lax regulation continue to be made whenever substandard nursing home care is exposed. For example, concerns about abuse of residents prompted the Minister for Aged Care to institute mandatory police checks from 2006 for staff and assessors.

Regulatory Mechanisms

What mechanisms do accreditation, certification and licensing bodies use to promote or enforce compliance with standards? This analysis applies a responsive regulation framework in considering the potential range of rewards and sanctions. The responsive regulation model advocates a dialogue-based approach to securing compliance but regulators must have the capacity to punish poor performers as well as reward quality performers (Braithwaite et al. 2007). Regulators choose among a range of supports and sanctions that escalate upwards in strength as required from persuasion to coercion, but crucially, the threat of enforcement must be available to drive regulation down towards the softer base of the regulatory pyramid. Accreditation and certification schemes generally have the capacity to apply a range of sanctions and supports – as shown on twin regulatory pyramids (see Figure 7.1).

Accreditation procedures schemes involve an intensive sequence over a three to four year cycle. An applicant organization pays a fee to an accreditation organization; the applicant conducts a self-assessment against standards devised by a standard-setting body and published in a manual; the accreditor undertakes a desk audit of submitted material; a survey team of two or three people (or larger for big hospitals) conduct an arranged site visit to assess how well the applicant complies with the standards; the surveyors may hold an exit conference where they advise the applicant of their interim conclusions; the survey team write a detailed report; and the accreditation body makes a decision and, if positive, awards a certificate. The accredited organization may be required to report on improvements during the cycle in order to retain accreditation and may receive unannounced inspection visits. The cycle begins again after perhaps three years. Licensing and certification in contrast usually involves a less comprehensive (or more focused) self-assessment report by the applicant of achievement against standards and may involve a one-off site visit by inspectors. Inspectors usually are employed by licensing and certification authorities while in an accreditation model the surveyors (assessors, reviewers) often are peer volunteers from other organizations.

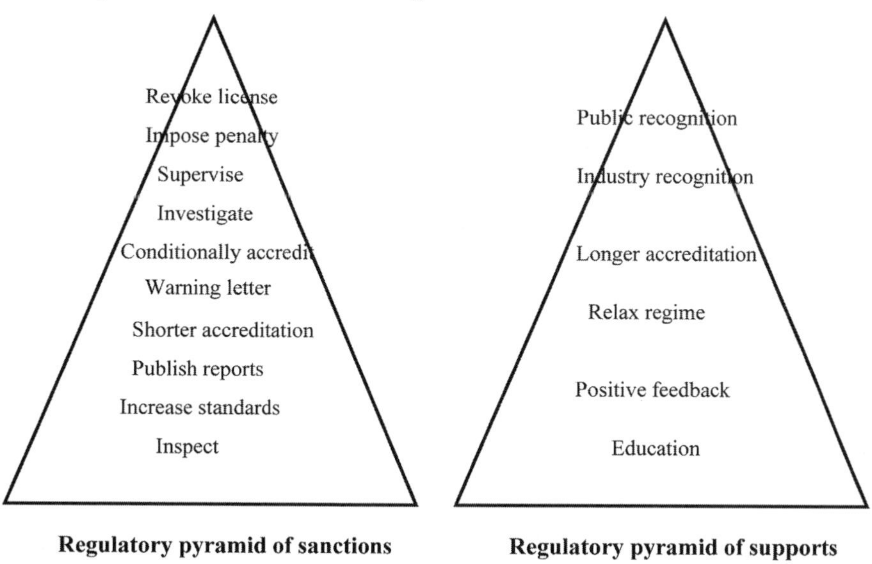

Figure 7.1 Regulatory pyramids of sanctions and supports in licensing and accreditation

Source: Adapted from Braithwaite et al 2007: 319

Regulatory Sanctions

A regulator should respond appropriately from a range of sanctions with the capacity, to escalate to stronger sanctions if organizations do not comply with reasonable requests. On a sanctions pyramid, options include extra inspection visits, a warning notice, a reduced accreditation period, or withdrawal of accreditation. Statutory authorities have legal powers of enforcement in contrast to non-government accreditation (Figure 7.1) organizations. The Care Quality Commission in England, for example, has powers under legislation to select from several actions where organizations fail to comply with standards including issuing a warning notice, imposing conditions, issuing a penalty notice, suspending registration, cancelling registration, and prosecuting for specified offences (Care Quality Commission 2009: 3). Regulators typically stop short of revoking a licence, however, since putting a facility out of business, especially a hospital, has ramifications for patients as well as politicians. Revocation of licence also suggests regulatory failure in that the regulator failed to identify and remedy problems earlier. The counter argument is that strong enforcement action is sometimes necessary in order to send an unmistakeable deterrent signal to others. Whether a mechanism is seen as a sanction or support, however, can depend upon how it is framed by a regulator and how it is viewed by a regulatee. For example, an on-site visit may be seen by an applicant organization as an investigation by suspicious inspectors intent on uncovering infractions (a sanctions visit), or as a developmental opportunity for staff to engage in educative conversations with industry peers in order to promote improvement (a supportive visit).

Inspect

Inspection visits are a stock-in-trade of review schemes and have prompted a suite of inspection tools and a large literature on how to score organizations against measurable standards. Accreditation manuals set out procedures for conducting site visits that may run over five days for a large hospital, which cover initial introductions and a facility tour, presentations by staff, group meetings, and a range of verification methods including observation, extensive interviews, document examinations and database analysis. A 'patient safety journey' methodology is being developed as an inspection tool where surveyors pull a random sample of patient medical records to explore points at which the safety of a patient's care was protected or compromised during his/her stay in hospital. For example, did the hospital have safe clinical handover procedures?

Unannounced inspection visits increasingly are used as regulators are well aware that applicants make a big effort for the site visit and thereafter subside back into their usual ways of working (Shaw 2003a). Hospital managers have websites for exchanging tips on how to ready their hospitals for inspection and how to impress surveyors. A study of nursing home regulation in three countries found many examples of premises being readied for the scheduled visit by inspectors. For example, staff in one nursing home complied with the standard on 'a homelike environment' by quickly slapping up magazine pictures of movie stars on walls, while other nursing homes hired pot-plants that were returned after the inspection (Braithwaite et al. 2007: Chapter 8). Some regulators undertake surprise visits in order to circumvent regulatory games thus causing panic among staff when the inspectors arrive. The US Joint Commission moved to unannounced visits in 2006 (but has since retreated somewhat) since scheduled visits had allowed hospitals to spruce themselves up for the occasion. The Australian nursing home accreditor, the Aged Care Standards and Accreditation Agency, undertakes some unannounced site visits, giving less than 30 minutes' notice of an impending inspection. Australian facilities are not enthusiastic about unannounced or 'short notice' inspections, however, given their potential for service delivery disruption.

Risk-based inspections aim to minimize costs and maximize benefits. Rather than inspect all organizations every time, some schemes concentrate upon those where there is indication of unacceptable risks to patients. The Netherlands Health Care Inspectorate (IGZ) has a three-phase risk-based working method. The first phase identifies institutions where there is evidence of higher than average risk (based on performance monitoring) and requests more information in order to assess the extent of risk. The second phase is an on-site inspection of institutions with apparent increased risks. In the third phase, supervision and enforcement is stepped up for poor performers in order to restore good quality care and products. In serious cases and 'failing hospitals', the IGZ investigates causes of problems and possible remedies and then undertakes crisis supervision.

'Regulatory ritualism' is an inherent danger in an inspectorial approach when the process becomes an end in itself (Braithwaite et al. 2007: chapter 8). First, the criteria by which a regulatory authority usually judges its success is throughputs (number of inspections) and outputs (number of certified organizations) rather than outcomes (improved performance). Second, 'gaming' can become an endemic problem. For example, when US nursing homes were financially rewarded for increasing the number of residents participating in an activity, John Braithwaite and colleagues observed sleeping residents in wheel chairs being wheeled into the room where a craft or game was going on so that they could be recorded in the head count. Managers can be very creative in fabricating quality to outflank instruments of regulation. This is not to deny that inspection is a crucial regulatory tool, but rather to point out the possible pitfalls of a rules-based stance. Inspections are not all empty rituals, of course, since many experienced inspectors find ways to resist ritualism and to respond positively to staff trying to do the best they can for their patients/residents.

Expand standards

The scope and scale of standards tend to increase over time. The US Joint Commission sets ever-expanding standards that its surveyors tick off on a checklist; for example, patient safety compulsory standards increased from 7 in 2001, to 11 in 2003, to 20 in 2007 (Joint Commission 2008). But specificity can defeat the good intention of achieving a comprehensive review. For example, nursing home standards in the United States were specified in ever increasing detail in order to narrow discretion and improve surveyor reliability, but paradoxically this produced worse inter-inspector reliability scores as inspectors could not cope with checking off hundreds of federal and state regulations (Braithwaite et al. 2007: chapter 7).

Australian accreditation standards have increased in number to achieve valid and reliable measures so resulting in greater complexity. The Australian Council on Healthcare Standards EQUIP 4 manual published in 2007 lists 45 criteria rated in five levels of achievement (including 14 mandatory criteria) producing a maximum possible score of 225 (45 criteria × 5 levels); the Standards for General Practices list 44 criteria under 15 standards; and the Aged Care Standards and Accreditation Agency lists 44 indicators under four areas.

Publish reports

Accreditation schemes must balance the preference of their members for confidentiality with demands by the public for transparency. In response to these pressures, accreditation is moving from an internal industry arrangement to public reporting on whether health facilities are safe and of good quality. Countries vary on whether public reporting is regarded is a standard accountability requirement or a regulatory sanction (see Chapter 8).

Both the market model US health sector and England's public health sector now require much greater performance transparency from hospitals. The US Joint Commission over a decade ago devised a public disclosure accreditation document and its website offers on-line searches on hospitals: accreditation compliance and/or scores, a comparison with state and national scores, and a 'quality report' of compliance with patient safety goals, such as reduced health care acquired infections. England's Care Quality Commission publishes 'health reports' that rate each hospital on several criteria.

Australian accreditation agencies, however, have been reluctant to adopt public disclosure. While all publish a list of accredited organization on their websites this means little since virtually all applicants get accredited. Accredited general practices are listed by the Australian General Practice Accreditation Ltd but no other information is given on how they shape up against standards. Hospitals are not 'named and shamed' by the Australian Council on Healthcare Standards as this is not compatible with a membership approach. For example, the ACHS does not name organizations refused or given conditional accreditation even the 26 hospitals in 2003 that were given 60 days to fix major problems. The ACHS lists accredited hospitals and their expiry date and accredited organizations from July 2007 were asked to agree a short joint statement with surveyors to be lodged on the ACHS website – few have done so and very few complied with earlier voluntary public reporting.

Nursing home accreditation is the most transparent as the Aged Care Standards and Accreditation Agency posts the full 30-page or so accreditation report – a case of too much information – as well as a summary. The Department of Health and Ageing names aged care homes that do not comply with one of more specific standards (24 homes in November 2009), and also names homes under sanction, the type of sanction and reasons, with five homes out of nearly 2800 named in November 2009 (see Box 7.2).

Box 7.2 Minister for Health and Ageing announces sanction on Victorian aged home

The Australian Government in January 2010 announced a sanction on the Lions Club of Sunbury Elderly Peoples Homes Inc in Melbourne. The Department of Health and Ageing imposed the sanction following unsatisfactory action by the provider to address areas of concern identified in late 2009 by the Aged Care Standards and Accreditation Agency. Although no immediate or serious risk to the 26 residents was identified, non-compliance with the *Aged Care Act 1997* included:

- A lack of systems and processes to guide staff practices in providing care and services to residents;
- Information systems not supporting appropriate care planning and identification of residents' needs;
- Failure to implement improvements in processes and procedures across a range of areas.

The provider is required to appoint an adviser with nursing experience (approved by the Commonwealth) for a period of six months to help the facility comply with its responsibilities. The nursing home will continue to be monitored closely. The Minister said: 'When aged care providers fail to meet their responsibilities the Government will

Source: Ministerial media release 7 January 2010

Reduce accreditation period

Duration of accreditation is a commonly used regulatory mechanism with high performers awarded the full period and poorer performers a shorter period. (Shorter accreditation periods also may be awarded to new applicants). A shorter accreditation period is a strong sanction, not just for reputational reasons, but because accreditation is costly in terms of staff time as an applicant organization must invest substantial resources in preparing its case and managing the process, and is also costly in terms of accreditation fees. The US Joint Commission charges a large teaching hospital around US$26,000 (A$33,000) for three-yearly accreditation (Gaul 2005). In Australia, the ACHS accreditation fee for a medium size hospital (100–400 beds) is around $15,000; ISO accreditation costs up to $30,000; and general practice accreditation costs around $1800 for each full-time doctor in the practice (Appleyard Ramsay and Associates 2008).

The Australian Council on Healthcare Standards accredits hospitals for varying periods: the full four years, two years with corrective action on some criteria within 12 months, conditional one-year accreditation subject to specified improvements, and refusal of accreditation. Less than the full four years of accreditation (according to ACHS reports) was given to around 20 per cent of applicants in 2002, 70 per cent in 2003 after mandatory criteria were introduced, 60 per cent in 2004, 10 per cent in 2005, 25 per cent in 2006, and 6 per cent during 2007 and 2008. The Aged Care Standards and Accreditation Agency renewed accreditation for less than one year for 63 aged care homes in 2008–09.

Issue warning letter

Accreditation and licensing agencies send a warning letter where breaches of standards are identified that gives the organization notice that they have a specified period of time to put things right before the next inspection, or else face withdrawal of licence or accreditation. Depending on the severity of the breach and the powers of the accreditor, a notice may be framed in softer terms as a warning letter or in stronger terms as a statutory warning notice.

Conditionally accredit

Conditional accreditation gives an organization an opportunity to remedy a breach of standards. This may entail progress reports by the organization and extra inspection visits. The Australian Council on Healthcare Standards may give registration for one year conditional upon any serious breaches of standards being remedied within 60 days (5 per cent of organizations over 2007 and 2008), or may offer an applicant 60 days to fix problems before a decision on final accreditation status (68 organizations in 2007–08 were given 60 days to fix a problem). In its first round in 2002, Australian General Practice Accreditation Ltd awarded conditional accreditation to two-thirds of applicants and asked them to improve problem areas but most achieved full accreditation in subsequent rounds (Department of Health and Ageing 2005: 491). The Aged Care Standards and Accreditation Agency required four homes in 2008–09 to rectify problems urgently with conditions or 'sanctions' placed on their accreditation meanwhile.

Investigate

Accreditation NGOs do not have investigative powers under law although in practice can investigate complaints as part of an accreditation cycle. Statutory agencies may have powers under their legislation to require further information and to undertake an investigation where there is reason to believe that performance is seriously substandard and may pose risks to patients. In England, the Care Quality Commission investigates where there are serious concerns as does the Health Care Inspectorate (IGZ) in the Netherlands. Australia has no external national authority with the capacity to initiate and systematically carry out investigations into poor performance by a health care organization – a major regulatory gap and one under discussion. Aged care homes are the exception as the Aged Care Standards and Accreditation Agency can inspect homes and the Australian Government Department of Health and Ageing as the licensing authority also can investigate. State health departments, however, do have investigative powers over hospitals as the licensing body for private hospitals and as the administrative authority for public hospitals. A state health minister can request an investigation by the department, by a statutory health complaints commissioner or can set up a public inquiry.

Supervise performance

Some regulators undertake supervision in cases where accreditation/certification is conditional or limited or may require the facility to appoint an adviser/supervisor. The emphasis is upon remedying problems rather than punishing the organizations – and from this perspective might be classified as a support rather than a sanction. An alternative strategy for identifying poor performers requires the collection of indicators from all organizations in order to benchmark and compare performance. Such a national (or regional) performance indicator scheme usually is a government function. Countries that monitor hospitals via performance indicators include Denmark, England, Germany, the Netherlands and Sweden. Under-performing organizations are asked to explain and to remedy poor performance while seriously substandard organizations incur extra inspections. The intention is to identify 'failing hospitals' before they collapse into crisis and to supervise their return to better performance. The regulatory emphasis may be to identify and remedy outlier poor performers rather than work with all to continually improve quality so that the focus is upon the laggards rather than the leaders: raising the floor rather than raising the ceiling.

Impose a penalty

Fines are a commonly used sanction by all regulatory regimes. Financial penalties are less used in the health sector, however, where many hospitals are public sector organizations, although a fine would impact upon an autonomous public agency that must manage its own budget. Statutory authorities in some countries have the legislative authority to impose a financial penalty. In England, the Care Quality Commission can issue a financial penalty notice in lieu of prosecution (Care Quality Commission 2009). Fines have not been used so far by accreditation/licensing schemes in the Australian health sector.

Revoke accreditation/licence

At the sharp end of the regulatory pyramid, non-accreditation may follow serious and continuing failure in standards, but accreditors in the health sector very seldom revoke accreditation even when compulsory minimum standards are not met. Withdrawing accreditation has major ramifications, such as loss of funds, patients and staff. Revoking a licence (usually a state function) is even more serious since this means that an organization cannot continue to function legally. The state must weigh the risks to patients or residents of closure of a facility versus the risks of allowing substandard care to continue. The closure of a hospital could leave people without access to health services; the closure of a nursing home could result in deaths of frail people moved elsewhere. On the other hand, accreditation agencies may have more credibility with the public if they were seen to take sterner action on poor standard facilities.

Accreditation agencies differentiate themselves from licensing authorities in that loss of accreditation does not necessarily mean loss of licence. For example, the president of the US Joint Commission, as quoted by a newspaper journalist, said that its role was to help hospitals meet standards not to punish them. 'We can't fine you or close you,' O'Leary said. 'It's right in the articles of incorporation. Our role is to evaluate and educate' (Gaul 2005).

In Australia, general practices are not refused accreditation, hospitals and other health services virtually never (except some day clinics), and nursing homes very seldom. Nursing homes also can appeal against a decision not to accredit or against a short period of accreditation. The Australian Council on Healthcare Standards refused accreditation for less than 1 per cent of organizations in 2003 and 2004, apparently none in 2005 and 2006, and one in 2007 and 2008. In relation to nursing homes, things have to be very bad for a finding of non-compliance with standards, as 99 per cent (of nearly 3,000 aged care homes) were judged fully compliant (with all 44 standards) in 2005, compared to only 72 per cent in England, with enforcement tougher in the United States (Braithwaite et al. 2007: chapter 6). The high level of compliance with standards by Australian nursing homes suggests that standards are set at a low level attainable by everyone, or else there was dramatic improvement in the industry.

Prosecute

A statutory regulatory agency may have the power to bring a prosecution or to recommend a prosecution, such as to crown prosecutors. In England, the Care Quality Commission has the power to prosecute for specified offences with maximum court fines set under the 2008 legislation, for example, £50,000 for failure to comply with conditions in relation to registration.

Regulatory Supports

On the supports pyramid (Figure 7.1), a regulator can offer positive feedback, relax the inspection regime, award a longer period of accreditation, or publicize the achievements of the facility. Some supports are the obverse of sanctions, such as conferring a full period of accreditation, or praising rather than naming and shaming

Educative conversations

Regulatory conversations between surveyors and health care staff are an important but under-estimated tool for improving quality. A site visit presents an opportunity for staff to obtain expert advice from surveyors on how to improve their organization and their own professional practice. Accreditation reviewers engage more in developmental conversations than do licensing inspectors, as peer reviewers can play an educative role while inspectors are required to search for infractions. Accreditation surveyors take on a demanding task since they need professional knowledge about many aspects of a health care organization and should possess both review skills and quality improvement skills. A site visit can present an especially learning opportunity for an organization in a first accreditation application, and offers a valuable quality assurance opportunity for people who work in professionally isolated situations, such as small rural hospitals.

John Braithwaite and colleagues have observed the many skills exercised by experienced inspectors in their conversations with nursing home staff during both supportive and compliance-oriented site visits. These conversations produced changes in understanding that resulted in undertakings to improve care for the residents/patients, especially when the inspectors sought to be supportive and to build on the strengths of the staff. The conversational mechanisms used by inspectors that were observed to improve compliance with standards include the following: praises, reminds, commits, shows, fixes, educates, asks questions, proposes corrections, stimulates problem-solving, proposes analysis, triggers improvement, triggers a consultancy, builds self-efficacy, promotes triple-loop learning, nominates for awards and grants, empowers, and enlists a third party in reinforcing compliance (Braithwaite 2009).

The visitatie scheme run by Dutch professional associations also emphasizes educative conversations and reflective practice with the site visits framed as a supportive peer review of hospital clinical units (Lombarts and Klazinga 2001). In their adoption of continual quality improvement (CQI) concepts, accreditation schemes encourage conversations about ways to achieve and surpass standards. But does there come a point where no further improvements can possibly be made? Can organizations ingeniously continue to find evidence of continuous improvement?

Relax regulatory regime

Accreditation agencies can reward high performing organizations with long periods of accreditation, the converse of short periods for poor performers. Accreditation standards in Australia are framed in broader terms than in the United States and so are more open to interpretation and discretion. The Australian Council on Healthcare Standards has varied considerably over time in its award of full four-year accreditation: 81 per cent of organizations in 2002, only 30 per cent in 2003 after some mandatory criteria were introduced, 39 per cent in 2004, 89 per cent in 2005, 75 per cent in 2006, and 94 per cent in the 2007 and 2008 cycle. The Aged Care Standards and Accreditation Agency awarded full accreditation to 92 per cent of nursing homes in 2004–05 and also in 2008–09, claiming that over 98 per cent of aged care homes were fully compliant with all 44 standards. Being fully compliant is easier when there is room for interpretation, for example, standard (3.6) reads: 'Each resident's right to privacy, dignity and confidentiality is recognized and respected.'

Publicize success within the industry

Accreditation agencies are important actors in their capacity to spread news throughout the industry about excellence and innovation. For example, the Australian Council on Healthcare Standards awards 'outstanding achievement' (36 organizations in 2007 and 2008) and 'extensive achievement' awards, and publishes summaries of named high-achieving organizations. Organizations in the information age have become increasingly transparent in their workings and engage in 'democratic experimentalism' (Dorf and Sabel 1998) in that they observe the successes and failures of others and then decide which initiatives may work in their own organizations. Double-loop learning, that is, lessons spread from one organization to others (Parker 2002) is a common form of learning in the health sector. This also works well where organizations engage in collaboration rather than competition. Experimentation is especially important as the evidence base on safety and quality mechanisms is still evolving. Accreditation agencies are an important source of information about good practice and can spread these ideas among their members.

Confer public recognition

Public recognition, whether in the form of gold stars or awards, is a powerful incentive to inspire high performance since such recognition brings market and reputational benefits. Public recognition as a high-performing organization is taken notice of by funders, professionals and consumers. For example, national awards for quality are highly prized by health care organizations in Europe. In Australia, public awards are conferred on high-achieving health professionals and the health sector should make more use of public awards for high-achieving organizations.

Conclusion

This chapter has shown that several types of schemes for externally reviewing health care organizations are being adopted around the world. Accreditation is one of the best-known schemes and increasingly is expected or required, its main focus being to continuously improve quality. Governments are increasing pressure upon hospitals to seek accreditation and are pushing the various review schemes to harmonize their requirements. The other main strategy is to set minimum standards and to enforce compliance with these standards so that the public can be confident that an organization offers safe and satisfactory care. A minimum standards approach might be undertaken through mandatory certification schemes and/or monitoring performance indicators to identify and remedy substandard performers. The first conclusion from this international overview is that countries are adding a mandatory standards approach to quality improvement. Organizations in breach of standards are more likely to incur sanctions, even loss of certification, than under a quality improvement approach. Reviews of external review schemes argue that a dual approach works best: voluntary schemes for improving quality such as peer audit and accreditation, and mandatory and statutory regulation such as licensing and inspections to ensure compliance with basic standards (Heaton 2000; Klazinga 2000; Legido-Quigley et al. 2008). Reforms to the Australian accreditation/certification system propose to maintain a quality framework while adding compulsory national minimum standards (Australian Commission on Safety and Quality in Health Care 2008a). Second, accreditation and certification schemes have the capacity to select from a large range of rewards and sanctions to promote compliance and are potentially effective regulatory strategies. Third, little rigorous evaluative research has so far been undertaken on the impact of external reviews on safety and quality although more research is underway. This concluding section turns now to an examination of what is known about the impact of external review schemes.

Accreditation schemes have received more research attention so far and can produce evidence that organizations do improve their structures and procedures over time as part of their accreditation cycles, but there is little rigorous research on the impact of accreditation on patient outcomes. The reasonable assumption has been that well-designed and well-run hospitals produce good patient outcomes (Robinson 1995). An analysis in the mid 1990s concluded that accreditation was more art than science and more a management consultancy approach than a tool for measuring performance (Scrivens 1995). By the early 2000s, there was still little hard evidence on whether accreditation improved health outcomes for patients given the absence of outcome measures and trend data (Ovretveit 2003; Shaw 2003a). A systematic review of the hospital accreditation research literature, while noting the paucity of rigorous studies, reached some conclusions: there was consistent evidence that accreditation promotes change in organizations and supports professional development, results were inconsistent on the relationship between accreditation and quality measures, and little relationship was found between a specified quality measure and an accreditation outcome (Greenfield and Braithwaite 2007). A recent study of 19 Australian health service organizations by Jeffery Braithwaite and colleagues noted a weak but positive association between accreditation and clinical performance, and found that organizations with a positive culture and good leadership achieved better accreditation scores (Braithwaite et al. 2010).

In the case of the nursing home industry in three countries (Australia, the United Kingdom and the United States), John Braithwaite and colleagues conclude that after over two decades of regulation the smaller and less competent nursing homes had disappeared, and that overall quality had improved, at least judging by US time trends on measures such as less use of restraints and fewer pressure ulcers (Braithwaite et al. 2007: chapters 6, 10).

There is little analysis of the relationship between accreditation and patient outcomes such as 30-day post hospital mortality, while process standards generally lack validation. For example, does information technology, such as electronic patient medical records, actually improve patient care? Since most health facilities are accredited and the validity of an overall score is unclear, the question may not be a binary yes or no as to the impact of accreditation on patient outcomes, but rather the extent of the relationship between specific standards and specific clinical performance measures. For example, is the presence of an infection team within a hospital associated with a reduction of rates of hospital acquired infection?

Evidence on the impact of accreditation schemes upon patient safety is even more elusive. A structured review of the literature found no convincing research evidence on whether accredited hospitals have fewer adverse events (Trowbridge and Wachter 2001). Measuring adverse events as an indicator of patient safety remains problematic, however, given substantial under reporting. While an entire system should not be rejected because of a few failures, in some notable cases accreditation has failed to detect patient safety problems. The US Joint Commission was criticized for accrediting several hospitals later revealed to be seriously substandard in some areas (Gaul 2005). The Bundaberg Hospital in Queensland was accredited in mid 2003, two months after Dr Patel began as director of surgery, with disastrous outcomes for at least 13 of his patients, while later public inquiries revealed serious failures of hospital management (Davies Report 2005). Problems that threaten the safety of residents also periodically come to light in accredited nursing homes.

Accreditation schemes are devising measurable standards that align better with outcome measures. For example, the US Joint Commission is testing a set of hospital performance measures, the ORYX initiative, which enables hospitals to choose their own bench-mark measures and compare their performance against national scores. The Australian Council on Healthcare Standards has collected data from its members since 1989 on clinical indicators (currently 308 indicators from over 650 hospitals), which offers hospitals an opportunity to track progress and to relate accreditation standards to performance measures (Australian Council on Healthcare Standards 2006). Australia proposes to establish a national data collection and reporting system to measure and track progress on performance outcomes among accredited hospitals to enable them to 'benchmark' their performance against others, although the proposed 'national entity' would not publish 'league tables' (Australian Commission on Safety and Quality in Health Care 2007: 19).

A new era of research is underway, however, with the development of sector-wide indicators on the performance of health care facilities with participation required under legislation in some countries, which potentially will enable the impact of various external review schemes to be tracked against independent measures of patient outcomes. These stronger regulatory strategies are discussed in the next chapter.

References

Appleyard Ramsay & Associates (2008), Cost Analysis of Safety and Quality Accreditation in the Australian Health System. (Canberra: Australian Commission for Safety and Quality in Health Care).

Australian Commission on Safety and Quality in Health Care (2006), *Discussion Paper: National Safety and Quality Accreditation Standards*. (Sydney: Australian Commission on Safety and Quality in Health Care).

Australian Commission on Safety and Quality in Health Care (2007), Draft: An Alternative Model for Safety and Quality Accreditation. (Sydney: Australian Commission on Safety and Quality in Health Care).

Australian Commission on Safety and Quality in Health Care (2008a), *Final Report on the Review of National Safety and Quality Accreditation Standards*. (Sydney: Australian Commission on Safety and Quality in Health Care).

Australian Commission on Safety and Quality in Health Care (2008b), *Windows into Safety and Quality in Health Care 2008*. (Sydney: ACSQHC).

Australian Commission on Safety and Quality in Health Care (2009), *Windows into Safety and Quality in Health Care 2009*. (Sydney: ACSQHC).

Australian Council on Healthcare Standards (2006), *ACHS Clinical Indicator Report for Australia and New Zealand 1998–2005*. (Ultimo NSW: Australian Council on Healthcare Standards).

Australian Institute of Health and Welfare (2005), *Australia's Welfare 2005*. (Canberra: AIHW).

Australian Institute of Health and Welfare (2008), *Australia's Health 2008*. (Canberra: AIHW).

Berrill J and Healy J (2009), 'Hospital licensure, certification and accreditation'. In Healy J and Dugdale P. *Patient Safety First: Responsive Regulation in Health Care*. (Crows Nest NSW: Allen & Unwin): 273–298.

Blum J (2008), 'A revisionist model of hospital licensure.' *Regulation and Governance* 2(1): 48–64.

Braithwaite J (2009), 'Leading from behind with plural regulation'. In Healy J and Dugdale P. *Patient Safety First: Strategies for Regulating Health Care*. (Crows Nest NSW: Allen and Unwin): 24–43.

Braithwaite J, et al. (2010), 'Health service accreditation as a predictor of clinical and organizational performance: a blinded, random, stratified study.' *Quality and Safety in Health Care* 19: 14–21.

Braithwaite J, et al. (2007), *Regulating Aged Care: Ritualism and the New Pyramid*. (Cheltenham. Northampton MA: Edward Elgar).

Brennan T (1998), 'The role of regulation in quality improvement.' *Milbank Quarterly* 76: 709–731.

Busse R and Riesberg A (2004), *Health care systems in transition: Germany*. (Copenhagen: European Observatory on Health Care Systems and Policies).

Caillet R and Baillet S, 2000, 'Accreditation: the French experience.' *Hospital: Official Journal of the European Association of Hospital Managers* 1: 23–24.

Care Quality Commission (2009), Enforcement Policy. (London: Care Quality Commission).

Council of Europe (2005), *Guide to the Preparation, Use and Quality Assurance of Blood Components*. (Strasbourg: Council of Europe Publishing).

Davies Report (2005), *Queensland Public Hospitals Commission of Inquiry Report*. (Brisbane: State of Queensland).

Department of Health and Ageing (2005), *General Practice in Australia: 2004*. (Canberra: Commonwealth of Australia).

Dorf M and Sabel C (1998), 'A constitution of democratic experimentalism.' *Columbia Law Review* 98: 267–473.

Dwan K and Boyce R (2003), 'Competition policy and intra-professional conflict: re-regulating general practice.' *International Journal of Public Sector Management* 16(2): 141–152.

Engels Y, et al. (2005), 'Developing a framework of, and quality indicators for, general practice management in Europe.' *FamilyPractice* 22: 215–222.

Francis Report (2010), *Independent Inquiry into Care Provided by Mid-Staffordshire NHS Foundation Trust January 2005–March 2009*. (London: The Stationery Office).

Gaul GM (2005), Accreditors blamed for overlooking problems. (Washington, DC: Washington Post).

Geraedts M, et al. (2007), 'Hospital quality reports in Germany: patient and physician opinion of the reported quality indicators.' *BMC Health Services Research* 7: 157.

Gibson D (1998), *Aged Care: Old Policies, New Problems*. (Melbourne: Cambridge University Press).

Greenfield D and Braithwaite J (2007), *A Review of Health Sector Accreditation Research Literature*. (Sydney: Centre for Clinical Governance Research, University of New South Wales).

Health Policy Monitor, Hospital audit and licensing, (2 March 2009 2 March 2009) http://www.hpm.org/index.jsp

Heaton C (2000), 'External peer review in Europe: an overview from the ExPeRT project.' *International Journal for Quality in Health Care* 12(3): 177–182.

International Hospital Federation and World Health Organization (2007), *The Performance of Hospitals under Changing Economic Conditions: A Global Study on Hospital Sector Reform*. (Geneva: World Health Organization).

Joint Commission (2009), National Patient Safety Goals 2008, 22 February http://www.jointcommission.org/PatientSafety/NationalPatientSafetyGoals/

Klazinga N (2000), 'Re-engineering trust: the adoption and adaption of four models for external quality assurance of health care services in western European health care systems.' *International Journal for Quality in Health Care* 12(3): 183–189.

Knudsen J (2009), *From professional to regulatory driven quality improvement in Danish healthcare*. International Society for Quality in Healthcare, (Dublin).

Legido-Quigley H, et al. (2008), *Assuring the Quality of Health Care in the European Union: A Case for Action*. (Brussels: World Health Organization and European Observatory on Health Systems and Policies).

Lombarts M and Klazinga N (2001), 'A policy analysis of the introduction and dissemination of external peer review (visitatie) as a means of professional self-regulation amongst medical specialists in the Netherlands in the period 1985–2000.' *Health Policy* 58: 191–213.

Nabitz U, et al. (2000), 'The EFQM excellence model: European and Dutch experiences with the EFQM approach in health care.' *International Journal for Quality in Health Care* 12(3): 191–201.

Ovretveit J (2003), What are the best strategies for ensuring quality in hospitals? *Health Evidence Network*. (Copenhagen: World Health Organization Europe).

Parker C (2002), *The Open Corporation: Effective Self-Regulation and Democracy*. (Cambridge: Cambridge University Press).

Robinson R (1995), 'Accrediting hospitals.' *The British Medical Journal* (310): 755–756.

Runciman W (2006), 'Shared meanings: preferred terms and definitions for safety and quality concepts.' *Medical Journal of Australia* 184(10 (Supplement)): S41–S43.

Schoen C, et al. (2009), 'A survey of primary care physicians in eleven countries, 2009: Perspectives on care, costs and experiences.' *Health Affairs* 28(6): w1171–w1183.

Scrivens E (1995), *Accreditation: Protecting the Professional or the Consumer?* (Buckingham. Philadelphia: Open University Press).

Scrivens E (1998), 'Policy issues in accreditation.' *International Journal for Quality in Health Care* 10(1): 1–5.

Shaw C (2000), 'Editorial: The role of external assessment in improving health care.' 12(3): 167.

Shaw C (2003a), 'Editorial: evaluating accreditation.' 15(6): 455–456.

Shaw C (2003b), *Toolkit for Accreditation Programs*: International Society for Quality in Health Care).

Standards Australia, What is a standard?, (29 January 2007 29 January 2007) http://www.standards.org.au

Sweeney J and Heaton C (2000), 'Interpretations and variations of ISO 9000 in acute health care.' *International Journal for Quality in Health Care* 12(3): 203–209.

Swerissen H, et al. (2000), *A Review of Quality Improvement Approaches in Health and Community Services*. (Canberra: Commonwealth of Australia).

Trowbridge R and Wachter R (2001), 'Chapter 55: Legislation, accreditation, and market-driven and other approaches to improving patient safety'. In Shojania K, Duncan B, McDonald K, et al. *Making Health Care Safer: A Critical Analysis of Patient Safety Practices*. (Rockville MD: Agency for Healthcare Research and Quality): 601–610.

Walshe K (2003), *Regulating Healthcare: A Prescription For Improvement?* (Maidenhead. Philadelphia: Open University Press).
Weingart S (2005), 'Editorial: Beyond Babel: prospects for a universal patient safety taxonomy.' *International Journal for Quality in Health Care* 17(2): 93–94.

Chapter 8
Regulation by Enforcement: Laws, Money, and Monitoring

Enforcement Strategies

Regulation often is assumed to be about an authority enforcing rules and standards set out in legislation. A responsive regulation perspective, however, regards enforcement as one of many strategies that in terms of greater strength and lesser frequency of use is located at the apex of a regulatory pyramid. Enforcement is an essential strategy, however, whether used or whether hanging like the sword of Damocles above the head of a recalcitrant individual or organization. An alternative term, 'command and control', coined in reference to command economies (now very few) also refers to aspects of government systems where authority is vested in, and maintained by, a central authority. The contemporary state in practice uses command and control sparingly and prefers to brandish it as a deterrent or use it as a last resort (Braithwaite and Drahos 2000). Also, as the contemporary state 'steers rather than rows' the economy, it must harness additional networks of power to the task of governance (Osborne and Gaebler 1992). This is particularly so in the case of health systems, since most are not run by a sole and central government agency, involve both public and private sectors, and contain influential professional groups. In governing the health sector, the state uses meta-regulation and co-regulation strategies far more than command and control.

Meta-regulation means the regulation of self-regulation, where an external regulator checks that internal regulators meet externally acceptable standards. It offers the twin benefits of encouraging problem-solving creativity among self-regulators, while providing an assurance that a minimum standard of performance is met (Braithwaite et al. 2005: 28). Co-regulation involves a partnership, often between external and internal regulators, and is a common form of regulation in health systems, such as between the state and the professions. An external regulator needs mechanisms to require and to check that an internal regulator is doing a satisfactory job, however, such as agreed standards, on-site inspections and performance indicators. New forms of governance do not mean the complete rejection of enforcement mechanisms, such as laws and inspections, since enforcement is necessary when laws are broken and appropriate when the public must be protected.

Regulatory authority generally derives from legislation with protection of the public a key rationale, such as laws governing the licensing of hospitals and registration of health professionals. Some countries are adopting a legal strategy to assure patient safety; others are stepping up performance indicator monitoring; while others use financial instruments to steer behaviour. This chapter discusses stronger strategies for regulating the safety and quality of health care in relation to three broad mechanisms: laws, money, and monitoring.

Regulation through Legal Instruments

Governments and their agents, unlike other regulatory actors, can apply direct legal means to secure compliance. Legal instruments include legislation, regulations under an act, rules, directives, government endorsed standards, tort law, and contracts. A legal framework ranges upwards in strength from guidelines to laws in a hierarchy of mechanisms from 'soft' to 'hard' law. Soft law (a term coined in international law) refers to quasi-legal instruments that do not have binding force, or whose binding force is less than in traditional law referred to as 'hard law'. The soft law term is used to describe various quasi-legal instruments, such as codes of conduct and guidelines (Scott 2004).

The status of guidelines issued by a government authority often is ambiguous. Are departmental guidelines an example of soft law? Health departments issue a constant stream of guidelines for staff that appear to be mandatory in theory but voluntary in practice – or vice versa. Does a guideline become a directive if full compliance is expected in practice, or if it becomes a legal document in a test case? Guidelines issued by a central government agency are a well-established convention throughout the civil service. Hurwitz quotes the following exchange with Lady Thatcher in the *Scott Inquiry into Arms for Iraq* (Hurwitz 1998: x):

> Ms Baxendale QC: Some of the witnesses we have had have described these guidelines as a framework, within which to work … Does that fit in with how you saw the guidelines?
> Lady Thatcher: They are exactly what they say, guidelines, they are not the law. They are guidelines.
> Ms Baxendale QC: Did they have to be followed?
> Lady Thatcher: Of course they have to be followed, but they are not strict law. That is why they are guidelines and not law and, of course, they have to be applied according to the relevant circumstances.
> Ms Baxendale QC: They are expected to be followed?
> Lady Thatcher: Of course they have to be followed. They need to be followed. They need to be followed for what they are, guidelines.

Patient Safety Legal Frameworks

Some countries adopt the law as a key regulatory strategy in health sector governance while others assign it a more limited role within an armoury of strategies. For example, the dramatic rise in litigation by patients prompted US state legislatures to pass laws mandating reporting of adverse events (The Commonwealth Fund 1 August 2005); New Zealand's patient safety legal framework includes laws on clinical negligence, independent investigations of complaints, and standards that health providers must meet (Minister of Health 2003); and several European Union countries have patient safety legislation, principally Denmark, Germany, the Netherlands and the United Kingdom (Legido-Quigley et al. 2008). A review of patient safety legal instruments in five countries (Australia, Denmark, New Zealand, United Kingdom, United States) identified a shift to legal frameworks of oversight that displace or supplement those that traditionally allowed health providers a significant degree of autonomy (Downie et al. 2006: iv). Laws applying to various aspects form a body of patient safety law:

> in that it functions to protect the patient by reducing unsafe acts within the health care system. The different areas of law that affect patient safety (for example, tort law, professional regulation, institutional regulation) are not usually conceived of as an integrated system of law. However, conceiving of patient safety law as an integrated entity has value since it allows the discussion to move away from thinking in terms of narrow siloed categories of law to thinking of the larger systemic objectives the legal framework should enable regarding the governance of patient safety.(Downie et al. 2006: v)

While governments in Australia have not used law as the main strategy, and have not passed a patient safety law, legislation has accumulated in many areas that potentially impact upon patient safety. A legislative strategy is not easy to marshal in Australia's federal system of government. While the Australian Government is the main health sector funder and has legislative authority in several areas, constitutional responsibility for the governance of professionals, organizations and services lies mainly with the states. Each Australian state has legislation that could be invoked to regulate patient safety. Although the details differ, all states have similar health care legislation, and the Victorian example is given below as it has reviewed the legislation that bears upon health care in its jurisdiction (Victorian Department of Human Services 2007).

Legislation governing professionals

Health practitioner legislation dates from the nineteenth century when medical boards were established in each state, but the governance of the health professions now is being transformed (see Chapter 4). The states from the 1990s updated their legislation governing professional boards and Victoria notably set up a single regulatory framework for its 12 registered health professions under the *Health Professions Registration Act 2005* (Vic). The Australian Government now has entered the field and has established national boards for 10 professions under the *Health Practitioner Regulation (Administrative Arrangements) National Law Act 2008*, and the *Health Practitioner Regulation National Law 2009*. Professional standards were raised from the 1990s including tighter definitions of misconduct and malpractice, such as the *Professional Standards Act 2003* (Vic). Professionals also have more protection, however, under several pieces of legislation; for example, the confidentiality of quality assurance discussions on patient cases is protected under the *Health Insurance (Quality Assurance Confidentiality) Amendment Act 1992* (Cth) and similar state legislation, and the scope for patients to sue professionals has been restricted and liability payments capped, such as *Wrongs and Other Acts (Law of Negligence) Act 2003* (Vic).

Legislation governing organizations

State health departments have considerable power under legislation and in their capacity as employers. All states have omnibus legislation on the governance of public sector health agencies, and the funding and accountability of non-government agencies. The *Health Services Act 1988* (Vic) and pursuant regulations cover all public hospitals, community health services, aged care homes, and other residential and community services. The legislation sets out broad principles that allow for interpretation and later regulations; for example, Victoria required all its public hospitals from 2000 to undergo accreditation. Agreements with service providers generally contain a requirement that they provide quality services. Private hospitals and private day hospitals (but not public hospitals) must be licensed by state health departments, for example, the *Private Hospitals and Day Procedures Act 1988* (NSW). The Australian Government also funds health care organizations and schemes directly or via agreements with the states and so potentially can attach safety and quality requirements, such as under the *National Health Act 1953* (Cth). Under the *Aged Care Act 1997* (Cth), the Australian Government requires aged residential homes to meet certain standards. In addition, occupational health and safety legislation nationally and in each state protects the working conditions of staff.

Legislation governing technology

The Australian Government regulates the safety and quality of goods and services via several agencies. Therapeutic goods and medical devices are regulated under the *Therapeutic Goods Act 1989* (Cth). The *National Health Act 1953* (Cth) enables the establishment of bodies, such as the Pharmaceutical Benefits Advisory Committee and the Medical Services Advisory Committee. Australia is regarded as a world leader in its health technology assessment procedures and its cost-effective criteria for deciding on the drugs and services eligible for government subsidies (Ettelt et al. 2007).

Legislation protecting people

The Australian Government has powers under the 1901 Constitution to prevent diseases entering the country and has greatly expanded its disease prevention and health promotion responsibilities for communicable and non-communicable diseases. Each state has population health legislation and some clauses bear on health care delivery; for example, the *Health Act 1958* (Vic) enables the Minister to set up consultative councils. The protection of individual patients is embedded in several pieces of legislation in each state. These include the right to health information and privacy, such as the *Health Records Act 2001* (Vic), protection for mental health patients, such as the *Mental Health Act 1986* (Vic), the establishment of health ombudsman, such as the *Health Services Conciliation and Review Act 1987* (Vic), and coronial legislation, such as the *Coroners Act 1985* (Vic).

The next sections go on to examine legislative strategies for regulating the safety and quality of patient care, beginning with coronial inquiries.

Coronial Inquiries

Some state governments are increasing the statutory power of the coroner and his/her importance as a regulatory actor in patient safety (Freckelton 2009). Among the activities undertaken by coroners, three bear upon patient safety regulation: investigating deaths where an adverse event is believed to be a contributing factor; recommendations for system change; and learning from databases on deaths from medical error.

Coroners in most states investigate only ‘reportable’ deaths, which category varies across jurisdictions (Freckelton and Ranson 2006). However, questionable deaths in hospital are under-reported to coroners; for example, the death of a woman in hospital from cardio-respiratory arrest was not reported although the later coronial autopsy found this was due to perforation of the heart following a catheter exchange (Victorian Parliament Law Reform Committee 2005: 75–76). The Commission of Inquiry into Queensland public hospitals recommended strengthening the *Coroner's Act 2003* (Qld) after noting that only two out of 13 suspicious deaths at the Bundaberg Hospital had been reported to the Coroner (Davies Report 2005). Some argue that the coronial process offers a systematic and independent way to investigate deaths from adverse events in a clinical care setting, such deaths should be legally reportable, and a coroner should always be involved where a death involved an adverse event. Such coronial investigations certainly would require a substantial increase in coronial resources; for example, 183 deaths over six months in New South Wales public hospitals were associated with an adverse event (NSW Health 2008).

The traditional view is that the coroner is a public messenger whose task is completed on delivery of the message (Victorian Parliament Law Reform Committee 2005: 71). Coroners have had little power to make binding recommendations to Ministers and public authorities, and most Australian jurisdictions had no legal requirement for health providers to take action or to report back to the coroner (Bugeja and Ranson 2003; Bugeja and Ranson 2005). Victoria now has strengthened its *Coroners Act 2008* (Vic) and requires authorities to report back to the coroner on the action taken on coronial recommendations (Freckelton 2009).

Learning from adverse events could be improved by better working relations between coroners, health departments and health professionals (Victorian Parliament Law Reform Committee 2005: 74–75). The Victorian Coroner's

Office runs a Clinical Liaison Service that employs doctors, nurses and lawyers who recommend an appropriate coronial process after examining the medical records of all deaths reported to the coroner that occur in hospital or within seven days of discharge (Bohensky et al. 2005), while the CLS *Coronial Communiqué* summarizes cases of interest to clinicians that are reported to the Coroner's Office (Ranson and Emmett 2003). The National Coroners Information System collects information on every death reported to an Australian coroner, searches the database to discern fatality patterns, and reports these in its publication, *Fatal Facts*. The vast majority of so-called accidents are said to be preventable:

> We see constant repetitions of the same kind of accidents: yet as human beings we don't learn from them … Part of Johnstone's [the then Victorian Coroner] philosophy is that … systems should be in place to accommodate human error and, by shifting the emphasis in society away from focusing on blame and towards inquiring how an incident happened and how safety measures can be put in place, Australia could realize the potential for slashing the national accidental death toll. (Williams 25 October 2004)

Patient Complaints

Patients have both internal and external avenues for seeking resolution to grievances about encounters with health care providers (apart from going to lawyers, the media and politicians). They can complain directly to the professional or organization concerned and many organizations now have internal complaints procedures. They can complain to a professional registration board, or to a health ombudsman who aims to 'secure the fair, simple, speedy and efficient resolution of complaints'. Their function is to respond to citizen/consumer grievances in order to ensure the accountability of societal institutions and to safeguard the civil liberties of citizens:

> When complaints are freely heard, deeply considered, and speedily reformed, then this is the utmost bound of civil liberty attained that wise men look for. (John Milton *Areopagitica*, 1664)

Each of the Australian states has established health ombudsman (health complaints commissioners) who are independent and non-partisan (Table 8.1). The legislation varies on whether commissioners cover the private as well as the public sector, and with the exception of Queensland, their powers are restricted to responding to consumer complaints and to Ministerial requests for reviews. Complaints to commissioners have risen in recent years but are not a reliable indicator of health care standards since relatively few patients lodge complaints (for example, the NSW Commission received over 3000 complaints in 2007–08). An analysis of complaints to eight health complaints commissioners found most had to do with quality, such as unsatisfactory treatment and inadequate communication (Australian Commission on Safety and Quality in Health Care 2009: chapter 5).

Table 8.1 Health care complaints commissions, Australian states

State	Commissioner	First est.	Current legislation
NSW	Health Complaints Commissioner	1984	Health Care Complaints Act 1993 Health Care Complaints Amendment (Special Commission of Inquiry) 2004 Medical Practice (Amendment) Act 2008
Vic	Health Services Commissioner	1988	Health Services (Conciliation and Review) Act 1987 2001 Amendment; Health Records Act 2001
Qland	Health Quality & Complaints Commissioner	1991	Health Quality & Complaints Commission Act 2006
WA	Office of Health Review	1996	Health Services (Conciliation and Review) Act 1995
SA	Health Quality & Complaints Commissioner	2004	Health & Community Services Complaints Act 2004
Tas	Health Complaints Commissioner	1997	Health Complaints Act 1995
ACT	Community & Health Services Complaints Commissioner	1994	Community & Health Services Complaints Act 1993
NT	Health & Community Services Complaints Commissioner	1998	Health & Community Services Complaints Act 2003

Source: commission websites

An ombudsman can respond to complainants in a range of ways that can be classified within a typology of dispute settlement roles (Black and Baumgartner 1998). An ombudsman acts as an *adviser* in encouraging a person to complain directly to the service provider, termed 'direct resolution', so that many inquiries do not proceed to a written complaint. An ombudsman *assesses* whether a complaint is reasonable, its seriousness, whether the complainant has tried to resolve the matter with the provider, and whether the complaint could be resolved through commission procedures or should be referred to another body, such as a professional registration board. The *conciliation* role varies in degrees of intervention but aims for 'early resolution' and most complaints are resolved with an explanation and/or apology from the health provider. A *mediation* process encourages the parties to reach a mutually agreeable settlement, typically a compromise. An ombudsman acts as an *investigator* when inquiring into a grievance in a formal procedure, and some can adopt an inquisitorial role with powers under legislation to require responses and obtain information on serious matters. The term *arbitration* is not used but in effect the two parties may undertake to abide by an agreement reached in commission proceedings. Ombudsmen are not part of the formal justice system, and the rationale is to avoid expensive and adversarial litigation, and so they do not act as a *judge* and nor can they enforce a determination. Ombudsmen pass matters involving civil or criminal liability to *prosecutors* to institute legal proceedings, such as the director of public prosecutions.

Most commissioners pursue conciliation rather than investigation and prosecution both as a function of the legislation and as a philosophical preference (Newby 2002). The NSW Health Care Complaints Commission takes a more adversarial approach with more cases proceeding to formal conciliation, investigation and prosecution, while the Victorian Commissioner prefers a conciliation approach in assisting the parties to come to an agreement. She believes that conciliation offers a speedier and more effective route for complainants than litigation:

> Nearly all patients who come to our Commission with complaints are seeking quality changes. They usually want to know what happened, why, and they want to make sure that what happened to them does not happen to someone else. We hear this every day. It is very common for conciliation agreements to include assurances from the health service that the complaint has led to changes of practice so that the same mistakes won't reoccur … Conciliation can also result in apologies being made and accepted (apologies are very powerful in complaints resolution and are really important to people) and payments of compensation and explanations'. (Wilson 2004)

Litigation by Patients

'Regulation by litigation' is seen by some as a key instrument for regulating patient safety (Mello et al. 2005). Compensation for medical injuries in common law countries, including Australia, is a fault system based predominantly on the tort of negligence: someone is alleged to have wronged the complainant. The relationship between a health care provider and a patient involves a duty of care under tort law, torts being civil wrongs where some form of compensation is sought. Judicial determinations under common law apply a civil standard of proof on the 'balance of probabilities', while charges brought by the state under criminal law must argue 'beyond reasonable doubt' that the defendant committed the offence, that is, a higher standard of proof is required. Several categories of charges by patients against health professionals may arise under law (McIlwraith and Madden 2006):

- Contract: The nature of the relationship between the health care provider and patient involves an implied, oral or written contract under civil law.
- Negligence: A finding of civil negligence under tort law enables damages to be awarded to a person who suffers injury resulting from health care, where negligence on the part of the provider is proven on the balance of probabilities.
- Defamation: The tort of defamation is designed to protect the individual's reputation. It may be defamatory to accuse a health professional of incompetence. Truth is a defence to a civil action for defamation and the onus of proving the statement true lies with the person who made the statement.
- Battery: Battery under criminal law covers any touching of a person without their consent and so may be relevant if a health care procedure is performed without patient consent.
- Criminal charges: A health practitioner may be charged with fraud, with negligently causing serious injury, or charged with assault, or charged with manslaughter as a result of the death of a patient.

Reforms to tort law are much debated in common law countries including the United States, United Kingdom and Australia (Kerridge et al. 2005: 71). The arguments in favour of patients being able to sue health care providers are that it is a necessary avenue of last resort for aggrieved patients, and has a salutary impact upon doctors and hospitals in ensuring safer and better care (Hirsch 2009). The counter argument is that recourse to litigation is not in the best interests of the general public since it deters health care professionals from learning from their mistakes: 'the conflicts between the tort system and error reduction programmes are fundamental and severe' (Brennan and Berwick 1996: 271). In addition, the costs of litigation are excessive for patients and doctors, the experience of litigation is traumatic on both sides, and claims data do not add knowledge given the small and skewed number of cases (Runciman et al. 2007: chapter 4).

Litigation rates are rising in the United States where doctors are lobbying state legislatures to enact further caps on claims and damages (The Commonwealth Fund 10 January 2005); patients are suing their doctors more often in the United Kingdom (National Audit Office 2001); and rising litigation in Australia led to a doubling of medical indemnity claims by doctors between 1998 and 2002 (Fowler 2005: 3). Rises in malpractice suits by patients, consequent rises in medical indemnity claims, and increases in payouts by insurance funds and courts, followed by rising indemnity insurance premiums, prompted the Australian Government to set up a review of tort law headed by Mr Justice Ipp.

The Ipp Report clarified many aspects of malpractice tort law; for example, a plaintiff's claim may relate to the standard of treatment or to a failure to warn of the risks (Ipp Report 2002). In determining medical negligence, a court must decide whether an appropriate standard of health care was provided. The Ipp Committee recommended that the court adopt a version of the *Bolam* test, under which conformity with practices approved by a responsible body of expert opinion would defeat an allegation of negligence, with the court having the final say (Bennett and Freckelton 2006). The salient definition of negligence in the Ipp Report is as follows:

> A medical practitioner is not negligent if the treatment provided was in accordance with an opinion widely held by a significant number of respected practitioners in the field, unless the court considers that the opinion was irrational. (Ipp Report 2002)

Legislation Protecting Professionals

The states embarked on a flurry of legislation to reduce civil and professional liability following the Ipp Review. The context was the rise in civil litigation in many areas of society by the Australian public (who increasingly were suing companies, governments and neighbours) prompting legislators to reduce the ambit and the costs of civil cases, to establish personal liability principles, and to define personal responsibility for risks. A raft of changes to national and state legislation during 2002–04 curbed the frequency and economic effect of liability litigation (Finance Ministers Communiqué 2005). The collapse in 2002 of the largest medical indemnity insurer, United Medical Protection (see Chapter 4) also hastened changes to medical negligence laws. (Medical indemnity is a form of professional liability insurance that protects the insured against the consequences of being legally liable for injury or damage to third parties, in this case patients.) The two main areas of legislative reform in Australia intended to protect health professionals are changes to medical negligence laws and confidentiality protection for peer review discussions.

Medical negligence laws

The import of changes to medical negligence legislation was to reduce civil liability, set upper limits on damages, reduce the time period for making a claim, limit claims for psychological distress, and ensure that an apology did not represent an admission of guilt. All Australian jurisdictions reduced the opportunities for patients to sue health care providers and reduced the ambit of claims and the size of the awards (Bennett and Freckelton 2006). For example, South Australia passed the *Wrongs (Liability and Damages for Personal Injury) Amendment Act 2002*, the *Law Reform (Ipp Recommendations) Act 2004*, and the *Professional Standards Act 2004*. Who were the winners and losers from these tort law reforms? Medical practitioners gained protection and lower medical indemnity premiums, lawyers had their income-earning opportunities reduced, and patients had their litigation opportunities restricted – against which there are benefits for patients generally in removing a barrier to quality improvement activities. Some argue that these changes will have little impact on the arbitrary nature of a tort-based compensation system, however, and call for a no-fault compensation system providing also that a health provider puts in place prevention strategies to reduce future such adverse events (Corbett 2006).

No fault accident schemes are in place in several countries (Denmark, Sweden, Finland, Iceland, New Zealand). Rather than going to court to prove negligence, patients claim compensation from an insurance scheme where an expert panel assess whether the injury was caused by health care and determines compensation (Fowler 2005; Kerridge et al. 2005: 154–156). The New Zealand scheme, under the *Accident Rehabilitation and Compensation Insurance Act 1992* (NZ), applies to all accidents, as well as medical errors, and covers medical costs, compensation and rehabilitation (French et al. 2001). There is no evidence that the lack of a tort deterrent in New Zealand has any impact, positive or negative, on the quality of health care, however, since the number of patient complaints has continued to rise and the incidence of adverse events is similar to other countries (Bismark and Paterson 2006).

'Qualified privilege' for health professionals

The fear of medico-legal consequences is said by medical practitioners to be a major barrier to their participation in quality improvement activities, such as peer review and learning from adverse event reports. 'Freedom of information' legislation in Australia in the 1980s gave patients access to their own medical information and raised the possibility that medical records could be subpoenaed in a court case. In order to protect health professionals, the Australian Government enacted the *Health Insurance (Quality Assurance Confidentiality) Amendment Act 1992* (Cth), followed by legislation in most states, for example, *Health Services (Quality Improvement) Act 1995* (WA). The legislation confers confidentiality on approved quality activities, 'qualified privilege', in order to keep the information out of the public domain, and nor can an aggrieved patient (or an aggrieved professional alleging defamation) obtain the records of a 'privileged' peer review meeting (Australian Council for Safety and Quality in Health Care 2003a). In most states, a quality improvement committee must apply for privileged status to a minister for health and argue that such confidential proceedings are 'in the public interest'.

Despite the legislation, many health professionals remain uncertain about the extent of protection, since the legislation differs somewhat between the states and interpretations by courts and tribunals also differ. A national guideline was proposed for a standard qualified privilege procedure (Australian Council for Safety and Quality in Health Care 2003a), but had not been endorsed by Health Ministers as at late 2009. Does 'qualified privilege' sometimes 'let doctors off' when negligence or substandard practice is involved? There is a tension, moreover, between the protection of confidential discussions among professionals and a patient's right to information. Do presumed benefits for the patient population trump transparency for individual patients?

Legislation Protecting Patients

The rights of patients are protected by legislation in several areas in Australia, principally rights to one's own medical information, and the right to informed consent for any medical procedure, while the rights of patients are being asserted to be told about any medical error in their treatment. Such rights make for greater transparency and enable a patient to become a more active partner in his/her own health care.

Patient rights to medical information
Public disclosure laws had spread to around 70 countries by 2006 following the lead of Scandinavian and English-speaking countries (Florini 2007). Australia passed the *Freedom of Information Act 1982* (Cth), followed by legislation in all states establishing a right of access by citizens to information about them contained in government records. As this raised privacy issues all jurisdictions later passed legislation protecting a person's rights to privacy and confidentiality of personal information including in their health records. For example, Victoria passed the *Health Records Act 2001* (Vic) that entitles a patient to obtain their own medical record but prevents external persons (including researchers) from seeing that record without the patient's consent. Other hospital records (not covered by privacy legislation) may be obtained 'in the public interest' by third parties. The 'Guthrie Cards' affair in Victoria illustrates the type of privacy concerns that can arise in relation to medical information (see Box 8.1).

Box 8.1 Security of genetic information

Media stories in Victoria in 2004 highlighted privacy issues in relation to the collection and storage of blood testing cards, Guthrie Cards, arising from genetic screening in Victoria of infants for various diseases (for example, phenylketonuria). This major public health programme had been operating for over 30 years and had accumulated records containing genetic information on a large number of Victorians. Given concerns about the security of the records, the Health Services Commissioner brought various parties together to develop transparent guidelines for access, use and research.

Source: Health Services Commissioner Victoria 2004.

Informed consent by patients
The doctrine of informed consent has altered the relationship between clinician and patient. Informed consent is 'voluntary authorization, given to the physician by the patient, with full comprehension of the risks involved, for diagnostic or investigative procedures and medical and surgical treatment' (Medical Dictionary Online). A medical practitioner is legally responsible in many countries for giving information to a patient about the risks associated with receiving, or not receiving, a particular form of treatment. Informed consent is 'based on the principle that

a competent individual has the right to determine what will or will not be done to him or her' (Pizzi et al. 2001). The ethics and legality of what constitutes informed consent involve considerable debate (Kerridge et al. 2005: chapter 13). While upholding the principle, some ethicists argue that the consent procedure is overly onerous in requiring 'full disclosure' of a more comprehensive nature than that required in any other transaction (Clarke 2003). Understanding the risks, for example, implies that a patient can make an informed decision on the ability of a particular surgeon to perform the operation in question (Clarke and Oakley 2004). The requirement to give a full explanation is a radical shift in the doctor-patient relationship from earlier eras when a patient was not necessarily even told the diagnosis.

The High Court of Australia has made a number of rulings that require doctors to inform their patients of any material risks associated with a procedure, and these rulings have been codified in civil liability legislation in most jurisdictions (Bennett and Freckelton 2006). The best known case is Rogers v. Whittaker in 1992 where the High Court held that a doctor has a duty to disclose and warn of risks specific to the particular patient being treated, both of undergoing the procedure and not undergoing the procedure. Failure to obtain adequate informed consent constitutes medical malpractice and can lay a doctor open to a charge of negligence or battery.

Open Disclosure

While the law requires a doctor to obtain informed consent before a procedure, a patient who suffers an adverse event is not necessarily legally entitled to be told. Some ethicists argue that clinicians are ethically required to disclose medical error to their patients irrespective of legal or financial consequences (Oakley and Cocking 2001; Gallagher et al. 2003). The fiduciary obligations of the doctor-patient relationship could also extend to creating a legal duty that any adverse health event be reported promptly to the patient involved (Faunce and Bolsin 2005). An open disclosure procedure is defined as follows:

> Open disclosure is the open discussion of incidents that result in harm to a patient while receiving care. The elements of open disclosure are an expression of regret, a factual explanation of what happened, the potential consequences and the steps being taken to manage the event and prevent recurrence. (Australian Council for Safety and Quality in Health Care 2003b: 1)

While many doctors agree that harmful errors should in principle be disclosed, in practice they 'choose their words carefully' to avoid actually stating that an error had occurred, fearing that an apology will create legal liability. Also, doctors understandably find it difficult to tell bad news to patients and families let alone to admit to errors: 'forgiveness is something that I think is tougher for physicians to give themselves than to get from the patient' (Gallagher et al. 2003: 1005):

> The thing that really galvanises surgeons in a hospital is when they, or one of their colleagues, have a near miss. Or particularly when an actual adverse event occurs because then the surgeon has got to do the open disclosure and tell the patient and undergo the RCA investigation and the whole thing. Surgeons don't like doing that, of course, who would? (Hospital medical director)

Open disclosure policies have been adopted in several countries including Canada, the United Kingdom and the United States. The US Department of Veterans Affairs introduced an open disclosure policy in 1995 with positive effects both for patients and the department (Kraman and Hamm 1999). Several US states have passed laws requiring that patients be informed about 'unanticipated outcomes' in their care, and the US Joint Commission has made open disclosure a requirement for hospital accreditation (Gallagher et al. 2003). While open disclosure may be the policy, it is not known to what extent it actually is practised. For example, a US survey found that only 30 per cent of respondents who had experienced a medical error said that they had been informed of this by a health professional (Blendon et al. 2002).

The Australian states have not enacted legislation that mandates open disclosure, but they have civil liability legislation that protects against an apology being regarded in court as an admission of liability, although the definitions and ensuing protection vary somewhat (Bennett and Freckelton 2006: 403). Not all health care providers are convinced that open disclosure is ethically necessary or financially wise, however, and some hospital managers say that their insurers warn against it. The Health Ministers in 2008 agreed to 'work towards' the implementation of a National Open Disclosure Standard in all Australian hospitals that gives legal protection in expressing regret or making an apology, giving a factual explanation, explaining the consequences of the incident and its management, and discussing the steps being taken to prevent any recurrence (Australian Commission on Safety and Quality in Health Care 2008: 62). Some health departments, such as New South Wales, have now adopted open disclosure as a mandatory policy. Open disclosure of medical injury is an important accountability mechanism but it will require a great deal of persuasion, training and perhaps enforcement to become standard practice (Studdert 2009). The '100 patients stories' project (see Box 8.2) is interviewing patients and families who received an open disclosure explanation from a clinician after an adverse incident, with a view to improving the procedure and designing training (Iedema et al. 2008).

Regulation through Financial Mechanisms

Market model forms of governance were introduced into the health sectors of many countries from the 1980s onwards. Economists argue that regulation is most effective when based on explicit economic incentives and penalties. Competition is an indirect mechanism for promoting quality, for example, and offering a financial

Box 8.2 One story from the 100 patients stories project

> (Family member) [The adverse event] just [felt] like bad luck and that's how [the clinician] described it, you know, it was like the Swiss Cheese Syndrome. I just shook my head and he said 'what it is, you know the Swiss Cheese Syndrome, all the holes line up and she just fell through the holes' and I just thought [sarcastically] that was really great, bad luck Mum sort of thing.'

Source: Australian Commission on Safety and Quality in Health Care 2009: 44

incentive for good performance is a direct mechanism. Health sectors in many countries (both market and quasi-market health systems) use economic regulatory levers to exert pressure for a satisfactory standard of performance. For example, corporate purchasers can offer incentives for high quality care and refuse to pay for unsafe care.

Funding Agreements

Governments have the capacity to use financial levers to enforce standards, such as through funding agreements with organizations to administer or provide health services. About half the recurrent funds for public hospitals in Australia have come from the national government, formalized in five-year bilateral agreements under the *Health Care (Appropriation) Act 1998* (Cth). These Australian Health Care Agreements originally were intended to compensate the states for additional costs incurred after the introduction of Medicare and to insure continued free access to hospitals for public patients (Duckett 2000: 35). The negotiations are always accompanied by considerable political noise'; for example, the 2003–08 Agreement was signed 'after vituperative debate and intransigence from the Commonwealth that vitiated the negotiation process' (Duckett 2004). The Agreements over several rounds from 1993 onwards earmarked money for quality initiatives. The Australian Government in 2007 proposed to step up accountability and tie public hospital funds to the states with a requirement they publish statistics on the quality of hospital performance (Metherell 2007). A proposal for a National Funding Authority to oversee the performance of public hospitals was abandoned in mid 2010, however, and it remains to be seen whether the new Health and Hospitals Network Fund will insist upon publicly reported hospital performance indicators.

Regulation through Market Competition

The Australian Competition and Consumer Commission (ACCC) investigates, warns and prosecutes individuals and organizations for breaches to the law on anti-competitive conduct and protection for consumers (Australian Competition and Consumer Commission 2003a). Australian jurisdictions from 1995 onwards were required to review their legislation in light of National Competition Policy and to remove anti-competitive clauses. In relation to the health sector, the *Trade Practices Act 1974* (Cth) applies to professionals in private practice, private hospitals and clinics (for-profit and non-profit), laboratories, pharmacies, professional associations, and private health funds. The ACCC takes an interest in exclusionary medical practices that limit supply, so that the professions must demonstrate that any monopoly practices have clear benefits to the public in order to be granted exemptions from competition policy (Althaus 1996). In response to protests from the health sector, the ACCC Chairman said that 'the health sector really has to learn to live with the TPA in the same way that businesses in every other sector of the Australian economy do' (Fels 1998).

The *Trade Practices Act* prohibits anti-competitive practices including market share and price fixing agreements, collective boycotts, misuse of market power, anti-competitive exclusive dealing, resale price maintenance, and anti-competitive practices such as price-fixing, and unconscionable conduct (taking unfair advantage). The ACC has taken court actions against doctors for allegedly fixing prices and for collusion. It also scrutinized the professional colleges in relation to alleged anti-competitive behaviour including functioning as 'closed shops' and controlling entry to a specialty so that the incumbents can maintain their share of patients and incomes (Fels 1998). The ACCC pushed for the Royal Australian College of General Practitioners (RACGP) to hand over training to an independent but government-owned organization in 2001(Dwan and Boyce 2003). An ACCC decision in 2003 also ended the Royal Australasian College of Surgeons (RACS) monopoly over surgeon training and entry requirements: 'The 'closed-shop' arrangements and culture, represented by the Royal Australasian College of Surgeons, which unduly influence the selection, training and assessment of Australian surgeons and the accreditation of hospitals must be overcome' (Australian Competition and Consumer Commission 2003b).

The *Trade Practices Act* protects consumers by prohibiting misleading or deceptive conduct by business, ensures compliance with product safety standards, makes manufacturers and importers liable for defective goods, and prohibits unconscionable conduct. The ACCC required the bar upon advertising by doctors to be lifted by medical boards as this was construed as a constraint upon competition, although doctors are not permitted to endorse therapeutic products, under the *Therapeutic Goods Act 1989* (Cth). The ACCC has taken court action on many health scams, such as misleading advertising on products and devices.

Pay-for-Performance

Pay-for-performance (P4P) schemes come in various forms. The softest form, a bonus scheme, offers a health provider an extra payment for completing a certain task, such as immunizations. The next level up, a payment aligned to quality, aims to change the behaviour of medical practitioners by rewarding improvements in clinical practice and clinic procedures (Epstein et al. 2004). Some P4P schemes may be compulsory rather than voluntary, and in a further leap may financially punish poor performance. Medical practitioners, of course, prefer financial incentives to deliver high quality care not payment cuts for poor performance (Institute of Medicine 2002). Some US payers impose financial disincentives for poor performance, for example, by withholding money from hospitals for medical error costs, in other words, they pay for good care not poor care: 'By saying no to unacceptable errors, payers will strengthen incentives for hospitals, doctors, and other health professionals to provide high-quality, safe care' (Leape and Davis 2005).

The main advantage of pay-for-performance is that good quality care is rewarded, and depending on the formula, there may be financial sanctions for poor quality care. The disadvantages are philosophical and technical. The medical profession is divided over the desirability of pay-for-performance: some oppose the idea of rewarding 'good' physicians and punishing 'bad' physicians, while others regard P4P as undermining professional service and treating medicine as a commodity. The technical disadvantage is the difficulty of arriving at an acceptable definition of what constitutes good (or quality) performance as measures of quality are many and various. Since a pay-for-performance formula cannot take all aspects of performance into account, it must select from among evidence-based indicators; for example, the proportion of patients who smoke who are advised to cease.

Pay-for-performance schemes for doctors are common in the highly privatized health care sector in the United States. The Leapfrog Group identified 100 different types of pay-for-performance programmes that vary along a number of dimensions including type of sponsor, size of the bonus, formula for determining the bonus, and type of clinical area targeted (Greene and Nash 2009). Many health plans offer a bonus to physicians with quality and safety systems in place, such as electronic medical records, and pay bonuses for performance measures, such as generic drug utilization and patient satisfaction (The Commonwealth Fund 27 June 2005). Medicare and Medicaid offer doctors a 1.5 per cent increase in payments to report data on at least three quality measures. Some urge Medicare to deny payments for the costs associated with preventable adverse events as do some Health Maintenance Organizations (HMOs); for example a large Minnesota HMO refuses to pay for 27 types of medical mistakes (The Commonwealth Fund 18 December 2006).

In England's National Health Service (NHS), a large portion of GP income now is based on pay-for-performance. Most general practitioners (GPs) are 'independent contractors' who supply medical services to the NHS under an agreed national contract. The 1990 contract introduced financial incentives for some preventive health tasks and these were expanded in subsequent contracts. The 2004–07 contract set aside money to pay GPs according to their success in meeting 146 criteria for quality patient care for 10 chronic diseases, plus money for better clinic procedures and increased patient satisfaction. In the first year, GPs met all clinical indicators for 83 per cent of eligible patients and so received substantial additional payments that boosted their annual income by 23 per cent, so that this unexpected budgetary blow-out contributed to the large NHS deficit (Doran et al. 2006).

In Australia, general practitioners are mostly self-employed private professionals although most of their income derives from public sources: about 68 per cent comes from Medicare for bulk-billed services (Department of Health and Ageing 2005: 60). GPs are paid on a fee-for-service basis by patients and by Medicare so that payment is based on quantity (number of consultations and tests), not quality in terms of processes and outcomes. The Australian Government from the late 1990s onwards began to introduce some performance bonuses (Department of Health and Ageing 2005: 478). The Practice Incentives Programme (PIP) offers financial incentives to improve quality of care for diabetes, asthma, mental health and cervical screening, offers financial incentives to improve IT infrastructure, and requires them to become accredited practices – over half of general practices participated in the programme in 2006. Under the Enhanced Primary Care scheme, GPs can claim Medicare rebates for undertaking care plans for patients with chronic medical conditions. Service Incentive Payments target chronic diseases: asthma, cervical screening, diabetes and mental health. The extra payments from these schemes are significant since the PIP programme in 2003 provided around 10 per cent of GP income. There is also evidence that financial incentives improve quality since 20 per cent more PIP GPs ordered a HbA1c test (a blood sugar test) for their diabetes patients than did GPs not members of the scheme (Scott et al. 2009).

Regulation through Monitoring

The monitoring of performance indicators has become a major regulatory strategy. Many countries have set up programmes to collect and analyse performance data from health care providers and research is underway on improving methods of measurement. This section discusses four types of monitoring programmes: database registers as a well-accepted professional mechanism; adverse event reporting as a recent policy priority; performance indicators as a meta-regulation mechanism; and the monitoring of insurance fraud by health professionals.

Registers and Databases

Professional groups establish registries to collect data to track conditions and activities with a view to improving professional performance (see Chapter 4). 'Clinical registries are databases that systematically collect health-related information on individuals who are treated with a particular surgical procedure, device or drug, diagnosed with a particular illness or managed via a specific health care resource. The system or organization governing the register is known as the registry' (Buchan et al. 2009: 72). Registers are well-accepted by the medical profession and their advocates argue that targeted reporting on specific phenomena, backed up by professional authority, is a better way to audit practice than a broader adverse event reporting system. Clinical registers run by professional groups are based on voluntary reporting and peer audit that aim to develop a consensus on standards and protocols. Registers are maintained on certain types of mortality, such as cancer, anaesthesia and surgical mortality, the management of organ transplants and therapeutic devices and equipment, as well as surveillance of adverse drug reactions and hospital acquired infection. For example, Sweden has over 70 clinical registers and Australia has 28 (McNeil et al. 2010). Registries aim to strengthen participation by clinicians, improve their methodology and governance, form national networks, and link to international registries to enable cross-national comparisons.

Hospital acquired infection, for example, is an important area of surveillance through either voluntary or mandatory registers. Reporting is mandatory in some US states, while the National Nosocomial Infection Survey covers about 300 hospitals and produces confidential inter-hospital comparisons (Centers for Disease Control and Prevention). In Australia, some but not all state health departments have surveillance systems to monitor hospital acquired infections and efforts are underway to establish a national surveillance programme (Australian Commission on Safety and Quality in Health Care 2009: chapter 4). Anaesthesia registers are another example as anaesthesia has long been recognized as a potentially risky procedure and anaesthetists were active safety advocates in studying 'critical incidents' that consequently led to improvements in equipment design. The reason for vigilance in anaesthesia is captured well in the following quotation:

> The body is paralysed, the brain rendered unconscious, and machines are hooked up to control breathing, heart rate, blood pressure – all the vital functions. Given the complexity of the machinery and of the human body, there are a seemingly infinite number of ways in which things can go wrong. And yet anaesthesiologists have found that if problems are detected they can usually be solved. (Gawande 2002: 64)

Adverse Event Reporting Systems

There are two main arguments for a reporting system. First, the performance indicator argument is that a database can be used to ascertain the scope and scale of adverse events, compare others against a performance average, and set a benchmark in order to monitor progress. This measurement rationale is problematic since estimates are unreliable in the absence of agreed definitions, and especially given under-reporting by health professionals. As Lucian Leape put it politely, 'physicians have been reluctant partners in reporting' (Leape 2002: 1633). Interpreting the numbers also is problematic since more reports may not indicate worsening patient safety but rather that people are reporting more, and conversely apparently fewer events may be due to less reporting.

The second rationale, the quality argument, is that incidents should be identified and analysed to provide evidence upon which to base improved procedures and practices. This requires a large database since medical errors come in many types and mostly in low frequencies. A hospital may regard some errors as too infrequent to warrant attention and not realize that these are cumulatively significant across hospitals, while the occurrence of a rare event can be catastrophic for a patient. The Quality in Australian Health Care Study (QAHCS) study found that the top ten categories of frequency accounted for only 25 per cent of all adverse events (Runciman and Moller 2001: 19). Also, the small number of serious adverse events that individual doctors encounter over their careers means that many downplay the risks and are surprised at the scale when extrapolated to national estimates (ibid).

Incident reporting in the aviation industry is cited as a model to emulate, but the health sector situation is rather different. Lucian Leape quotes the architect of the Aviation Safety Reporting System as attributing its success to three factors: reporting is safe (pilots are immune from disciplinary action if they report promptly), simple (a one-page report), and worthwhile (experts analyse the 30,000 confidential annual reports and disseminate recommendations to pilots and the Federal Aviation Administration). Leape comments that in the health sector, in contrast, reports made to mandatory programmes are seldom simple, safe or worthwhile: reporting is cumbersome, carries considerable risks (loss of licence or accreditation, damage to reputation, loss of business), and lessons learned from investigations into adverse events are seldom shared (Leape 2002).

Adverse event reporting systems have been established in many countries as a measurement mechanism for monitoring patient safety, and as a quality mechanism for learning from and preventing future adverse events. Reporting systems are an expensive regulatory strategy since substantial resources must be expended in establishing and maintaining them so policy makers must believe that the benefits outweigh the costs. Countries vary on whether they have national or regional system, and whether reporting is mandatory or voluntary on the part of hospitals and professionals.

United States: Many US states have reporting systems but national trends cannot be extrapolated given under-reporting and varying definitions (Leape 2002). Mandatory error reporting was required in 22 US states in 2004 (Davis 2004), and hospitals must have reporting systems to achieve accreditation (Joint Commission 2005a). In the voluntary camp, the Institute for Safe Medication Practices claims that its reporting programme has improved the policies and practices of pharmaceutical and device manufacturers and governments (Cohen 2000: 72), and the Veterans Affairs Administration has voluntary reporting in its health care facilities (Bagian et al. 2001, 2002).

United Kingdom: The National Patient Safety Agency launched its National Reporting and Learning System (NRLS) in England and Wales in 2004 for staff in NHS organizations to report incidents and near misses. Reporting by individuals is voluntary, can be anonymous, and is made locally or centrally on an electronic report form. The NRLS extracts and analyses data from local reporting systems, but incident investigation is the responsibility of local NHS managers.

European Union: A survey of 25 EU member states in 2005 found that 7 countries (Czech Republic, Denmark, England and Wales, Germany, Ireland,

Slovak Republic and Sweden) had national systems in place, although the type and scope differed, and the Netherlands was implementing a system (SIMPATIE 2007). Apart from England, Denmark has the best-established system that began in 2004 with reporting by hospitals mandatory to a national database run by the National Board of Health, and individuals are protected from disciplinary action.

Australia: Australia has eight state reporting systems for public hospitals although the desirability of a national system has been extensively discussed (Runciman 2002). These systems do not add up to a national database given different software and different incident classifications. Four states (New South Wales, Western Australia, South Australia, Northern Territory) use the Australian Incident Monitoring System (AIMS) software, Victoria and the Australian Capital Territory use Riskman, Queensland developed its own software, and Tasmania (in 2007) had not decided. While public hospitals must participate in their state system, reporting is voluntary on the part of staff (in legal terms although most hospitals as employers expect staff to report), except in the case of serious adverse events and so-called sentinel events.

Sentinel events

A *sentinel event* signals 'the need for immediate investigation and response' defined as 'an unexpected occurrence involving death or serious physical or psychological injury, or the risk thereof' (Joint Commission 2005b). These are regarded as 'never events' that should not occur. The US Joint Commission began to issue sentinel event alerts after identifying some serious and unacceptable errors from hospital reports to the Commission's database. The concept of a subset of serious adverse events offers a rationale for compulsory reporting. The Australian Health Ministers in 2004 selected eight types of errors (see Table 8.2) as 'sentinel events' (somewhat strange categories according to critics) and required the states to forward data for national publication:

The subsequent report disclosed 130 sentinel events occurred in public hospitals around Australia in 2004–05, the largest category (41 per cent) being procedures on the wrong patient or body part (Australian Institute of Health and Welfare and the Australian Commission on Safety and Quality in Health Care 2007). The report sparked considerable media publicity: as one journalist commented 'everyone's nightmare about undergoing the wrong operation appears to be true'. Reporting over the next two years showed that some errors increased (for example, medication error), while the big increase in 2006–07 in 'procedures involving the wrong patient or body part' was redefined downwards in 2007–08 (Table 8.2). Some states publish reports on sentinel events each year without identifying hospitals but hospital managers brace themselves for publicity:

> When the health department published a sentinel event report last year there was headline on page two of the newspaper saying 'Public hospital hangs head in shame'. Unfortunately these incidents get sensationalised. All we can do is to

work with the media to understand we are trying to improve. (Hospital safety and quality coordinator)

How do reported numbers compare to the numbers that might be expected? This is hard to assess. Sentinel events represent perhaps 10 per cent of all serious events (Australian Commission on Safety and Quality in Health Care 2009: 63). The Quality in Australian Health Care (QAHCS) study found that 280 serious events occur each year in a large public hospital (Runciman and Moller 2001). New South Wales reported 429 serious (SAC1) events for all 222 acute public hospitals in 2004–05, but 1.9 events per hospital (compared to the QAHCS prediction of 280 for a large hospital) suggests substantial under-reporting or else a dramatic but unlikely improvement in patient safety over the decade.

Table 8.2 Sentinel events in public hospitals Australia 2005–06 to 2007–08

Sentinel event type	2005–2006	2006–2007	2007–2008
Procedures involving the wrong patient or body part (*resulting in death or permanent loss of function)	66	159	21*
Suicide of a patient in an inpatient unit	25	41	32
Retained instrument or other material after surgery requiring re-operation or further surgical procedure	28	28	34
Intravascular gas embolism resulting in death or neurological damage	2	3	1
Haemolytic blood transfusion reaction resulting from blood type ABO incompatibility	1	2	4
Medication error leading to death of patient reasonably believed to be due to incorrect administration of drugs	5 11	21	
Maternal death or serious morbidity associated with labour or delivery	12 13	22	
Infant discharged to the wrong family	0	0	2
TOTAL	139	257	137

* Revised sentinel event definition

Source: Australian Commission on Safety and Quality in Health Care, 2009: 64

Near misses

Jim Bagian, a pioneer of adverse event reporting, argues that near misses are the 'main game' of opportunities to learn (Bagian et al. 2002). Near misses are far more frequent than actual adverse events (Institute of Medicine 2004: 226); for example, comparisons of potential and actual adverse drug events suggest a five-fold difference (Bates et al. 1995). While learning from near misses clearly makes sense, in practical terms reporting would be a huge task for a hospital. Taking the estimate that near misses are five times more frequent than actual events, and taking estimates of adverse events based on the QAHCS study, a large Australian teaching hospital over a year may have 1,400 near misses for serious incidents (280 incidents × 5). These numbers suggest that logging near misses in the hospital sector currently is not realistic – although England's reporting system aims to collect near misses. News of a near miss spreads rapidly throughout a hospital, however, and has a salutary effect in improving compliance with patient safety protocols:

> The reason the [safe surgery] protocol gained traction in our hospital was because there were three near-miss clinical incidents. They weren't serious but enough to make three different groups of surgeons take notice because of the angst caused to them and to their patients. The surgeons also realised that while those were near misses on minor surgery, it showed the potential for error with major surgery. It opened their minds to the issue. (Hospital CEO)

Measuring and Monitoring Health Care Performance

Measuring and monitoring clinical indicators is now well-established. The thrust is to identify an activity that is easy to measure and to track over time, or if this is not possible, then a proxy measure of performance is sought. The choice of indicator often is pragmatic depending on what data can be gathered conveniently, what data are least ambiguous (such as death), and what data are less amenable to gaming. Research on performance indicators aims to identify, validate and standardize measures in order to assess health care quality (McGlynn 1998). Measures of health care quality can be classified in terms of structural indicators (systemic aspects of how health care is organized), process indicators (what health professionals do to people), and outcome indicators (what happens to people in terms of their health outcomes) (Brook et al. 2000: 281).

Structural indicators do not necessarily correlate well, however, with process and outcome measures. For example, does an adverse event reporting system produce safer patient care? *Process* indicators (for example, waiting times for elective surgery) are often used, partly because they are easiest to collect although not necessarily associated with improved outcomes. Do shorter waiting times produce better clinical outcomes? *Outcome* indicators are the most difficult to collect and to interpret but are the most direct measures of patient safety and quality. Using 30-day post-surgical patient mortality rates, for example, requires adjusting for patient case mix and other external factors. Definitions of hospital quality outcomes are hotly contested. Research on Australian standardized hospital mortality ratios (deaths per 100 patients) concluded that such measures are best regarded as screening tools rather than as measures of quality (Ben-Tovim et al. 2009). Measures of quality also are beginning to include patient views and to develop survey instruments (such as the Dutch consumer quality index), while some countries, such as England and the Netherlands, publish surveys on the experiences of users and name these services.

Poorly designed monitoring can increase regulatory burden and provoke perverse behaviour. Hospitals collect huge amounts of data and staff hate more reporting requirements. There are many stories about the ingenious manipulations of performance indicators that occur when providers 'game the numbers' in order to improve their scores. For example, a NHS target was that patients be seen in less than four hours by a hospital emergency department, the anecdotal reports being that patients are kept outside in ambulances so that they are not officially in the hospital and so the triage clock does not start ticking (Cameron 2007).

Performance indicators that aim to track health care quality are used to compare performance at several levels: clinicians, organizations and whole health systems. The OECD Health Care Quality Indicators Project collects a core set of comparable measures that enables a comparison of medical care quality across several countries (Mattke et al. 2006). National quality reports are produced in several countries based on performance indicators across their health system. For example, the US National Healthcare Quality Report measures progress in 57 areas on processes (for example, service use) and outcomes (for example, mortality rates) (Agency for Healthcare Research and Quality 2008). In Australia, a national report charted trends in clinical performance indicators, such as effectiveness (for example, treatment of high blood pressure), appropriateness (for example, unacceptably high caesarean section rates), patient safety (for example, surgical mortality), access to care (for example, waiting times in emergency departments), responsiveness (for example, patient satisfaction with health services), and disparities in health care (for example, access to services for renal disease) (Australian Council for Safety and Quality in Health Care 2004). Some states also publish quality reports, notably New South Wales, where annual state-wide safety and quality measures are tracked for 13 clinical specialties (Clinical Excellence Commission 2007).

From a regulatory perspective, a monitoring programme can identify substandard clinical areas and substandard health care providers that require remedial attention. Monitoring the proportion of patients who receive clinically appropriate treatment, for example, indicates the extent of compliance with evidence-based clinical guidelines. A US study found that only 54.9 per cent of US adults had received the recommended care, varying across 30 conditions from 78.7 per cent down to 10.5 per cent of patients, based on a telephone survey of 13,275 patients in 12 metropolitan areas (McGlynn et al. 2003). Similar results were found with children: only 46.5 per cent of children received the recommended care, varying across clinical conditions from 92 per cent down to 34.5 per cent, based on an examination of 1,536 paediatric outpatient medical records across 12 metropolitan areas (Mangione-Smith et al. 2007).

Public Reporting on Performance as a Regulatory Strategy

Publicly reporting on the performance of named health care providers is now a major regulatory strategy. Several countries (for example, England, Denmark, Germany, United States) publish performance indicators that name hospitals. These measures are presented as gold stars, ranges, ranks, scores, or as 'league tables' when rank order comparisons are made between providers. There are three main arguments in favour of public reporting. First, the personal autonomy argument is that people need reliable information in order to make informed decisions about health care treatment (Clarke and Oakley 2004). Second, the market argument is that public reporting enables purchasers to choose between providers and consequently demand will rise for high performers and drop for poor performers. Third, the quality argument is that health providers care about their reputations, will seek to do better and so standards will rise. These arguments assume that choice exists, that providers want more money and patients, and that providers care about their reputations.

There are also arguments against publishing performance indicators that identify individual clinicians and hospitals. Even advocates of public reporting regard it as a 'two edged sword whose effects can motivate and reward but also discourage and punish' (Leatherman and McCarthy 1999). Public reporting of performance involves ethical and technical issues and strongly held views (Clarke and Oakley 2004; Clarke and Oakley 2007). A host of objections commonly are raised as barriers to performance transparency:

> This dilemma arises repeatedly in the quality of care field. People want valid and reliable measures of quality of care but they do not want to pay for them. They vigorously oppose any system that has demonstrable error in it that could be improved with a better data collection system because it is not fair to risk the reputation of a single hospital or a single doctor through bad data about quality. On the other hand, when one proposes a more detailed clinical data collection system, the complaints are that it costs too much, is not feasible, and probably is not that important. (Brook et al. 2000: 287)

Practicality is an issue since installing additional and specialized reporting is expensive and an added burden on staff. There is increasing interest, therefore, in identifying existing datasets that could be used to monitor safety and quality. Hospital standardized mortality ratios are one source, but more as a screening tool to investigate outlier hospitals (Ben-Tovim et al. 2009). Improving routinely collected data may be a cost-effective mechanism to measure some indicators. For example, an analysis of Victorian administrative datasets used for calculating hospital casemix payments, with adverse events identified by International Classification of Diseases diagnostic codes, found that 6.88 per cent of patients were coded as experiencing at least one adverse event – close to the 10 per cent of cases identified in retrospective reviews of patient medical records (Ehsani et al. 2006).

Technical issues are raised in relation to measurement reliability and validity. Variance can be hard to explain; for example, an 'unplanned readmission' might say more about a lack of post-hospital services than treatment shortcomings in the previous admission. Providers with sub-optimal scores typically claim that the measures did not adjust sufficiently for their sicker patients. Performance indicator studies are possible only with a high volume of cases sufficient to be statistically confident that the outcomes have not arisen by chance (Marshall et al. 1998). Technical issues that need addressing include diagnostic coding, lack of risk-adjustment models for all conditions, and statistical tools to handle random error in sample sizes (Scott and Ward 2006). Methods that adjust for severity of the patient's condition include the Charlson index that uses using ICD-10 codes as well as codes that indicate a pre-admission complication (Sundararajan et al. 2004). Another technical issue is how best to present the results when the aim is to inform public choice. 'League tables' are the most popular with the public but not methodologically sound given the large confidence intervals that often surround the data. Public reporting on adverse events is particularly problematic given problems with reporting reliability, so that the danger in 'naming and shaming' is that safety conscious hospitals are punished because their staff conscientiously report incidents:

> I don't have a problem with transparency and making things public. Sometimes making things public is a great motivator. But Australian hospitals have a big cultural problem with public reporting of adverse incidents. Misinformation is highly political. The number of reports by a hospital to the reporting system may be high because you're bloody awful and have many incidents that should not be occurring. Or it may be high because you have a culture of safety and everyone is reporting. You can have two hospitals that are poles apart on the safety issue but from the data are identical and both get hammered. The hospital that is doing badly probably thinks it wasn't as bad as it could have been. The hospital who is doing well thinks why do we bother? So you may destroy the safety culture they have built up. I'm quite cynical of incident reporting from that perspective. I think reporting is only useful for identifying where there may be opportunities for improvement. I don't think it is useful for quantification. (Director of Surgery)

Third, 'gaming', that is the manipulation of measures by providers is an ever-present issue. Does public reporting actually improve performance or only appear to do so? Ideally, a lagging hospital would take remedial action, but in practice might just look for ways to massage the numbers. The 'gaming' phenomenon has received considerable attention. For example, the introduction of report cards on death rates among those operated on by cardiac surgeons in New York State was followed by a substantial increase in the reported severity of patients with chronic problems, although not matched by more objective markers of chronic disease, so that statistical adjustment for apparently sicker patients produced improved outcomes. It was impossible to ascertain whether this severity coding creep was real or the combined effect of sicker patients and the exaggeration of patient severity (Hannan et al. 1998).

Finally, what follows from a regulatory perspective? Is the detection of poor performers followed by correction? Hospitals in poorer areas often perform less well on performance indicators suggesting that insufficient allowance was made for sicker patients and fewer resources to treat them (Appleby and Mulligan 2000). This was also a concern when the Australian Government in 2010 began report cards' on schools (see Box 8.3).

Box 8.3 Public reporting of school results

The Australian Government launched the My School website in January 2010, just before the new school year, to acclaim from parents and vociferous opposition from teacher unions. The website published test results that named each school on reading, writing, spelling, grammar and punctuation, and numeracy, for Years 3 and 5 for primary schools, and Years 7 and 9 for high schools. Like schools were grouped together and scores adjusted for a school's geographic socio-economic status. The website crashed on the first day under an avalanche of hits. While the website does not rank schools, newspapers immediately published lists of schools in their state against test results for the state and nationally that allowed 'league table' comparisons. Politicians pontificated on schools in their state in comparison to other states, teachers complained that their fears that schools (and hence their pupils) would be 'named and shamed' were realized, while parents welcomed the information. It remains to be seen whether parents will move their children from schools with poor results to those with high results (given that public schools are geographically zoned), and whether governments will take remedial action including allocating more resources to poor performing schools.

Public reporting in several countries

The *United States* places a high priority on information strategies for consumers and purchasers. Public reporting on clinical performance dates from the 1980s when New York State introduced 'report cards' on cardiac surgeons based on death rates among their patients. Since then several NGOs have made it their mission to develop and publish indicators. The Hospital Quality Alliance compares the quality of hospitals nationwide on measures of heart attack, heart failure, and treatment of pneumonia (The Commonwealth Fund 11 April 2005), the National Committee for Quality Assurance publishes indicators on doctors and health plans (National Committee for Quality Assurance 2005), and the National Quality Forum developed 36 measures on the quality of physician care in outpatient settings (The Commonwealth Fund

8 August 2005), while the Leapfrog Group in the private sector publishes hospital ratings (Leapfrog Group 2005). In the government sector, the Centers for Medicare and Medicaid Services website publishes information on over 4,000 hospitals against national and state averages including on three types of conditions: heart attack, heart failure, and pneumonia (The Commonwealth Fund 4 April 2005).

In the *United Kingdom*, the Care Quality Commission publishes annual 'health checks' on named hospitals (excellent, good, fair, weak) on two measures: quality of services, and use of resources. The Darzi Review called for all NHS healthcare providers to be legally obliged to publish 'quality accounts' on safety, patients' experiences, and clinical outcomes (Kmietowicz 2008). The Care Quality Commission website shows annual survival rates for hospital units and for surgeons for all cardiac surgery (on average 96.6 per cent) and for two common types of heart surgery: coronary artery bypass grafts and aortic valve replacement surgery (Neil et al. 2004; Mayor 2006). Dr Foster, a private company set up in 2001, offers the public a website search on quality and waiting lists for hospitals, doctors and complementary practitioners.

In *Australia*, state health departments are not enthusiastic about public reporting. But some have been pushed, partly by public inquiries, into making hospital data public. For example, the Queensland Government now publishes clinical indicators on their 74 public hospitals, such as risk-adjusted inpatient mortality rates (Queensland Health 2006; Scott and Ward 2006). The data on an array of clinical indicators are analysed using the variable life adjusted display (VLAD) statistical method (Duckett et al. 2007). Public reporting is now on the policy agenda. A report on health system reform called more public reporting (National Health and Hospital Reform Commission 2009). The Australian Commission for Safety and Quality in Health Care, is working on a core set of hospital-based outcome indicators in the following areas: hospital standardized mortality ratios, in-hospital mortality rates for several conditions, unplanned hospital readmissions for several conditions, health care associated infections, and serious obstetric trauma (Australian Commission on Safety and Quality in Health Care 2009: 86). It remains to be seen which agency will collect this data from hospitals and under what authority, and whether hospitals will be identified in published reports.

Medicare Payments: Monitoring Fraud and Over-Servicing

The regulation of medical and pharmaceutical benefit payments to claimants is considered here for several reasons. First, this is a huge area in terms of the volume and variety of regulatory activities. Second, 'medifraud' costs the Australian Government (and hence taxpayers) a large amount. Third, Medicare Australia applies an array of regulatory instruments ranging from education to prosecution. Fourth, more could be done to regulate quality as do insurance funds in other countries (Germany, Netherlands, the United States). Finally, Medicare Australia regulates over-servicing (one aspect of clinical performance) through a form of peer review.

Medicare Australia (formerly the Health Insurance Commission) administers the national health insurance scheme that offers a full rebate of the Medical Benefits Schedule fee for GP consultations, and 85 per cent of the schedule fee for consultations with specialists. Doctors who charge no more than the schedule fee can bulk-bill Medicare and the majority of services (about 75 per cent) are bulk-billed. The Pharmaceuticals Benefits Scheme (PBS) subsidizes the purchase of pharmaceuticals on its approved list. Claims on consultations and prescriptions provide an enormous database for statistical interrogation.

Fraud is an unambiguous concept under s129 of the *Health Insurance Act 1973* (Cth) that prohibits making false or misleading statements on documents used to obtain medical or pharmaceuticals benefits (for example, falsely claiming for consultations). This legislation and the *Health Legislation (Powers of Investigation) Amendment Act 1994* (Cth) give Medicare Australia considerable regulatory power, including to obtain a search warrant, and to require a person to give information and to produce a document. Over-servicing and over-prescribing are more complex matters, referring to services not reasonably required for the adequate medical care of a patient (for example, repeated consultations without medical justification), and unnecessary medication (for example, excessive repeat prescriptions).

While the great majority of doctors and pharmacists are honest, there are financial temptations. A series of reports since the early 1980s by parliamentary committees and auditors have complained about fraud and over-servicing by up to 7 per cent of medical practitioners. Termed 'leakage', this was estimated to cost around 2 per cent of the Medicare and Pharmaceutical budget in 1997 and required strong regulatory action (Auditor-General 1997). A TV programme in 2004 titled 'Doctoring the Figures' aired disagreements on how much was being 'rorted': a Health Insurance Commission official thought less than 1 per cent while others said 5–10 per cent. The Health Insurance Commission was characterized as a regulatory rabbit rather than a watch dog as it generally counselled and warned rather than punished doctors (Moynihan 1998). According to the HIC 2003–04 annual report, 603 doctors were interviewed for suspected 'inappropriate practice', 75 were investigated for fraud, 15 were partially or fully suspended as Medicare providers, nine were prosecuted with charges proven against one but no conviction recorded, and one doctor was convicted. The convicted doctor was charged by the Director of Public Prosecutions on 27 counts of making false statements and was disqualified as a Medicare provider (Health Insurance Commission 2004). Despite the scale of the 'rorts', the Health Insurance Commission seldom escalated up the regulatory pyramid to prosecutions and convictions.

The Health Insurance Commission, relabelled Medicare Australia, was restructured in 2005 as a government agency under the Department of Human Services and brought under closer Ministerial control. Medicare Australia operates an extensive and sophisticated 'national compliance programme' to detect fraud and over-servicing through prevention, detection, and correction. It aims to encourage a culture of voluntary compliance ranging from 'soft' strategies at the bottom of its regulatory pyramid to 'hard' instruments at the apex.

Prevention: *Information and education* mechanisms include attempts to reduce over-servicing by countering drug company promotional material with other information on rational prescribing, articles in the agency newsletter, and information sessions for new providers.

Detection: *Data analysis* involves sophisticated techniques including scanning provider profiles for outlier practitioners and prescribers. For example, one indicator of 'inappropriate practice' is the rendering of 80 or more consultations on 20 or more days within a 12-month period (dubbed the 80/20 rule). *Reports of fraud* are invited from the public and many investigations result from people being 'dobbed in'. *Random audits and targeted audits* are carried out regularly. Audits have increased from 1 per cent to 4 per cent of health professionals with 2700 medical practitioners reviewed in 2008–09. Targeted audits also are carried out, for example, on prescriptions of high-cost medicines. *Investigations* are carried out on over 3,000 reports each year and investigators can search premises and seize material where fraud is detected. For example, the 'Prescription Shopping Project' investigated cases where patients consulted multiple prescribers.

Correction: *Correction* of non-compliance is through feedback to the individuals concerned, interviews with medical practitioners and pharmacists by agency staff, recovery of benefits paid ($6.18 million in 2008–09), investigations, and where fraud is detected referral for criminal prosecutions to the Commonwealth Director of Public Prosecutions. *Counselling and peer review* is the main approach taken on suspected over-servicing and Medicare Australia staff can interview the doctor or refer the case to the Professional Services Review Scheme (see later). *Fines* can be levied and a requirement to pay back defrauded funds. *Disqualification* from Medicare or PBS can be recommended, either complete or partial, for a stated period of time. *Adverse publicity* involves those successfully prosecuted being named in the agency's annual compliance report. *Deregistration* as a medical practitioner or pharmacist is a matter for the professional boards. *Prosecution*, the strongest instrument available is used sparingly, with successful prosecutions mounted in 2008–09 against four medical practitioners, one pharmacist, and 43 members of the public.

Peer review of 'inappropriate practice'

Medicare investigations on whether a medical practitioner was intensively servicing or over-servicing (euphemistically termed 'inappropriate practice') have involved peer review since the 1980s. Medicare employed doctors to question those with apparently excessive billing or prescribing patterns, and alleged cases of 'inappropriate practice' then were referred to a panel of medical practitioners who could recommend sanctions to the Minister. The Professional Services Review scheme (PSR) was established in 1994 under the *Health Insurance Act 1973* (Cth) to formalize such investigations. After a referral from Medicare Australia (137 cases in 2008–09), the PSR can assign staff to investigate the medical practitioner, engage medical consultants, requisition medical records, compel answers under oath in a formal hearing, and recommend a range of sanctions including prosecution (see Box 8.4).

The PSR applied 'naming and shaming' in 2006 when it mailed a report to all Medicare providers (over 45,000 doctors) naming 26 doctors who were disqualified, reprimanded or forced to repay Medicare Australia, plus details of court decisions on 13 doctors found guilty (Professional Services Review 2006). For example, one doctor, 'the busiest general practitioner in Australia', had claimed on 80 or more patients each day in the 32 day review period (ten minutes per patient over an eight-hour day or vice versa?).

Litigious doctors and lawyers' fees make the PSR an expensive regulatory mechanism. Doctors not surprisingly fight vigorously through the courts to defend fraud charges, to protect their reputations, and to maintain registration as Medicare providers and hence their livelihood. The PSR scheme is estimated to have cost an average of almost $70,000 to resolve each of the 447 referrals over 11 years (1994–2005) with action taken as follows:

- 447 referrals/requests received;
- 189 PSR committees established;
- 98 Final determinations issued;
- 31 Appeals to PSR Tribunals; and
- 47 cases that resulted in substantive Federal Court actions (Bell 2006: 120).

Conclusion

Do Legal Strategies Improve Safety and Quality?

A body of law is accumulating that bears upon patient safety in several ways including patients' complaints procedures, changes to medical negligence legislation, legal protection for quality activities, and protection of patients' rights. Patient safety legislation in some countries also enables enforcement, and while important symbolically, its direct impact so far is unknown.

Consumer complaints to health ombudsmen
Ombudsmen are an important integrity mechanism in democratic societies. Health complaints commissioners cite many success stories in obtaining redress for individuals. Grievance procedures are said to result in better care for individual patients, and further, the resolution of individual complaints often leads to systemic health care improvements for all patients (Paterson 2001). Consumer satisfaction surveys are less positive with complainants wanting stronger disciplinary action than conciliation (Daniel et al. 1999; Newby et al. 2004). The second main role of an ombudsman is as a public 'watchdog' although Commissioners vary in their powers and preferences. There is a patient safety case for expanding their powers, for example, to initiate independent reviews as do statutory auditors. Health ombudsmen agree that complaints management extends beyond the resolution of individual grievances, since complainants want, not just a resolution to their own grievance, but an explanation of

why the problem arose and what is being done to prevent it happening again (Wilson 1999; Barbour 2007). The absence of research, however, means that there is no hard evidence on whether the health ombudsmen achieve systemic changes in hospitals and so make health care safer for all patients (Thomas 2002).

Box 8.4 Medical practitioner suspended for three years for upcoding

After analysing data, Medicare Australia was concerned that a medical practitioner working in a skin cancer clinic may have been billing skin lesion items at a higher level of benefit than was warranted by the size of the lesion. We referred the case to the Director of the Professional Services Review Scheme. From an examination of the medical practitioner's medical records it appeared that the patients received inappropriate and unnecessary treatments. In some instances the medical practitioner had upcoded the MBS item to obtain a higher benefit. The medical practitioner acknowledged inappropriate practice and agreed to repay $400,000 in Medicare benefits and be disqualified from using MBS items related to skin cancer for five years.

Source: Medicare Australia 2009

Litigation by patients

The dilemma is that the tort law system compensates a few patients who suffer from adverse events but may undermine a safety culture intended to assure better and safer care for all patients. McDonald concludes that tort law is a weak regulatory instrument for achieving systemic change given its many barriers and tortuous procedures (McDonald 2008). The main argument for litigation is that is an important last resort for patients who claim to have suffered negligent health care (Hirsch 2009). Four main reasons are given why litigation by patients does not have a positive impact on doctors' behaviour in relation to quality and safety. The first argument is that tort law systems have not produced significant improvements in patient safety (Ipp Report 2002). Countries with tort law systems do not have lower levels of adverse events than those with 'no fault' systems (Davis et al. 2003). For example, high rates of litigation in the United States have not produced better patient safety outcomes (Brennan and Berwick 1996), but on the other hand, malpractice litigation prompts hospitals to take patient safety measures more seriously (Brennan 1998).

Second, despite the 'defensive medicine' argument, there is no clear evidence that the threat of litigious patients makes doctors more careful, nor for the counter claim that defensive doctors order unnecessary medical tests, procedures and referrals and so expose their patients to unnecessary risks (Schoenbaum and Bovbjerg 2004). Studies of US obstetricians (the most ruinously litigious area for doctors) have found no evidence that fear of malpractice litigation produces changes in practice (Brennan and Mello 2003: 269).

Third, the largely anecdotal but influential argument is that patient litigation undermines learning from medical errors (Kachalia et al. 2008). Doctors say that the fear of being sued deters them from reporting adverse events, and from participating in quality improvement activities (despite qualified privilege legislation) such as peer review. Litigation is not a good learning strategy for detecting medical error (since very few affected patients sue), and is not a positive learning experience since the tort law system is overly adversarial and traumatic for both doctors and patients (Vincent 2003; Vincent et al. 2006)).

Patients rights mechanisms
Legislation from the 1980s onwards in many countries, including all Australian jurisdictions, extends the rights of patients to access their own medical information, and requires health professionals to obtain informed consent from patients before any medical procedures. Studies of informed consent have not investigated its impact upon patient safety although the assumption is that clearer communication should reduce the risk of an adverse event (Pizzi et al. 2001). Doctors generally are not legally required to inform patients of errors in their treatment, although policies and legislation on open disclosure are being debated and studies are underway on the impact of open disclosure on quality and safety (Studdert 2009). The ethics argument is that patients are entitled to an explanation and an apology when an error occurs. The pragmatic argument is that people who receive an explanation and an apology are less likely to sue. The best evidence so far comes from a US Veterans Affairs Medical Centre in Kentucky where a policy of open disclosure since 1987 resulted in reduced malpractice costs, since many patients accepted an apology and an assurance that the problem had been fixed, while the 88 malpractice claims (over 6 years) were settled for lesser amounts than in comparable facilities and few proceeded to court (Weeks and Bagian 2000; Kraman and Hamm 1999). Some commentators argue that this experience cannot be generalized: 'the Veterans Affairs system is not representative of the world of medical practice in the United States. Its patient population consists mainly of older men of limited means, a group that may have finite expectations and a low level of litigiousness.' (Wu 1999: 971). Some US studies have found that open disclosure reduces the likelihood of litigation by patients, other studies are less certain whether open disclosure will have a claim-inhibiting or a claim-prompting effect (Studdert et al. 2007).

Do Financial Strategies Improve Safety and Quality?

Does 'money talk'? Experiments are underway on combining methods of paying for health care to offset the disadvantages inherent in any single method. One method, pay-for-performance (P4P), is seen as having potential for improving quality. Structured reviews of purchaser-driven P4P programmes have found improvements in provider performance although any independent effect was difficult to interpret as these programmes generally were part of larger quality efforts (Maynard 2006: 152; Christianson et al. 2008; Greene and Nash 2009).

In England, the contract between the NHS and general practitioners resulted in most GPs meeting performance criteria and claiming their bonus payments. An analysis of over 8100 GP practices suggested three alternative explanations: GPs markedly improved their practice, performance targets were set too low, or GPs gamed the system by excluding patients whose care did not offer opportunities to meet the criteria (Doran et al. 2006). Pay-for-performance is used widely in the United States where purchasers clearly believe that it influences provider behaviour, but while payment has improved performance reporting, its impact on quality is largely untested and the US Agency for Healthcare Research and Quality is being urged to fund more research.

Some argue that P4P is over-sold as the answer to all health system problems; for example, it is not designed to achieve costs savings, since most measures target underuse and so reward physicians and hospitals for delivering more services (Rosenthal 2005). P4P schemes also contain some pitfalls. The mix of incentives must be aligned if adverse quality consequences are to be avoided: physicians may concentrate upon targeted areas and neglect others; bonus payments for high-performing physicians may mean lower base payments for others; physicians caring for lower socioeconomic patients may seek to reduce access for such patients; financial incentives may threaten professionalism and self-regulation; and financial incentives for quality may shake the public's faith in physicians (Epstein et al. 2004).

Does Performance Monitoring Improve Safety and Quality?

The monitoring of clinical performance has expanded dramatically and is a major regulatory strategy although one that can involve considerable effort and cost. Monitoring can be undertaken as an enforcement and inspectorial process or as a self-regulation and peer review learning process. Research evidence is accumulating that monitoring performance indicators, and auditing clinical cases and procedures, do improve performance.

Peer audit of databases

Peer audit is a formal procedure that draws on registers of clinical databases to establish best practice standards and to detect and correct poor practice. The evidence is that well-established registries accompanied by peer audit can improve the performance of clinicians (Dreyer and Garner 2009; Buchan et al. 2009; McNeil et al. 2010). The Scottish Audit of Surgical Mortality, a leader in the field, conducts peer reviews on all reported surgical deaths in hospital, virtually all Scottish surgeons participate, and is credited with achieving significant performance improvements (Scottish Audit of Surgical Mortality 2009). The Danish Lung Cancer Group registry also exemplifies the quality improvement potential through communicating indicators of high-quality care to clinicians and is credited with improving survival rates of people with lung cancer (McNeil et al. 2010). A Western Australia audit of surgical mortality offers peer review comments to the surgeon involved, and feedback to the surgical community through de-identified results on overall mortality and on specific procedures, such as coronary artery bypass grafts. The audit is credited with changing clinical behaviour and consequent improvements in patient outcomes (Semmens 2007). The Australian and New Zealand College of Anaesthetists (ANZCA) also believes that anaesthesia mortality registers and associated peer reviews have been instrumental in reducing mortality, although findings are limited by the lack of a national standardized reporting system and lack of mandatory reporting (Mackay 2002: 6). It is unclear from these studies, however, to what extent improvement can been attributed the monitoring process itself, that is, the knowledge that one's performance is monitored, or to the peer review process and insights gained from comments on particular cases.

Adverse event reporting systems

The international consensus is that a national policy calls for a country to put in place some form of adverse event reporting. There is no rigorous research evidence, however, whether adverse event reporting produces safer patient care, which is a major research gap given the effort and cost involved. The UK National Patient Safety Agency runs the largest reporting system so that studies of its impact are awaited with interest. It is unclear, for example, whether it is better to have one broad reporting system or multiple specialized reporting systems. Should reporting by health professionals be mandatory or voluntary (most are voluntary)? Should hospitals be legally (as opposed to administratively) obliged to participate in adverse event reporting? For example, a shift from voluntary to mandatory reporting in England of hospital acquired infections increased the number of reported incidents by almost 50 per cent (Collignon et al. 2005).

A systematic review of early research found that most reporting systems, of whatever type, failed to capture the majority of errors, and that wide variations in adverse event rates probably had more to do with reporting incentives and local cultures than health care safety (Wald and Shojania 2001). Lucian Leape concluded that while much of the evidence on the positive impact of adverse event reporting is anecdotal, there are many success stories (Leape 2002). The Joint Commission credits its reporting system with providing the evidence for sentinel event alerts that led to action, such as the removal of concentrated potassium chloride from hospital wards. The Institute for Safe Medication Practices cites cases where reports led to changes in drug names and labelling and the withdrawal or restricted use of drugs. The US Pharmacopeia reporting system made hospitals more careful with drugs involved in medication errors, such as insulin, heparin, and warfarin. The National Nosocomial Infection Survey showed that hospitals that participated in reporting had 32 per cent lower infection rates than those not in the programme.

Does public reporting improve performance?

'The legitimate public interest in healthcare quality makes it very difficult to argue against the public release of performance data' (Douglas et al. 2001: 267). While there is a strong public interest case, does public reporting produce better and safer health care? Studies in the 1990s found little empirical evidence that public reporting had any impact upon the behaviour of providers and purchasers and found no impact upon consumers (Coles 1999; Collopy 1999; Leatherman and McCarthy 1999; Mebius 1999). Patient outcomes data for individual cardiac surgeons, 'surgeon report cards', has been publicly reported since the early 1990s in the US states of New York, Pennsylvania and New Jersey. But most cardiologists in the early days of public reporting said they did not discuss this information with their patients and it did not influence their referrals to surgeons (Schneider and Epstein 1996; Hannan et al. 1994; Hannan et al. 1998), while a literature review of over a decade of public reporting of cardiac surgery success rates in New York state found that while some studies claimed it had led to major quality improvements, other researchers disputed this finding on the grounds that NY surgeons no longer operate on high-risk patients (Trowbridge and Wachter 2001).

More recent systematic reviews have found evidence that public reporting does improve the quality of health care (Marshall and Brook 2002; Fung et al. 2008). A systematic review of 21 peer-reviewed studies found that while public reporting had little impact upon patients (the potential users of the data), it did impact upon doctors and hospitals (the sources of the data) (Marshall et al. 2000). A controlled study showed that making clinical performance data public pushes hospitals to make improvements because they believe the reports will affect their public image (Hibbard et al. 2005). US researchers argue, in relation to hospital acquired infection rates, that thousands of lives and billions of dollars could be saved if hospitals had to publicly report as they would then be shamed into doing more about prevention (Nash 2006).

John Braithwaite and colleagues conclude that despite equivocal evidence on whether referrers, consumers and corporate purchasers make choices based on performance indicators, public reporting does change the behaviour of health providers for two reasons (Braithwaite et al. 2007). First, most providers care about the opinion of their peers and their public reputations. Second, health providers, particularly in the United State, worry that accreditation agencies, indemnity insurers and medical malpractice lawyers may target them if they get a poor public report (Marshall et al. 2004). These findings suggest that the power of public reports to improve quality might be enhanced by thinking of them less as a tool for strengthening markets and more as a tool for bolstering regulation via reputational threats. The power of public reporting may lie in the protection of a public image:

> In sum, the pattern of evidence suggests that a good policy might be open publication on the internet of quality report cards without a large investment in publicising them. No point in ritualistically flogging a dead (market) horse. Just publishing them would be sufficient to make them available to bankers, professional reputational networks, inspectors and internal quality assurance staff who might make some strategic use of them, and in honouring good governance values of transparency. (Braithwaite et al. 2007: 270)

References

Agency for Healthcare Research and Quality (2008), *National Healthcare Quality Report 2007*. (Rockville MD: Agency for Healthcare Research and Quality).

Althaus C (1996), 'National competition policy: progress and prospects.' *Australian Journal of Public Administration* 55(2): 65–70.

Appleby J and Mulligan J (2000), 'Performance measures: the public's choice'. In Appleby J and Harrison A. *Health Care UK: Spring 2000: Performance Management*. (London: King's Fund).

Auditor-General (1997), *Medifraud and Inappropriate Practice: Health Insurance Commission Performance Audit*. (Canberra: Australian National Audit Office).

Australian Commission on Safety and Quality in Health Care (2008), *Windows into Safety and Quality in Health Care 2008*. (Sydney: ACSQHC).

Australian Commission on Safety and Quality in Health Care (2009), *Windows into Safety and Quality in Health Care 2009*. (Sydney: ACSQHC).

Australian Competition and Consumer Commission (2003a), The ACCC and the health sector, ACCC Update, 12

Australian Competition and Consumer Commission (2003b), News Release: ACCC requires reform of surgeons' training program. (Canberra: ACCC).

Australian Council for Safety and Quality in Health Care (2003a), *Improving the Consistency of Approaches to Qualified Privilege Schemes*. (Canberra: Commonwealth of Australia).

Australian Council for Safety and Quality in Health Care (2003b), *Open Disclosure Standard: A National Standard for Open Communication in Public and Private Hospitals, Following an Adverse Event in Health Care*. (Canberra: Commonwealth of Australia).

Australian Council for Safety and Quality in Health Care (2004), *Charting the Safety and Quality of Health Care in Australia*. (Canberra: Australian Council for Safety and Quality in Health Care).

Australian Institute of Health and Welfare and the Australian Commission on Safety and Quality in Health Care (2007), *Sentinel Events in Australian Public Hospitals 2004–05*. (Canberra: AIHW).

Bagian J, et al. (2002), 'The Veterans Affairs root cause analysis system in action.' *Joint Commission Journal on Quality Improvement* 28(10): 531–545.

Bagian J, et al. (2001), 'Developing and deploying a patient safety program in a large health care delivery system: you can't fix up what you don't know about.' *Joint Commission Journal on Quality Improvement* 27(10): 522–532.

Barbour B (2007), 'The impact of external administrative law review: courts, tribunals and ombudsman.' *Australian Institute of Administrative Law (AIAL) Forum* (57): 50–58.

Bates D, et al. (1995), 'Incidence of adverse drug events and potential drug events: implications for prevention.' *Journal of the American Medical Association* 274(1): 1–98.

Bell R (2006), 'Medicare regulation through professional services review - lessons learned'. In Freckleton I. *Regulating Health Practitioners*. (Annandale, NSW: The Federation Press).

Bennett B and Freckelton I (2006), 'Life after the Ipp reforms: Medical negligence law'. In Freckelton I and Petersen K. *Disputes and Dilemmas in Health Law*. (Leichhardt NSW: The Federation Press).

Ben-Tovim D, et al. (2009), *Measuring and Reporting Mortality in Hospital Patients*. (Canberra: Australian Institute of Health and Welfare).

Bismark M and Paterson R (2006), 'No-fault compensation in New Zealand: harmonizing injury compensation, provider accountability, and patient safety.' *Health Affairs* 25(1): 278–283.

Black D and Baumgartner M (1998), 'Toward a theory of the third party'. In Black D. *The Social Structure of Right and Wrong*. (San Diego, London, Boston, New York, Sydney, Tokyo, Toronto: Academic Press).

Blendon R, et al. (2002), 'Views of practising physicians and the public on medical errors.' *New England Journal of Medicine* 347(24): 1933–1940.

Bohensky M, et al. (2005), 'Experience with practice guidelines for medico-legal death investigations: the case of falls-related deaths in hospital.' *Medicine and Law* 24:727-742.

Braithwaite J and Drahos P (2000), *Global Business Regulation*. (Cambridge: Cambridge University Press).

Braithwaite J, et al. (2005), *The Governance of Health Care Safety and Quality*. (Canberra: Commonwealth of Australia).

Braithwaite J, et al. (2007), *Regulating Aged Care: Ritualism and the New Pyramid*. (Cheltenham. Northampton MA: Edward Elgar).

Brennan T (1998), 'The role of regulation in quality improvement.' *Milbank Quarterly* 76: 709–731.

Brennan T and Berwick D (1996), *New Rules: Regulation, Markets and the Quality of American Health Care*. (San Francisco, CA: Jossey-Bass).

Brennan T and Mello M (2003), 'Patient safety and medical malpractice: a case study.' *Annals of Internal Medicine* 139(4): 267–275.

Brook R, et al. (2000), 'Defining and measuring quality of care: a perspective from US researchers.' *International Journal for Quality in Health Care* 12(4): 281–295.

Buchan H, et al. (2009), 'Voluntary initiatives by clinicians'. In Healy J and Dugdale P. *Patient Safety First: Strategies for Regulating Health Care*. (Crows Nest NSW: Allen & Unwin): 71–97.

Bugeja L and Ranson D (2003), 'Coroners' recommendations: do they lead to positive health outcomes?' *Journal of Law and Medicine* 10(4): 399–400.

Bugeja L and Ranson D (2005), 'Coroners' recommendations: a lost opportunity.' *Journal of Law and Medicine* 13(2): 173–175.

Cameron P (2007), *The dangers of measurement*. 5th Australian Conference on Safety and Quality in Health Care, (Brisbane: Australian Healthcare Association).

Centers for Disease Control and Prevention (2006), National Nosocomial Infections Surveillance System, 15 February http://www.cdc.gov/ncidod/dhqp/nnis.html

Christianson J, et al. (2008), 'Lessons from evaluations of purchaser pay-for-performance programs: a review of the evidence.' *Medical Care Research and Review* 65(Supplement): 5S-35S.

Clarke S (2003), 'Informed consent without bureaucracy.' *Journal of Clinical Neuroscience* 10(1): 35–36.

Clarke S and Oakley J (2004), 'Informed consent and surgeons' performance.' *Journal of Medicine and Philosophy* 29(1): 11–35.

Clarke S and Oakley J, eds. (2007), *Informed Consent and Clinician Accountability: The Ethics of Report Cards on Surgeon Performance*. (Cambridge: Cambridge University Press).

Clinical Excellence Commission (2008), Quality of Care in NSW: A Chartbook 2007, 13 May www.cec.health.nsw.gov.au/moreinfo/chartbook.html

Cohen M (2000), 'Why error reporting systems should be voluntary.' *British Medical Journal* 320: 728–729.

Coles J (1999), 'Public disclosure of health performance reports: a response from the UK.' *International Journal for Quality in Health Care* 11: 104–5.

Collignon P, et al. (2005), 'Staphylococcus aureus bacteremia, Australia.' *Emerging Infectious Diseases* 11(4): 554–561.

Collopy B (1999), 'Public disclosure of health performance reports: what do we lose in giving information?' *International Journal for Quality in Health Care* 11: 98–101.

Corbett A (2006), 'Regulating compensation for injuries associated with medical error.' *Sydney Law Review* 28: 259–296.

Daniel A, et al. (1999), 'Patients' complaints about medical practice.' *Medical Journal of Australia* 170: 598–602.

Davies Report (2005), *Queensland Public Hospitals Commission of Inquiry Report*. (Brisbane: State of Queensland).

Davis K (2004), Top 10 health policy stories of 2004. (New York: The Commonwealth Fund).

Davis P, et al. (2003), 'Preventable in-hospital medical injury under the 'no fault' system in New Zealand.' *Quality and Safety in Health Care* 12(4): 240–241.

Department of Health and Ageing (2005), *General Practice in Australia: 2004*. (Canberra: Commonwealth of Australia).

Doran T, et al. (2006), 'Pay-for-performance programs in family practices in the United Kingdom.' *New England Journal of Medicine* 355(4): 375–385.

Douglas N, et al. (2001), *Inquiry into Obstetrics and Gynaecology Services at the King Edward Memorial Hospital 1990–2001*. (Perth: Department of Premier and Cabinet).

Downie J, et al. (2006), *Patient Safety Law: From Silos to Systems: Final Report*. (Halifax, Nova Scotia: Health Law Institute, Dalhousie University).

Dreyer N and Garner S (2009), 'Registries for robust evidence.' *Journal of the American Medical Association* 302(7): 790–791.

Duckett S (2000), *The Australian Health Care System*. (South Melbourne: Oxford University Press).

Duckett S (2004), 'The Australian Health Care Agreements 2003–2008.' *Australia and New Zealand Health Policy* 1(1): 1–5.

Duckett S, et al. (2007), 'Identifying variations in quality of care in Queensland hospitals.' *Medical Journal of Australia* 187: 571–575.

Dwan K and Boyce R (2003), 'Competition policy and intra-professional conflict: re-regulating general practice.' *International Journal of Public Sector Management* 16(2): 141–152.

Ehsani J, et al. (2006), 'The incidence and cost of adverse events in Victorian hospitals 2003–04.' *Medical Journal of Australia* 184(11): 551–555.

Epstein A, et al. (2004), 'Paying physicians for high-quality care.' *New England Journal of Medicine* 350: 406–410.

Ettelt S, et al. (2008), Policy Brief: The Systematic Use of Cost-Effectiveness Criteria to Inform Reviews of Publicly-Funded Benefits Packages, 2 February http://www.international-comparisons.org.uk/themes.html

Faunce T and Bolsin S (2005), 'Fiduciary disclosure of medical mistakes: the duty to promptly notify patients of adverse health care events.' *Journal of Law and Medicine* 12(4): 478–482.

Fels A (1998), *Competition health: two years on*. Australian Medical Association: Competition in Health Conference.

Finance Ministers Communiqué (2005), Reform of Liability Insurance, Progress as at 8 April 2005.

Florini A (2007), 'Introduction: the battle over transparency'. In Florini A. *The Right to Know: Transparency for an Open World*. (New York: Columbia University Press): 1–6.

Fowler S (2005), 'Medical indemnity: crisis and response.' *Centre for Health Economics Research and Evaluation Discussion Paper* No 56.

Freckelton I (2009), 'Non-disciplinary pathways in practitioner regulation'. In Healy J and Dugdale P. *Patient Safety First: Strategies for Regulating Health Care*. (Crows Nest NSW: Allen and Unwin): 167–191.

Freckelton I and Ranson D (2006), 'The evolving institution of the coroner'. In Freckelton I and Petersen K. *Disputes and Dilemmas in Health Law*. (Leichhardt NSW: The Federation Press).

French S, et al. (2001), *Health Care Systems in Transition: New Zealand*. (Copenhagen: European Observatory on Health Care Systems).

Fung C, et al. (2008), 'Evidence that publishing patient care performance data improves quality of care.' *Annals of Internal Medicine* 148: 111–123.

Gallagher T, et al. (2003), 'Patients' and physicians' attitudes regarding the disclosure of medical errors.' *Journal of the American Medical Association* 289(8): 1001–1007.

Gawande A (2002), *Complications: A Surgeon's Notes on an Imperfect Science*. (New York: Metropolitan Books, Henry Holt and Company).

Greene S and Nash D (2009), 'Pay for performance: an overview of the literature.' *American Journal of Medical Quality* 24: 140–163.

Hannan E, et al. (1994), 'Improving the outcomes of coronary artery bypass heart surgery in New York State.' *Journal of the American Medical Association* 271: 761–766.

Hannan E, et al. (1998), 'Public release of cardiac surgery outcomes in New York.' *American Heart Journal* 134: 55–61.

Health Insurance Commission (2004), Compliance Program 2004–05. (Canberra: Australian Government Health Insurance Commission).

Health Services Commissioner Victoria (2004), 2004 Annual Report. (Melbourne: Health Servies Commissioner).

Hibbard J, et al. (2005), 'Hospital performance reports: impact on quality, market share, and reputation. Evidence from a controlled experiment shows the long-term effects of reporting hospitals' performance ratings to the public.' *Health Affairs* 24(4): 1150–1160.

Hirsch D (2009), 'Does litigation against doctors and hospitals improve quality?' in Healy J and Dugdale P. *Patient Safety First: Strategies for Regulating Health Care*. (Crows Nest NSW: Allen and Unwin): 254–272.

Hurwitz B (1998), *Clinical Guidelines and the Law: Negligence, Discretion and Judgement*. (Oxford: Radcliffe Medical Press).

Iedema R, et al. (2008), 'The national open disclosure pilot: evaluation of a policy implementation initiative.' *Medical Journal of Australia* 188: 397–400.

Institute of Medicine (2002), *Leadership by Example: Coordinating Government Roles in Improving Health Care Quality*. (Washington DC: The National Academies Press).

Institute of Medicine (2004), *Patient Safety: Achieving a New Standard of Care*. (Washington DC: Institute of Medicine, The National Academies Press).

Ipp Report (2002), *Review of the Law of Negligence: Final Report*. (Canberra: Commonwealth of Australia).

Joint Commission (2005), Home page, 9 August www.jcaho.org

Joint Commission (2006), Sentinel events, 9 October http://www.jointcommission.org/SentinelEvents/PolicyandProcedures/

Kachalia A, et al. (2008), 'Beyond negligence: avoidability and medical injury compensation.' *Social Science and Medicine* 66(2): 387–402.

Kerridge I, et al. (2005), *Ethics and Law for the Health Professions*. (Annandale, NSW: Federation Press).

Kmietowicz Z (2008), 'Darzi review: Annual 'quality accounts' will help improve services and increase choice for patients, says Lord Darzi.' *British Medical Journal* 337: a646.

Kraman S and Hamm G (1999), 'Risk management: extreme honesty may be the best policy.' *Annals of Internal Medicine* 131(12): 963–967.

Leape L (2002), 'Reporting of adverse events.' *New England Journal of Medicine* 347(20): 1633–1639.

Leape L and Davis K (2005), To err is human; to fail to improve is unconscionable. *From the President*. (New York: The Commonwealth Fund).

Leapfrog Group (2005), Home page, 11 August www.leapfroggroup.org

Leatherman S and McCarthy D (1999), 'Public disclosure of health care performance reports: experience, evidence and issues of policy.' *International Journal for Quality in Health Care* 11(2): 93–98.

Legido-Quigley H, et al. (2008), *Assuring the Quality of Health Care in the European Union: A Case for Action*. (Brussels: World Health Organization and European Observatory on Health Systems and Policies).

Mackay P, ed. (2002), *Safety of Anaesthesia in Australia: A Review of Anaesthesia Related Mortality 1997–1999*. (Melbourne: Australian and New Zealand College of Anaesthetists).

Mangione-Smith R, et al. (2007), 'The quality of ambulatory care delivered to children in the United States.' *New England Journal of Medicine* 357(15): 1515–1523.

Marshall E, et al. (1998), 'Reliability of league tables of in vitro fertilisation clinics: retrospective analysis of live birth rates. Commentary: how robust are rankings?' *British Medical Journal* 316: 1701–1705.

Marshall M and Brook R (2002), 'Public reporting of comparative information about quality of healthcare (editorial).' *Medical Journal of Australia* 176: 205–206.

Marshall M, et al. (2004), 'How do we maximise the impact of the public reporting of quality of care?' *International Journal for Quality in Health Care* 16(Supplement 1): i57-i63.

Marshall M, et al. (2000), 'The public release of performance data: what do we expect to gain? A review of the evidence.' *Journal of the American Medical Association* 283(14): 1866–1874.

Mattke S, et al. (2006), 'The OECD Health Care Quality Indicators Project: history and background.' *International Journal for Quality in Health Care* September (Special issue): 1–4.

Maynard A (2006), 'Incentives in healthcare: the shift in emphasis from the implicit to the explicit'. In Dubois C-A, McKee M and Nolte E. *Human Resources for Health in Europe*. (Maidenhead, Berkshire: Open University Press): 140–154.

Mayor S (2006), 'UK website publishes cardiac surgery survival rates.' *British Medical Journal* 332(7549): 1049.

McDonald F (2008), 'Working to death: the regulation of working hours in health care.' *Law & Policy* 30(1): 108–140.

McGlynn E (1998), 'Choosing and evaluating clinical performance measures.' *The Joint Commission Journal on Quality Improvement* 24(9): 470–479.

McGlynn E, et al. (2003), 'The quality of health care delivered to adults in the United States.' *New England Journal of Medicine* 348(26): 2635–2645.

McIlwraith J and Madden B (2006), *Health Care & The Law*. (Pyrmont NSW: Lawbook Company).

McNeil J, et al. (2010), 'Clinical-quality registries: their role in quality improvement.' *Medical Journal of Australia* 192(5): 244–245.

Mebius C (1999), 'Public disclosure of health performance reports: comments and reflection from Sweden.' *International Journal for Quality in Health Care* 11: 102–3.

Medicare Australia (2009), National Compliance Program 2008–09. (Canberra: Australian Government).

Mello M, et al. (2005), 'Fostering rational regulation of patient safety.' *Journal of Health Politics, Policy & Law* 30(3): 375–426.

Metherell M, Abbott wants hospital rankings, The Sydney Morning Herald, 22 July 2007

Minister of Health (2003), *Improving Quality (IQ): A Systems Approach for the New Zealand Health and Disability Sector*. (Wellington: Ministry of Health).

Moynihan R (1998), *Too Much Medicine?* (Sydney: ABC Books).

Nash DB (2006), 'Editorial: Hospital-acquired infections: raising the anchoring heuristic.' *American Journal of Medical Quality* 21(6 (supplement)): 5S-6S.

National Audit Office (2001), *Handling Clinical Negligence Claims in England*. (London: The Stationery Office).

National Committee for Quality Assurance, Home page, (16 August 2005 16 August 2005) http://www.ncqu.org

National Health and Hospital Reform Commission (2009), *A Healthier Future for all Australians: Final Report June 2009*. (Canberra: Australian Government).

Neil D, et al. (2004), 'Public reporting of individual surgeon performance information: United Kingdom developments and Australian issues.' *Medical Journal of Australia* 181(5): 266–268.

Newby L (2002), 'Concluding commentary'. In Thomas D. *Medicine Called to Account: Health Care Complaints Mechanisms in Australasia*. (Sydney: University of New South Wales): 111–118.

Newby L, et al. (2004), *Bringing in the Consumer Perspective: Final Report*. (Melbourne: Health Issues Centre).

NSW Health (2008), Incident Management in the NSW Public Health System, January to June 2008. (North Sydney: NSW Department of Health).

Oakley J and Cocking D (2001), *Virtue Ethics and Professional Roles*. (Cambridge: Cambridge University Press).

Osborne D and Gaebler T (1992), *Reinventing Government: How the Entrepreneurial Spirit is Transforming the Public Sector*. (Boston: Addison-Wesley).

Paterson R (2001), Patients' rights in New Zealand: Lessons for Ontario? (Auckland, NZ: Office of the Health and Disability Commissioner).

Pizzi L, et al. (2001), 'Section H: Role of the patient'. In Shojania K, Duncan B, McDonald K, et al. *Making Health Care Safer: A Critical Analysis of Patient Safety Practices*. (Rockville MD: Agency for Healthcare Research and Quality): 544–572.

Professional Services Review (2006), *Director's Report to the Professions 2005–06*. (Canberra: Professional Services Review).

Queensland Health (2006), *An Investment in Health. Queensland Public Hospitals Performance Report 2005–06*. (Brisbane: Queensland Health).

Ranson D and Emmett S (2003), 'Falls and fall-related injuries: far-reaching implications.' *Journal of Law and Medicine* 11: 16–17.

Rosenthal M (2005), *Examining Pay-for-Performance Measures and Other Trends in Employer-Sponsored Health Care*. (New York: The Commonwealth Fund).

Runciman WB, et al. (2007), *Safety and Ethics in Healthcare: A Guide to Getting it Right*. (Aldershot: Ashgate).

Runciman W and Moller J (2001), *Iatrogenic Injury in Australia*. (Adelaide: Australian Patient Safety Foundation).

Runciman WB (2002), 'Lessons from the Australian Patient Safety Foundation: setting up a national patient safety surveillance system - is this the right model?' *Quality and Safety in Health Care* 11: 246–251.

Schneider E and Epstein A (1996), 'Influence of cardiac surgery performance reports on referral practices and access to care: a survey of cardiovascular specialists.' *New England Journal of Medicine* 335: 251–256.

Schoenbaum S and Bovbjerg J (2004), 'Malpractice reform must include steps to prevent medical injury.' *Annals of Internal Medicine* 140(1): 51–53.

Scott A, et al. (2009), 'The effects of an incentive program on quality of care in diabetes management.' *Health Economics* Online DOI: 10.1002/hec.1536.

Scott C (2004), 'Regulation in the age of governance: the rise of the post-regulatory state'. In Jordana J and Levi-Faur D. *The Politics of Regulation: Institutions and Regulatory Reforms for the Age of Governance*. (Cheltenham. Northampton.: Edward Elgar).

Scott IA and Ward M (2006), 'Public reporting of hospital outcomes based on administrative data: risks and opportunities.' *Medical Journal of Australia* 184(11): 571–574.

Scottish Audit of Surgical Mortality, About SASM, (5 May 2009 5 May 2009) www.sasm.org.uk

Semmens J (2007), *Technology allows the rite of passage: the use of record linkage for research into health*. 5th Australian Conference on Safety and Quality in Health Care, (Brisbane: Australian Healthcare Association).

SIMPATIE (2007), *Final Report of the Mapping Exercise*. (Utrecht: CBO).

Studdert D (2009), 'Disclosure of medical injury'. In Healy J and Dugdale P. *Patient Safety First: Responsive Regulation in Health Care*. (Crows Nest NSW: Allen & Unwin): 237–253.

Studdert D, et al. (2007), 'Disclosure of medical injury to patients: an improbable risk management strategy.' *Health Affairs* 26(1): 215–226.

Sundararajan V, et al. (2004), 'New ICD-10 version of the Charlson comorbidity index predicted in-hospital mortality.' *Journal of Clinical Epidemiology* 57: 1288–1294.

The Commonwealth Fund (1 August 2005), Washington Health Policy Week in Review: legislation aimed at reducing medical errors cleared by House. (New York: The Commonwealth Fund).

The Commonwealth Fund (4 April 2005), Washington Health Policy Week in Review: soaring Medicare payments to physicians may speed pay-for-performance. (New York: The Commonwealth Fund).

The Commonwealth Fund (8 August 2005), Washington Health Policy Week in Review: quality forum endorses quality measures for physician care. (New York: The Commonwealth Fund).

The Commonwealth Fund (10 January 2005), Washington Health Policy Week in Review: Bush calls upon Congress to pass medical malpractice legislation this year.

The Commonwealth Fund (11 April 2005), Washington Health Policy Week in Review: experts see 'fundamental change' in drive to improve health care quality. (New York: The Commonwealth Fund).

The Commonwealth Fund (18 December 2006), Washington Health Policy Week in Review: Rating the winners and the losers in the Medicare Package.

The Commonwealth Fund (27 June 2005), Washington Health Policy Week in Review: Reps. Thomas, Johnson ask CMS help in changing Medicare's 'irrational' payment system. (New York: The Commonwealth Fund).

Thomas D (2002), 'Introductory overview'. In Thomas D. *Medicine Called to Account: Health Care Complaints Mechanisms in Australasia*. (Sydney: University of New South Wales): 1–14.

Trowbridge R and Wachter R (2001), 'Chapter 55: Legislation, accreditation, and market-driven and other approaches to improving patient safety'. In Shojania K, Duncan B, McDonald K, et al. *Making Health Care Safer: A Critical Analysis of Patient Safety Practices*. (Rockville MD: Agency for Healthcare Research and Quality): 601–610.

Victorian Department of Human Services (2007), A selection of Victorian legislation and supporting information relevant to health service providers, 10 April http://www.health.vic.gov.au/legislation/

Victorian Parliament Law Reform Committee (2005), *Coroners Act 1985: Discussion Paper*. (Melbourne: Parliament of Victoria).

Vincent C (2003), 'Compensation as a duty of care: the case for 'no fault'.' *Quality in Australian Health Care* 12: 240–241.

Vincent C, et al. (2006), 'Learning from litigation: the role of claims analysis in patient safety'. In Walshe K and Boaden R. *Patient Safety: Research into Practice*. (Maidenhead, Berkshire: Open University Press): 41–65.

Wald H and Shojania K (2001), 'Chapter 4: Incident reporting'. In Shojania K, Duncan B, McDonald K, et al. *Making Health Care Safer: A Critical Analysis of Patient Safety Practices*. (Rockville MD: Agency for Healthcare Research and Quality): 41–50.

Weeks W and Bagian J (2000), 'Developing a culture of safety in the Veterans Affairs Administration.' *Effective Clinical Practice* 3: 270–276.

Williams S, Death's lessons for the living, The Australian,

Wilson B (1999), 'Health disputes: a 'window of opportunity' to improve health services'. In Freckelton I and Petersen A. *Controversies in Health Law.* (Sydney: Federation Press).

Wilson B (2004), *Does shaming, naming and blaming improve the quality of our health services? Adversarial versus conciliatory approached to investigating health complaints.* 10th Conference of the Australian Bioethics Association, (University of New South Wales.

Wu A (1999), 'Handling hospital errors: is disclosure the best defense?' *Annals of Internal Medicine* 131(12): 970–972.

Chapter 9
Regulation by Patients

Concepts of Patients

The patient has been the missing person in regulatory debates as the health care safety movement paradoxically has paid little attention to the patient's perspective (Vincent and Coulter 2002; Jorm et al. 2009). This is changing, however, as health services look to redesign their procedures and practices around 'patient-centred care' (Picker Institute Europe 2007; Darzi 2009). Patients also are being acknowledged as regulatory actors although the reality seldom matches the promising rhetoric. This chapter analyses the processes through which individual patients can have a say over their own health care and reviews the evidence on the impact of consumer/citizen participation. While the term 'patient' is used in this chapter, the language in this area is tricky as alternative words also carry dubious connotations; for example, the terms consumer and customer can imply that health care is a commodity:

> Patients should remain patients because it helps remind doctors of their professional and ethical obligations. No doctors I know think of their patients as customers. Health care is a partnership involving a host of ethical and contractual obligations that are built on the doctor-patient relationship, not on a relationship with a customer. (Walton 1998: 180)

Virtually everyone during their life consults health professionals, takes medication and undergoes procedures and through these encounters influences the health system. People might also exert influence through groups that range from self-help groups based on mutual assistance between peers, to formal organizations run by a board and employing professional staff. Non-government organizations (NGOs) advocate on behalf of their clients or a population group and might engage in research, prevention and treatment. Many groups and organizations are single-issue entities, however, arising from longer-term health concerns, such as arthritis, breast cancer, cystic fibrosis, and diabetes. Safety and quality concerns relating to specific conditions, however, may apply generally to all patients.

The metaphors of 'exit' and 'voice' suggest how individuals can influence the behaviour of service providers (Hirschman 1970). 'Voice' is a political concept that fits a citizen participation paradigm, referring to the ability of a person to influence a service provider while continuing to use the service. This assumes an active not passive person who can ask for information, negotiate options, fill out surveys, use complaint procedures, and join a group. 'Exit' is an economic concept that fits a market model paradigm and refers to a person's ability to leave a service and go elsewhere, which assumes that a person has the capacity to leave a service, that other options are available, that the person is able to obtain or pay for another service, and can make an informed choice – all somewhat problematic assumptions in health care.

The concept of a patient as a regulatory actor invokes the principle of personal responsibility. But is it fair to ask people to take responsibility for the quality and safety of their own health care? This should not absolve providers, of course, since it is not construed as a patient's fault if she does not check and takes the wrong medicine offered by a nurse. Further, there may be several barriers to assigning responsibility to patients and expecting them to engage as regulatory actors: a personal barrier of lesser capacity during illness, a class barrier of lesser resources both educational and financial, a cultural barrier of different expectations and language, a knowledge barrier given the esoteric nature of medical expertise, and a power barrier given the unequal relationship between doctors and patients. The willingness and ability of patients to monitor their own care depends on demographic characteristics, such as age and ethnicity, as well as psychological and social factors (Koutantji et al. 2005; Johnstone and Kanitsaki 2006). The main reason for engaging people in monitoring their own health care, however, is the pragmatic reason that they are the ones that suffer most keenly the consequences of medical errors.

Regulatory Mechanisms

This chapter discusses people as regulatory actors in terms of five roles: informed patients, selective consumers, vocal complainants, entitled citizens, and active partners. Patients can exert influence in various ways to improve the safety and quality of their own health care using mechanisms that range upwards in a regulatory pyramid from voluntary strategies at the base (asking for information, giving consent), to market strategies (responding to a survey, making a complaint), to enforcement strategies (asserting one's legal rights, suing for negligence). These concepts are depicted in Figure 9.1 with informed patients as more passive regulatory actors at the base of the pyramid rising to active partners at the apex.

Informed Patients

The model of a doctor-patient relationship is changing from a centuries-old medical tradition that held up doctors as the experts who need only reassure their patients: 'trust me, I'm a doctor'. The doctor in this paternalistic model decided the treatment and offered little information to the patient other than to secure compliance with the regime: 'take the antibiotics with each meal'. Patients were not asked for their views and were expected to follow instructions:

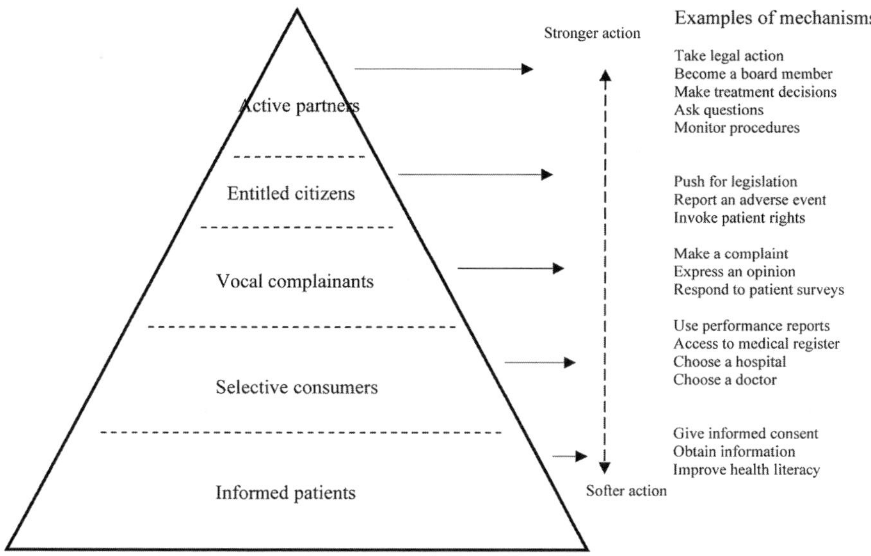

Figure 9.1 Patients as actors on a regulatory pyramid

> Little more than a decade ago, doctors made the decisions; patients did what they were told. Doctors did not consult patients about their desires and priorities, and routinely withheld information – sometimes crucial information, such as what drugs they were on, what treatments they were being given, and what their diagnosis was. (Gawande 2002: 210)

Health authorities now devote considerable effort to improving two-way communications between doctors and patients. The earlier focus on doctor-patient communications was how best to convince patients to comply with medical instructions. The communication rationale now has been reframed, however, not in terms of issuing instructions and expecting compliance (although compliance can be crucial), but in terms of offering information and explaining the treatment. The aim nowadays is to enable patients to make informed decisions. Communications need more work, however, as a systematic literature review concluded that non-compliance is more widespread than health professionals realize and often due to misunderstandings and that a wide range of solutions have been tried with mixed results (Pizzi et al. 2001).

Good professional practice calls for a doctor to explain and obtain consent before a procedure, and moreover 'informed consent' is a legal requirement in many countries. A manual or 'toolkit' produced for health professionals in Australia suggests practical strategies for better communication with patients, sets out principles, and gives case study scenarios (National Health and Medical Research Council 2006). Improving informed decision-making is regarded as a quality process that also leads to better outcomes for patients. In addition, it establishes another layer of protection against adverse events, according to a systematic review of consent procedures (Pizzi et al. 2001). Exactly what constitutes an 'informed' consent to tests and treatment remains a matter for considerable conjecture, however, while offering a readily understood explanation is a challenge when people lack health literacy.

Health literacy is a crucial attribute if people are to make informed decisions and to monitor their own health care (Nutbeam 2008). Defined as the capacity to acquire, understand and use information for health, health literacy is an important risk factor in poor health outcomes: such patients have higher risks of hospitalization, have longer hospital stays, are sicker when they seek medical help, are less likely to comply with treatment, and are more likely to make errors with their medication (Institute of Medicine 2004). In other words, poorly informed patients experience lower quality and less safe health care. A survey conducted in Australia in 2006 found that, alarmingly, nearly 60 per cent of adults lack basic health literacy and so may lack the capacity to follow health advice or to engage in decisions about their own health care (Australian Bureau of Statistics 2006). Recommendations on reforms to the Australian health care system therefore included calls for action to improve health literacy (National Health and Hospital Reform Commission 2009).

Health services are trying ways to make their communications more 'patient-friendly' including better designed administrative forms and information brochures (Coulter and Ellis 2007). Systematic reviews of studies on communication tools found that these do increase patients' understanding (Trevena et al. 2006), such as the fairly basic practice of giving parents both written and verbal information when children are discharged from hospital (Johnson et al. 2006). Most people can relate to the experience of coming away from a consultation with a doctor and being unclear what was said, not necessarily because the doctor did not explain, but because anxiety got in the way of asking, listening, understanding and remembering.

Health departments and NGOs publish an enormous amount of material on many health topics and increasingly make information available on websites. Since a myriad Internet websites offer information (and misinformation) on health conditions and treatments, governments have set up websites that provide authoritative information. For example, the Australian Department of Health and Ageing runs Health*Insite*, an internet gateway that offers information on health and well-being and provides links to other specialist websites.

E-health enthusiasts point out that the Internet has dramatically improved public access to health information and offers opportunities to network with other patients, exchange information, and organize pressure groups (Yellowlees 2000). Participation in the electronic information age depends upon Internet access, however, which varies across countries and socio-economic groups with high population penetration in OECD countries, such as Sweden with 89 per cent and Australia with 80 per cent (Internet World Statistics 2009). The information revolution has not overcome the usual socio-economic bias inherent in consumer participation. Rates of internet access in Australia are higher in capital cities, among higher income households, and among people with higher educational attainment, those in the workforce, and younger people (Australian Bureau of Statistics 2007). In other words, wealthier, employed, well-educated and younger people have more e-health opportunities.

Selective Consumers

Policy makers promoted consumer choice and provider competition in the neo-liberal reforms that swept across health sectors from the 1980s onwards. Consumer exit, more than citizen voice, was the preferred demand-side regulatory mechanism. The concept of a selective consumer involves three elements. First, people are able to articulate what they want from health professionals and health services. Second, they have access to information for making informed choices. Third, they are able to leave a service and go elsewhere. While consumer choice is an important principle, there are limitations to the concept of a selective health care consumer. Some patients may be too ill, confused, or lack the knowledge and confidence to question doctors and nurses. Relying on patients as selective consumers to regulate their own health care is not feasible in some cases:

> We are a major trauma hospital and patients aren't competent in much of our emergency work. In some we don't even get consent because they are straight to theatre. Also, most of our patients are really sick. Second, if a patient has something that is not pretty simple, it's difficult to get them to tell you that back reliably. Also, I don't think many patients are confident enough to challenge professionals. Unless you are part of the health culture, it's difficult to question professional advice; people just tend not to do it. And their view is that the doctors know what they're doing, although that may be a generational thing as older patients tend not to be very questioning about their care. (Hospital director)

What people want from doctors and health services

Making patient-centred care the foundation that under-pins high quality health services (Bergeson and Dean 2006) requires finding out what people want. What criteria do people use to choose 'Dr Right'? Community surveys in Europe report that being a good communicator tops the ten priorities that people look for in a general practitioner (Baker et al. 2006: 220). Surveys of patients conducted by the Picker Institute Europe found their top priorities for good care from health services included good communications, being treated with respect, and fast access to care (Picker Institute Europe 2009). A survey of over 72,500 English NHS hospital patients concluded that if hospitals wish to improve the quality of their care they should focus on several domains important to patients: consistency and coordination of care, treat patients with respect, involve patients in decisions, improve communications, ensure cleanliness, and improve pain control (Sizmur and Redding 2009). Surveys in Canada produced slightly different results to the European surveys in that respondents rated highly the importance of medical skills and for doctors to be up to date (competence), as well as good communications and accessible services (Table 9.1).

Table 9.1 What people want from their health care providers

Relative order	Hospitals: what information should the public be told?	Primary care: what performance priorities should apply to family physicians?
1	Skills of medical staff	Physician knowledge/skills up to date
2	About serious medical errors	Physician skilled in identifying/treating problems
3	Use of latest technology and equipment	Ability to explain things
4	Patient satisfaction with care	Makes referrals when needed
5	Whether nurses are sensitive and caring	Patient satisfaction with care
6	Coordination between hospital and other services	Physician is sensitive and caring
7	Whether discharge information is satisfactory	Spends adequate time with patients
8	Job satisfaction of hospital staff	Accessible after hours care
9	ER waiting times	Sends reminders
10	Elective surgery waiting times	Short waiting time for appointment

Source: Adapted from Sandoval 2007; Berta et al. 2008

Exercising choice

Patient choice of doctor is a strongly held principle in some countries: a person can choose a medical practitioner, consult several practitioners if he/she wishes, and move between practices. Choice is a key consumer principle that also is expected to push health services to improve since people can 'exit' and go elsewhere if they are unhappy with the service. People in Denmark, England and Finland must enrol with a general practitioner in their geographic area, in the Netherlands they must enrol but are free to choose their general practitioner, while in Australia, New Zealand, France and Sweden they can consult any general practitioner and can claim a public subsidy without being registered with a particular practice (Ettelt et al. 2006). While patients in Australia have unfettered choice, studies show that two-thirds stick with 'their' general practitioner (General Practice Strategy Review Group 1998: 68–71). While even small movements in patient demand can be influential in theory, in practice in Australia consumer demand outstrips GP supply in many areas so that GPs do not have to compete for patients.

Patient choice in relation to specialists and hospitals also varies between countries. In England, Finland, the Netherlands and Sweden, patients must have a referral from a general practitioner to qualify for reimbursement for specialist care. In some countries, patients are able to bypass a general practitioner gatekeeper and go direct to specialists if they pay out-of-pocket or accept higher co-payments for publicly-funded care (Ettelt et al. 2006). Until recently, patients in France and Germany could bypass a referral and directly consult a specialist without incurring any charges.

Patients in Australia can discuss with their GP a referral to a specialist or a hospital (patients need a GP referral to make a Medicare claim). But since patients have little comparative information on which to base such a decision, they presumably rely upon the opinion of their GP. A person wanting an elective procedure (non-emergency surgery) as a private patient in either a public or private hospital may have a choice, but patients usually opt for the nearest appropriate hospital and usually do not want to travel perhaps another 20 kilometres to a more distant hospital. In preferring one's own doctor and hospital, patients appear to follow historical medical advice:

> As if you would call a physician, that is thought good for the cure of the disease you complain of but is unacquainted with your body, and therefore may put you in the way for a present cure but overthroweth your health in some other kind; and so cure the disease and kill the patient. (Francis Bacon sixteenth century 1979)

Some governments use patient choice as a demand-side regulatory mechanism, the economic rationalist assumption being that patients will choose high performers and so put pressure to improve upon poor performers. The UK Government in 2006 urged GPs to offer their patients an elective surgery choice between four to five hospitals (King's Fund 2006). The expectation was that some patients would opt for hospitals with shorter waiting lists and so bring down overall waiting times, or would opt for hospitals with good performance indicators and so signal a demand for good care. Since funds follow the patient, even a small minority of patients switching their preferences would impact on hospital budgets, although early studies had found that most patients opt for their local hospital (Appleby 2005). In many countries, however, patient choice does not drive quality since public hospitals do not need to compete as they already have more patients than they can cope with: patient demand exceeds service supply.

The consumer choice principle also assumes that patients can make an informed choice. One of the reasons that people entrust others to purchase health services on their behalf, whether governments or health insurance funds, is that it is difficult for a lay person to make an informed decision on a procedure, doctor or hospital, because this often requires considerable medical and technical knowledge – it is easier to trust one's doctor to make the decision (Dugdale 2008: 132). The role of health broker in negotiating decisions is undertaken by a person's general physician in many health systems, and by a health maintenance organization in the case of the United States private health insurance model. The increasing complexity of health care has prompted the role of a trusted intermediary (broker, case manager, advocate) who can manage interactions on behalf of a patient with health services and insurance funds.

What information can the public find out about doctors and hospitals?
It is not easy for a person to access information on which to base an informed choice even though more information is available than in earlier decades. The intention of a medical register, for example, is to provide an assurance to the public that a doctor is accepted as a professionally qualified practitioner of good standing. Access by the public to a medical register is the norm in many countries. In the United Kingdom, for example, the General Medical Council offers an online search on a doctor's registration status, whether any restrictions apply, qualification details, and information on fitness to practise and any disciplinary orders, while the Federation of State Medical Boards in the United States posts information on a doctor's whole disciplinary history. Public access to information on medical practitioners in the Australian states has varied considerably. A search of the eight state medical boards in 2007 found that while most offered a free on-line search on whether a practitioner was registered, few other details were provided, and only three states listed de-registered doctors and posted tribunal disciplinary orders (Healy et al. 2008). Under the *Health Practitioner Regulation National Law 2009* (Cth), a national register for each of the 10 health professions will be set up that offers the public access to information on practitioners including their qualifications and any restrictions or conditions placed on practice by a board or tribunal.

Public reporting is another key regulatory strategy whereby patients can exert power as selective consumers. The citizen rights rationale is that people are entitled to information that can directly affect them; the informed consumer rationale is that people need reliable information on success rates and risks in order to choose between providers and procedures; the market rationale is that informed consumers will choose high performers and so motivate others to improve. Public reporting on performance is increasingly common in many countries (see Chapter 8). For example, government agencies in the United States and the United Kingdom post information on hospital scores, as do private sector agencies, such as the US Leapfrog Group and the UK 'Dr Foster' website. In Australia, state health departments have been slow to publish performance indicators on their public hospitals, so that an Australian can look up a US or UK hospital on the Internet but can find virtually nothing about the performance of his/her local hospital.

Vocal Complainants

Patient 'voice', that is, the expressed views of patients, can be used to exert pressure to improve the safety and quality of health care. Patient views may be expressed in different ways, the two main avenues being consumer surveys and formal complaints procedures.

Express an opinion

Patient opinion now is regarded as a legitimate indicator, among other measures, of health care quality (World Health Organization 2000). Such surveys are a mechanism through which patients can express a view and influence the delivery of health services – assuming that an organization takes notice of the results. Patient satisfaction is a measure of quality from the patient's perspective and so different from the myriad other collections of health services data. As an outcome indicator, patient satisfaction is a proxy measure of whether services are of appropriate quality and meet patients' needs. The UK Care Quality Commission, for example, conducts regular surveys of consumer experiences and uses the results to assess NHS performance as well as in regulatory activities such as registration, monitoring ongoing compliance and reviews of organizations. Patient satisfaction surveys have become the norm in many health services. The Picker Institute Europe urges health organizations to undertake regular patient surveys in order to inform the design of their service delivery and provides guidance in designing and administering a questionnaire and implementing the findings (Picker Institute Europe nd).

Consumer surveys must be interpreted with caution since an overall satisfaction question generally obtains an over 80 per cent satisfaction rating, which level of approval is strikingly discordant with more focused and more in-depth evaluations (Carr-Hill 1992; Baker et al. 2006). There are also technical problems in measuring patient satisfaction. First, satisfaction is a multi-dimensional construct that involves many variables with no agreement on a standard instrument. Questions about experiences and health outcomes are more informative than just a broad question on patient satisfaction. Second, in analysing results, there is little agreement on the statistical adjustment of variables; for example, sicker patients undergo more treatments and generally are less satisfied with hospital care (Perneger 2004). Finally, although many consumer surveys are undertaken, as the phrasing of the questions and the technical quality vary there are insufficient good-quality published studies to generate systematic literature reviews.

In Australia, a review of patient satisfaction surveys carried out in public hospitals found that although the methodology differs, the questionnaires generally contain core questions on similar aspects of patient experiences, and so offer potential for developing a national minimum dataset comparable across hospitals and across states (Pearse 2005). The states all conduct patient satisfaction surveys as do many hospitals (Steering Committee for the Review of Government Service Provision 2006). Victoria has conducted surveys since 2001, publishes the results of an annual patient satisfaction survey in 95 hospitals, and requires hospitals to report what action they take in response to these results; South Australia runs regular patient satisfaction surveys in its public hospitals (Hordacre et al. 2005); and New South Wales includes patient satisfaction questions in its regular computer-assisted telephone interview (CATI) surveys of a random population sample. NSW Health also published the results of a postal survey of patients treated in February 2008 in most public healthcare facilities and compared results for categories of patients and for peer facilities across the state (NSW Health 2008).

It is notable that these surveys seldom ask a patient whether he/she had experienced any adverse event in their use of a health service. It is perfectly possible to ask such a question. The Commonwealth Fund asked people who reported poor health (that is, regular health care users) from six countries (Australia, Canada, Germany, New Zealand, United Kingdom, United States) about their experiences with health care. Between 22–34 per cent of respondents in the six countries said that they had experienced a medical mistake, medication error, or test error in the previous two years (Schoen et al. 2005).

While consumer surveys are a relatively reliable way of gauging patient views, anecdotal accounts can be telling. While many are testimonials by grateful patients, others tell tales of poor treatment. A notable account, written by a former hospital CEO now suffering a life-threatening chronic illness that requires treatment at four Australian public hospitals, despite her familiarity with the way hospitals work, complained of being treated with a lack of respect and encountering poor communication and little continuity of care (Cahill 2004). Another patient described the chaotic recording of her patient medical information and the near misses that ensued due to poor communication and mistakes (Stevens 2005). The personal stories of patients who experienced a medical error (the 'voice' metaphor) involves patients as partners in change and can be a powerful way of influencing policy makers (Newell et al. 2010).

Making a complaint

Patients usually can complain directly to a health care provider either informally or through formal internal complaints procedures (or an independent complaints body such as an ombudsman or to a professional registration board). It is surely more satisfactory for a person to have a complaint dealt with by a health provider, quickly and cheaply, rather than going through more complex and lengthy external procedures. Seeking external avenues of redress may be too daunting, slow and adversarial for many people (Handler 1986).

Large public hospitals usually have procedures for responding to complaints from patients and family, often through a designated staff member (patient services adviser, patient's guide, patient advocate, patient representative, complaints liaison officer). In Australia, all public hospitals have internal complaints procedures as intergovernmental hospital funding agreements since 1993, the Australian Health Care Agreements, have required a public hospital to set out the process by which a person can complain to the hospital or make a complaint to an independent complaints body. Hospital brochures often avoid the word 'complaint', however, preferring the circumlocution 'what would you like to tell us?' A large literature now deals with consumer grievance procedures both in the public and private sectors. For example, an Australian handbook sets out guidelines on how health care providers should manage complaints by patients (Australian Council for Safety and Quality in Health Care 2005). It is not clear whether internal complaints by patients have any systemic impact upon hospital procedures and practices. An analysis of complaints lodged by patients attending Victorian hospitals between 1997 and 2001 concluded that patient complaints were a good indicator to service quality, however, and should be used more often as a quality assurance tool (Taylor et al. 2004).

Patients could also make a complaint when they suffer from an adverse event. Patients could be regulatory actors in monitoring and reporting any adverse event they might experience but they are not invited to do so although this is technically possible via an electronic reporting system or a telephone number, anonymously if they prefer. The US Joint Commission, for example, offers patients access to its reporting system in order to report any adverse events or near misses that they experience in hospital. The substantial under-reporting of adverse events by providers suggests that more errors might be picked up if health care users were encouraged to report. For example, patients in a Boston teaching hospital were interviewed about any near misses, mistakes or injuries that had occurred during their stay in hospital: 8 per cent of patients said that they had experienced an adverse event, and 4 per cent a near miss of which several were serious or life threatening (Weingart et al. 2005).

Entitled Citizens

The fundamental right of citizens to good health care is set out in some countries in a constitution, bill of rights, or legislation, and specific patient rights in transactions with health services and health professionals may be codified. Such formal entitlements offer individuals and groups legal leverage in demanding quality health care. Many countries are signatories to international treaties that have implications for patients' rights symbolically and from which national legislation sometimes follows. The United Nations 1948 Universal Declaration of Human Rights recognizes 'the inherent dignity' and the 'equal and unalienable rights of all members of the human family'. The idea of patient rights flows from this concept in relation to person's fundamental right to good health and to good health care, and in relation to how health services should respond to a patient as a human being. The European Convention on Human Rights and Fundamental Freedoms, for example, has implications for the doctor-patient relationship, such as the right to informed consent for a medical procedure (Hewson 2000). In addition, a number of documents, while not legally binding, carry moral authority, such as the WHO 1994 Amsterdam Declaration on the Promotion of Patients' Rights.

Access to good health care and remains an elusive 'right' in many poor countries, of course, and also for poor people in some rich countries.

Views on patients' rights differ across countries depending upon social and political norms and transactions are shaped by different expectations of a patient-doctor relationship. Patients are not necessarily regarded as entitled citizens who have a right to demand, and be given, full information about their own condition and own health care. For example, patients have few rights under the Soviet-style medicine practised in the central Asian republics (McKee et al. 2002).There are still some echoes in western hospitals, however, of attitudes depicted in Solzhenitsyn's novel *Cancer Ward* where patients must battle with the doctors for information about their conditions and treatments:

> [Doctor] It's strictly against the rules for patients to read medical books …
> [Patient] What is the diagnosis?
> [Doctor] Generally speaking, we don't have to tell our patients what's wrong with them …
> [The director] insisted too on discharging those who were doomed. As far as possible their deaths should occur outside the clinic. This would increase the turnover of beds, it would be less depressing for those that remained and it would help the statistics, because the patients discharged would be listed not as 'deaths' but as 'deteriorations' … .(Solzhenitsyn 1971)

Nordic countries led the way in passing patients' rights legislation that also formalized the relationship between doctor and patient. Such legislation provides a framework within which health care providers must consider how best to protect consumer rights to safe and good quality health care. For example, Norway passed the *Act on Patients' Rights 1999* that includes the right to choose a hospital, to have access to a specialist evaluation within 30 days of referral, to a second opinion, to be fully informed, to give informed consent, and to have access to complaints procedures (Myklebust 2000). New Zealand also stresses a rights approach in its Code of Health and Disability Services Consumers' Rights (Paterson 2002). Australia does not have a 'bill of rights' (except in the Australian Capital Territory) in relation to citizen rights in general or to patients' rights in particular. No legislation at national or state level sets out a comprehensive statement of patient rights, but some legislation sets out rights in relation to specific areas, such as confidentiality of medical information. The law in Australia has been concerned with ensuring that a person gives consent to health care, about breach of contract between a doctor and patient involving medical negligence, and a person's right to access their own medical information (McIlwraith and Madden 2006).

While many countries have informed consent legislation, patients are not necessarily legally entitled to know when an error occurs – and they should be. Most patients want to be told of any error in their treatment and to receive an explanation about why it happened and how a recurrence will be prevented (Hobgood et al. 2002). For example, a UK survey found that 34 per cent wanted an apology or explanation and 23 per cent wanted an enquiry into the causes (Chief Medical Officer 2003). A US survey of patients where a medical error was recorded in their medical file found that 70 per cent had not been informed by the doctor involved (Kaiser Family Foundation and AHRQ 2004). Despite differences across countries there is a growing international consensus that patients have the right to expect confidentiality, information, self-determination and choice from health services (see Box 9.1).

Box 9.1 International trends in patient rights

- confidentiality of their medical information
- access to their own medical records
- consent to treatment or to refuse treatment
- right to discharge oneself from hospital
- to be informed about any risks in undergoing, or not undergoing, a procedure
- access to complaints procedures
- right to interpreter assistance
- open disclosure when an adverse event occurs (in some countries)
- right to a second opinion (in some countries)
- choice of doctor (in some countries)
- choice of hospital (in some countries)
- access to performance information on doctors and services (in some countries).

What standard of service can patients expect?

Patients need a statement on the standard of care that they should be able to expect from health services, while health care providers also need reminding of patients' reasonable expectations. 'Patient charters' that set out what a patient has a right to expect from a health care provider have been produced in many countries (Massion 2000). For example, England issued a Patient's Charter in 1991 that set out 10 rights and codified the standards that people could expect from National Health Service providers (Department of Health 1995). Such charters encapsulate standards, rather than legally enforceable 'rights', and the adoption of a charter by health providers generally is voluntary. Charters are mandatory in some US states, however, and patients' rights have legislative force although they are seldom enforced (Silver 1997).

The Australian Health Care Agreements since 1993 have required the states to ensure that their public hospitals have a patient charter, that a charter is published in community languages, that there are distribution strategies, and that a charter is publicly available. A charter must inform patients they are entitled to free access to public hospital treatment, to be treated as a public or a private patient within a public hospital, set out the process by which patients can complain about hospital services, and also explain how complaints can be made to an independent complaints body. State health departments all post a charter on their websites that set out rights of patients as well as their responsibilities. The Australian Charter of Healthcare Rights, endorsed by the Health Ministers in 2008 on the basis that patients should be able to expect nation-wide consistency, sets out seven broad principles that health consumers should be able to expect, including the right to receive safe and high quality care (see Table 9.2). The charter lays out a set of aspirations rather than enforceable rights or measurable standards and it is unclear to what extent such aspirations are implemented in practice.

Table 9.2 Australian Charter of Healthcare Rights

What can I expect from the Australian health system?	
My Rights	**What This Means**
ACCESS: I have a right to health care	I can access health services to address my healthcare needs
SAFETY: I am a right to receive safe and high quality care	I receive safe and high quality health services, provided with professional care, skill and competence
RESPECT: I am a right to be shown respect, dignity and consideration	The care provided shows respect to me and my culture, beliefs and values and personal characteristics
COMMUNICATION: I am a right to be informed about services, treatment, options and costs in a clear and open way	I receive open, timely and appropriate communication about my health in a way I can understand
PARTICIPATION: I have a right to be included in decisions and choices about my care	I may join in making decisions and choices about my care and about health service planning
PRIVACY: I have a right to privacy and confidentiality of my personal information	My personal privacy is maintained and proper handling of my personal health and other information is assured
COMMENT: I have a right to comment on my care and to have my concerns addressed	I can comment on or complaint about my care and have my concerns dealt with properly and promptly

Source: Australian Commission on Safety and Quality in Health Care 2009

Active Partners

Citizen participation strategies are pursued in the health sector with the intention of redressing the traditionally unequal power relationship between professionals and patients (Healy 1998). The citizen participation concept suggests a democratic paradigm where a person is an active partner in decision-making. This approach aligns with community development principles that broadly are about removing conditions of domination (for example, by health professionals), and increasing the self-determination of individuals by lifting restrictions (for example, overcoming poor health) and by increasing capacity (for example, through information and empowerment). In transactions between people and health services, the therapeutic argument is that involving patients as partners in the process of health care results in satisfied patients and better health outcomes. The quality argument is that patients understand their own needs best and can help ensure the safety and quality of their own care. The governance argument is that consumers can regulate their own health care: in market terms they are co-producers of their own health care, and in citizenship terms they are active participants.

A classic paper by Arnstein applied a power analysis to citizen participation in depicting a ladder with eight rungs beginning with the bottom rung of manipulation and ascending upwards through therapy, information provision, consultation, placation, partnership, delegated power, to the top rung of citizen control (Arnstein 1969). But while most people are willing to step onto the bottom rung to answer a consumer survey, very few want to climb to the top three rungs and become a board member. A criticism of a consumer participation strategy is that, given a socioeconomic bias in who participates, it can easily become a way by which the elite manipulate the system in their favour (Midgley et al. 1986). A large literature addresses the citizen participation issues of who participates, on which matters, and at which level, as well as the barriers to securing meaningful participation (Healy 1998: 29–31).

Many health sector boards and committees now include consumer representatives but the issue of who best represents health care consumers remains problematic. Three types of representation have been defined, with the boards of health service organizations for practical reasons more likely to seek members from consumer organizations (substantive representation), than to aim for a microcosm of the consumer population (descriptive representation), or to seek members through a democratic voting procedure (formal representation) (Marmor and Morone 1980). At the management level, many health services now include citizens/patients on management boards or have set up citizen advisory councils.

At the international level, Council of Europe recommendations to governments urge more citizen participation in health system decisions and for governments to ensure that a patient can become 'an active participant in his own treatment' (Rec (80)4). The WHO World Alliance for Patient Safety has embraced the concept of patients as active partners in patient safety issues and has developed an international network of patient organizations in order to enlist consumers in helping to drive the patient safety movement. The consumers steering group is chaired by Susan Sheridan, co-founder of the US Consumers Advancing Patient Safety, founded in 2003 after two separate serious medical errors in which Sheridan's husband died and her son was brain damaged. In consequence, she has become a very active advocate for patient safety at national and international forums.

Health services are beginning to enlist patients as partners in a range of activities that involve them in contributing to treatment decisions, checking the accuracy of records and processes, monitoring their own treatment and being involved in self-management (see Box 9.2). This will require considerable patient education, however, since many studies find that patients are overly trusting and tend to assume that health care professionals 'will take care of everything'.

Box 9.2 Patients as partners in health care

- Making informed choice about providers
- Helping to reach an accurate diagnosis
- Sharing decisions about treatments and procedures
- Contributing to safe medication use
- Participating in infection control initiatives
- Checking the accuracy of medical records
- Observing and checking care processes
- Identifying and reporting treatment complications and adverse events
- Practising effective self-management, including treatment monitoring
- Shaping the design and improvement of services.

Source: Coulter and Ellins 2006, p. 143

To give some examples, patients are being asked to be more active in patient identification procedures. A health worker should ask 'Can you tell me your name' rather than asking 'Are you Mrs Smith'? While patients can get irritated about repeatedly being asked this question, it is a crucial patient safety practice given the numerous adverse events that arise from patient misidentification. Brochures for hospital patients explain the reason for this information check. Patients now have the right to read their own medical record, which previously was regarded as the sole property of the health care provider, and asking patients to verify information is an effective safety check given the many errors that can creep into medical records. Patients increasingly are being involved in monitoring and managing their own health, particularly those with chronic conditions such as asthma and diabetes.

Encouraging patients to speak up

While people in theory can be active partners in monitoring their own health care, in practice many, or perhaps most, need to be reassured that it is OK to question let alone challenge doctors and nurses. This reticence on the part of patients is deeply embedded in the health care culture and in the doctor-patient relationship. Patients are reluctant, for example, to remind doctors or nurses that they should wash their hands before physically examining them (World Health Organization 2007). A very telling survey of patients in English NHS hospitals found that although 71 per cent said that patients should be involved in improving hand hygiene only 26 per cent said they were willing to remind staff to clean their hands (Davis et al. 2008). It would be interesting to compare whether attitudes differ between public and private patients. The relationship between health professionals and patients clearly is not one of partnership so that health systems need to find ways to engage patients in speaking up if patients are to take on an effective role as regulatory actors.

In order to legitimize the role of patients in monitoring their own health care, many countries have produced brochures that in effect give patients permission to become active partners in their own health care. For example, a US brochure, 'Ask Me 3', urges patients to ask at least three questions during a visit to the doctor: 'What is my main problem? What do I need to do? Why is it important for me to do this?'(Partnership for Clear Health Communication 2007). The brochure also gives several tips for clearer communication: for example, 'I will bring a list of all my medicines when I visit the doctor'. The lead US government patient safety agency in its publication, '20 Tips to Help Prevent Medical Errors', leads as its first tip: 'The single most important way you can help to prevent errors is to be an active member of your health care team' (Agency for Healthcare Research and Quality 2000). While safety tips for patients vary somewhat across countries the basic message is to encourage patients to speak up. In Demark, the first tip is to 'Speak up if you have any questions or concerns' (Danish Society for Patient Safety and TrygFonden 2007). In Australia, Tip 2 in the 'Ten Tips for Safer Health Care' exhorts people to 'Speak up if you have any questions or concerns' (see Box 9.3). An accompanying brochure points out that improving safety is not just the business of health professionals but also of patients: 'By taking an active role in your health care, you can help to make sure you get the best possible care for your needs'(Australian Council for Safety and Quality in Health Care 2003). The Health Ministers in 2004 required all public hospitals to distribute 'Ten Tips' to

Box 9.3 Ten Tips for Safer Health Care

1. Be actively involved in your own health care
2. Speak up if you have any questions or concerns
3. Learn more about your condition or treatments
4. Keep a list of all the medicines you are taking
5. Make sure you understand the medicines you are taking
6. Get the results of any test or procedure
7. Talk about your options if you need to go into hospital
8. Make sure you understand what will happen if you need surgery or a procedure
9. Make sure you, your doctor and your surgeon all agree on exactly what will be done
10. Before you leave hospital, ask your health care professional to explain the treatment plan you will use at home.

Source: Australian Council for Safety and Quality in Health Care 2003

their patients, but so far, there has been no evaluation on whether patients receive or act upon these tips, let alone whether there is any discernable impact upon patient safety – admittedly a very difficult research task in terms of outcomes.

A book by the late Stephen Schneider, who was diagnosed with a rare type of lymphoma, is an example of a patient who was an active partner in discussing and deciding his treatment decisions with top US clinicians (Schneider 2005). The title of the book says it all: 'The patient from hell: how I worked with my doctors to get the best of modern medicine and how you can too'. The author acknowledges, however, that he was better able than the average patient to research the condition and treatment options, and that many patients may need a knowledgeable advocate to help them along the way on their patient journey.

Conclusion

Can Patients Improve Safety And Quality?

Systematic reviews have examined patient participation in processes but there is much less research on the impact of patient participation on outcomes. Systematic reviews on process studies have looked at ways to improve access to, and use of, health services, ways to involve patients in having a say over health care, and ways to improve health literacy. For example, the Cochrane Consumers and Communication Group based at La Trobe University generally focuses on the impact of processes 'to educate, communicate with, inform, support, involve and seek the participation of consumers of health care'. There is considerable research on methods to improve patient health literacy, such as the impact of patient education materials and procedures to improve compliance. For example, a systematic review of interventions for enhancing medication adherence found that many people do not take their medication as prescribed, and that while short-term adherence can be improved, including by counselling, written information and personal phone calls, most interventions showed little improvement in long-term adherence (Haynes et al. 2006). A structured review of patient safety interventions that directly enlist patients concluded that as the role of patients as regulatory actors has only recently been recognized research was still in its early stages (Coulter and Ellis 2006).

The frequent claim is that 'research shows that patients who are more involved with their care tend to get better results' (Agency for Healthcare Research and Quality 2000). For example, involving patients as partners in the process of health care results not only in more satisfied patients but also in better health outcomes, as shown in randomized cancer treatment trials (McPherson and Britton 1999). But systematic reviews have found few studies that rigorously examine the impact of patient participation on health care safety partly because such outcome studies are difficult to undertake (Pizzi et al. 2001). A criticism of the evidence-based health care movement is that the reasons why only limited evidence of the impact of consumer participation has emerged is, first, because systematic review criteria reject many studies of patient participation as insufficiently rigorous in research design, and second, because systematic reviews are more interested in health outcomes than in patient experiences and patient satisfaction (Horey and Hill 2005).

While the policy thrust now is to involve patients in monitoring the safety of their own care, research on the outcomes of patient involvement is in the early stages. A structured literature review found that the health sector has not facilitated a role for patients in reducing medical errors in their own health care, except in the area of chronic disease, where the review found a positive impact from patients' involvement in improving the quality and safety of care in a range of chronic diseases (Pizzi et al. 2001).

Patient choice also appears to be a weak mechanism for regulating safety and quality. While there is a strong public interest case, public reporting so far appears not to prompt people to choose better performing health services (in contrast to purchasers and other providers), and patient choice appears not to drive the production of better health care. Systematic reviews have found that public reporting has very little impact upon patient choice (Marshall et al. 2000; Marshall and Brook 2002). The overall research consensus is that few patients look at published performance data and even fewer seek to identify and then go to the best doctor and best hospital.

What might be the reasons for the lack of impact of public reporting on patient choice? First, these are early days for public reporting and the public are not yet familiar with this type of information. Future studies may find different results. Second, the information usually is way too complex since the data presentation is oriented to professionals, and there is low health literacy among the general population as well as low research literacy. Policy makers must make public reporting more reader-friendly if they want people to make choices that drive improvements. This requires the publication of quality indicators that the public finds easier to understand than reams of statistical data and tediously long reports. Third, people may opt for convenience and familiarity in going to the nearest or known provider. Fourth, the public retains a disproportionate trust in health care providers and may believe that all providers are equally good. Finally, all these reasons may apply. Public reporting is likely to have more impact in future as the concept of performance indicators become better understood by the public, and as people become more discerning users of health care given greater public knowledge about the variability of health care quality and the risks involved in health care treatment.

References

Agency for Healthcare Research and Quality (2007), 20 Tips to Help Prevent Medical Errors, 2 May http://www.ahrq.gov/consumer/20tips.htm

Appleby J (2005), 'Impact of choice on hospital viability'. *Health Service Journal* 115(5945): 23.

Arnstein S (1969), 'A ladder of citizen participation'. *American Institute of Planners Journal* 35(4): 216–224.

Australian Bureau of Statistics (2006), *Health Literacy, Australia 2006*. (Canberra: ABS).

Australian Bureau of Statistics, Patterns of internet access in Australia, 2006, 8146.0.55.001, (14 January 2007 14 January 2007) http://www.abs.gov.au/AUSSTATS

Australian Commission on Safety and Quality in Health Care Australian Charter of Healthcare Rights (2 March 2009) http://www.safetyandquality.gov.au/internet/safety/publishing.nsf/Content/PriorityProgram-01

Australian Council for Safety and Quality in Health Care (2003), *10 Tips for Safer Health Care: What Everyone Needs to Know*. (Canberra: Commonwealth of Australia).

Australian Council for Safety and Quality in Health Care (2005), *Complaints Management Handbook for Health Care Services*. (Canberra: Commonwealth of Australia).

Baker R, et al. (2006), 'Improving the quality and performance of primary care'. In Saltman R, Rico A and Boerma W. *Primary Care in the Driver's Seat? Organizational Reform in European Primary Care*. (Maidenhead: Open University Press) : 203–226.

Bergeson S and Dean J (2006), 'A systems approach to patient-centred care'. *Journal of the American Medical Association* 296(23): 2848–2851.

Berta, W. et al. (2008), 'In the eyes of the beholder: population perspectives on performance priorities for primary care in Canada'. *Healthcare Policy* 4(2): 86–100.

Cahill A (2004), 'A tale of a few hospitals'. Australian Health Review 27(2): 1–4.

Carr-Hill R (1992), 'The measurement of patient satisfaction'. *Journal of Public Health Medicine* 14: 236.

Chief Medical Officer (2003), *Making Amends: A Consultation Paper Setting Out Proposals for Reforming the Approach to Clinical Negligence in the NHS*. (London: Department of Health).

Coulter A and Ellins J (2006), *Patient-Focused Interventions: A Review of the Evidence*. (London: The Health Foundation).

Coulter A and Ellins J (2007), 'Effectiveness of strategies for informing, educating and involving patients'. *British Medical Journal* 335: 24–27.

Danish Society for Patient Safety and TrygFonden (2007), *Patient Handbook: A Patient's Guide to a Safer Hospital Stay*. (Hvidovre: Danish Society for Patient Safety).

Darzi A (2009), *High Quality Care For All: NHS Next Stage Review Final Report*. (London: Department of Health).

Davis R, et al. (2008), 'How willing are patients to question healthcare staff on issues related to the quality and safety of their healthcare? An exploratory study'. *Quality and Safety in Health Care* 17(2): 90–96.

Department of Health (1995), NHS: *The Patient's Charter: A Charter for England*. (London: HMSO).

Dugdale P (2008), *Doing Health Policy in Australia*. (Sydney: Allen & Unwin).

Ettelt S, et al. (2006), *Policy Brief: Health Care Outside Hospital: Accessing Generalist and Specialist Care in Eight Countries*. (Brussels: European Observatory on Health Systems and Policies).

Francis Bacon 16th century (1979), 'So cure the disease and kill the patient'. In. *The Oxford Dictionary of Quotations*. (Oxford: Oxford University Press) : 26.

Gawande A (2002), *Complications: A Surgeon's Notes on an Imperfect Science*. (New York: Metropolitan Books, Henry Holt and Company).

General Practice Strategy Review Group (1998), *General Practice: Changing the Future through Partnerships*. (Canberra: Commonwealth of Australia).

Handler J (1986), *The Conditions of Discretion: Autonomy, Community, Bureaucracy*. (New York: Sage).

Haynes R, et al. (2006), 'Interventions for enhancing medication adherence'. In Collaboration C. *The Cochrane Database of Systematic Reviews*: John Wiley & Sons).

Healy J (1998), *Welfare Options: Delivering Social Services*. (Sydney: Allen & Unwin).

Healy J, et al. (2008), 'A national medical register: balancing public transparency and professional privacy'. *Medical Journal of Australia* 188(4): 247–249.

Hewson B (2000), 'Why the Human Rights Act matters to doctors'. *British Medical Journal* 321: 780–781.

Hirschman A (1970), *Exit, Voice and Loyalty: Responses to Decline in Firms, Organizations and States*. (Cambridge, Massachusetts: Harvard University Press).

Hobgood C, et al. (2002), 'Medical errors - what and when: what do patients want to know?' *Academic Emergency Medicine* 9(11): 1156–1161.

Hordacre A-L, et al. (2005), 'Assessing patient satisfaction: implications for South Australian hospitals'. *Australian Health Review* 29(4): 439–446.

Horey D and Hill S (2005), Engaging consumers in health policy. 3rd Health Policy Roundtable, (Parliament House, Canberra: Australian Institute of Health Policy Studies).

Institute of Medicine (2004), *Health Literacy: A Prescription to End Confusion*. (Washington DC: National Academies Press).

Internet World Statistics (2009), Internet Usage Statistics: World Internet Statistics and Population Statistics 12 November http://www.internetworldstats.com/stats.htm

Johnson A, et al. (2006), 'Written and verbal information versus verbal information only for patients being discharged from acute hospital settings to home'. In Collaboration C. *The Cochrane Database of Systematic Reviews*: John Wiley & Sons).

Johnstone M and Kanitsaki O (2006), 'Culture, language, and patient safety: making the link'. *International Journal for Quality in Health Care* 18(5): 383–388.

Jorm C, et al. (2009), 'Should patient safety be more patient centred?' *Australian Health Review* 33(3): 390–399.

Kaiser Family Foundation & AHRQ (2004), *National Survey on Consumers' Experiences with Patient Safety and Quality Information*. (California: Kaiser Family Foundation).

King's Fund, Patient choice, (23 November 2006 23 November 2006) www.kingsfund.org.uk/resources/briefings/patient_choice.html

Koutantji M, et al. (2005), 'The patient's role in patient safety: engaging patients, their representatives, and health professionals'. *Clinical Risk* 11(3): 99–104.

Marmor T and Morone J (1980), 'Representing consumer interests: imbalanced markets, health planning and the HSAs'. *Health and Society* 58(1): 125–165.

Marshall M and Brook R (2002), 'Public reporting of comparative information about quality of healthcare (editorial)'. *Medical Journal of Australia* 176: 205–206.

Marshall M, et al. (2000), 'The public release of performance data: what do we expect to gain? A review of the evidence'. J*ournal of the American Medical Associatio*n 283(14): 1866–1874.

Massion J (2000), 'The ethical characteristics of patients' rights in Europe'. *Hospital: Official Journal of the European Association of Hospital Managers* 2(1): 11–13.

McIlwraith J and Madden B (2006), *Health Care & The Law*. (Pyrmont NSW: Lawbook Company).

McKee M, et al., eds. (2002), *Health Care in Central Asia*. (Buckingham. Philadelphia: Open University Press).

McPherson K and Britton A (1999), 'The impact of patient treatment preferences on the interpretation of randomised controlled trials'. *European Journal of Cancer* 35: 1598–1602.

Midgley J, et al. (1986), *Community Participation, Social Development and the State*. (London: Methuen).

Myklebust A (2000), 'Patients' rights in the 1999 reforms in Norway'. *Hospital: Official Journal of the European Association of Hospital Managers* 1: 16.

National Health and Hospital Reform Commission (2009), *A Healthier Future for all Australians: Final Report June 2009*. (Canberra: Australian Government).

National Health and Medical Research Council (2006), *Making Decisions about Tests and Treatments: Principles for better communication between health consumers and health professionals*. (Canberra: Commonwealth of Australia).

Newell S, et al. (2010), 'Partnership with patients to improve patient safety'. *Medical Journal of Australia* 192(2): 63–64.

NSW Health S (2008), NSW Health Patient Survey. (Sydney: NSW Department of Health).

Nutbeam D (2008), 'The evolving concept of health literacy'. *Social Science & Medicine* 67: 2072–2078.

Partnership for Clear Health Communication (2007), Ask Me 3, 6 March http://www.askme3.org/for_patients.asp

Paterson R (2002), 'The patients' complaints system in New Zealand'. *Health Affairs* 21(3): 70–79.

Pearse J (2005), Review of Patient Satisfaction and Experience Surveys Conducted for Public Hospitals in Australia. (Canberra: Steering Committee for the Review of Government Service Provision).

Perneger TV (2004), 'Editorial: Adjustment for patient characteristics in satisfaction surveys'. *International Journal for Quality in Health Care* 16(6): 433–435.

Picker Institute Europe (2007), Patient Centred Professionalism, 10 January http://www.pickereurope.org/page.php?id=9

Picker Institute Europe, Being patient centred, (10 February 2010 10 February 2010) http://www.pickereurope.org/patientcentred

Picker Institute Europe, Using patient feedback: a practical toolkit, (14 November 2009 14 November 2009) http://www.pickereurope.org/usingpatientfeedback

Pizzi L, et al. (2001), 'Section H: Role of the patient'. In Shojania K, Duncan B, McDonald K, et al. *Making Health Care Safer: A Critical Analysis of Patient Safety Practices*. (Rockville MD: Agency for Healthcare Research and Quality): 544–572.

Sandoval G (2007), 'Sustained public preferences on hospital performance across Canadian provinces'. *Health Policy* 83: 246–256.

Schneider S (2005), *The Patient from Hell: How I Worked With My Doctors To Get The Best Of Modern Medicine And How You Can Too*. (Cambridge, MA. Perseus Books).

Schoen C, et al. (2005), 'Taking the pulse of health care systems: experiences of patients with health problems in six countries'. *Health Affairs* Web exclusive 3 November 2005: W5 509–525.

Silver M (1997), 'Patients' rights in England and the United States of America: the Patient's Charter and the New Jersey Bill of Rights: a comparison'. *Journal of Medical Ethics* 23: 213–220.

Sizmur S and Redding D (2009), *Core Domains for Measuring Inpatients' Experience of Care*. (London: Picker Institute).

Solzhenitsyn A (1971), *Cancer Ward*. (Harmondsworth, Middlesex: Penguin Books).

Steering Committee for the Review of Government Service Provision (2006), *Report on Government Services 2006*. (Canberra: Productivity Commission).

Stevens S (2005), 'Information sharing in health care: a patient's perspective'. *Australian Health Review* 29(4): 398–400.

Taylor DM, et al. (2004), 'Analysis of complaints lodged by patients attending Victorian hospitals, 1997–2001'. *Medical Journal of Australia* 181(1): 31–35.

Trevena L, et al. (2006), 'A systematic review on communicating with patients about evidence'. *Journal of Evaluation in Clinical Practice* 12: 13–23.

Vincent CA and Coulter A (2002), 'Patient safety: what about the patient?' *Quality and Safety in Health Care* 11: 76–80.

Walton M (1998), *The Trouble with Medicine: Preserving the Trust between Patients and Doctors*. (St Leonards NSW: Allen & Unwin).

Weingart S, et al. (2005), 'What can hospitalized patients tell us about adverse events? Learning from patient-reported incidents'. *Journal of General Internal Medicine* 20(9): 830–836.

World Health Organization (2000), *The World Health Report 2000. Health Systems: Improving Performance*. (Geneva: World Health Organization).

World Health Organization, World Alliance for Patient Safety: Patient Safety Solutions, (2 May 2008 2 May 2008) http://www.who.int/patientsafety/solutions/en/

Yellowlees P (2000), *Your Guide to E-Health: Third Millenium Medicine on the Internet*. (St Lucia: University of Queensland Press).

Chapter 10
Responsive Regulation: Trust and Transparency

Pressures for Greater Accountability

This book has traced the substantial shifts in health care governance in the regulation of both professionals and organizations in the early twenty-first century. Governments have cast aside their reluctance to regulate doctors and health services, have passed legislation, and have established state and quasi-state bodies who engage in regulatory strategies ranging from persuasion to coercion. Regulatory activities have increased dramatically in number and in scope, including external mechanisms such as mandatory public reporting, and internal mechanisms such as peer audit. Health care providers aim to build patient safety cultures, continually improve quality, and learn from adverse events. The amount of activity in the short space of a decade is very impressive. The intention is to ensure that health care is of a high standard and as safe as possible – which is good news for patients. The new regulatory frameworks being constructed stress trust and transparency as key principles. Health care depends upon trust in professionals and hospitals – but trustworthiness comes at a price: the price the state has set is insistence on external accountability and transparency in clinical performance.

Principles in Regulatory Design

Regulatory mechanisms have expanded rapidly but in a haphazard way. As unplanned growth does not result in coherent regulation, policy makers seek to link the bodies within these regulatory constellations and build governance networks, such as councils and commissions, which connect the multiple regulatory actors. The actors in these forums should then engage in 'regulatory conversations' to develop shared understandings of principles and actions (Black 2002). Arriving at common understandings is important for three reasons. First, the responsive regulation model argues that beliefs and values must be understood in order to craft effective regulatory mechanisms capable of changing behaviour. This is crucial in the health sector where the many occupational groups hold firm views on principles and practices. Second, principles can mobilize regulatory actors behind a common purpose. The adoption of a general principle can serve an instrumental purpose in rallying people behind a common goal, while agreeing on principles at a high level of generality is easier than reaching agreement on specific mechanisms

(Braithwaite and Drahos 2000: chapter 21). Third, regulatory conversations illuminate areas of compatibility and conflict in principles and procedures. These areas need to be negotiated since complex health system issues require multiple and ongoing regulatory mechanisms – a one-off single intervention is seldom enough.

Governance networks, or nodes of governance, should work towards constructing a regulatory framework that harmonizes the different principles and practices. The push for harmonization is prompted partly by the issue of 'regulatory burden'. The principle of proportionate regulation has come to the fore given the dramatic increase in regulation across many sectors of the economy. Is the risk to the public sufficient to warrant regulation? If so, what is the minimum intervention necessary for achieving the desired impact while posing the minimum compliance burden? The issue of regulatory burden upon health care providers is of concern in the health care sector given the heavy demand by patients upon health care workers and the supply constraints in terms of human resources and budgets.

Table 10.1 lists over a dozen principles identified as desirable in the international literature on designing regulatory frameworks (Better Regulation Task Force 2003; Organisation for Economic Co-operation and Development 2005). The UK Better Regulation Commission highlights five principles in designing a regulatory framework intended to reduce regulatory burden by simplifying and harmonizing procedures: accountable, transparent, coherent, proportionate, and targeted (Better Regulation Task Force 2003). The UK's Care Quality Commission lists three key principles in its regulatory strategy: proportionate, transparent and consistent (Care Quality Commission 2009). While many principles in the long wish list are compatible with each other, some principles conflict so a trade-off between respective advantages and disadvantages must be devised. For example, the principle of subsidiarity (regulation handled by a competent authority closest to those being regulated) may conflict with equity (fairness to all), and also may conflict with accountability to the state and the public. The state has rejected subsidiarity in relation to reliance on professional bodies to govern the health professions, however, and now requires more accountability to the state and the public.

Table 10.1 Regulatory design principles

Principles	Definitions
Trustworthy	Confidence in trustworthiness of regulators and regulatees
Transparent	The public can find out about regulatory deliberations and their outcomes
Evidence-based	Regulatory mechanisms as far as possible based on evidence of effectiveness

Principles	Definitions
Accountable	Accountable to the state, the public, and other key stakeholders
Coherent	Internally consistent and complementary with other regulatory regimes
Proportionate	Regulation warranted to protect the public against significant risk with the minimum intervention necessary to achieve objectives with minimum compliance burden
Targeted	Clear goals so regulatees can plan how best to achieve them and regulators can assess progress
Enforceable	Capable of being enforced
Responsive	Responsive to the context, culture and behaviour of those being regulated
Minimum standards	Set minimum standards that must be met, that is, compliance is mandatory
Continuously improved	Doing better every year in terms of a regulatory objective
Mutually recognised	Regulatory actors recognise one another's rules even if these rules differ
Harmonized	Different regulatory actors should agree on the same rules
Clear	User friendly and understandable
Equitable	Fair to all regulatees
Cost-effective	The most regulatory protection at the least cost
Participative	Stakeholders are involved in formulation and implementation
Subsidiarity	Regulation handled by a competent authority closest to those being regulated

Contests of principles can be difficult to resolve since principles derive in large part from norms and values. One approach is to invoke the *cui bono* adage that asks 'to whose benefit?' The health care sector throws up many conflicts of principle between interest groups. For example, quality improvement mechanisms, such as peer review and accreditation, mainly are designed to be confidential and accountable to professional and industry groups. Should the principle of public transparency trump professional 'privilege' and confidentiality? Is public transparency conducive to quality improvement discussions? Health professionals want confidentiality in discussing and learning from cases of less than optimal practice and regard such discussions as an internal professional activity.

Governance in the health sector has been radically overhauled over the last decade. Old assumptions have been overthrown in the lively debate on governance principles. The UK's Chief Medical Officer, Sir Liam Donaldson, has set out a comprehensive list of standards that should be expected of health care governance bodies (Chief Medical Officer 2006) (see Box 10.1). The key points about this set of standards is that they stress principles of accountability to the state and to the public, not just accountability to the health professions and the health industry, and stress transparency in procedures and decisions with the onus placed upon these bodies to demonstrate their impartiality. The following sections discuss two important regulatory principles that have emerged in the health care sector regulatory discourse: trust and transparency.

Box 10.1 Principles for health care regulatory bodies

- Regulatory bodies are accountable to the public and Parliament for their actions and performance. The Government must, and will, act to put right any deficiencies.
- Regulatory bodies must set clearly expressed standards of the knowledge, skills, experience, attitudes and values necessary for continuing practice.
- Regulatory bodies must concern themselves with the competence and conduct of practitioners at all stages in their careers.
- Regulatory bodies must not delay in taking action to protect patients from serious adverse outcomes of care when such circumstances arise.
- Regulatory bodies must demonstrate their objectivity in making assessments and forming judgements about performance.
- Regulatory bodies must show their procedures are free of racial and other forms of bias or discrimination.
- Regulatory bodies must take proper account of the health service context when making interventions.
- Regulatory bodies involved in education must produce clearly stated standards for professional education and training by which the providers of education and training can be monitored and held to account.
- Regulatory bodies must operate clear and independent disputes procedures.

Source: Chief Medical Officer 2006: 166)

Trust

Trust is integral to good governance in society. The many and varied definitions of trust depend on the disciplinary perspective and the phenomena of interest, but trust as a broad concept mostly is defined as an attitude or mental state where a person has confidence in the goodness of others, and expects that others will behave benevolently towards him/her (Braithwaite 1998). One's trusting outlook on life, or attitude towards a particular person or institution, may rest on an emotional or psychological basis and/or on a rational basis that calculates the likelihood of benevolent behaviour by others. Trust involves both a relational aspect, that is, people being ready to trust other individuals, and a rational aspect, that is, people being ready to trust the institutions of government (Job 2007). Both aspects of trust are relevant to the public's trust in health professionals and in health institutions. A simple definition of patient trust in relation to a doctor is 'the belief that a doctor is working in the patient's best interests' (McKinstry et al. 2009: 3). Trust in one's doctor has a personal aspect (trust in a known individual) and an impersonal aspect (trust in the profession of medicine).

Trust is an important concept in health care for two reasons. First, 'trust is a relational notion' and many challenges in the health sector involve trust and relationship issues (Gilson 2003). The medical profession, and the other health professions, enjoy their privileged societal position in large part due to public trust (Kerridge et al. 2005: 119). While people may be disinclined to trust other officials, the willingness to trust doctors, and indeed the necessity to so do when injured or ill, is a key characteristic of the doctor-patient relationship. But empirical evidence since the mid 1990s has indicated a decline in trust in health systems as part of a general decline in social trust (trust in strangers) and a decline in trust in social institutions (organizations and government) although the extent of the decline varies between countries; for example, studies in the United States report more erosion of trust than do studies in the United Kingdom (Calnan and Sanford 2004).

Research on trust in the health field focuses on three aspects: whether people have confidence in their own doctor, in the health professions, and in the health system as a whole. The relationship between these aspects is complex; for example, it is not clear whether people who trust their own doctor are more likely to trust the health system. A survey of adults in England and Wales (n = 1,187) found that people expressed higher levels of confidence in the perceived quality of health care given by doctors (for example, 'patients are taken seriously') than in the perceived performance of the health care system (for example, waiting times, cost cutting) (Calnan and Sanford 2004).

People trust doctors (their own doctor, doctors generally) more than disembodied health systems. Further, while surveys in some countries indicate a trend towards declining trust in health systems or aspects of health systems, trust in the medical profession (compared to other professions) appears not to have declined, although it is unclear to what extent respondents equate trust in the medical profession with trust in one's own doctor. MORI polls in Britain between 1983 and 2009 report increasing proportions of respondents trust doctors (92 per cent in 2009) above other professional groups 'to tell the truth'. In light of the many medical scandals in Britain, the President of the Royal College of Physicians commented with some relief that 'it is heartening to know that the public's level of trust in doctors has been maintained'. In Australia, doctors and other health professionals remain highly regarded according to an annual 'image of professions' survey. In 2008, respondents ranked nurses top of the list of 29 professions on honesty and ethical standards followed by pharmacists and doctors, with dentists in sixth place, public servants ranked 16, politicians and journalists were lower down, and car salesmen were bottom at number 29 (Roy Morgan Research 2008).

The attributes that people say underlie trust in their doctor, according to a structured review of the research literature, generally stress interpersonal attributes (that is, relational aspects) above technical attributes (that is, medical competence) (McKinstry et al. 2009: 3). Five dimensions form the basis of trust in doctors based on US patient surveys: technical and interpersonal competence (the doctor is knowledgeable and experienced and has good communication skills); fiduciary responsibility and agency (the doctor is financially ethical and can be trusted to act as the patient's advocate); control (the doctor controls medical decisions not employers or payers); disclosure (the doctor will disclose any conflicts of interest); and confidentiality (the doctor will not reveal private matters to others) (Mechanic and Meyer 2000).

Trust in one's doctor is important for patients for two reasons. First, the pragmatic reason is that patients, even the well-informed and knowledgeable, must rely on their doctors. They have little choice since health care is complex and most people do not have the necessary medical and technical knowledge but must trust their doctor. Second, the effectiveness argument is that trust in doctors is an essential component of the doctor-patient relationship since trust (or confidence) has an impact on health outcomes: patients are more likely to comply with their treatment regime if they trust their clinicians, and further, trust in one's doctor in itself has a therapeutic effect (Mechanic and Meyer 2000).

Is less, not more, trust in health providers a better regulatory principle?

Trust traditionally is the basis of regulation in the health care sector rather than law and inspections. Professionals and organizations have been trusted to provide good health care: regulatory strategies have relied upon voluntary action by individuals and upon self-regulation by the professions and industry. But by the early twenty-first century, the state (and supposedly the public) had lost confidence in the willingness of the health professions (especially the medical profession) to discipline its members, and in the willingness of health providers to put the interests of patients first. For example, public inquiries over the last decade give little grounds for thinking that health departments can be trusted to put the interests of patients before the organizational interests of senior managers and before the political interests of health ministers. The state in many countries has undertaken regulatory reforms including strengthening external regulation with the stated intention of restoring public trust in professionals and institutions. 'All patients want good doctors they can trust' (Irvine 2007: 256). This is the explicit rationale in the UK White Paper titled 'Trust, assurance and safety: the regulation of health professionals in the twenty-first century':

> Patients in the United Kingdom rightly have great confidence in their health professionals. When we need care, we entrust ourselves to doctors, nurses and a range of other skilled and dedicated professionals because we know from our

> own experiences and the experiences of others that our trust is well placed and will not be abused. (Secretary of State for Health 2007: 1)

A second theme in regulatory reform, enlisting patients as regulatory actors, is a recent strategy. This calls for patients to trust their health care providers less not more. This strategy conflicts with the restoration of trust rationale. The safety and quality argument is that 'blind trust' is misplaced as it means abrogating personal responsibility and trusting implicitly in health providers. A person may be reluctant to ask a doctor questions about his/her competence, ask about the risks of a proposed procedure, seek a second opinion when doubtful, give truly informed consent, check their medication, and check they are about to undergo the correct procedure. It remains to be seen to what extent patients take on a role as a regulatory actor, such as checking a doctor's credentials on the medical register, asking questions in a consultation, reminding health professionals to clean their hands, lodging a complaint, reporting adverse events, and reading performance reports on hospitals and doctors.

> Patients trust us so implicitly and completely that it's scary. They don't understand how vulnerable they are. But government does not want to say 'Health care is risky business and you could be harmed so take care that we don't hurt you.' (State safety and quality coordinator)

Engaging people as regulatory actors in their own health care is proving difficult, even though a prudent view of trust requires some rational calculation as to whether a health professional always can be trusted implicitly to act in one's interests. For example, a doctor may be too tired, too busy, too inexperienced, too out-of-date, or may be over-servicing and over-charging. First, a rational calculation requires a cultural shift in the doctor-patient relationship since many people are reluctant or unable to question the competence or benevolence of their doctor. Second, the basis of trust in one's doctor (and other health professionals) is as much emotional as rational. Any change will require considerable public education and will require the health system to put in place mechanisms that 'give permission' and that encourage people to become regulatory actors in their own health care.

Transparency

In studying regulation in the globalizing economy, Braithwaite and Drahos found that transparency has become an over-riding principle in regulatory discourse and practice and has the moral power to trump other principles (Braithwaite and Drahos 2000). A broad definition of transparency is 'the degree to which information is available to outsiders that enables them to have informed voice in decisions and/or to assess the decisions made by insiders' (Florini 2007b: 5). A more legalistic view in relation to its regulatory purpose defines transparency as 'the capacity of regulated entities to identify, understand and express views on their obligations under the rule of law' (Organisation for Economic Co-operation and Development 2002).

Transparency involves both moral and instrumental claims: transparency is a key principle of democratic government, a human rights principle, a potent weapon in countering corruption, and a regulatory tool in promoting accountability (Florini 2007b: 2–3). First, the right to freedom of information is regarded as fundamental to the functioning of a democratic society since the essence of democracy is informed consent on the part of its citizens: this requires a government to disclose information on its policies and practices. Transparency is not just a mechanism for holding decision-makers accountable, but a mechanism for participation by citizens who increasingly demand a say in decisions that affect them. Second, the human rights argument regards freedom of information as a fundamental human right and as necessary to the realization of other rights, such as access to health care. The UN Declaration of Human Rights in article 19 gives 'the right to seek, receive and impart information and ideas through any media and regardless of frontiers'. Third, transparency is regarded as essential in ensuring integrity on the part of government, in particular in preventing and countering corruption. For example, the leading anticorruption international NGO, Transparency International, aims to 'promote transparency in elections, in public administration, in procurement and in business'. Finally, transparency is regarded as a key public policy principle: it is this regulatory function that is discussed here. Transparency is regarded as 'an administrative tool, a way of making increasingly large and complex government agencies work more efficiently and effectively, as well as with greater accountability to the citizenry' (Florini 2007a: 338).

Freedom of information is not an absolute principle, however, and most laws define areas of exemption, as do organizations in their principles and practices, such as areas of national security, diplomacy, intellectual property, commercial confidentiality, professional confidentiality, and personal privacy. Regulators must balance calls for transparency with calls for confidentiality since some matters may be better discussed 'behind closed doors'. Global governance studies have examined the struggle by civil society organizations to embed more openness in international organizations, such as the World Bank, as these were founded when secrecy was the norm and by people to whom secrecy was second nature. 'Diplomats, central bankers, generals, and corporate lawyers founded the international institutions that exercise power in the globalized world today. It is no wonder that the habits of confidentiality ingrained in these men (and they were almost all men) became the ethos of the institutions they started' (Blanton 2007: 247). The same observation holds for health care institutions in that the principle of confidentiality is ingrained in medical practitioners.

Regulation by revelation

Disclosure now is widely used as a regulatory mechanism. 'Regulation by revelation' means that 'disclosure can also serve as a direct regulatory tool, in some cases as a more efficient and effective regulatory approach than traditional command and control mechanisms' (Florini 2007a: 339). Regulation through disclosure is used as a tool to promote accountability in a wide range of areas and across local to international organizations. At the international level, for example, the International Monetary Fund and the World Bank make fiscal and performance reporting a condition of their aid packages, and the European Union makes transparency in policies and procedures part of its requirement that member countries meet democratic standards (Hale 2008). Health care meta-regulators now require more transparency from internal regulators, such as whether safety and quality procedures actually are implemented, and on patient outcomes in order to track progress.

The big gap in the regulatory research, however, is that we know very little about how disclosure actually functions to produce accountability by altering the behaviour of the disclosers. Regulation by disclosure has concentrated on procedures rather than outcomes, with regulators intent on establishing procedures for gathering, analysing and disseminating information, on the assumption that making the information public will result in changed behaviour. An analysis of transparency as a regulatory tool should begin by asking the following questions: who discloses information, to whom is the information disclosed, about what, and to meet what ends (Gupta 2008)? Further, if transparency is to promote accountability, two components must be linked: the ability to know what an actor is doing, and the ability to make that actor do something else: transparency clearly speaks to the first, but can it, despite its 'softness', produce the latter (Hale 2008: 74)? Can transparency alone in the absence of direct powers of enforcement by a regulator, promote accountability, that is, make actors answerable for releasing information that produces the effect of pushing them to change their behaviour? Most studies explore transparency as an informal process and gloss over the question of how the disclosers are made to alter their behaviour in a 'transparency action cycle': the disclosure of information changes the perception of the information users, who alter their behaviour accordingly; and this shift is perceived by the discloser who responds appropriately (Hale 2008: 76).

Regulation by revelation appears to work but its success depends on what information is provided, in what form, to what audience, and crucially, it depends on what options that audience has to induce the discloser to act differently (Florini 2007a: 341). A review of disclosure-based regulatory systems ranging from nutritional labelling to corporate financial reporting found that although disclosure is widely used as a form of regulation its impact is variable. The reviewers concluded that transparency works better when three pre-conditions apply: (a) the potential recipients make less than ideal choices because they lack information; (b) they could and would change their behaviour if they had the appropriate information; and (c) their changed behaviour would cause the disclosers, in turn, to act in ways more desired by the regulators (Weil et al. 2006). The health sector meets the first pre-condition but less so the other two: (a) health care users lack information to make informed choices; (b) the information available often is not appropriate (too technical, information overload) and many patients are unable to exercise 'exit' or voice', and (c) changes in patient behaviour will not change provider behaviour if providers are impervious to public opinion and have no incentives to increase their market share of consumers.

The question is how might transparency work in bringing about a change in provider behaviour? Hale identifies three tools of enforcement that can have a regulatory impact on actors (in this case global actors) that brings about a change in their behaviour when their actions are made transparent: market pressure, external discourse, and internal norms (Hale 2008: 73).

Market pressure: The market model argument is that transparency reduces information asymmetry: it enables people to make informed choices and select the product/service that offers the best value, and so prompts providers to compete on quality and price. Consumers may also consider other factors such as the social and environmental impact of a product or organization; for example, the public might consider a range of performance indicators, as well as waiting times, in choosing between doctors and hospitals. Market pressures also are exerted by the labour market and health professionals are crucial regulatory actors in the context of skilled labour shortages. For example, the 'magnet hospital' movement seeks to recruit and retain nurses by offering environments that value quality care. Many analysts argue that the single most important source of demand for disclosure comes from civil society. Case studies on transparency provide many examples of civil society groups mobilizing consumer and political coalitions to demand more information disclosure. But civil society has been slow to exert pressure on the health system, apart from in the United States.

Public discourse: The public discourse generally favours transparency, and conversely, transparency facilitates the public discourse between the discloser and interested parties. Transparency mechanisms enable a discourse based on strategic facts (or at least on reasonably credible information) as opposed to speculation (Hale 2008: 86). Hale quotes a *New Yorker* cartoon that asks 'If this is the information age, how come nobody knows anything?' Public opinion may influence actors to change their behaviour in order to maintain their good reputation. There are many examples in the environmental area where transparency has pushed organizations to seek to maintain their reputations as good corporate citizens. Reputations also matter to health providers so that public reports on their performance exert a reputational pressure to do better next time (Marshall et al. 2004). Public opinion is a powerful regulatory tool since the health professions depend upon the state for their professional mandate and income. The status and power of the medical profession previously had shielded it from external scrutiny but health policy makers now require greater transparency.

Internal norms: Regulation also is carried out internally within groups although here the impact of transparency as a tool is less tangible. Hale discusses the conceptual literature on self-reflection, or reflective practice, carried out by individuals and groups where the actors are guided by internal norms and by information on 'best practice' (Hale 2008: 82). The health sector is characterized by its strong norms and values, and internal transparency is most apparent in the well-established tradition of peer review. But transparency has its dilemmas. Reflecting on transparency issues in surgical practice, Gawande comments that professional solidarity makes surgeons unwilling to report the errors of others, since they are acutely aware that surgery is an imperfect science and that one day they will make a mistake of omission or commission (Gawande 2002).

Reluctant Regulators

While patient safety is now a much higher priority than at the end of the twentieth century, there is little evidence so far of improved outcomes, despite the emergence of new safety and quality regulatory bodies, an avalanche of information, and a ferment of activities (Leape and Berwick 2005; Wilson and Van Der Weyden 2005). It is unrealistic, however, to look for a 'big bang' change. The patchy evidence on progress is unlikely to be because nothing has changed, but rather because it is difficult to undertake large-scale research so that progress may have to be measured by cumulative studies across many areas.

One proposal is that regular national 'report cards' should be published, perhaps by an international organization such as the World Health Organization or the OECD, that grades the progress of countries on patient safety. Australia, Denmark, England, the Netherlands, New Zealand and the United States have emerged as leaders in the patient safety field although they pursue different strategies and differ on whether they favour 'soft' or 'strong' regulation. One patient safety expert gave the United States an overall grade of C+ on progress: A- on regulation, C for error reporting systems given the lack of programmes to turn reports into meaningful changes, B- for information technology, D+ for lack of progress on malpractice litigation, and B for workforce and training issues (Wachter 2004). A report card for Australia also could be scored overall as a C+: C- in terms of mandatory regulatory requirements, C+ for error reporting systems despite the lack of a national database, C+ for efforts to improve information technology, B for changes to malpractice legislation, and C on workforce training.

This study has identified the many actors involved in efforts to make health care better and safer for patients and a large array of promising regulatory mechanisms. Most regulation occurs towards the base of the responsive regulation pyramid, and soft regulation generally is an appropriate first choice in the health sector. Good governance should be built on a foundation of cultural strengths and the health care sector has impressive strengths in its commitment to patient care, the creativity of its professionals, and their learning model approach. The regulatory problem is that when persuasion fails there is little capacity or willingness to escalate upwards to stronger mechanisms at the apex of the regulatory pyramid – so that any crisis risks immediate recourse to a heavy top-down political intervention rather than a more graduated regulatory response.

Regulatory reluctance is receding, however, with the rise of meta-regulation by external authorities with the capacity to insist on transparency and to apply remedial and enforcement actions. Stronger regulation to ensure patient safety is on the policy agenda in most health sectors. Patient safety regulation also is on the cusp of change in Australia with the introduction of national professional registration boards, an overhaul of accreditation schemes, a return to local hospital boards, and public reporting of hospital performance. The complacency of earlier eras has been banished.

References

Better Regulation Task Force (2003), *Principles of Good Regulation*. (London: Crown).

Black J (2002), 'Regulatory conversations.' *Journal of Law and Society* 29(1): 163–196.

Blanton T (2007), 'The struggle for openness in the international financial institutions'. In Florini A. *The Right to Know: Transparency for an Open World*. (New York: Columbia University Press): 243–278.

Braithwaite J and Drahos P (2000), *Global Business Regulation*. (Cambridge: Cambridge University Press).

Braithwaite V (1998), 'Communal and exchange trust norms: their value base and relevance to institutional trust'. In Braithwaite V and Levi M. *Trust and Governance*. (New York: Russell Sage Foundation): 46–74.

Calnan M and Sanford E (2004), 'Public trust in health care: the system or the doctor?' *Quality and Safety in Health Care* 13: 92–97.

Care Quality Commission (2009), Enforcement Policy. (London: Care Quality Commission).

Chief Medical Officer (2006), *Good Doctors: Safer Patients: Proposals to strengthen the system to assure and improve the performance of doctors and to protect the safety of patients*. (London: Department of Health).

Florini A (2007a), 'Conclusion: whither transparency?'in Florini A. *The Right to Know: Transparency for an Open World*. (New York: Columbia University Press): 337–348.

Florini A (2007b), 'Introduction: the battle over transparency'. In Florini A. *The Right to Know: Transparency for an Open World*. (New York: Columbia University Press): 1–6.

Gawande A (2002), *Complications: A Surgeon's Notes on an Imperfect Science*. (New York: Metropolitan Books, Henry Holt and Company).

Gilson L (2003), 'Trust and the development of health care as a social institution.' *Social Science and Medicine* 56: 1453–1468.

Gupta A (2008), 'Transparency under scrutiny: information disclosure in global environmental governance.' *Global Environmental Politics* 8(2): 1–7.

Hale TN (2008), 'Transparency, accountability, and global governance.' *Global Governance* 14(1): 73–94.

Irvine D (2007), 'Everyone is entitled to a good doctor.' *Medical Journal of Australia* 186(5): 256–261.

Job JA (2007), Ripples of Trust: Reconciling Rational and Relational Accounts of the Sources of Trust. *Regulatory Institutions Network*. (Canberra: Australian National University).

Kerridge I, et al. (2005), *Ethics and Law for the Health Professions*. (Annandale, NSW: Federation Press).

Leape L and Berwick D (2005), 'Five years after *To Err is Human*: what have we learned.' *Journal of the American Medical Association* 293(19): 2384–2390.

Marshall M, et al. (2004), 'How do we maximise the impact of the public reporting of quality of care?' *International Journal for Quality in Health Care* 16(Supplement 1): i57–i63.

McKinstry B, et al. (2009), 'Interventions for improving patients' trust in doctors and groups of doctors (Review).' *The Cochrane Library* (4): 1–26.

Mechanic D and Meyer S (2000), 'Concepts of trust among patients with serious illness.' *Social Science and Medicine* 51: 657–668.

Organisation for Economic Co-operation and Development (2002), *Regulatory Policies in OECD Countries: From Interventionism to Regulatory Governance*. (Paris: OECD).

Organisation for Economic Co-operation and Development (2006), The OECD Reference Checklist for Regulatory Decision-Making, 24 October http://www.oecg.org/dataoecd/20/10/35220214.pdf

Roy Morgan Research (2009), Morgan Poll: Image of Professions Survey, 21 July http://www.roymorgan.com/news/polls/2008/4283/

Secretary of State for Health (2007), *Trust, Assurance and Safety - The Regulation of Health Professionals in the 21st century*. (London: The Stationery Office).

Wachter R (2004), The end of the beginning: patient safety five years after 'To Err is Human'. *Health Affairs web exclusive*. (New York: The Commonwealth Fund).

Weil D, et al. (2006), 'The effectiveness of regulatory disclosure policies.' *Journal of Policy Analysis and Management* 25(1): 155–181.

Wilson RM and Van Der Weyden M (2005), 'The safety of Australian healthcare: 10 years after QAHCS.' *Medical Journal of Australia* 182(6): 260–261.

Index

Scope too broad – does it deliver?

↓ All too much

Regulation + impact?

↓ p.17 Compl[illegible] All not excluded ...

then P114?

'Rehabilitation' – not feature much in book – somewhat misleading?

/ 264 Medical[illegible] [illegible]

tends to be descriptive / many short items P146

– Needlessly long – larger boxes from other books / positions

– Revalidation ✗

– Comparative work – too superficial – jumps about from place to place → structure not logical

Typos – yet occasional nice flourish ...

UK Aust... eg P116

Refs not always provided.